THE LEAN HANDBOOK

Also available from ASQ Quality Press:

Lean Kaizen: A Simplified Approach to Process Improvements
George Alukal and Anthony Manos

The Certified Six Sigma Master Black Belt Handbook
T.M. Kubiak

Lean-Six Sigma for the Public Sector: Leveraging Continuous Process Improvement to Build Better Governments
Brandon Cole

Lean Acres: A Tale of Strategic Innovation and Improvement in a Farm-iliar Setting
Jim Bowie

A Lean Guide to Transforming Healthcare: How to Implement Lean Principles in Hospitals, Medical Offices, Clinics, and Other Healthcare Organizations
Thomas G. Zidel

Lean Doctors: A Bold and Practical Guide to Using Lean Principles to Transform Healthcare Systems, One Doctor at a Time
Aneesh Suneja and Carolyn Suneja

Profitability with No Boundaries: Optimizing TOC and Lean-Six Sigma
Reza (Russ) M. Pirasteh and Robert E. Fox

The Logical Thinking Process: A Systems Approach to Complex Problem Solving
H. William Dettmer

The Executive Guide to Understanding and Implementing Lean Six Sigma: The Financial Impact
Robert M. Meisel, Steven J. Babb, Steven F. Marsh, and James P. Schlichting

The Certified Six Sigma Black Belt Handbook, Second Edition
T.M. Kubiak and Donald W. Benbow

Six Sigma for the New Millennium: A CSSBB Guidebook, Second Edition
Kim H. Pries

The Certified Six Sigma Green Belt Handbook
Roderick A. Munro, Matthew J. Maio, Mohamed B. Nawaz, Govindarajan Ramu, and Daniel J. Zrymiak

Lean ISO 9001: Adding Spark to your ISO 9001 QMS and Sustainability to your Lean Efforts
Mike Micklewright

Optimizing Student Learning: A Lean Systems Approach to Improving K-12 Education
Betty Ziskovsky and Joe Ziskovsky

Root Cause Analysis: Simplified Tools and Techniques, Second Edition
Bjørn Andersen and Tom Fagerhaug

Quality Function Deployment and Lean-Six Sigma Applications in Public Health
Grace L. Duffy, John W. Moran, and William J. Riley

To request a complimentary catalog of ASQ Quality Press publications, call 800-248-1946, or visit our website at http://www.asq.org/quality-press.

THE LEAN HANDBOOK

A Guide to the Bronze Certification
Body of Knowledge

Anthony Manos and
Chad Vincent, editors

ASQ Quality Press
Milwaukee, Wisconsin

American Society for Quality, Quality Press, Milwaukee 53203
© 2012 by ASQ
All rights reserved. Published 2012
Printed in the United States of America
16 15 14 13   5 4 3

Library of Congress Cataloging-in-Publication Data

The lean handbook / Anthony Manos and Chad Vincent, editors.
  p. cm.
  Includes bibliographical references and index.
  ISBN 978-0-87389-804-1 (alk. paper)
  1. Total quality management.   2. Industrial efficiency.   I. Manos, Anthony,
1963– II. Vincent, Chad.

  HD62.15.L4324 2012
  658.4'013—dc23

                                                    2012010040

Publisher: William A. Tony
Acquisitions Editor: Matt Meinholz
Project Editor: Paul Daniel O'Mara
Production Administrator: Randall Benson

ASQ Mission: The American Society for Quality advances individual, organizational, and community excellence worldwide through learning, quality improvement, and knowledge exchange.

Attention Bookstores, Wholesalers, Schools, and Corporations: ASQ Quality Press books, video, audio, and software are available at quantity discounts with bulk purchases for business, educational, or instructional use. For information, please contact ASQ Quality Press at 800-248-1946, or write to ASQ Quality Press, P.O. Box 3005, Milwaukee, WI 53201-3005.

To place orders or to request a free copy of the ASQ Quality Press Publications Catalog, visit our website at http://www.asq.org/quality-press.

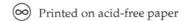 Printed on acid-free paper

 Quality Press
600 N. Plankinton Ave.
Milwaukee, WI 53203-2914
E-mail: authors@asq.org

ASQ **The Global Voice of Quality**™

To Jennifer, who puts up with all my antics. To Judy, who taught me her version of continuous improvement—"Do not rest on your laurels." And to George, for supporting me and for helping me reach a higher level of accomplishment.

—Tony Manos

To my wife, Holly, and my kids, Austin and Miranda, who gave up their time with a husband and father to make this book possible, and whose continued support provides me strength to pursue my dreams.

—Chad Vincent

Table of Contents

List of Figures and Tables

Foreword

Robert D. Miller
Executive Director
The Shingo Prize for Operational Excellence
Jon M. Huntsman School of Business
Utah State University

*T*he Lean Handbook is a terrific compilation of sections written by practitioners who bring their individual and unique experience and expertise to this body of knowledge. I appreciate the connections made with many of the dimensions and principles identified in the Shingo model. We must each be on a journey of continuous improvement, which means we must be constantly looking for new perspectives and approaches to bring about personal and organizational improvement.

Anthony Manos is correct when he says that the most difficult and yet important work we will do with lean is to change the culture of the organization. For lean to be successful, the many tools outlined in this handbook must be supplemented with an equally devoted effort to influence the mind-sets and behaviors of people in the organization. At the Shingo Prize we have learned that the best way to do this is to, as Stephen Covey would say, "begin with the end in mind." In other words, while you are learning to use these great tools, you must also keep the deeper meaning, or the "why" behind the tools, very clear. *The Lean Handbook* can help each of us act our way into a new way of thinking, and then think our way into a new way of acting. By putting the wisdom of this handbook to work every day by every person and never taking your eyes off the prize—a new culture that is deeply embedded in the principles of lean—we will greatly increase the odds of a sustainable business transformation.

As you put this work into practice, you will recognize the shifting roles of leaders and managers in your organization. It is not enough for leaders to just keep doing what they have always done, nor is it enough for them to merely support the work of others. Rather, leaders must lead the cultural transformation and build the principles behind all of these great tools into the mind-sets of their associates. Similarly, managers have to do more than participate in kaizen teams. The emerging role of managers is to focus on designing, aligning, and improving the systems of the business so that they drive ideal behaviors that cause people to change their thinking of what excellence really looks like.

Using *The Lean Handbook* as a roadmap will no doubt be a powerful tool in helping you avoid many of the mistakes made by others over the years. I invite you to visit http://www.shingoprize.org to see how the key points illustrated here support the Shingo model for operational excellence. My thanks to all of the contributing authors!

Preface

WELCOME TO *THE LEAN HANDBOOK*

What a remarkable journey this has been. Working on this book has been a terrific experience. We have had the great pleasure of working with a number of wonderful and giving individuals. Lean practitioners are truly an amazing and unique family. The energy and willingness of the individuals who helped create this book are evidence of the great profession and network of people of which we take part. So many different points of view and applications of knowledge made for great discussions, contemplation, and collaboration. With so much knowledge and understanding, it was difficult to find a point at which to stop talking and start putting these discussions on paper. In the end, we believe this book embodies the Lean Body of Knowledge (BOK) in a way that is much like the lean journey—ever evolving and always adaptable.

Lean has been a culmination of multiple individuals, philosophies, systems, tools, and applications throughout history. The challenge has been that all these different contributions are found in different places, called different things, and applied in different manners—making it difficult for the lean practitioner to gain an understanding of lean at a level of its full body of knowledge without great effort, research, experience, and networking. While this book is not a substitute for the effort, research, experience, and networking every seasoned lean practitioner goes through, we hope it provides a sound starting point for those just beginning or expanding their knowledge of lean.

NOT AN EXAM PREPARATION MANUAL

First and foremost, this book is not a Lean Certification exam preparation manual. The Lean Bronze Certification exam questions are based on material from the five recommended reading books (see Appendix B, "Recommended Reading List for Lean Certification Exam Preparation"):

- *Learning to See*
- *Lean Thinking*
- *Gemba Kaizen*
- *Lean Production Simplified*
- *Lean Hospitals*

Make no mistake—this book takes nothing away from the great lean works that have preceded it. As a matter of fact, we believe that this book complements and pays tribute to those works as being pieces of the larger Lean BOK. But that is exactly what they are—pieces. Our intent was to put these pieces together in a manner to provide a higher-level overview of the Lean BOK. We realized early on in the project that this task was not something we could do alone.

This handbook's intention is to gather information related to the Lean BOK (see Appendix A, "Lean Certification Body of Knowledge") into one source. This book will enhance your understanding of the BOK as a whole and give you a more holistic look at lean. As great as the five recommended reading books are, they were not written with the intent of covering all aspects of the Lean BOK individually. Additionally, this book does not rehash the content of the five recommended reading books. What we have done is put together a book whose sole purpose is to embody the entire Lean BOK, section by section. This book is, by design, written at the Bronze Level for certification knowledge. This means that the weightings used in the Lean BOK for the Bronze Certification were considered for the depth and breadth of material considered for each rubric. Therefore, it is by no means all inclusive of every principle, system, and tool at every level of application related to lean.

By addressing the Lean BOK at the Bronze Level, this book provides a basic understanding of the lean principles, systems, and tools at a tactical level to drive improvements with measureable results. The intent is to revise the book over time to encompass the topics of the Silver Level (an integrated application on value stream transformations for lean leaders) and the Gold Level (for strategic application of lean across the entire enterprise, with emphasis on assets, systems, processes, and people). Therefore, this book, much like a lean journey in an organization, will be adapted as the Lean BOK evolves and more knowledge is integrated.

Given that the intent of this book is not to rehash the certification reference books, we hope that this book serves as a good starting point for those practitioners who want a holistic view of the Lean BOK, with links to many other lean references for greater detail and understanding. While there are many references, we tried to stay true to the terminology and applications discussed in the core books of the certification reading list.

One of the difficulties we faced in creating a book of this magnitude was how to structure it. While we could have structured it alphabetically by topic, organized it by case studies or by organizations, or arranged it by some other method, we wanted to stay true to the Lean BOK structure. While this structure does not allow for a nice flow from one topic to another for easier reading, the writing conforms to the Lean BOK and the Shingo Prize model. We thought that this would provide a traceable reference for those individuals and organizations utilizing those structures for the pursuit of operational excellence.

When lean is applied in an organization, the knowledge of the processes and the generation of ideas do not come from the organization's designated lean experts. They come from those who perform the work on a daily basis. We took the same approach with this book. It would have been easy for us to read all the books and then pull information from those books to create another book. But then it would have been just that—another book. We needed to take a lean approach with this book. So, just as you would create a team of individuals who perform the work in a kaizen event, we assembled a team of individuals who perform the work and who apply lean in their organizations every day.

MANY VOICES AND MANY STYLES

We were lucky to have some of the best minds in lean contribute to this endeavor (see "Contributing Authors and Editors"). There are many voices, many contributors, many styles of writing, and more than one point of view. The contributing authors come from many different backgrounds. Such different life experiences weave a wonderful lean tapestry. This book is not just lean for manufacturing—or lean for service or lean for healthcare. The examples given in this book can fit any type of organization. We hope you find these different points of view helpful while finding your voice in lean.

It has been a pleasure to not only be authors and share our knowledge of lean but also be editors and work closely with others like us. The great thing about working with all these individuals was learning how they apply the same things we apply, but maybe just a little differently. These differences provided us a different perspective on our version of lean and were wonderful opportunities to expand our personal lean knowledge base.

> *Coming together is a beginning. Keeping together is progress. Working together is success.*
>
> —Henry Ford

We wish you the best of luck and fair weather on your lean journey!

Acknowledgments

It would be nearly impossible to mention everyone who had an influence on the creation of this lean handbook, but we would like to make a few special mentions.

First and foremost we would like to thank all the contributing authors, who worked tirelessly to help construct and shape this handbook. Their willingness to share their knowledge and experience was exceptional. To learn more about these extraordinary lean thinkers, see "Contributing Authors." A special acknowledgment goes to all the people and organizations that the contributing authors and editors have worked with over the years to help develop and deepen our understanding of lean and influence us as we continue to learn more.

This handbook would not have been possible without the support of the Lean Enterprise Division (LED) of the American Society for Quality (ASQ) and the LED Leadership Team—Kiami Rogers (chair), Frank Murdock (chair-elect), and Tammy Miller (secretary). We would also like to thank George Alukal, founding member of the LED and the driving force behind lean's becoming an integral part of ASQ and a resource for its members.

The Lean Certification is supported by the four alliance partners: the Society of Manufacturing Engineers (http://www.sme.org), the Association for Manufacturing Excellence (http://www.ame.org), the Shingo Prize (http://www.shingo prize.org), and of course ASQ (http://www.asq.org).

We would like to thank Kris Nasiatka from the Society of Manufacturing Engineers (SME) for all her efforts in creating the Lean Certification and for her continued support of the partner organizations and this lean handbook. Also from SME, Kelly Lacroix leads the Lean Certification Oversight and Appeals Committee, which continually monitors and improves the certification process.

If it wasn't for our friends Matt Meinholz and Paul O'Mara at ASQ Quality Press, this book never would have been completed. We appreciate their patience and advice while working on this endeavor.

Last, but not least, we would like to give our utmost gratitude to Robert Damelio. As a member volunteer, Robert not only was the driving force behind ASQ's LED adopting the Lean BOK, but he also guided the certification initiative at ASQ. Without his tireless efforts, ASQ would not have been a partner member of the Lean Certification.

A Brief History of the Lean Certification Body of Knowledge

Kris Nasiatka, SME

HOW IT STARTED

The publication of *The Machine that Changed the World*, in 1990, brought the concept of lean to the masses. It also provided opportunities for many different flavors of lean to be born. With that came a myriad of education, training, and consulting practices, each bringing its own version of lean to the market.

In 2001, members of the Society of Manufacturing Engineers (SME) and the Association for Manufacturing Excellence (AME), and constituents of the Shingo Prize came together and determined that some type of validation for professional practice of lean was necessary. There was a need to align practitioners with a common foundation (fundamentals) of lean practice and, more importantly, provide a roadmap to support workforce development and training efforts. After a few stops and starts, development was under way in earnest in 2004.

The parties involved agreed that the Shingo Prize model should serve as the basis for the program's Body of Knowledge (BOK). The initial BOK went deeply into evaluating lean practitioners' job tasks. The model was modified to make it applicable to people and workforce development efforts versus being a corporate lean transformation model. The proposed Lean BOK was validated in a study in early 2005, thus launching version 2.0.

KAIZEN BLITZ WEEK

Shortly after version 2.0 was launched, a core development committee was established. With the preliminary validation of the BOK in place, a straw man for program components was outlined. SME hosted a "blitz week" to expedite development of the program. Nearly 60 lean practitioners, representing a breadth of manufacturing industries, consulting practices, and academia, gathered for a week to develop the components of this new certification program. During the blitz, development teams were established to focus on exams, portfolios, and the mentoring requirements for this new program. Throughout the entire development process, nearly 200 lean practitioners were involved in the creation of this program not including the couple of thousands that participated in the study.

The first Bronze exam was offered to the public in March 2006. The Silver exam was available in June 2006, and the Gold exam was launched in December of that year. The formal Lean Certification Oversight and Appeals Committee was established and met for the first time in March 2006.

UPDATED VERSION OF THE BOK

With the program "live" for a year, a second BOK validation study was conducted. It was desired to structure the certification BOK similar to the Shingo Prize model. The Shingo Prize was restructuring its model, which created an opportunity for the certification program to validate proposed changes to the BOK received by certification candidates as well as the oversight body.

The validation study was completed in 2007. The Lean Certification Oversight and Appeals Committee used the findings to restructure the BOK and launched version 3.0 in 2008 (see Appendix A). Although the topics did not change, the BOK was reorganized for better flow and improved alignment of topics within each category. Each BOK validation study is structured in a way that derives a weighting factor for each section of the BOK. The weighting factors identify the percentage of exam coverage for each BOK area and help the committee identify priority areas for building the exam bank.

THE FUTURE OF THE BOK

Validation studies will be conducted every five to seven years. The studies are intended to verify that current topics are still relevant in contemporary practice of lean and to identify any new or emerging topics that should be added to the BOK.

Special Dedication

Kiami Rogers
Chairperson, ASQ Lean Enterprise Division

This handbook is dedicated in loving memory to Wayne Paupst (1957–2010), past chairman of the Lean Enterprise Division (LED). In August 2010, Wayne lost a long battle with cancer. Wayne was a quality professional's "quality professional." He never complained about his condition. In fact, many of us on the Leadership Team, which worked closely with Wayne, were not even aware of the severity of his condition. Wayne possessed a wonderful sense of humor and had a kind word for everyone. He was always ready with a joke, and always ready to laugh at jokes offered by others. His leadership, instruction, kindness, and humor will be missed by family and friends as well as organizations such as ASQ.

I first met Wayne at a meeting of the founders of the LED prior to the LED becoming a forum and subsequently a division. Wayne had been a member of ASQ since 1988. He had more than 25 years in the quality profession, holding positions such as quality engineer, quality systems coordinator, inspector, and quality assurance manager. He had been instructing certification courses for the Lehigh Valley Section of ASQ since 1996 and also had provided instructional courses for many of the top companies in the Lehigh Valley as well. Wayne also held several ASQ certifications: Six Sigma Black Belt, Quality Engineer, Quality Manager, Quality Auditor, Quality Technician, Quality Inspector, Process Analyst, and Quality Improvement Associate. It was during Wayne's tenure as LED division chair that ASQ introduced the Lean Certification, in partnership with SME, AME, and the Shingo Prize organizations. I have no doubt that Wayne would have pursued obtaining the ASQ Lean Certification himself, as well as teaching and mentoring other lean professionals pursuing this certification. It is with great honor that we dedicate this handbook to Wayne.

Prologue

Kiami Rogers
Chairperson, ASQ Lean Enterprise Division

The purpose of this handbook is to provide a reference guide for lean principles and methods. This handbook on its own is not intended to prepare one for the ASQ Lean Certification (in partnership with SME, AME, and the Shingo Prize organizations). The user of this handbook is a lean professional who has some knowledge of and experience with lean principles and methods. Material from several lean practitioners with differing levels of disclosure of their experiences has been gathered to create this handbook and has been edited to be presented in a consistent and unified format.

With 6000 members worldwide, the ASQ Lean Enterprise Division (LED) is a global network of professionals helping individuals and organizations apply proven and leading-edge lean principles and practices to achieve dramatic results for personal and organizational success. Whether or not you are a member of the ASQ LED, we hope you find this handbook a useful guide in your lean journey.

Contributing Authors and Editors

This handbook was a large collaborative effort, and we would especially like to thank all the contributing authors, who shared their time and wisdom to help make this endeavor possible.

CONTRIBUTING AUTHORS

Christopher Abrey is a program manager with Northstar Aerospace in Bedford Park, Illinois. He earned a bachelor of engineering in manufacturing systems engineering from Coventry University, UK. He is a senior member of the Society of Manufacturing Engineers (SME) and a member of the Association of Manufacturing Excellence (AME). Christopher has more than 20 years of lean experience in manufacturing and recently completed the Lean Bronze Certification. He can be reached at cabrey@nsaero.com.

Section

2.2.5.   Total Productive Maintenance (including predictive)

Andy Carlino is cofounder and partner of the Lean Learning Center. In addition to over 20 years' experience in real-world senior management, including president and COO, he has for the past 20 years been providing consulting, training, and coaching services from the boardroom to the shop floor to organizations across the globe. He has published numerous articles and is coauthor of *The Hitchhiker's Guide to Lean: Lessons from the Road*. Andy is a frequent speaker for a variety of professional organizations and corporate conferences, including guest speaker for Clemson and Harvard University. He holds a BS in engineering and a BA in psychology and is a member of SME, SAE, AME, ASQ, and numerous other industry and professional associations.

Sections

1.2.1.   Planning & Deployment

1.2.2.   Create a Sense of Urgency

1.2.3.   Modeling the Lean Principles, Values, Philosophies

1.2.7.   Motivation, Empowerment & Involvement

Adil Dalal is CEO of Pinnacle Process Solutions, Intl.; a keynote speaker; thought leader in lean, project management, and leadership; and author of *The 12 Pillars of Project Excellence: A Lean Approach to Improving Project Results*. He has earned MS degrees in engineering management and mechanical engineering. He is a Certified Lean Bronze Professional, Certified Quality Engineer (CQE), Project Management Professional (PMP), and Board Certified Executive Coach. He is the chair of ASQ's Human Development & Leadership Division, and certification chair of the Lean Enterprise Division. He served on the Lean Certification Oversight and Appeals Committee. He can be reached at adil@pinnacleprocess.com.

Sections

1.   Cultural Enablers

1.1.   Principles of Cultural Enablers

1.1.1. Respect for the Individual

4.3.5. Competitive Impact

Grace Duffy is president of Management and Performance Systems. She holds an MBA from Georgia State University and has coauthored numerous books: *The Quality Improvement Handbook, Executive Guide to Improvement and Change, Executive Focus: Your Life and Career, The Public Health Quality Improvement Handbook, QFD and Lean Six Sigma for Public Health, Modular Kaizen: Dealing with Disruption*, and *Tools and Applications for Starting and Sustaining Healthy Teams*. She is an ASQ Certified Manager of Quality/Organizational Excellence (CMQ/OE), Improvement Associate, Auditor, Lean Six Sigma Master Black Belt (LSS MBB), and ASQ Fellow.

Section

2.2.8. Strategic Business Assessment

David S. Foxx is a senior manager and Champion of the Continuous Process Improvement Community of Practice at Deloitte Consulting. He earned an MBA at the University of Phoenix and a bachelor of science in industrial engineering at the University of Texas at El Paso. David is a leader in enterprise transformation and specializes in innovation, product, process, and service design. David presented "Total Quality Design—An Imperative for Survival" at the Annual Quality Congress. He is a senior member of ASQ and a member of the ASQ Quality Press Standing Review Board, the Institute of Industrial Engineers (IIE), and the International Society of Six Sigma Professionals (ISSSP). His certifications include ASQ Certified Six Sigma Black Belt (CSSBB), LSS MBB, Lean Master, and Design and Innovation Master Black Belt. He can be reached at sixsigmalean@aol.com.

Sections

2.1.2.2. 7 Wastes (Muda), Fluctuation (Mura), and Overburden (Muri)

2.3.5. Product and Service Design

2.3.5.1. Concurrent Engineering

Dr. Gwendolyn Galsworth is president and founder of Visual Thinking, a training, research, and consulting firm, and the VTI/Visual-Lean Institute, which offers licensing and train-the-trainer in nine core visual workplace courses. Over some 30 years of hands-on implementations, Gwendolyn has nearly single-handedly created the models, concepts, and methods of workplace visuality that define visual's distinct and powerful contribution to enterprise excellence—and to sustainable cultural and bottom-line results. Gwendolyn serves as a Shingo Prize examiner. She is the author of *Visual Systems: Harnessing the Power of the Visual Workplace*; *Smart, Simple Design: Using Variety Effectiveness to Reduce Total Cost and Maximize Customer Selection*; two Shingo award-winning books, *Visual Workplace, Visual Thinking: Creating Enterprise Excellence through the Technologies of the Visual Workplace* and *Work That Makes Sense*; and many DVDs. She can be reached at gwendolyn@visualworkplace.com.

Section

Bruce Hamilton is president of the Greater Boston Manufacturing Partnership, headquartered at the University of Massachusetts Boston campus. He attended Bowdoin College and earned a BA from the University of Arizona. Bruce is the creator of *Toast Kaizen* and other lean training videos, and also coauthor with Pat Wardwell of the *e² Continuous Improvement System Manual*. He posts weekly to his blog: http://www.oldleandude.org. Both a recipient of the Shingo Prize and an inductee into the Shingo Prize Academy, Bruce is also a Shingo Prize examiner and a member of the Shingo Prize Board of Governors. He can be reached at pokayoke@comcast.net.

Sections (with Pat Wardwell)

2.1.2.5. Make End-to-End Flow Visible

2.1.2.6. Manage the Flow Visually

2.3.7.1. Mistake and Error Proofing (Poka Yoke)

2.3.7.4. Right Sized Equipment

2.3.7.5. Cellular Flow

John Kendrick is a principal with Fujitsu in Sunnyvale, California, and has more than 15 years of lean experience in manufacturing, finance, telecommunications, and healthcare. John holds a master of engineering degree in simulation and modeling from Arizona State University, a master of applied statistics from Penn State, and a master of business administration in finance from the University of Pittsburgh. He is a Certified Six Sigma Master Black Belt (CSS MBB) and a senior member of ASQ. He is also a CSSBB, Certified Reliability Engineer (CRE), Certified Software Quality Enginleer (CSQE), and CMQ/OE and holds two Lean Certifications.

Sections

2.3.1.   Work Flow Analysis

2.3.1.1. Flowcharting

2.3.1.2. Flow Analysis Charts

2.3.1.3. Value Stream Mapping

2.3.1.4. Takt Time Analysis

4.2.1.   Measurement

4.2.1.1. Understand Interdependencies between Measures and Measurement Categories

4.2.1.2. Align Internal Measures with What Matters to Customers

4.2.1.3. Measure the Results from the "Whole" System

4.2.1.4. Measure Flow and Waste

4.2.3.   Analysis—Understand What Moves the Dial on Measures

4.2.4.   Reporting

4.2.4.1. Visible Feedback Real-Time

Matthew Maio is a quality manager at Raytheon IDS in White Sands, New Mexico. He earned bachelor's degrees in business and computer science from the College of Santa Fe, New Mexico. He is the author of *Quality Improvement Made Simple . . . and Fast!* and coauthor of *The Six Sigma Green Belt Handbook* (both from ASQ Quality Press). Matthew is a member of the International Test and Evaluation Association and the Directed Energy Professionals Society. He is a senior member of ASQ and past regional director (board member) and section chair of ASQ. He holds ASQ certification as a CQM/OE, CSSBB, Certified Six Sigma Green Belt (CSSGB),

CSQE, and Certified Quality Auditor (CQA) and Defense Acquisition University Lean Six Sigma Yellow Belt (LSSYB) and Process Quality Management (PQM) certification/recognition. He can be reached at Matt_Maio@comcast.net.

Sections

1.2.4. Message Deployment—Establishing Vision and Direction

1.2.5. Integrating Learning and Coaching

1.2.6. People Development—Education, Training & Coaching

1.2.8. Environmental Systems

1.2.9. Safety Systems

2.1.5.1. Quality at the Source

2.1.5.4. Multi-Process Handling

2.2.6. Standard Work

2.2.7. Built-in Feedback

2.2.15. Knowledge Transfer

2.3.7.3. One Piece Flow

2.3.7.4. Right Sized Equipment

2.3.7.6. Sensible Automation

2.3.7.8. Source Inspection

David Mann is principal at David Mann Lean Consulting. He is the Shingo Prize–winning author of *Creating a Lean Culture: Tools to Sustain Lean Conversions* (Productivity Press). David serves on the editorial board of AME's publication, *Target*, on the management science faculty at the Fischer College of Business at Ohio State University, and as a Shingo Prize examiner. He earned his PhD in psychology from the University of Michigan. He can be reached at dmann@dmannlean.com.

Sections

2.1.1. Process Focus

3.1.1.3. Closed-Loop Thinking to Assure Effective Feedback of Organizational Learning

Anthony Manos is a catalyst with Profero and lean champion at 5S Supply in Frankfort, Illinois. He earned an MBA in entrepreneurial studies from the University of Illinois at Chicago. He is the coauthor of *Lean Kaizen: A Practical Approach to Process Improvement* (ASQ Quality Press), a senior member of ASQ, senior member of SME, cofounder and past chair of ASQ's Lean Enterprise Division, and a member of the Lean Certification Oversight and Appeals Committee. He is Lean Bronze Certified. He can be reached at anthony.manos@proferoinc.com.

Sections

1.1.2.   Humility

1.3.5.   Coaching & Mentoring

2.2.1.1. 5S Standards and Discipline

3.2.2.   Policy Deployment/Strategy Deployment

4.3.5.1. Customer Satisfaction

Brian H. Maskell is president of BMA in Cherry Hill, New Jersey, and St. Albans, Hertfordshire, England. He has an engineering degree from the University of Sussex, England. Brian is certified with the Chartered Institute of Management Accountants (CIMA) in London, the American Institute of Certified Public Accountants (AICPA), and the Institute of Management Accountants (IMA). He is a Fellow of the American Production and Inventory Control Society (APICS). Brian is the author of eight books, including *Making the Numbers Count: The Accountant as Change Agent on the World Class Team* (second edition) and *Practical Lean Accounting: A Proven System for Measuring and Managing the Lean Enterprise* (second edition). He can be reached at bmaskell@maskell.com.

Section

4.2.1.5. Lean Accounting

Timothy F. McMahon is the founder of and a contributor to *A Lean Journey Blog* (http://aleanjourney.com). He has a BS in chemical engineering from the University of Massachusetts and holds a Lean Certification and Six Sigma Black Belt from Central Connecticut State University. Tim is a member of the regional board of directors for AME and currently serves as the VP of program for northeast region. He can be reached at Tim@aleanjourney.com.

Sections

1.3.1.   Cross Training

1.3.3.   Instructional Goals

1.3.6.   Leadership Development

1.3.7.   Teamwork

1.3.8.   Information Sharing (Yokoten)

1.3.9.   Suggestion Systems

2.2.14. Pull System

2.3.6.   Organizing for Improvement

2.3.6.1. Kaizen Blitz Events

2.3.7.   Countermeasure Activities

2.3.7.1. Mistake and Error Proofing (Poka Yoke)

2.3.7.2. Quick Changeover/Setup Reduction (SMED)

2.3.7.3. One Piece Flow

2.3.7.4. Right Sized Equipment

2.3.7.5. Cellular Flow

2.3.7.7. Material Signals (Kanban)

Dr. Mark W. Morgan is the associate vice president for institutional effectiveness and research at Seminole State College of Florida. Mark earned his doctorate in educational leadership from the University of Florida and is a three-time examiner for the Malcolm Baldrige National Quality Award. Mark was an improvement consultant for Fortune 500 companies for more than 10 years and is the author of three books on measurement and performance improvement, including his latest, *The Path to Profitable Measures: 10 Steps to Feedback That Fuels Performance* (ASQ Quality Press).

Section

4.1.   Principles of Business Results

Frank Murdock is senior process engineer at Plymouth Tube Company in West Monroe, Louisiana. He earned a BS in engineering science at Purdue University, an MS in applied mathematics at the University of Michigan, and an MS in industrial engineering at Wayne State University. Frank spent 28 years with the Ford Motor Company, 8 years as an independent consultant, and 6 years as an adjunct professor at Lawrence Technological University. A senior member of ASQ and an ASQ Certified Six Sigma Black Belt, Frank is chair-elect for the Lean Enterprise Division as well as chair of the ASQ Voice of the Customer Committee. He can be reached at fmurdock@plymouth.com.

Section

4.2.1.6. Voice of the Customer

Mike Osterling has been a lean management practitioner and leader since the mid-1990s and is the lead consultant at Osterling Consulting, a San Diego–based firm. He earned an MBA in international business at San Diego State University and a BS in production and operations management. Mike coauthored *The Kaizen Event Planner: Achieving Rapid Improvement in Office, Service, and Technical Environments.* He is a certified trainer for the implementation of lean manufacturing (University of Kentucky) and a Lean Six Sigma Black Belt (University of California San Diego). He is certified in production and inventory management (APICS). He can be reached at mike@mosterling.com.

Sections

2.1.5.   Jidoka

2.1.7.   Seek Perfection

Mark Paulson is a quality manager for CDI in Minneapolis, Minnesota. He holds a bachelor of science degree in business administration. Mark is a senior member of ASQ, president of the Association for Manufacturing Excellence (AME)—North Central Region, former Minnesota Quality Award examiner/team leader, approved trainer for Bronze Lean Certification refresher class and associated exam, and member of the Lean Certification Oversight and Appeals Committee. He is an ASQ Certified Manager of Quality/Organizational Excellence, Quality Engineer, Quality Auditor, and Bronze Lean Certified.

Sections

2.1.4.   Scientific Thinking

2.1.4.1. Stability

2.1.4.2. Standardization

2.1.4.3. Recognize Abnormality

2.1.4.4. Go and See

2.1.5.   Jidoka

2.1.5.1. Quality at the Source

2.1.5.2. No Defects Passed Forward

2.1.5.3. Separate Man from Machine

2.1.5.5. Self Detection of Errors to Prevent Defects

2.1.5.6. Stop and Fix

2.1.7.1. Incremental Continuous Improvement (Kaizen)

2.1.7.2. Breakthrough Continuous Improvement (Kaikaku)

Robert (Bob) Petruska works as a performance improvement consultant in Charlotte, North Carolina. He has a master of science degree in manufacturing systems from Southern Illinois University. Bob is a senior member of ASQ and a CSSBB. Bob is authoring a book titled *Gemba Walks for Service Excellence: The Step-by-Step Guide for Identifying Service Delighters*, to be published in 2012 by Productivity Press.

Sections

3.2.1.   Enterprise Thinking

3.2.1.1. Organize around Flow

3.2.1.2. Integrated Business System and Improvement System

3.2.1.3. Reconcile Reporting System

3.2.1.4. Information Management

Govind Ramu is a senior manager for global quality systems for SunPower Corporation. Prior to this role, he was Six Sigma Master Black Belt for JDS Uniphase Corporation. Govind is a professional engineer (mechanical) from Ontario, Canada, and an ASQ Fellow. He holds six ASQ certifications. Govind has had articles published in *Quality Progress* and in the Six Sigma forum. He coauthored ASQ's *The Certified Six Sigma Green Belt Handbook*, for which he received the ASQ Golden Quill Award in 2008. Additionally, Govind was a 2006 and 2011 examiner for the California Awards (CAPE) and a 2010 examiner for the Malcolm Baldrige Award. He can be reached at ramu.govind@gmail.com.

Sections

2.1.5.1. Quality at the Source

2.1.7.1. Incremental Continuous Improvement (Kaizen)

2.2.9.   Continuous Improvement Process Methodology

2.2.9.1. PDCA

2.2.9.2. DMAIC

2.2.9.3. Problem Solving Storyboards

2.2.10. Quality Systems

2.2.11. Corrective Action System

2.3.3.3. Failure Mode and Effects Analysis

2.3.4.   Presenting Variation Data

2.3.4.1. Statistical Process Control Charts

2.3.4.2. Scatter and Concentration Diagrams

2.3.5.2. Quality Function Deployment

2.3.5.4. Design for Product Life Cycle (DFx)—Cradle to Cradle

2.3.5.6. Design for Manufacturability

Rama Shankar is the managing partner at Delta Management Associates in Glenview, Illinois. She has a master's degree in engineering management from Northwestern University and a master's degree in materials management from Indian Institute of Materials Management, India. Rama is the author of *Process Improvement Using Six Sigma: A DMAIC Guide* (ASQ Quality Press). She is a senior member of ASQ and a past chair, section director, and training institute director of the ASQ Chicago Section. Rama is a past Malcolm Baldrige Award examiner, an ASQ CSSBB, and a CQA. She is also a certified trainer by NIST for lean.

Sections

2.1.5.   Jidoka

2.1.5.1. Quality at the Source

2.1.5.2. No Defects Passed Forward

2.1.5.3. Separate Man from Machine

2.1.5.4. Multi-Process Handling

Gregg Stocker is an operational excellence advisor at Hess Corporation in Houston, Texas. He earned an MBA from the University of Houston and a BA from Michigan State University. Gregg is the author of *Avoiding the Corporate Death Spiral: Recognizing & Eliminating the Signs of Decline* (ASQ Quality Press). He is a certified purchasing manager from the Institute for Supply Management. He can be reached at gstocker1111@gmail.com.

Chad Vincent is a lean manufacturing specialist with Greif in St. Louis, Missouri. He earned a BS in engineering management from Missouri University of Science and Technology. Chad is a senior member of ASQ and SME, and the current ASQ Lean Enterprise treasurer. He serves on the Lean Certification Oversight and Appeals Committee. Chad is a CQE, CRE, CMQ/OE, CSSBB, and Lean Bronze Certified. He can be reached at chadvincent88@gmail.com.

Sections

Pat Wardwell is the chief operating officer at Greater Boston Manufacturing Partnership in Boston, Massachusetts. She holds a BA from the University of Maine and an MBA from Bentley College. Pat is the coauthor of *e² Continuous Improvement System*. Her accomplishments include SME Lean Gold Certified, past chair of the Lean Certification Oversight and Appeals Committee, Shingo Prize recipient and examiner, AME Manufacturing Excellence Awards committee member and examiner, AME Northeast Board of Directors, and member of SME Boston Chapter Leadership Committee. She can be reached at pwardwell@gbmp.org.

Sections (with Bruce Hamilton)

2.3.7.1. Mistake and Error Proofing (Poka Yoke)

2.3.7.4. Right Sized Equipment

2.3.7.5. Cellular Flow

Jerry M. Wright, P.E., is the senior vice president of lean and enterprise excellence for DJO Global in Vista, California. He earned an MBA in 2002 from the University of Phoenix and is a registered professional engineer in the state of California. He is the annual international conference chair for AME for Chicago in 2012 and also a west region director for AME. He is also the chair of the So Cal Lean Network, an affiliation of more than 75 companies focused on lean and sharing in Southern California, as well as a Shingo Prize examiner and a previous Baldrige Award examiner. He can be reached at jerry.wright@djoglobal.com.

Sections

3.3.1.   A3

3.3.2.   Catchball

3.3.3.   Redeployment of Resources

EDITORS

Anthony Manos is a catalyst with Profero, where he provides professional consulting services, implementation, coaching, and training for a wide variety of organizations (large and small, private and public) in many industries focusing on lean enterprise and lean healthcare. Tony has extensive knowledge of lean and quality in a wide range of work environments. He is trained and certified by the National Institute for Standards and Technology (NIST) U.S. Department of Commerce in all elements of lean manufacturing. Tony also is a lean champion for 5S Supply.

Relying on his diverse knowledge of business, manufacturing techniques, and applications, Tony has assisted numerous clients in implementing a lean enterprise and lean healthcare. Over the past 10 years, he has helped over 150 companies in several aspects of lean implementation, including team building, standardized work, 5S workplace organization and visual workplace, quick changeover, plant layout, cellular, kanban, total productive maintenance, kaizen events, and hoshin planning. Tony is an internationally recognized speaker and expert on lean and presents at several conferences a year. As an ASQ faculty member, he teaches a two-day course in lean enterprise and a one-day course on kaizen. Tony is the past chair of the Lean Enterprise Division of ASQ. He is a senior member of SME and a member of AME. Tony is coauthor of the book *Lean Kaizen: A Simplified Approach to Process Improvement* and author of many articles on lean and its allied subjects. He serves as an ASQ representative to the Lean Certification Oversight and Appeals Committee. Tony is Lean Bronze Certified and was part of the original team to develop the Lean Certification.

Tony served in the US Navy nuclear propulsion program. He holds an MBA from the University of Illinois at Chicago.

Chad Vincent is a lean manufacturing specialist and corporate operational excellence team member with Greif, Inc. in St. Louis, Missouri, where he provides professional guidance, facilitates implementation, and coaches and trains personnel at manufacturing facilities on lean enterprise and operational excellence. Prior to Greif, he worked as a quality engineer in the medical device field and as a project engineer in the construction industry; he also has worked in management in the logistics and transportation industry.

Chad has served as a senior lead examiner and judge for the Governor's Quality Award (Arkansas' equivalent of the Malcolm Baldrige National Quality Award) and is past president of the Leadership Arkansas Alumni Association Board of Directors. Chad is an advocate for ASQ's Socially Responsible Organization (SRO) Initiative and a member of SME's Lean to Green Committee. He has written articles, such as "Back in Circulation" for *Quality Progress*, on the utilizing of lean to achieve socially responsible and environmentally favorable results within organizations and on defining the 8 Green Wastes for environment, health, and safety (EHS) professionals to apply lean in their areas of expertise. He is a voting member of the US Technical Advisory Group (TAG) for the ISO 26000 Guidance for Social Responsibility.

Chad earned a BS in engineering management, specializing in quality engineering, from the Missouri University of Science and Technology, in Rolla, Missouri. He is a senior member of ASQ and SME, and is currently the ASQ Lean Enterprise treasurer and serves on the SME/AME/Shingo/ASQ Lean Certification Oversight and Appeals Committee. Chad is a CQE, CRE, CMQ/OE, and CSSBB, and he is Lean Bronze Certified.

Module 1
Cultural Enablers

Culture is the widening of the mind and the spirit.

—Jawaharlal Nehru

The first section of the Lean Body of Knowledge is dedicated to culture. Although lean is about the tools, it is more about creating a culture of people who truly believe in continuous improvement. This portion of the book focuses on what it takes to create, change, and lead an organizational culture into operational excellence. There is no lean without people. This section explores the importance of leading with humility, showing respect for people, having a well-crafted plan with a sense of urgency, and developing the people and leaders in your organization.

1.1

Principles of Cultural Enablers

According to Pascal Dennis (2007, 145), author of *Lean Production Simplified*, "Intensity is the soul of lean production, and team members are its heart." In other words, people are the most critical element of lean production, and the *culture* the team members create is the major source of fuel required to propel lean systems forward in any organization.

In a vast majority of cases, the success or failure of any lean, Six Sigma, or other corporate initiative will depend on the people who execute it rather than on any equipment, consultant, software, or other tools and techniques. Thus, organizations that consider people as the prime appreciating asset and invest adequate time, effort, and money in hiring and developing the right people will get unmatched results (Dalal 2011, 584).

What Is a Culture?

A *culture* is the sum total of all behaviors, relationships, comprehension, and interactions that fuel overall alignment via collective thoughts, words, and actions.

What Is a Lean Culture?

Lean is an approach to improve quality, increase productivity, reduce costs, and increase customer satisfaction by eliminating waste and creating value.

A *lean culture* is the sum total of all the lean tools, techniques, and knowledge that exist within an organization at the root level and that fuel the overall organizational alignment via collective lean thoughts, words, and actions toward the elimination of waste and the creation of value.

Organizations that have a strong lean culture do two things:

1. They promote at least five key *cultural enablers* (safety, standards, leadership, empowerment, and collaboration), which allows the lean culture to exist

2. They build their business on the core fundamentals of respect for individuals

An Example of a Strong Lean Culture

The consistent growth, prosperity, innovation, and operational excellence of Toyota are clearly results of the Toyota Production System (TPS), which is built on the foundation of a strong and dynamic culture and sophisticated "human systems" consisting of highly motivated and well-trained people in plants, dealerships, and offices around the globe. In *Toyota Culture*, authors Jeffrey Liker and Michael Hoseus (2008) explain Toyota's four-stage process for building and keeping quality people: attract, develop, engage, and inspire. The "people-centric" culture of Toyota is carefully designed by:

- Finding competent, able, and willing employees

- Beginning the training and socializing process as they hire the people

- Establishing and communicating key business performance indicators at every level of the organization

- Training the people to solve problems and continuously improve processes in their daily work

- Developing leaders who live and teach your company's philosophy

- Rewarding top performers

- Offering help to those who are struggling (Liker and Hoseus 2008, 44)

What Is a Cultural Enabler?

Just as a sapling requires critical factors like the right soil, adequate sunlight, and water to survive and grow into a strong tree, culture requires factors that allow it to stabilize and pervade throughout the organization. These factors are known as cultural enablers.

Cultural enablers are critical to the people on the journey of building a culture of operational excellence within an organization.

What Constitutes as Cultural Enablers of a Lean Culture?

Cultural enablers of a lean culture include the basic principles of safety, standards, leadership, empowerment, and collaboration.

Basic Principles of Safety

There are only two types of organizations: safe or lucky.

Safety is the prime cultural enabler, as only safe environments can be productive and profitable. Lean organizations believe that merely adhering to all requirements of the Occupational Safety and Health Administration (OSHA) is not sufficient in order to have a safe working environment.

The following two principles are engrained in the culture of lean organizations:

1. Safety is the responsibility of every employee within the organization

2. A proactive versus a reactive approach is required in order to create and maintain a clean, safe, ergonomic, and sustainable work environment

Lean organizations realize that to attain all-encompassing safety standards, they must focus on education and awareness in safety practices related to people's health and wellness, and interface with people and equipment and environmental aspects.

Personal Safety

Personal safety focuses on security and protection from accidents, injuries, fire hazards, equipment malfunction, and any other aspect threatening the health and well-being of every individual in the organization.

Fatigue Prevention

Fatigue results from a poorly designed workplace, work environment, tools, equipment, and policies and procedures. Practicing workplace ergonomics, which optimizes the comfort of employees while they are interacting with all the elements of their workplace, is the key to reducing fatigue and increasing employee efficiency.

Environmental Safety

Environmental safety involves reducing the carbon footprint of products and processes on the surrounding environment. It encompasses product and process design from cradle to grave, including use of environmentally conscious raw materials, supplies, and packaging materials requiring minimal transportation and minimal waste, along with proactive implementation of recycling or reuse programs.

Some top enablers for creating a culture of safety are the following:

- Focus of top leadership
- Organizational emphasis on safety
- Clearly defined organizational structure
- Clearly defined lines of authority and accountability
- Unambiguous communications
- Trust and engagement
- Ability of organization to learn from failures
- Safety training and sharing of lessons learned

Some top barriers for creating a culture of safety are the following:

- Lack of support from top leadership
- Minimal emphasis or pseudo-emphasis on safety
- A culture of blame and retribution
- Lack of training or sharing of lessons learned

Basic Principles of Standards

Standards are baselines from which improvements can be easily measured. All standards related to safety, communications, operations, human resources, policies, procedures, and tasks need to be standardized across the entire organization. Standardization is not static but dynamic and requires continuous improvement using the Plan-Do-Check-Act model of the Deming cycle (ASQ).

Taiichi Ohno is credited with saying, "Where there is no standard there can be no kaizen." Thus, a *standard* is "the best known method/process/system at a particular point of time" and is a dynamic point of reference that becomes the baseline for future improvements. Every continuous improvement activity must result in the establishment of a new standard. This "new standard" may require establishing a new standardized work sequence, recalculating takt times and establishing new inventory levels, updating visual work instructions, and setting new inspection or quality control standards.

According to Masaaki Imai (1997, 54–56), author of *Gemba Kaizen*, standards have the following key features:

- Represent the best, easiest, and safest way to do a job

- Offer the best way to preserve the know-how and expertise

- Provide a way to measure performance

- Show the relationship between cause and effect

- Provide a basis for both maintenance and improvement

- Provide objectives and indicate training goals

- Provide a basis for training

- Create a basis for audit or diagnosis

- Provide a means for preventing recurrence of errors and minimizing variability

Basic Principles of Leadership

Without support from the top leaders and executives, lean initiatives cannot survive in an organization. The leader is not only required to support lean initiatives in good times but also required to show persistence and constancy of purpose during tough times. The leader needs to develop a clear vision for lean, communicate it effectively to his or her employees, and empower them to adopt it as their own mission. Thus, leadership is the key cultural enabler that determines whether lean is established as a culture in the organization.

Good leaders understand that in an environment of continuous improvement, failures are imminent. But rather than blame people for failures, they ask "why" five times, approach the problem, and create a plan to strengthen the people (Dennis 2007, 130).

According to Dalal (2011, 471–85), there are three types of failures:

1. System level failures

2. Process level failures

3. Human level failures

Great lean leaders avoid focusing on the human level failures, as this would create an environment of fear, distrust, and a culture of risk aversion lacking creativity and innovation. Instead, great lean leaders:

- Focus on system failures ("why")

- Spend more time to prevent the failure

- Believe that 80% of the failures are avoidable by 20% of planning
- Perform root cause analysis to prevent failures
- Implement dynamic risk assessment to identify and plan for failures
- Use Plan-Do-Check-Act cycle to prevent failures
- Establish a creative and open environment for lessons learning (Dalal 2011, 471–85)

Figure 1.1-1 shows a representation of an empowered culture of trust created by leaders using these techniques.

Basic Principles of Empowerment

A Japanese saying alludes to the fact that a statue of Buddha will not mean much without putting a soul in it (Imai 1997, 242). The soul of a lean organization is employee empowerment.

The prime responsibility of a leader in a lean organization is to develop effective problem solvers and decision makers. The only way a leader can achieve an empowered workforce is by helping to set a vision and relinquishing some authority in order to allow the capable employees to make decisions and influence corporate policies. Empowered employees get to the depths of understanding of lean technology and go beyond the know-how of lean and experience and apply lean with a deeper understanding of the know-why. Thus, lean leaders rely on their

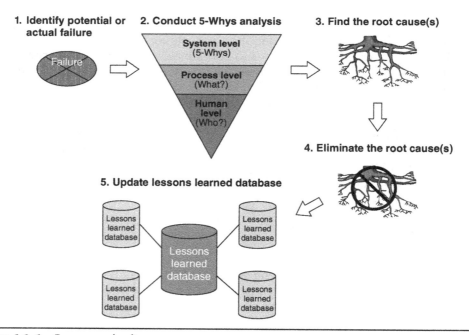

Figure 1.1-1   Empowered culture.
Source: Dalal (2011, 471–85).

empowered employees to optimize the benefits of lean initiatives, ensuring superior levels of customer satisfaction.

Employee empowerment must be done in six steps:

Step 1: Leaders make a commitment to have an engaged workforce

Step 2: Roles and responsibilities are clearly defined

Step 3: Training is conducted for managers, supervisors, staff, and shop-floor personnel

Step 4: Training is conducted for all administrative and support staff

Step 5: A formal idea-suggestion or idea-sharing program that involves all employees is implemented

Step 6: Action is taken to assign responsibility and accountability

Basic Principles of Collaboration

The cultural enabler "collaboration" is the backbone of lean. Lean initiatives do not depend on the knowledge of one but achieve breakthrough results due to the deployment of the collective wisdom of many. In lean organizations, collaboration exists across:

- Various functions

- Different departments

- Staff and union workers—and even between executives and operators

Collaboration and partnerships extend beyond the four walls of the organization and include suppliers, contractors, and, in some cases, competitors.

By design, lean tools allow for a collaborative culture throughout the organization. *Nemawashi*, A3 form, kaizen events, and several other lean tools are designed for automatic collaboration.

1.1.1. RESPECT FOR THE INDIVIDUAL

One of the most critical aspects of lean cultures is the inherent importance placed on valuing individuals and treating each individual with dignity.

In lean organizations, respect starts with the top leaders and permeates throughout the organization. However, "respect for every individual" does not end at the four walls of the organization; rather, it extends to all customers, suppliers, and stakeholders, including the community in which the organization does business.

Respect allows the lean culture to achieve the following goals:

- Create a culture of cohesive teamwork

- Create a culture of continuous improvement

- Increase employee involvement

- Empower employees

- Encourage diversity

A key requirement and an underlying quality required by employees of lean organizations is humility.

Leaders and employees all practice humility as a technique that allows the process of continuous improvement to go on via open collaboration. In lean cultures, everyone is open to learning from one another and to raising their game incrementally on a daily basis in order to generate superior value and increase customer satisfaction.

The key traits of a humble environment are as follows:

- An open learning environment
- People form a critical element of the value stream
- A long-term relationship based on mutual loyalty
- A mentor-mentee, sensei-student relationship throughout the organization
- Lack of discrimination throughout the organization and the entire supply chain

Thus lean organizations and their leaders focus on operational excellence via a people-centric approach by ensuring an empowered, safe, and collaborative environment based on standards and a philosophy of a wholehearted pursuit of long-term excellence.

1.1.2. HUMILITY

> *Humility leads to strength and not to weakness. It is the highest form of self-respect to admit mistakes and to make amends for them.*
>
> —John J. McCloy

Humility ties in directly with respect for the individual (see Section 1.1.1, "Respect for the Individual"). Humility is considered the quality of being modest, unassuming in attitude and behavior. It also can be taken as feeling or showing respect and deference toward other people. Don't think of humility in the lean sense as being meek, shy, and timid or of lesser value. Of course, the opposite of being humble is being arrogant, overconfident, condescending, or egotistical or displaying hubris. Humility is a principle that enables the people in your organization to learn, improve, and excel.

Consider two types of humility: personal humility and leading with humility. This approach helps us understand what it takes to develop our own personal style, along with the similarities and differences in leading people.

Personal Humility

Personal humility can be thought of as having pride (not boastful), self-respect, and dignity. These traits are created over the years with a commitment to integrity, honor, and pursuing lifelong learning. Being humble means that you understand that you don't know everything and can continually learn from those around you. As you learn, you improve. This also involves understanding your strengths and weaknesses. Understanding your strengths allows you to be a better team member, as you bring certain skills to your workplace. Appreciate your weaknesses (or opportunities for improvement) so you can continually develop and progress as a person. Another important role of humility includes being able to accept personal responsibility for your actions. Admit when something doesn't go as planned. *Hansei* is a Japanese word that means "self-reflection" or to acknowledge a mistake and pledge to improve. It is perfectly acceptable to say, "I don't know; let's find out." Humility also includes being authentic to yourself and to others and staying true to your principles or virtues. Another important skill for fostering humility is to perfect your active listening skills and be present for the other person. Humility is also being mindful of others, in your thoughts, speech, and actions. In Stephen Covey's *The 7 Habits of Highly Effective People* (1989, 235), habit 5 says to "seek first to understand, then to be understood." This is a classic example of showing your humility. By reserving your desire to jump in, speak up, and be heard and truly trying to understand the other person's point of view you create a better relationship and find overall solutions to problems. In a way, humility can be thought of as living by the golden rule: Treat others as you would like to be treated. This leads to workplace satisfaction and gratification of a job well done.

Leading with Humility

Leading with humility is not only for the CEO or the president of your organization. Leading with humility should permeate all the way through the ranks to the level of the value-adder. At any one time, everyone has a chance to lead, from daily meetings or training to large-scale projects. Gary Convis (2011) tells of his mentor at NUMMI, Kan Higahsi, telling him his greatest challenge would be "to lead the organization as if I had no power." This is a sure sign of humility.

In his book *Good to Great*, Jim Collins (2001) talks about Level 5 Leadership, of having personal humility and professional will. Table 1.1.2-1 shows a summary of Level 5 Leadership personal humility traits, adapted from the book.

Leading by Deeds

Building trust to become trustworthy as a leader starts with personal humility. Building trust can take time. Your words and actions demonstrate your ability to

Table 1.1.2-1   Level 5 Leadership—personal humility traits.

- Demonstrates a compelling modesty, shunning public adulation; never boastful
- Acts with quiet, calm determination; relies principally on inspired standards, not inspiring charisma, to motivate
- Channels ambitions into the company, not the self; sets up successors for even greater success in the next generation
- Looks out the window, not in the mirror, to apportion credit for the success of the company—to other people, external factors, and good luck

Source: Adapted from Collins (2001, 39–40).

do what you say. An example of this is a leader who says that the customer comes first but then makes it difficult for the customer to contact him or her—making the customer search a website for a telephone number or navigate lengthy phone menus that lead nowhere. As a humble leader, you will need to know how to be patient in developing your people. While there are always deadlines, proper planning, tapping into the creativity of your employees, and having the patience to stay the course will pay off dramatically as you create a more engaged workforce. Always make sure to give credit to others for their contributions to the success of the organization, and take personal responsibility for any letdowns. Learn how to shine the spotlight on others; let them shine in the eyes of the company. If you can learn how to talk to the CEO and the value-adding worker in the same way, you are developing the type of skills that will make you invaluable to your institution. As a leader, design your systems with respect and humility.

Dwight Davis (2011), associate vice president of Utah State University, on the topic of leading with humility, says, "Humility is a key element in building teams, unifying organizations, unleashing employee capabilities, optimizing relationships, designing systems of accountability and achieving a culture of discipline. Humility simply enables individual and organizational learning and improvement."

> We come nearest to the great when we are great in humility.
>
> —Rabindranath Tagore

REFERENCES

ASQ. "Project Planning and Implementing Tools." http://asq.org/learn-about-quality/project-planning-tools/overview/pdca-cycle.html.

Collins, Jim. 2001. *Good to Great.* New York: Harper Business.

Convis, Gary. 2011. "Lean Leadership: The Toyota Way." Keynote speech at the AME conference, Dallas, Texas.

Covey, Stephen. 1989. *The 7 Habits of Highly Effective People.* New York: Simon and Schuster.

Dalal, Adil. 2011. *The 12 Pillars of Project Excellence: A Lean Approach to Improving Project Results.* Boca Raton, FL: CRC Press.

Davis, Dwight. 2011. "Lead with Humility, Respect Every Individual." *GembaWalkabout* blog, October 17. http://gembawalkabout.tumblr.com/post/11595991420/lead-with-humility-respect-every-individual.

Dennis, Pascal. 2007. *Lean Production Simplified: A Plain-Language Guide to the World's Most Powerful Production System.* 2nd ed. New York: Productivity Press.

Imai, Masaaki. 1997. *Gemba Kaizen: A Commonsense, Low-Cost Approach to Management.* New York: McGraw-Hill.

Liker, Jeffrey, and Michael Hoseus. 2008. *Toyota Culture: The Heart and Soul of the Toyota Way.* New York: McGraw-Hill. http://www.lean.org/BookStore/ProductDetails.cfm?SelectedProductId=270.

1.2

Processes for Cultural Enablers

Just as there are principles for cultural enablers, there are also processes. These processes are the ongoing systems and inherent culture of the organization as it continues to improve itself.

1.2.1. PLANNING & DEPLOYMENT

There is an old saying that poor planning guarantees poor execution. It's actually quite shocking how little time and effort companies put into planning their lean implementation. The more common approach is to simply choose a convenient tool, 5S being the most popular (see Section 2.2.1.1, "5S Standards and Discipline"), and apply it with a broad brush across the organization. Certainly this approach can have some positive results, but it is neither sustainable nor comprehensive. Good planning doesn't guarantee good execution, but it gives you the best chance of success. Also, there should not be a "one plan fits all" approach. Every lean implementation should be designed on the basis of specific objectives and characteristics of the particular organization. Additionally, every plan should include at least three basic pillars as the foundation (see Figure 1.2.1-1).

The first pillar is "quick and measurable improvement." It is obvious that the primary objective of any lean transformation is to significantly improve the performance of all critical measures. Lean isn't implemented because it's the nice thing to do for the business; it's implemented because it is the right, and sometimes critical, thing to do for the business. Experience suggests that if the lean implementation is

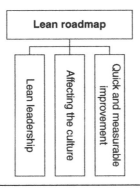

Figure 1.2.1-1 Lean roadmap.

11

not providing significant returns in key performance indicators in the first 12–18 months, someone (usually in finance or accounting) will challenge both the relative effectiveness and the need for lean and decide that resources might be better spent elsewhere. Quick results can be achieved through kaizen events (rapid process improvement), targeted lean demonstration projects, or even some basic tool implementation aimed at quick wins. But be cautious that these relatively quick and measurable wins can become a crutch that limits further lean transformation. Be careful of your transformation becoming what is called "event lean."

The second pillar, and absolute complement to the first pillar, is the development of a lean culture, embedding lean into daily behaviors. Culture is about shared and common principles, practices, and behaviors that will ultimately determine outcome. There is a very simple formula for pillar number two: principles (thinking) drive behaviors, behaviors drive action, and action drives results. Simply put, the desired thinking will get the desired results. There are two ways that lean thinking can be embedded into the organization. The first is through continued repetition. The messages and experiences simply cannot be repeated enough. Remember how you learned the multiplication tables in school? It was all repetition and it stayed with you for life. The second is through application. A principle or practice must be aggressively applied and applied in varying environments if there can be any expectation of embedding the behaviors. This can be accomplished by taking a slice (inch wide/mile deep) of the organization and deeply immersing it in the principles and practices of lean. Then, based on the lessons learned, expand throughout the organization, slice after slice.

The third pillar is the principle of lean leadership. The decision makers in the organization, regardless of level, must be engaged in the lean transformation. This means they provide the direction, participate in the lean activities, provide some of the education, create the tension and need, and certainly exhibit the desired behavior. This can be accomplished through active engagement of leadership in the lean activities and by establishing some sort of lean management structure similar to a steering committee or leadership council. Ideally, the three pillars are implemented simultaneously, but this can be difficult to achieve, as identified in the next section.

Any lean transformation requires, or should require, a framework for the implementation. Lean is a journey, and as with any journey, you need a roadmap (see Figure 1.2.1-2).

Your roadmap's route should be based on a series of issues and concerns that must be considered. A few examples include:

- Business conditions—If the business is just trying to survive, you can forget culture. Just get quick results.

- Baggage—Prior experiences cause people to carry around thinking that might affect implementation. For example, a prior failed continuous improvement implementation can create "program of the month" baggage.

- Resources—The availability, or lack thereof, of resources to support the lean transformation will affect the pace of the implementation. Be very cautious of managing expectations.

- Culture—A risk-adverse culture will require assurances and safety nets. A frugal culture will require proof of return on investment.

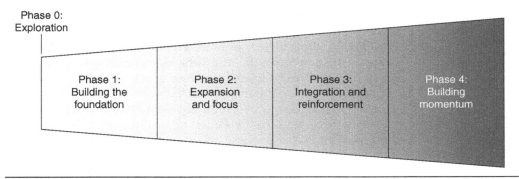

Figure 1.2.1-2   Roadmap for transformation.

These and any other issues and concerns must be considered when developing the roadmap. Also consider designing the roadmap in phases and defining each of the following characteristics in each phase:

- Objectives

- Application

- Education

- Tools and methods

- Communication

- Infrastructure

- Leadership

- Expected results

The roadmap should be developed with three levels of varying detail. Level one generalizes the content of the roadmap for communication across the organization. It's like a map that shows only the major cities and primary roads and thus has lots of white space. Level two provides enough detail for the area/department or even the entire organization to assess where it is on the lean journey and what it must do to advance. This is like adding the small towns and secondary roads to the map and provides more guidance and options. Level three is very detailed and provides the specifics for active implementation. This is like adding all the cities, towns, and communities and all the primary, secondary, and tertiary routes to the map.

I can't stress enough how important it is to develop a roadmap. A very well-known Fortune 500 company often benchmarked for its lean implementation openly admits that it did not develop a roadmap but should have. The company is developing one now after what it considers three false starts. How many false starts can you afford?

1.2.2. CREATE A SENSE OF URGENCY

Creating a sense of urgency can be difficult in good times but is typically easy in bad times when the economy or business conditions are threatening survival. Futurist Joel Barker, in his video *Tactics of Innovation*, discusses five pairs of tactics to get someone to accept a new idea. In the video he makes it very clear that, when things are tough, the only tactics you need are Upside/Yes (there is a lot to be gained) and Downside/No (there is little to no risk). In tough times, it's easy to get people to change—just show them the numbers. However, most lean practitioners and leaders will be challenged to create a sense of urgency in an organization when it is doing well or when the employees believe that the organization is doing well. The real challenge is to overcome the belief that an organization needs to improve and improve significantly. Beliefs are embedded in the thinking of the organization. The way to change these beliefs is by building tension in the organization. Tension is not the same as stress. Whereas stress suggests a feeling of helplessness, tension is about recognizing the gap between where you currently are and where you would like to be. Very simply put, tension is about having a deep understanding of the current state and a well-defined vision of the ideal state. Tension can be used to improve a task, an entire process, or even an entire company by narrowing the gap.

It all starts with a deep understanding of the current state. There are several means to both understand and document the current state:

- Value stream mapping

- Detailed process mapping

- Direct observation

- Videotaping

- Data collection

Regardless of the method used, the key is to understand the *real* current state—not what is desired, not what is documented, but what is real. It is surprising how organizations almost always feel that their current state is better than what is discovered. One of the simplest means to relieve tension, relieve the sense of urgency, is to believe that things are better than they actually are. It's simple but not helpful.

Deeply understanding the current state is only half the formula. The other half is having a well-defined vision of the ideal state. Notice I did not say future state. Future states are simply intermediate gains. The ideal state is a step gain. There may be one or even more than one future state as you move toward ideal, but you must never lose sight of ideal. For example, one company may try to figure out how to fasten a nut and bolt faster (future state), while another company is trying to eliminate the need for the nut and bolt altogether (ideal state). On the surface it may sound difficult to define the vision of an ideal state, but it is actually quite simple. Simply develop a bulleted list of the ideal characteristics of an activity, a process, a department, or even a company. The only restriction is that it must be possible. You can't violate the laws of nature or science. For example, one consumer goods company defined the ideal state for its warehouse receiving process as:

- 100% quality incoming parts

- Correct count (standardize lot sizes)

- Containerization (direct to line)

- Radio frequency

- Bar coding

- Just-in-time

Nothing in the aforementioned ideal-state description is *not* possible, maybe very difficult but possible. For example, getting 100% quality from a supplier may be very difficult, but it is not outside the realm of possibility. Also, cost should never be considered when defining the ideal state. It might be a barrier that prevents achieving ideal, but it does not make the ideal state impossible. The likelihood of achieving the ideal state is low, especially because ideal is often a moving target. However, if you do not focus on the ideal, you will not make the big step gains, only incremental small gains. Remember, there may be one or more future states as you move toward ideal.

A deep understanding of the current state and a well-defined vision of the ideal state will expose the organization to the gap and therefore create the tension, the sense of urgency. The next challenge is to simply identify and remove the barriers to achieving the ideal state. You will most likely not remove all barriers, but the more barriers you do remove, the closer you get to ideal. So, in summary, if you want to create a sense of urgency, follow these three simple steps:

1. Deeply understand the current state

2. Clearly define the ideal state

3. Narrow the gap between steps 1 and 2

1.2.3. MODELING THE LEAN PRINCIPLES, VALUES, PHILOSOPHIES

Webster's dictionary defines *modeling* as "to display by wearing, using or posing." That could not be a better definition for modeling lean. You must *use* it both in your professional practice and in your personal practice, and you must *wear* lean on your sleeve for others to see. It is about exhibiting through action and dialogue the lean thinking and behavior desired of others on a lean journey. Actions always speak louder than words, but both are in their own way a means to model lean behaviors.

Waste elimination is the lifeblood of any lean implementation. It's not enough to ask others to surface waste and then simply support their activities. Every individual, regardless of his or her level in the organization, must be involved in waste elimination. This means that every individual should be performing waste walks routinely and frequently. Develop a standard form for documenting the identified waste and a standard process for providing feedback or entering the suggestions into a structured waste elimination system. Waste walks can be done individually or in teams. It's preferable, however, to do the waste walks in cross-level and cross-functional teams for two reasons. The first reason is the obvious visibility. The second reason is the opportunity to dialogue. In fact, you will find that the real value and opportunity to model lean is not in the actual application of lean tools (waste walks, 5Ss, process maps, etc.) but in the dialogue that is required to plan and implement the tool.

You must be a teacher. Simply subrogating the teaching, either formally or informally, to others is unacceptable. This doesn't mean just standing in front of a classroom. The transfer of skills and knowledge is too important not to share on a daily basis. While this can be about actually scheduling time to teach, it's more about taking advantage of situations that could be teaching moments. It might be helping to solve a problem, implementing a tool, resolving a crisis, or responding to any other situation that is a candidate for a lean solution. These teaching moments occur routinely in the daily practices of the organization. You can't expect a signal (andon) when a teaching moment surfaces. You must seek out these opportunities.

There must be an environment for learning. The lean transformation will require experimentation, action, and new thinking. In many cases these activities may involve risk. The challenge is to create an environment to encourage and support experimentation and new thinking. Learning occurs when people are asked to step out of their comfort zone. This doesn't mean chaos and unorganized change. Stepping out of the comfort zone must be purposeful by setting clear goals and providing effective mechanisms. When people step too far out of their comfort zone, they enter their fear zone. So, in addition to minimizing their comfort zone, you must also eliminate fear. You must provide physical, emotional, and professional safety. If an individual is ridiculed for making a suggestion, you can fully expect that he or she will not venture beyond his or her comfort zone. Regardless of the validity of the idea, it should be a teaching and learning moment, not a moment of embarrassment.

Simply proclaiming support of the lean transformation is not enough. Both active and visible participation are required. Support is easy; participation is far more difficult. Back in the early 1990s one of the big three auto companies had its first kaizen event. A member of that kaizen team was the president of the company. He was in jeans and a company T-shirt and came ready to do whatever was asked of him that entire week. Twenty years later that experience still resonates through the organization, even though that president is long gone. The right "model" is not about watching from the sidelines; it's about active engagement. It's about committing the time to actively participate. Maybe it is waste walks as mentioned earlier. Or it could be a kaizen event, problem solving, building process maps, or implementing lean tools. This is certainly a case where actions speak louder than words.

Lean must also be part of everyone's daily activities. It is not about others applying lean. It's about every individual applying lean to his or her self. It's about individuals aggressively applying lean to daily job functions by developing clearly structured processes for how they perform work and how they spend their time. This can manifest itself in many ways. Performing 5S in your own area is an obvious and simple answer, but it is far more comprehensive than that. Is there scheduled and structured time for reflection? Do you follow a structured problem-solving model? Do you look for the opportunity and the time to teach or coach others? Do you schedule certain critical activities and never vary? Are you auditing the lean implementation?

There are likely many more examples of how individuals can model lean principles, values, and philosophies, but it all comes down to two things: (1) exhibit the behavior you desire of others and (2) encourage and participate in the dialogue to develop lean thinking.

1.2.4. MESSAGE DEPLOYMENT—ESTABLISHING VISION AND DIRECTION

In their book, *Fail-Safe Leadership*, Martin and Mutchler (2003) use the analogy of a game of tug-of-war. In this game, two teams are placed at opposite ends, each holding one end of a rope. The objective is to pull the middle of the rope over a line. On one side, the team members are lined up and ready to pull in the same direction. On the other side, the team members are disorganized and ready to pull the rope in different directions. Which team do you think will win? Obviously the team that is aligned and pulling in the same direction will win. What does this have to do with message deployment? Everything! It all starts with the development of the vision, or direction, for the organization. More specifically, in the context of this handbook, what is the vision of the organization's lean system? What will be the driving force? Perhaps it is, "To eliminate waste and improve customer focus." Or, "To align our processes with the customers' needs and eliminate waste, while achieving Shingo recognition." The message has to fit *your* organization.

To achieve any vision, the organization must be aligned. One obstacle typically encountered on any lean journey is the fear that doing things right the first time and faster will result in cutbacks or layoffs. The emergence of this fear is a direct result of the vision and message deployment. The lean vision should not focus on the reduction of personnel but rather on the leveraging of those resources now available to grow. Growth can be in skills, new product lines, reduced overtime, and so on.

Martin and Mutchler (2003) prescribe clear methods to achieve fail-safe leadership, but key to lean is the alignment described as ensuring that, top to bottom, every employee understands the vision and has goals that directly relate to results. Their model is shown in Figure 1.2.4-1.

In the lean journey, this approach, or a similar approach, will ensure that the organization is aligned and that all functions are striving for the same results. The

Figure 1.2.4-1 Message alignment.

Source: Adapted from Martin and Mutchler (2003).

vision is established at the top and communicated across the organization through meetings, webinars, and webcasts or by any other effective means. Be wary of just making posters, hanging them up, and expecting the vision to be achieved—this is not communication or message deployment. Allowing for personal interaction and holding question-and-answer sessions will help with alignment.

After the vision is defined, strategies, goals, actions, and measures are established. Measures are not always needed and are typically driven by the organization's culture and size; however, they are helpful in ensuring alignment and fact-based decisions regarding progress. These are established at a level where they are functional to personnel and need to be reviewed to ensure they do not conflict—remember the tug-of-war—from one function to the other. For example, a facility may want to lower electricity costs by shutting down the lights and the heating system at night, but production may want to operate some machines at night to perform maintenance.

Personnel will establish goals and actions that align with functional goals and strategies (critical success factors). To achieve this message, deployment has to occur not only for the vision but also for the functional level, after strategies and functional goals or actions are reviewed to ensure there are no conflicts with other functions. This is an investment in time and energy that pays rapid dividends through everyone pulling the rope in the same direction at the same time.

Developing the vision at the top, then, involves more levels as each successive item that works in the organization is defined. In other words, don't change how you do things to fit the model above, but use the model within the organization's system to ensure alignment and results. Involve appropriate subject matter experts and formal and informal leaders to define the functional goals, actions, and measures.

Communicate the overall vision and functional goals to all levels. Ensure each person has goals and actions (one to three is the norm) that align with the overall vision and the function in which he or she works. Check and communicate progress regularly and make adjustments when necessary. Use the checks to ensure continued alignment. Stress the importance of achieving the vision and the benefits. Commit to the lean journey and ensure that it has little or no impact on staffing levels and that it is used to grow skills, people, and business results.

1.2.5. INTEGRATING LEARNING AND COACHING

To help the organization shift to a lean culture, learning and coaching must be part of the equation. Learning allows for the sharing of knowledge, personnel growth, removal of barriers, and the demonstration of leadership commitment. Coaching is a method used to enable learning and improvement. Integrating these into the planning and deployment, along with sustainment, provides continual benefits through improved morale, execution, idea generation, and retention.

All personnel, from individual contributors to executive leadership, must be involved with the learning process. A key concept of learning is to ensure continual application of the knowledge gained. In other words, once personnel learn a skill or gain knowledge, there should be an established expectation that that skill or knowledge is applied regularly in support of organizational and lean objectives.

As part of the lean culture shift and integrated learning, there will be formal and informal learning. Formal learning includes goal setting, teaching or facilitation (classroom, web-based, etc.), verification of knowledge gain (completion of exercises, case studies, testing, projects, etc.), and reinforcement of knowledge gain (a knowledge check following completion of the learning experience). Informal learning includes on-the-job training and coaching and mentoring. Formal learning is structured to account for adult learning styles and needs.

A formal learning process includes the following:

- Stated objectives

- Lesson plans

- Formal verification of knowledge gain

- Knowledge check

- Optional qualification or certification

Lean Bronze Certification, through the Society of Manufacturing Engineers (SME), the Association of Manufacturing Excellence (AME), the Shingo Prize, and the American Society for Quality (ASQ), is an example of formal learning. Organizations develop their own formal learning with a focus on their implementation of lean. Learning is usually broken down to meet different objectives of awareness, execution, project leadership, and program design. This learning may also include subsets within execution and project leadership based on the expectation (e.g., Lean Bronze, Silver, and Gold or Six Sigma Green Belt, Black Belt, and Master Black Belt). Not all learning is performed at one time, nor is all learning developed at the same level of difficulty, time invested, and length of course.

As the lean culture shift starts, all personnel receive lean awareness training, but those leading the initiative receive more in-depth training. Lean awareness training explains the organization's goals of lean, leadership's commitment, what will occur, how it impacts personnel, expectations for personnel involvement, top-level training, deployment schedules, and so on. This awareness training should emphasize that the goal of a lean culture is to execute smarter, eliminate waste, and grow skills and capability—it is not intended as a program that reduces the workforce. Reduction in personnel is typically a major workforce concern, and thus leadership must emphasize that it is not a goal or intention.

In formal training, on-the-job training is done at the lowest levels possible. It usually has top-level goals (e.g., ensure new hire can operate machines in work area effectively and efficiently) but no set agenda, timeline, and so on. It may have some level of competency testing, but it is usually completed when the trainer believes the trainee is able to execute correctly, safely, and efficiently.

In formal training, that critical knowledge transfer from one employee to another is something lean wants to leverage throughout time. Every person executing an activity, working with a tool or machine, or dealing with a process knows what works well and what doesn't. They know the value-added activities and waste (muda). The ability to tap into this knowledge, especially during area lean blitzes or kaizen events, is crucial to success and sustainment of changes and gains. If this knowledge is not captured, leveraged, and utilized once the blitz or kaizen event is done, personnel will revert to their way of doing things.

Additionally, understanding how things are really done will help the organization make effective changes and improve worker safety.

Coaching generally uses a nurturing approach to achieve an end goal. Good coaches keep the end goal in mind at all times; they recognize that there will be setbacks and know how to overcome them. When a setback occurs, a coach will assess the situation; adapt with small, incremental change (usually); and then guide the team to overcome the challenge and succeed.

Coaching relies on the ability to communicate and motivate, ensuring that "leanspeak" can be translated so that all involved understand. Coaching utilizes formal and informal leaders within the organization to ensure acceptance of the lean culture shift. The coaching method engages employees, improves performance, and reduces the effort needed to implement and sustain lean.

Learning and coaching are vital cultural enablers for lean. Learning ensures that personnel gain knowledge, apply the knowledge gained, and retain the knowledge, and it lays the foundation for culture shift and lean execution. Coaching reinforces learning, elevates employees to perform, and leverages personnel throughout the organization to adapt and embrace the culture shift and drive improvements to perform effectively and efficiently.

1.2.6. PEOPLE DEVELOPMENT—EDUCATION, TRAINING & COACHING

What does the organization do if it has a goal to penetrate a new product line or market? One method is that the organization first learns about that product line or market and then determines how to best leverage its performance to differentiate and penetrate that product line or market. This is an example of education, training, and coaching.

In lean, people development through education, training, and coaching is a key cultural component. Education can be formal or informal and external or internal to the organization. Training is also formal or informal and is usually internal to the organization or leverages external training that aligns with the organization's goals and lean system. Coaching leverages the education and training to guide people to achieve the desired results.

Education can take the form of degrees, courses, or certifications offered by external organizations like community colleges and universities or specialized organizations like ASQ and SME. Education is available in lean, components of lean, quality, and the like. In most cases, education involves a broad scope of the entire lean or functional area with depth in most, if not all, aspects of the area. Formal education is a needed investment for subject matter experts, especially those who will guide the organization and serve as coaches.

Training, on the other hand, is usually broken down into smaller aspects of lean. It begins with a top-level overview provided to the entire organization to achieve the alignment needed (see Section 1.2.4, "Message Deployment—Establishing Vision and Direction"). Then, more specialized training is available, or required, on the critical aspects of lean. The overview ties to the organization's vision and provides a high-level look at what lean is, how it works, what are its goals and objectives, and how people are engaged and contribute. Specialized training is used to expand on lean principles and tools like value stream mapping and 5S.

Specialized training is targeted to those involved with implementing the associated principles and tools to achieve the desired results. Training can include training within the industry and on-the-job training.

Coaching is more personal. It is provided by subject matter experts and leaders when and where needed. It may be to help get past a roadblock or to supplement skills where training is not available or needed to execute on a regular basis. For example, coaching may be done to help a team apply a lean principle or tool not ordinarily needed, and thus each individual does not need the training and ability to execute that specific principle or tool on their own. Coaching can also be used to make adjustments in execution to drive alignment.

Personnel development through education, training, and coaching provides everyone in the organization with needed skills enhancement and knowledge at the right time to ensure alignment and provide the foundation to achieve the desired results.

1.2.7. MOTIVATION, EMPOWERMENT & INVOLVEMENT

Education is not only important to a lean transformation, it's critical. However, a common mistake that organizations make is that they provide the education (the how) before they provide the purpose (the why). It is difficult to motivate individuals to accept a new idea, and especially difficult if they don't first understand the purpose or the value of the new idea. Most people will not accept what they don't value unless they do so only on blind faith. For example, a common lament is how difficult it is to sustain 5S. This is because most people believe the purpose of 5S is only about housekeeping and therefore is not seen as very valuable. What they don't realize is that the real purpose is the ability to see abnormal conditions and subsequently eliminate waste. They can see a lot more value in 5S when they understand the purpose, the why. Understanding the why establishes the value.

There are five phases to any change initiative:

Phase I—Enlightenment. This is simply about establishing the purpose—the "why"—before you provide the education. You can teach a new skill, but getting someone who doesn't see its value to use it will happen only by demand, not by desire.

Phase II—Education. This is self-explanatory. It's providing the "how." Providing someone with how to do or to accept something without first providing the why will likely diminish the chance for success.

Phase III—Empowerment. Once individuals know why and how, you must give them a chance to really learn through application and experimentation. *Very important*: Never have anyone assume new responsibilities before first providing him or her the skills. Empowerment requires the development of skills and/or knowledge first.

Phase IV—Experience. Empowerment provides the opportunity for multiple experiences, and subsequent multiple experiences will develop the expertise.

Phase V—Enrichment. This simply means "results." Any change initiative that follows the first four phases can fully expect to get the desired results.

As mentioned earlier, education is critical. Phase II is all about education. However, effectively transferring skills and knowledge can be difficult. A proven approach to effective education is "learn, apply, and reflect." Every educational experience should go through these three steps; some cases require more than one cycle.

1. *Learn.* Individuals must be provided the knowledge and skills required to achieve the desired expectations.

2. *Apply.* Knowledge without application will not be internalized. Adults in particular learn far better through application and the opportunity to discover on their own.

3. *Reflect.* Blinding acceptance that the skill or knowledge transfer has been effective is a common error. You must also reflect back on both the education and the applications to ensure that the knowledge or skills have been developed. If they have not been developed, it may be necessary to start the cycle again.

Understanding the five phases of change and the three-step approach to education is not easy, but it's important. They must be framed with some basic tactics for success. The use of tactics can be just as effective in getting people to accept lean, a new idea, as it is in getting people to accept a new product.

According to Joel Barker, tactics can be explained in pairs (see Figure 1.2.7-1):

Upside Yes/Downside No. The idea/concept must be presented from the user's point of view with a clear understanding of what is to be gained and what, if any, risks there might be. If the downside (real or perceived) is bigger than the upside, the idea will not be embraced.

Seemingly Simple/Small Steps. What new idea and concept can be offered from the user's current point of view, from what the user currently understands? If lean is a foreign term but continuous improvement is well understood, use continuous improvement as the introduction. You also need to start small. Learn from taking small steps and then accelerate the pace.

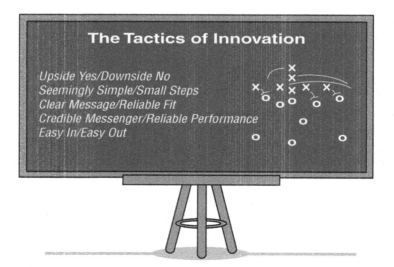

Figure 1.2.7–1   The tactics of innovation.

Clear Message/Reliable Fit. You must use language that the user is familiar and comfortable with. You can add to the vocabulary, but don't change it. Also, the more the idea matches what already exists, the easier it is to understand. For example, at one lead refinery, impurities skimmed off the top of a refining kettle are called DROSS. DROSS is an acronym that means *d*etermine, *r*emove, *o*rganize, *s*anitize, and *s*ustain. It's the same as 5S, but it's much easier for the organization to understand and accept.

Credible Messenger/Reliable Performance. There must be believability and respect from those presenting the idea. If you yourself don't have the credibility (may be new to the organization), get it from someone else. Also, failure is OK if you use it as a learning experience. Repeated failure, however, is unacceptable.

Easy In/Easy Out. Entry into a new idea, concept, or tool should be easy, low-cost, and relatively risk-free. Getting out or going back should also be easy and risk-free.

There is nothing easy about getting individuals and organizations to accept and implement lean. While there is no simple formula, if you consider all the aforementioned insights, you will have a much better chance for success. It is very important and must be stressed that motivating, empowering, and involving people in the lean journey cannot be an afterthought. It must be in the forefront of a lean implementation plan.

1.2.8. ENVIRONMENTAL SYSTEMS

A company must ensure that it assesses all aspects of the work environment in order to maximize the impact from lean activities. A company has two environmental systems priorities: those to the community and those to the employees. Social responsibility standards and environmental protection regulations, in part, address the community environmental concerns. Management system standards, worker protection regulations, improvement programs, and productivity measures address employee environmental systems.

The community priority is to ensure that the materials and processes used and the waste generated are properly obtained, controlled, utilized, and disposed. Since there are numerous regulations and variations associated with these regulations, this portion of environmental systems is highlighted to ensure awareness. Additionally, the company's view and commitment to social responsibility will have a significant influence on its willingness to address these requirements beyond regulations. If the company is committed to social responsibility, this commitment can leverage lean principles and reduce regulatory oversight. In the United States, the Voluntary Protection Program (VPP) of the Occupational Safety and Health Administration (OSHA) is an example of reduced oversight through a company's commitment to community and employee social responsibility. When implementing a lean program and assessing the potential for return on investment, reduced regulatory oversight and community satisfaction should be considered.

Work environment conditions, as they relate to employees, were the focus of many studies in the twentieth century. One of the most prominent is the Hawthorne Works (part of Western Electric) experiments in the 1920s and 1930s. These

1.2.8

experiments attempted to assess the impact of lighting and other conditions on employee productivity. Although there are questions about the validity of the data due to improvement sustainment issues, the debate is driven by trying to determine whether the productivity improvements were the result of the lighting changes or the attention the employees received. What should not be ignored is that there were productivity improvements.

When implementing a lean program, key considerations with regard to environmental systems include:

- Area cleanliness

- Lighting

- Heating, ventilation, and air conditioning (HVAC)

Area Cleanliness

Area cleanliness supports many aspects of the 5S process. From an environmental perspective, area cleanliness allows for easy identification of spills and other potential hazards, defective machinery, leaks, and so on. Additionally, area cleanliness helps eliminate potential safety issues like trip hazards. When assessing area cleanliness, as detailed in the 5S, provide for regular and deep cleaning. Regular cleaning consists of surface cleaning that occurs at the end of the task, shift, or day. Deep cleaning is intended to go a level or two deeper and includes mopping or waxing the floor, dusting light fixtures and HVAC ducting, cleaning storage areas, cleaning behind work stations, and so on.

Lighting

Lighting, as shown in the Hawthorne Works experiments, is important to ensure that employees can see adequately to perform the tasks assigned. Both general area lighting and task lighting appropriate to the work being performed should be provided. Lighting type, lumens (total light output), Kelvin (light temperature/color), wattage, source voltage type (line power, battery, etc.), and focus (pinpoint or flood) all must be considered to ensure proper light selection. Additionally, it might be necessary to assess how the lighting will affect the task being performed. For example, if the task involves assessment of color matching, then the light Kelvin should be considered to ensure it does not affect product quality. Lighting is an important part of the environment and can affect worker fatigue, productivity, quality, and so on, so the company should ensure it is evaluated as part of the overall environment.

HVAC

Heating, ventilation, and air conditioning (HVAC), like lighting, are environmental conditions that are typically controllable and could affect the workforce or product quality. There are many conditions (temperature, air flow rate, particle size and density, etc.) that need to be analyzed and understood. Their effect on employees, work tasking, and product should be understood and communicated. For example, work in a foundry is different from that in a semiconductor clean room. When assessing these environmental conditions, the company will need to prioritize product, task, and employee requirements. Communication of these priorities and what allowances can be made by the employees is necessary to ensure understanding. For example, semiconductor clean room or operating room environments require employees to wear certain protective clothing that differs from that worn by individuals who perform welding.

A company needs to know how the environment impacts it and how it impacts the environment. Assessments of work tasking and products are completed to help gain insight into impacts and identify controllable conditions. These controllable conditions are communicated to employees or the community, as appropriate. Then, working together, the controllable environmental conditions are adjusted to improve work conditions, employee satisfaction and productivity, product quality, and quality of life, along with safety.

1.2.9. SAFETY SYSTEMS

Safety systems are attributable to product and work environments. Product safety is the responsibility of the company and may be verified or tested by outside sources (e.g., Underwriters Laboratory). Safety applies to all work environments—from the office to manufacturing to engineering to the field.

Product Safety

Product safety may be regulated by external organizations, contractual requirements, or government agencies. The company must understand these external requirements and, similar to environmental regulations, determine whether to adhere to the minimal requirements or go beyond them. The decision to go beyond the minimum requirements may be driven by factors such as community and consumer (or end user) protection or a product/business differentiator. Examples of these business decisions to go beyond regulations are numerous in the automobile industry, where many automakers provided or offered seat belts, antilock brakes, accelerator override systems, and so on, before they were required by government regulations. Some companies, such as Volvo, shared safety advances with others even though they received patents to differentiate themselves from others and advance overall product safety.

Work Safety

Work environment safety systems are primarily used to improve work conditions, employee safety, and productivity—all goals of lean. Safety systems range from assessments to engineered controls. The company evaluates its work conditions (e.g., office, manufacturing) to identify potential safety hazards. Hazards can range from repetitive-motion issues to life-threatening hazards.

"Poor ergonomics has perhaps the biggest impact on safety. Ergonomic injuries comprise more than 50 percent of all workplace injuries in North America. . . . The most important ergonomic risk factors are posture, force, and repetition" (Dennis 2007, 22). Understanding these factors, work locations and placement, and movement will allow the company to reduce waste (muda) by

1.2.9

eliminating the non-value-added work. Additionally, the company and work-force can reduce injuries, resulting in a positive impact on the bottom line in areas such as insurance costs, lost time, and regulatory oversight. Assessment of ergonomics is done through survey and observation.

The survey can be generic or specific to the task and usually has questions that assess, at a minimum:

- Layout (work surface, storage, etc.)

- Body position versus work (reach, leg positioning, posture, seated, standing, walking, etc.)

- Task duration (how often performed, how long, position change frequency, etc.)

- Lifting (how often, how heavy, how big, etc.)

The survey can be automated or paper-based. Each category (layout, body position, etc.) has several questions and uses a Likert scale, a numbered or worded scale to rank the answer to a question (e.g., "always," "sometimes," or "rarely"). The data for each category are collected and scored to assess potential risk. Based on the score, an employee may take action, automatic workstation improvements may be implemented, or an ergonomic observation may be scheduled. An ergonomic observation is done by a trained person who watches the work being performed and determines actions that can be taken to reduce the potential for injury or eliminate wasted motion.

Like ergonomic study and change, engineered controls are assessed and implemented to prevent injury. Usually done during workstation or equipment design, engineered controls can also be done as part of improvement programs through upgrades or changes to the workstation or equipment. Examples of engineered controls include:

- Steel press cages preventing body or limb encroachment

- Machinery operating buttons that require both hands (with arms spread apart) to operate

Safety systems include awareness and training, surveys, and engineered controls. The purpose of safety systems is to prevent injury, improve product and work environment safety, and positively impact business operations and profit. Understanding the potential hazards, eliminating or reducing them, and providing appropriate awareness and training can influence employee satisfaction, community (customer) opinion, and profits.

REFERENCES

Barker, Joel. 2010. *Tactics of Innovation* (video). http://www.tacticsofinnovation.com.

Dennis, Pascal. 2007. *Lean Production Simplified: A Plain-Language Guide to the World's Most Powerful Production System.* 2nd ed. New York: Productivity Press.

Martin, Linda L., and David G. Mutchler. 2003. *Fail-Safe Leadership: Straight Talk about Correcting the Leadership Challenges in Your Organization.* Orlando, FL: Delta Books.

1.3

Cultural Enabler Techniques and Practices

L ean isn't as much about the tools as it is about changing a culture, a way of thinking. How does one go about making these changes? In this section, the key elements of techniques and practices are explained in order to create the new thinking that is required for a lean organization. It focuses on training, coaching and mentoring, and communication.

1.3.1. CROSS TRAINING

Cross training is a staple of lean manufacturing. Essentially, cross training involves teaching an employee to do a different part of the organization's work. It also refers to having multiple employees trained to do a single task, which establishes backups, leads to more well-rounded employees, and reduces the potential for bottlenecks. Cross training can be used in almost any position in almost any industry.

Reducing Bottlenecks

One of the greatest tools an organization can have is its own flexibility and ability to adapt to new situations, such as variations in supply and demand. One problem many companies face is bottlenecking. To reduce the bottlenecks in your business and maintain a happy and productive workforce in the lean tradition, your people must be cross trained as much as possible.

In lean companies, cross training is a prerequisite to supervisory and leadership positions, as the team leaders, group leaders, and even area managers are responsible for training, filling in for absent workers, and being intimately familiar with the processes they manage and possible problems within them.

Cross training employees provides flexibility. It allows leaders to shift people around to cover for breaks, vacations, and illnesses and to adjust staffing when demand shifts.

Cross training promotes continuous improvement with the rotation of a fresh set of eyes to observe and question the process. It also enables sharing and development of best practices across an organization.

A long-term investment in people through cross training pays off for everyone. Every employer has an obligation to promote cross training, as it creates a win-win-win situation: The employee, the company, and the customer all win.

Employee Development

There are many good reasons to cross train employees and to make cross training part of an overall employee development program:

- It provides staffing flexibility when an employee is on vacation, is out due to an emergency, or has moved to a new position. Cross-trained employees who can step in and fulfill open job responsibilities eliminate the need to spend money on temporary staff.

- Employees gain an understanding of the connections between departments and tasks to run the business. As a result, they are better able to answer customer questions and handle any problems that come up.

- Problems or suggestions for improvement may be identified when a different person performs the task.

- Employees experience a change in routine, thus reducing boredom.

- Employees feel valued because the employer is investing time and resources into their development.

- Candidates for higher-level jobs may be identified during the process.

Creating Cross-Training Plans

Take the following steps to create a successful employee cross-training plan:

1. Identify the tasks performed for various jobs and designate which ones could be successfully performed by other people.

2. Identify who is interested in participating in the program. It may be counterproductive to force someone to participate. Decide how to deal with this situation.

3. Identify who has the competencies to perform the tasks designated as cross trainable in step 1.

4. Develop a training process. Either the supervisor or the person currently performing the job can do the training. It is important to provide adequate instruction to the trainer on how to train. Don't assume the person has this expertise.

5. Reduce the employee's workload during training and while tasks are being performed. Otherwise, the person may feel resentful about the process.

6. Allow time for the employee to learn and practice skills. Don't assume he or she will pick up the new process and retain it forever. Outline a schedule for the employee to perform the new skill periodically and expect beginner mistakes while he or she is learning.

7. Recognize and reward employees who gain new skills and/or responsibilities.

8. Incorporate the cross-training process into an overall development plan for the employee.

Visual Cross-Training Records

As with many lean processes, a key to managing the cross-training process is to make it visible. The status of employee cross training is normally marked on a cross-training matrix that shows people along the side and jobs along the top. The level of training (generally something like "Trained," "In training," and "Not trained") is depicted. The matrix helps area leaders plan where to assign people. It is also the basis for forming a training plan.

Cross training not only offers employees the opportunity to learn more skills but also gives you ready backup for when your needs change on a dime. And, cross-trained employees can contribute even more to kaizen because they come to a process knowing how other processes function. They offer a fresh perspective.

Cross training is not a one-time event, however. It's a continuous process of tracking the skills and skill levels of each employee and scheduling additional training and reinforcement to fill in or prevent gaps.

1.3.2. SKILLS ASSESSMENT

A skill matrix is used to assess the training needs of the employees in an organization. A *skill matrix* is a table that is created by listing the skills required for a job position in an organization and then comparing this against the skills the employee already possesses. The skill set for every position in an organization is documented in a matrix format and compared with the employee's skills. Once documented, the skill set can be reviewed; any resultant blank spaces on the matrix are gaps in the employee's skill set that need to be addressed through training. The skill matrix therefore becomes a tool for managers, trainers, and human resource personnel, since it identifies training needs, unmet requirements, employee competency, and the core competency of the organization. Human resource managers can use the skill matrix to actively recruit personnel with the necessary talent and to identify where a desirable skill is missing.

The skill matrix is also a visual tool in that it shows managers the cross-trained employees (see Section 1.3.1, "Cross Training"), identifies candidates who can advance grades, and so on. In some instances, pay grades can be tied to the skill sets and competency levels, providing the organization with a clear-cut path for advancement of personnel. In lean, an emphasis is placed on training and advancing employees through education and personnel development.

In gemba, the skill matrix becomes indispensable as employees multitask in a cell and are responsible for a wide variety of activities. These activities may include managing multiple and different types of machines, working with suppliers, packaging, performing some amount of preventive maintenance, and so on. In these situations the supervisor needs to know what the employees are skilled in, and the employees need to know what they need to learn in order to perform their job adequately.

Developing a Skill Matrix

For every position in the organization, do the following:

1. Identify the skill set required for that position. This information can be obtained from many sources, such as standard operating procedures, work instructions, subject matter experts, experienced employees, machine manuals, and so on.

2. Identify all personnel in that department or functional area who hold that position in the organization.

3. For a simple matrix: Populate the matrix with an "X" or an "O" if the employee possesses that skill; if the employee does not possess that skill, leave the space blank. A blank space means that training is required or that a gap exists in the employee's skill set. Complex matrices can be created showing different levels of skills.

An example of a blank skill matrix is given in Figure 1.3.2-1. Each quadrant can be colored as the employee's proficiency level advances through training.

Managers can then look at the completed training matrix and identify gaps that can be addressed through training. Departmental training gaps can be aggregated to formulate an enterprise-wide training plan to address key requirements.

Once the training has been provided and the appropriate competency tested, the skill matrix can be updated. A typical legend for a skill matrix is presented in Figure 1.3.2-2.

The entire skill matrix needs to be reviewed and updated under all these conditions:

- New employee hire
- An employee transfers from one department to another
- An employee leaves the organization
- Changes to legal or regulatory requirements
- Requirements for a position change
- New technology demands certain skill sets

Figure 1.3.2-1 Skills matrix example.

Level	Description	Criteria	Symbol
0	Cannot do	• Insufficient knowledge or experience to perform to standard	
1	Knows all elements of task	• Has fully reviewed instructions and reference materials and is familiar with tools of the job	
2	Can do the basics	• Has received instruction from a level 4 instructor • Has performed task correctly before a level 4 instructor	
3	Can do fully	• Qualified by level 4 instructor	
4	Can teach others how to do	• Has taught or audited another person's work within 90 days	

Figure 1.3.2-2 Skills training matrix competency levels.

An annual review should be conducted, even if nothing has changed, to ensure that everything is accurate. A skill matrix, therefore, is an integral part of a visual management system that aids managers with resource planning and managing and monitoring skill levels within the organization.

1.3.3. INSTRUCTIONAL GOALS

A learning objective answers the question, "What is it that your students should be able to do at the end of the learning that they could not do before?" A learning objective makes clear the intended learning outcome or product of instruction, rather than what form the instruction will take.

Learning objectives focus on student performance. Action verbs that are specific, such as *list*, *describe*, *report*, *compare*, *demonstrate*, and *analyze*, should be used to describe the behaviors students will be expected to perform.

Generally, when writing instructional goals, consider the following:

- Every instructional goal should represent an intended learning outcome.

- Each instructional goal should begin with a verb that is general enough to cover a domain of student performance.

- Each instructional goal should be limited to one general learning outcome.

- Instructional goals should be free of specific subject matter or content.

- Instructional goals are further defined by a set of specific, representative learning outcomes.

Clearly defined goals and objectives form the foundation for selecting appropriate content, learning activities, and assessment measures. If both the instructor and the students do not clearly understand the objectives of the course, or if your learning activities do not relate to the objectives and the content that you think are important, your methods of assessment (which are supposed to indicate to both learner and instructor how effective the learning and teaching process has been) will be at best misleading and at worst irrelevant, unfair, or even useless.

1.3.4. ON-THE-JOB TRAINING

On-the-job training (OJT) is a very common form of training in the workplace. Both new employees and experienced employees can be trained on the job while learning a new skill set or becoming familiar with new technology. Due to rapidly changing tools and technology in today's workplace, OJT is the most common means of employee training. There are two aspects of OJT: (1) the person undergoing the training and (2) the trainer. For OJT to be successful, the requirements and evaluation criteria for the trainee must be determined prior to the training delivery, and the trainer needs to be well versed and experienced in the technology of the training being imparted. In other words, the trainer has to be able to transfer the knowledge and intricacies of what is being taught so that the trainee can be effective and perform the duties efficiently. Post-training evaluation is a must in these situations in order for the trainer and the manager to obtain an objective appraisal of the trainee's capabilities post-OJT.

A successful OJT program takes into consideration all of the following:

- Selecting and preparing a trainer
- Developing training materials
- Setting up post-training evaluation criteria
- Determining certifications
- Conducting lessons learned post-training

Selecting and Preparing a Trainer

A good trainer must know the job and be able to impart the knowledge to the trainee. The most experienced person in the workplace is not always the best trainer; what they may take for granted or deem trivial may not be imparted to the employee. A trainer or coach must possess certain traits, such as responsiveness, humor, enthusiasm, honesty, flexibility, and tolerance. Trainers should be given clear-cut expectations for how the success criteria for the program will be determined. This is done through involving the employee's manager and supervisor to establish the curriculum and identify desired skill sets.

Developing Training Materials

In some instances, training can be performed for multiple employees in a workshop-type session. If that is the desired format, appropriate training materials will need to be prepared according to a well-defined lesson plan. The trainer will need time for materials presentation and printing. Other logistics will also need to be considered: location of the training, schedules of all participants involved, and technology used to support the training.

Setting Up Post-Training Evaluation Criteria

One measure of the success of a training program is evaluating whether the trainee has gained the skills that were taught and can perform those tasks with minimum supervision. One way to evaluate training is to use a checklist and solicit feedback as to whether the trainee understands the material that was taught. This type of self-evaluation may have some drawbacks, in that the evaluation is subjective. A better method for post-training evaluation is through tests or audits. The best method for evaluation, however, is the supervisor's ability to directly link an improvement in the skill level of the trainee after OJT to the training.

Determining Certifications

Some organizations award certifications to the trainees after completion of OJT. Certification documents that the trainee has received the necessary skill sets to be able to conduct his or her duties in the workplace. In some instances, there may be levels of certification within an organization, such as with a Lean–Six Sigma program, in which there is an increase in complexity of the tools being taught and the trainees will need to complete basic requirements before they can progress to the next level.

Certifications may also be provided to trainers, in which trainers are certified according to certain guidelines. Trainer certification is important, as it ensures that the trainer knows the subject matter and is able to teach the necessary skills.

Conducting Lessons Learned Post-Training

As with any program, once OJT has been delivered, the program needs to be evaluated with respect to what went well, what did not go well, and what changes need to be made. This is in line with the Plan-Do-Check-Act (PDCA) methodology of continuous improvement, where the focus is on the training program itself. Lessons learned should be formally documented and conveyed to all the participants involved: trainer, trainee, supervisor, and management.

The biggest benefit of OJT is that it is cost-effective, since the training is done on-site using experienced employees. Additionally, the employee's manager is involved in setting up the training curriculum, and the employee receives real-time feedback.

1.3.5. COACHING & MENTORING

We expect greatness from all our people. We expect them to accept and conquer challenges that may seem overwhelming at first glance. The greatness in people comes out only when they are led by great leaders. We are all growing and learning, and we all need teachers and coaches to help guide us. We say at Toyota that every leader is a teacher developing the next generation of leaders. This is their most important job.

—Akio Toyoda, president of the
Toyota Motor Corporation

Coaching and mentoring by management and others are critical elements of understanding lean as a philosophy and respect for people. The primary task

Table 1.3.5-1   Coaching and mentoring qualities.

• Is accessible, makes time	• Gives useful feedback	• Is practical
• Adjusts as necessary	• Guides	• Shows respect
• Allows safe risk taking	• Provides insight	• Is a role model
• Is a good communicator	• Inspires	• Shares
• Counsels	• Has integrity	• Is supportive
• Is credible	• Instructs	• Teaches
• Has discipline	• Develops leaders	• Trains
• Directs	• Leads	• Tutors
• Has empathy	• Is a good listener	• Wants you to succeed
• Encourages with confidence	• Is motivated and motivates	
• Has and shows enthusiasm	• Has patience	

of Toyota's managers and leaders does not revolve around improvement per se, but around increasing the improvement capability of people (Rother 2010). Coaching and mentoring are two of the most important things management can do to develop people to help them reach their full potential. Managers must recognize their responsibility to strengthen their team members. Good managers recognize the difference between stretching their team members, which helps them grow, and overloading their team members, which does damage (Dennis 2007).

Coaching and mentoring carry many of the same traits, but there are also some subtle differences. Similar characteristics are shown in Table 1.3.5-1.

Sports Analogy for Coaching

The achievements of an organization are the results of the combined effort of each individual.

—Vince Lombardi

Think of individuals who coach sports and their role on the team. During training and practice they give advice and encouragement to players. If there are deficiencies, they take the time to show a player the correct way or form. They introduce new plays and have the team practice them. They watch how the players are feeling and whether there might be anything that prevents their top performance. Before the game they draw up the best starting lineup based on players' abilities and availability. They prepare a game plan. They confer with the other coaches, trainers, and doctors to make sure they are well informed. During the game, they monitor the performance of their players. They think steps or plays ahead; they may even call the plays. They look to see whether adjustments need to be made. They substitute players as needed. They look for ways to create the win.

Coaching Tasks

A coach can perform many tasks, including:

- Performing skills assessments—see what skills your team possesses and what skills are needed (gap analysis).

- Training, on-the-job training (OJT), and cross training—train others to follow standardized work and to seek opportunities for kaizen or improvements to the methods.

- Promoting teamwork—this can include stepping in when needed or helping team members who are going through difficulties.

- Developing leaders—identify potential leaders and find opportunities for them to help solve problems or improve processes.

- Information sharing (Yokoten)—make sure lessons learned are thoughtfully communicated to the people who can benefit from them.

- Monitoring and helping to implement ideas from suggestion systems— use these opportunities to see how team members think; what is their thought process? It is not about stepping in and solving the problem for them. Give them a safe environment to work on their solution.

- Solving problems—Use experience, education, skills, creativity, innovation, and "go see" to help solve problems. Practice Plan-Do-Check-Act (PDCA).

A coach does not always have to be a team leader, a supervisor, or a manager; a coach can be a coworker, someone more experienced at that particular skill or task who helps others. Sometimes the best coaches are those without fancy titles, people who are well respected for their work, enthusiasm, and willingness to share.

A key element to being a good coach is continually learning new things. It is important to not only stretch the knowledge of coaching a task but also include learning about human nature, teaching techniques for adults, communication effectiveness, and more. A coach is a lifelong learner. It is said that the teacher sometimes learns more than the student, meaning that by preparing to teach and observing human nature, the instructor builds more skills and becomes a better teacher as a result.

Mentoring

Mentoring is typically a long-term commitment between mentor and mentee, along with the willingness of both members to work together. A good fit of personalities is important. In a nutshell, mentors teach and give advice or guidance to a mentee, and the mentee works on the issue to learn and grow. The mentor should get himself or herself and the mentee to the point where "I don't know" is an acceptable and valid answer. And when "I don't know" is the answer, it is time to go and see (Rother 2010)!

Leaders may find different mentors for different stages of their career. Budding leaders should actively seek out mentors to help them on their improvement journey. Mentors may be one or two levels above the mentee's position, or in the case of executive management, they may be at the same level but from another discipline. Even top executives should seek out mentors to help them become better at what they do. Lifelong learning is important to those in leadership positions.

Table 1.3.5–2 Coaching and mentoring differences.

Coaching	Mentoring
• Typically one-on-one but can be done in small groups	• One-on-one
• Can be short in nature, like a coaching moment	• Longer-term commitment
• Performed by coworker/trainer, team leader, supervisor, or manager	• Performed by experienced person
	• Presents opportunities to challenge the mentee
	• Actively seeks out others who can help, uses network of contacts to provide needed expertise

Differences between Coaching and Mentoring

Coaching and mentoring share so many of the same elements that it is easy to think that they are the same thing. A closer look shows some understated differences (see Table 1.3.5-2).

Seek out coaches and mentors to help you on your lean journey and reciprocate by helping others.

It is often said that the best way to learn something is to teach it. Toyota takes this view to heart and expects that all leaders will be actively engaged in coaching and developing not just star performers or favorites but all staff members. In fact, it's often said at Toyota that the best measure of a leader's success is what is accomplished by those trained by the leader (Liker and Convis 2011).

1.3.6. LEADERSHIP DEVELOPMENT

Leadership development focuses on the development of leadership as a process. *Leadership* is the art of influencing people in order to achieve a result. Leadership means that you have to balance many factors in the real world, based on the situation at hand, to achieve a successful outcome. Leaders inspire, guide, and support their subordinates, gaining their commitment to the vision, mission, and objectives and encouraging them to perform creatively. Leaders need to balance the risks against the potential gains of any action. These decisions may be morally difficult with high-stakes consequences. Therefore, leaders have to rely on values and the art of leadership.

Leaders embody some core values and principles:

- Responsibility: Be proficient in your job, make timely decisions, supervise and make sure tasks are understood, and develop your people

- Respect: Keep people informed, build a team, and select the right people for the job in accordance with their capabilities

- Integrity: Know and understand yourself and continually seek improvement, take responsibility for your actions, and lead by example

Leaders face difficult problems of which there are no simple solutions. They must use their knowledge, skill, experience, and education to make the appropriate decision or take the necessary action.

The leadership environment is made up of critical elements that a leader must consider:

- Leaders are ultimately responsible for the consequences of decisions and the outcomes of all actions.

- Leaders are responsible for those reporting to them.

- Leaders constantly assess the environment and adapt accordingly; they demonstrate flexibility in selecting the appropriate techniques as a situation changes.

- Leaders must develop an effective two-way communication process. Good leaders actively listen and follow through on their commitments to build trust in others. Effective communication breaks down barriers, minimizes errors, and improves morale and awareness in the workplace.

- Leaders use a variety of styles to influence others. A leader's ability to read a situation and select the appropriate style enhances his or her ability to lead. When a leadership style is matched to the person's need, it results in increased competence, motivation, and growth in confidence on the part of the person.

Leadership development also focuses on the ability of the leader to motivate, coach persons, establish expectations, and manage change.

Motivation

Motivation can be intrinsic or extrinsic. *Intrinsic motivation* rests within the person and is driven primarily by enjoyment in performing the task itself. *Extrinsic motivation* is driven by outside needs to be rewarded and recognized or under the threat of punishment. Leaders need to understand what motivates the person. A number of motivational theories abound, prominent among them are Maslow's hierarchy of needs and Herzberg's two-factor theory.

Coaching for Performance

Leaders who coach well get their employees to examine their performance and work smarter. Coaching allows employees to build their skill level, which in turn motivates them to perform better. As employees become multiskilled, they become more capable and the leader's time can be devoted to other things.

Establishing Expectations

People perform better when they know what is expected of them, along with the sort of results. Expectations need to be made clear from the start. Mismatched expectations can cause problems in a reporting relationship, unnecessary anxiety and worry on the employee's part, and decreased productivity.

Change Management

Leaders understand that even a necessary change can be met with apprehension by people. Leaders know that these feelings of threat must be dealt with in order for a change to be effective in the workplace. Taiichi Ohno said that an organization is like the human body, which is designed to fight an infection with antibodies. An organization operates the same way. The antibodies create an organization's culture, which resists change. When a leader tries to bring about a change to the organization, he or she should include supports and resistors to the change.

1.3.7. TEAMWORK

Teams have become an essential part of work in organizations, but as you know from the teams you have led or belonged to, you can't expect a new team to perform exceptionally from the very outset. Team formation takes time, and usually follows some easily recognizable stages as the team journeys from being a group of strangers to becoming a united group with a common goal (see Figure 1.3.7-1).

Four Phases of Team Building

Psychologist Bruce Tuckman (1965) came up with the memorable phrase "forming, storming, norming, and performing" back in 1965. He used it to describe the path to high performance that most teams follow. Later, he added a fifth stage that he called "adjourning."

1. *Forming.* The first stage is characterized by a great deal of uncertainty about the group's purpose, structure, and leadership. Members test the waters to determine what types of behaviors are acceptable. This stage is complete when members begin to think of themselves as part of a team.

2. *Storming.* The storming stage is one of intragroup conflict. Members accept the existence of the team but resist the control that the group

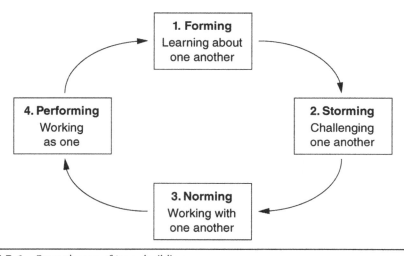

Figure 1.3.7-1   Four phases of team building.

imposes on individuality. Further, there is conflict over who will control the team. When the storming stage is complete, there will be relatively clear leadership within the team.

3. *Norming.* The third stage is one in which close relationships develop and members begin to demonstrate cohesiveness. There is now a stronger sense of team identity and camaraderie. The norming stage is complete when the team structure solidifies and members assimilate a common set of expectations of appropriate work behavior.

4. *Performing.* In the fourth stage, the structure is fully functional and accepted by team members. Their energy is diverted from getting to know and understand one another to performing the necessary tasks.

5. *Adjourning.* For permanent teams, performing is the last stage of their development. For temporary teams—those who have a limited task to perform—or kaizen teams there is an adjourning stage. In this stage the team prepares for its disbandment. A high level of task performance is no longer the members' top priority. Instead, their attention is directed toward wrapping up activities.

Tuckman's model explains that as the team develops maturity and ability, relationships are established and the leader changes leadership style. The leader's style begins with directing; moves through coaching, participating, finishing, and delegating; and ends with almost detached.

Contrary to what you might think, teams are not just groups of people (see Table 1.3.7-1). A *group* is two or more people who interact with each other to accomplish a goal. A *team* is a group with complementary skills that is committed to a common purpose, is defined by a set of performance goals, and holds itself mutually accountable. All teams are groups, but not all groups are teams. What distinguishes a team from a group? Table 1.3.7-1 helps identify the differences.

Groups don't become teams just because we use the term "team"; additionally, it is not about teamwork. Teams act like a collective unit with shared commitment, not like a band of individual contributors. As with lean, the whole—or in this case, the team—is greater than the sum of the individual parts. Teams often are more difficult to form because it takes time for members to learn to work together. Management must support and encourage the use of teams in the organization.

Work teams can be classified on the basis of their objectives. The five most common types of teams in an organization are functional teams, problem-solving teams, self-managed teams, cross-functional teams, and virtual teams.

1. *Functional teams* are composed of a manager and the employees in his or her department. Within this functional team, issues such as authority, decision making, leadership, and interactions are relatively simple and clear.

2. In *problem-solving teams*, members share ideas or offer suggestions on how work processes and methods can be improved. They meet regularly to discuss quality problems, and they generate and evaluate their own feedback.

Table 1.3.7-1   Teams versus groups.

Working group	Team
• Strong, focused leader	• Shared leadership roles
• Individual accountability	• Individual and mutual accountability
• Commitment to own silo/function/goals	• Common commitment
• Group's purpose is the same as the organization's mission	• Specific team purpose that the team itself delivers
• Performance is a function of individual work effort	• Performance is a function of collective work product
• Efficient meetings	• Time spent in open-ended discussion and active problem solving
• Measures its effectiveness via influence on other indicators (e.g., business unit financial performance)	• Measures performance directly by assessing collective work products
• Shares information; discusses, decides, and delegates to enhance individual performance	• Discusses, decides, and does real work together

Source: Katzenbach and Smith (2004).

3. Fully *self-managed teams* select their own members, and the members evaluate one another's performance. As a result, supervisory positions decrease in importance and may even be eliminated.

4. *Cross-functional teams* are made up of employees at about the same hierarchical level, but from different work areas, who come together to accomplish a task. Cross-functional teams are an effective means of allowing people from diverse areas within an organization to exchange information, develop new ideas, solve problems, and coordinate complex projects.

5. *Virtual teams* use computers and technology to tie together physically dispersed members in order to achieve a common goal. They allow people to collaborate online, whether they are only a room apart or a continent apart.

Organizations are finding that teams are a better way to utilize employee talents. Teams are more flexible and responsive to a changing environment than traditional departments or other permanent work groups. Additionally, teams can be quickly assembled, deployed, refocused, and disbanded.

The following are things to consider when picking team members:

- Balance of "hard" and "soft" skills
- Best experience possible
- Coverage of the knowledge areas needed
- Willingness to join

- Availability

- Leadership and/or management skills

- Maturity to take responsibility

- Good follow-through on commitments

- Good listening skills

- Willing to actively participate

- Can give and take feedback

- Can communicate clearly

Teams offer more than just increased efficiency and enhanced performance. They can serve as a source of job satisfaction. Because team members are frequently empowered to handle many of the things that directly affect their work, teams serve as an effective means for management to enhance employee involvement, increase employee morale, and promote workforce diversity.

1.3.8. INFORMATION SHARING (YOKOTEN)

Yokoten is a Japanese term that is roughly translated as "across everywhere." In the Japanese lean system, it means "best practice sharing." Toyota adopted the term to capture the idea of horizontal transfer of information and knowledge across an organization. Yokoten encourages sharing of data across the organization. To Yokoten is to "spread across or propagate." This is like the multiplying of saplings in nature from a large tree to many new trees. The new trees will grow in the proper soil and weather conditions. However, each new tree will grow and adapt differently to its unique environment. The trees are not clones, but they take on a life of their own. This is true of Yokoten as well. It is not just "go and see and then copy." Yokoten is horizontal, or more peer-to-peer, with the expectation that people go see for themselves and learn how another area did kaizen. In Yokoten at Toyota there is an expectation that copying a good idea will be followed by adding kaizen to that idea.

There is much untapped knowledge inside organizations. To combat this, companies have invested millions of dollars in knowledge management systems over the past two decades. The objective has been to capture the company's knowledge. Yokoten is a form of knowledge management. It encompasses the methods of documenting and distributing knowledge about what works and what doesn't. As a knowledge management device, Yokoten makes knowledge organizational, not individual. Yokoten is a two-way street, requiring proactive effort from both those acquiring and developing the knowledge and those who could benefit from greater understanding of the requirements for success.

If others are doing well, people tend to be interested in what they are doing and how they're doing it so that they, too, can be successful. Sharing best practices is a key attribute of the success of any organization. It's important to learn from individual experiences, but it's much easier and more effective to learn from the experiences, mistakes, and successes of others.

Much of best-practice knowledge is tacit—held in people's heads and not always easy to document. Therefore, most best-practice programs combine two key elements: explicit knowledge, such as a best-practice database (connecting people with information), and methods for sharing tacit knowledge, such as communities of practice (connecting people with people). *Communities of practice* are groups of people who share a concern or a passion for something they do and learn how to do it better as they interact regularly. These two approaches are complementary. A database can provide enough information for a potential user of the best practice to find it and decide whether it is worth pursuing further. However, the best way of sharing best practices is "on the job," and so communities and personal contact with others who have used the best practice are key.

Yokoten is an essential part of long-term success in a lean culture, but it can also have a big impact on short-term results. Yokoten is a success multiplier. Senior leaders must actively go see, recognize good work, and require others to go see. Management must organize presentations of successful kaizen projects and invite colleagues to attend and learn. Team and department leaders must actively engage members in studying kaizen examples, motivating them to start kaizen on their own. Project leaders and continuous improvement professionals must put Yokoten on their checklists and follow up rigorously.

Regardless of your path on the lean journey, focusing on the accumulation and transfer of knowledge and learning as embodied in the concept of Yokoten can have a tremendous impact on the overall results and success of lean programs.

1.3.9. SUGGESTION SYSTEMS

Employee suggestion programs can offer an organization a distinct competitive advantage with their many benefits, including cost savings; increased revenues; decreased waste; improved quality, safety, and customer service; improved corporate culture; employee motivation; and employee satisfaction. Employee suggestion systems have been in existence for over one hundred years in one form or another, ranging from the proverbial employee suggestion box to fully developed employee suggestion systems overseen by administrators, evaluators, and idea specialists.

The American-style suggestion system stresses the suggestion's economic benefits and provides economic incentives. These systems typically require considerable overhead: engineers costing out proposed improvements, managers reviewing ideas and making decisions, and administrators recording and routing information.

Suggestion systems at Toyota do not consist of a "box on the wall" where employees hand over ideas to management, as this type of system benefits neither those who submit ideas nor those who must implement them. The problem with this system is that management gets a long list of ideas and has limited resources to implement them, leading to frustration on the part of the originators because management doesn't implement their great idea (Liker and Hoseus 2008).

The following are essential components of Toyota's suggestion system:

- Idea acceptance is a given

- Recognition for suggestions (usually a small payment)

- Coaches help ideas grow

- Implement ideas yourself

The lean-style, kaizen-based suggestion system stresses the morale-boosting benefits of positive employee participation. In a lean organization it is understood that the suggestions of employees ultimately contribute to the bottom line, that employee suggestions provide a sense of ownership, and that workers have some control over their destiny. These feelings lead to greater overall satisfaction.

Key elements of a suggestion program are that it is simple (in all aspects, from idea submission through the approval process) and that responsibility for implementing the suggestion is maintained at the lowest possible level. Every person in the company can submit suggestions.

The approach follows the Plan-Do-Check-Act (PDCA) process for problem solving (see Section 2.2.9.1, "PDCA"). In this process a team member who has an idea works on defining the problem in terms of the current state, the goal, and the gap between the two. Using root cause analysis like the 5-Whys (see Section 2.3.3.2, "5-Whys"), the team member narrows the potential causes down to one. When the root cause is identified, potential countermeasures can be evaluated.

There is no review once the idea form is submitted, no decision of go or no-go. The review occurs at the lowest level possible, as quickly as possible. Ideally, this would be the supervisor of the person with the idea. The leader either approves the idea or coaches the member with hints to make the idea successful.

Figure 1.3.9-1 is an example of an idea board following the PDCA process.

The person who comes up with the idea works with his or her supervisor, who coordinates the timing and resources, to implement the idea. Because people are encouraged to come up with creative ideas for their own work area or process, it is rare that an idea involves such a large scope that the individual cannot contribute to its implementation. Lean as a true improvement system produces a steady stream of employee-suggested ideas for improvement.

There are a number of key points to make your process more successful:

- Get as many people involved as possible

- Focus on small ideas and small successes

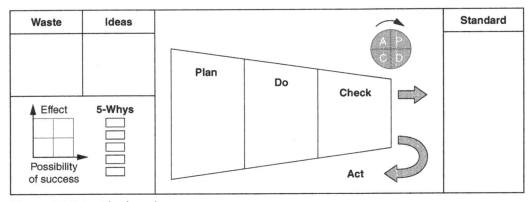

Figure 1.3.9-1 Idea board.

- Don't overpolice ideas

- Keep it visible

- Keep the recognition plan simple

- Realize that people want to be recognized even if they don't show it

In summary, the suggestion program should be designed for simplicity, intended for all employees to use, and free of barriers common to many programs (e.g., difficult to get and complete forms, ideas that must be cost justified, a cumbersome approval process for all suggestions, and small ideas that are not widely accepted). Most important, it should create a mind-set that everyone contributes to the overall success and growth of the company by providing their ideas.

REFERENCES

Dennis, Pascal. 2007. *Lean Production Simplified: A Plain-Language Guide to the World's Most Powerful Production System*. 2nd ed. New York: Productivity Press.

Katzenbach, J., and D. Smith. 2004. "The Discipline of Teams." In Harvard Business Review on Teams that Succeed, Harvard; HBR Paperback, pp. 1–25.

Liker, Jeffrey K., and Gary L. Convis. 2011. *The Toyota Way to Lean Leadership: Achieving and Sustaining Excellence through Leadership Development*. New York: McGraw-Hill.

Liker, Jeffrey K., and Michael Hoseus. 2008. *Toyota Culture: The Heart and Soul of the Toyota Way*. New York: McGraw-Hill.

Rother, Mike. 2010. *Toyota Kata: Managing People for Improvement, Adaptiveness, and Superior Results*. New York: McGraw-Hill.

Tuckman, Bruce. 1965. "Developmental Sequence in Small Groups." *Psychological Bulletin* 63 (6): 384–99. http://www.ncbi.nlm.nih.gov/pubmed/14314073.

Module 2
Continuous Process Improvement

2.1. Principles of Continuous Process Improvement
2.2. Continuous Process Improvement Systems
2.3. Continuous Process Improvement Techniques and
Practices

This module, on continuous process improvement, is broken into three main sections that correspond to the Shingo Transformational Process (Figure 2.0-1).

The principles provide overall guidance and vision for a continuous improvement culture within organizations striving for operational excellence. These are the basic philosophies of continuous improvement for lean organizations that provide

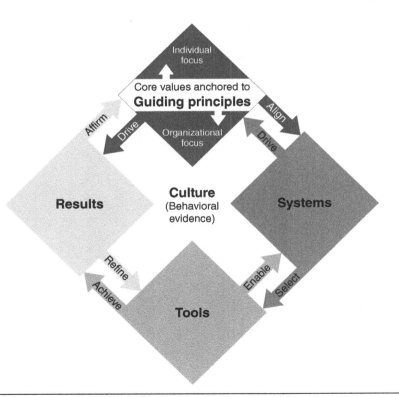

Figure 2.0-1 The Shingo Transformational Process.
Source: The Shingo Prize for Operational Excellence.

the foundation on which the rest of the organization is structured. As discussed in Section 2.1, the principles provide a foundation of organizational thinking and define why an improvement is needed.

Section 2.2 discusses continuous improvement in terms of systems. These are the systems that are required to successfully implement continuous improvement. The systems are structures that an organization puts in place to foster continuous improvement on a systematic and repeatable basis. The intent is that these systems are implemented on a permanent basis to drive behaviors related to the guiding principles of continuous improvement. They do not go away, as compared to tools that are used once and then not used again until needed. Systems are always in use. They define what and where improvements are needed.

Once these areas for improvement are identified, Section 2.3 identifies specific tools, or techniques and practices, that can be used to improve the organization to achieve results that align with the guiding principles. The intent of the tools is to support the systems of continuous improvement when needed. The tools identify how to make an improvement.

While reading the following sections, it is important to keep each section in context with the intent of principles, systems, and techniques/practices. Beginning practitioners may be confused because lean is generally taught with a focus on the tools. This method of lean learning blurs the lines between the differences among principles, systems, and practices. Seasoned practitioners understand this difference, which makes a significant difference in a successful lean transformation.

2.1

Principles of Continuous Process Improvement

Before continuous process improvement can begin, one must first understand what must be improved. Therefore, defining value in the eyes of the customer is of great significance. The value, as defined by the customer, must be clearly identified and communicated so processes can be continually modified to meet customer demand and requirements. This requires that every stakeholder in the process know what the value is in the eyes of the customer and what to do if the process is not creating value (*Model and Application Guidelines* 2010, 11). Dr. Shigeo Shingo said:

> Improvement means the elimination of waste, and the most essential precondition for improvement is the proper pursuit of goals. We must not be mistaken, first of all, about what improvement means. The four goals of improvement must be to make things: easier, better, faster, and cheaper. (*Model and Application Guidelines* 2010, 11)

Creating a culture of continuous process improvement is achieved by building a foundation of continuous process improvement principles. The following are the principles of continuous process improvement:

1. Process focus

2. Identification and elimination of barriers to flow

3. Match rate of production to level of customer demand

4. Scientific thinking

5. Jidoka

6. Integrate improvement with work

7. Seek perfection

2.1.1. PROCESS FOCUS

My first lean teacher, or sensei, was a former North American Toyota plant manager with an abrupt manner. He'd mutter to himself, "What is the process; what is the process?" as we walked the shop floor in the decidedly pre-lean plant where I used to work. I'll admit, I had no idea what he was talking about.

I was new to lean and thought its focus was on getting results—you know: safer, better, faster, cheaper. I was missing the point. It's not that lean thinkers

47

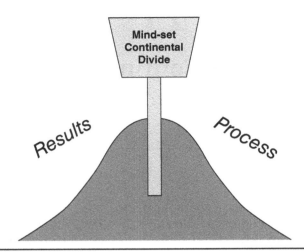

Figure 2.1.1-1 Lean mind-set and process versus results focus.

are indifferent to results, quite the contrary. Lean thinkers understand that results are so important that they can't take their eyes off the processes that produce the results. Apparently there isn't a Japanese phrase for "Take care of the process and the process will take care of you." It would have helped my sensei help me to understand a deeper, clearer picture of lean. Consider Figure 2.1.1-1 for the subtle but impactful difference in thinking between a lean mentality and a conventional, or batch, mentality.

Lean only *seems* like a systematic approach to get results such as reductions in lead time, cost, space, inventory, and so on. Lean is an improvement system first and foremost. In it, maximizing value-adding activity and reducing non-value-adding activity is the central tenet. Do those things, and cost, space, inventory, defects, and injuries will surely be reduced, but as side effects, collateral benefits. The main thing is to focus intensively on the process as it operates *to see where it misses, is delayed, or stumbles*. Those are among the clues for the best next places to work on improvement.

If you don't focus on the process, you miss the clues and are left wondering what went wrong. This is a common occurrence in a conventional, results-oriented world because measures of results are by their nature retrospective. How did we do yesterday? What were our results for last week? Last month? Last quarter? Last year? You can answer the question, because you almost certainly have many measures of results. But beyond the rare catastrophic event, without measures that reflect a focus on the process, you can't explain what caused the target to be missed. Without process focus, the trail grows cold and you're left speculating on what happened that undercut your results.

Focus on the Process

So, how do you focus on the process? Process focus, like many aspects of lean, is simple in concept. It isn't particularly difficult in practice, but it's quite different from a conventional, results-focused approach to managing an operation. For line managers, it entails both deploying at least some of your time differently and learning to look for, ask about, measure, and teach different things.

Allocate Time to the Floor

Yogi Berra said, "You can observe a lot just by watching." The first aspect of process focus is the standard lean advice: Go to gemba—weekly if you're an operations executive, most of your time if you're a team leader, and proportionally for positions in between. How much time? Thirty to 45 minutes a week for executives, and 80% of your time every day for team leaders in repetitive manufacturing, less for slower cycling processes.

Go to the place where and when the process is operating, *talk with the people* doing the work, *observe the process* as it is being executed. The idea is to ground yourself in regularly refreshed information about the reality of the process's operation. You can do this only by actually being there and watching it operate, conversing about the work with those performing it, and looking carefully at frequently updated process measures annotated by the task level performers.

Look at the Process in Actual Operation

To be most useful, your observations should allow you to compare what you see with a standard, with expected performance. Are you able to tell whether standardized work is being followed? Does the practice you see match the documented definition of the process where standardized work might not be able to be posted? Does the actual time to complete tasks match the expected time?

The main focus of floor time is to watch the process, ask the people doing the work how the process has been running, and look closely at the process measures. Consider how what you see and hear compares with what you expect. What is the reality the people on the floor regularly deal with? When actual outcomes fail to meet expected outcomes, ask people about it. What happened? How often does it occur? Where is it documented, and can you look at it? Is problem solving under way for this issue?

Measure the Process to Highlight Misses and Glitches

Most operations have a plethora of results measures but a dearth or complete absence of process measures. A process measure frequently (depending on the speed with which the process cycles) focuses on actual versus expected performance of the process. For a process that produces complex engineering drawings, frequently may mean daily or twice daily. For an order or claims processing area, frequently might mean four times a day. For a high-volume repetitive manufacturing process, frequently may mean every pitch, as often as every 9, 12, or 15 minutes or at a minimum every hour. With changeover times, whether of production equipment or hospital operating rooms, frequency means each changeover.

The purpose of process measures is to identify, isolate, and highlight process misses. This is the distinguishing characteristic of the mind-set continental divide in lean. In the conventional world, we've been trained and reinforced to work around problems, to cover them for now so we can hit the schedule. By contrast, the lean thinker devises measures to highlight problems, even if a temporary workaround is necessary. Process measures address the question, "How long do you want to wait to learn if your process is operating normally or if it's headed into a ditch?" When time is available, the lean thinker returns to the problem data captured on the process measures and mines them, looking for the root cause and then eliminating it—because lean is an improvement system.

Teach the Importance of Process Focus

When you're on the floor, people may ask, "Why do we need to track production so closely? Why are you micromanaging us? Don't you trust us?" Assuming you've put a daily accountability process in place, or some other means to respond to the process problems identified by floor-level value-adding workers, the answer is straightforward. It is the brief lesson on problems as opportunities to improve.

Process measures allow us to micromanage the *production process*, highlighting problems. Those problems are often "delegated up" to team leaders, supervisors, managers, or others who have the discretionary time to focus on them and drive them to root cause corrective action. Make the bargain explicit: "You identify the production problems that interrupt or slow you down, and we'll eliminate them or give you a good reason why not." When you keep your end of the bargain, it's very persuasive. Further, this discussion on the floor allows you to deliver a 90-second lesson about lean's focus on finding and eliminating the sources of delay, interruption, and frustration routinely experienced by those who perform the value-adding work.

In many ways, process focus is at the heart of putting lean into practice. When we concentrate on the health of the process, we can be more confident about the results it will produce. Process focus means leaders will have to learn some new skills, use some new measures, and reallocate some of their time to spend on the floor. But without doubt, when floor time is structured, intentional, and informed by the concepts and tools of process focus, the benefits are worthwhile. Leaders and task-level people alike are more engaged with each other and with improvement, you come to grasp the day-to-day reality of your production process, and you experience a steady stream of clues about the often small changes that cumulatively make a substantial difference in performance. In this way, process focus is an important key to unlocking the treasure chest of continuous improvement.

2.1.2. IDENTIFICATION AND ELIMINATION OF BARRIERS TO FLOW

At its most fundamental level, lean is about flowing value to the customer as quickly as possible. Sometimes this is referred to as "reducing the time between paying and getting paid," with an intentional focus on reducing the time to convert material or information into the customer's required product or service so that the producing organization quickly satisfies the customer and can be paid back for its investment as soon as possible.

Unlike traditional improvement activities, lean suggests that the focus of change initiatives should *not* be on cost reduction but on time reduction: time to design, time to buy, time to produce, time to sell, and time to collect cash. When the focus of improvement efforts is reducing the *time between paying and getting paid*, then, among other things, costs will be dramatically reduced. When lean principles serve as guiding principles, and the "tools of lean" are effectively engaged as a means to making value flow faster, processes can be systematically changed to better reflect "customer is first" thinking, a key philosophy of lean.

In order to flow value to customers faster, lean practitioners must understand the following:

- What customers value as well as how people and processes are combined to create, add, and deliver this value

- How to design processes that maximize value delivered while minimizing waste, fluctuation, and overburden

- Why businesses must organize around flows critical to customers, and why it is imperative to identify when flow is interrupted and how to eliminate those barriers to flow through countermeasures and continuous improvement

2.1.2.1. Flow and the Economies of Flow

In the early 1900s Frederick Winslow Taylor's (1911) *Principles of Scientific Management* incorrectly placed an emphasis on division of labor as the means to create an efficient process. Taylor's premise of a "best way" to produce was correct, but his endorsement of "division of labor" as a central concept of "best" is still apparent in many organizations and leads to a number of unexpected and very undesirable outcomes when it comes to flow of value.

Functional Arrangement

The concept of specialization within function (e.g., group all machining equipment together) was intended to improve standardization and skill levels, with an intended outcome of increasing efficiency at each operation. However, flow thinking has proved that specialization does not necessarily improve the overall efficiency of the entire value delivery system. Conversely, functional arrangements of operations often result in lack of flow due to lot and process delays, and require that a whole new complement of side services be set up to move material and prioritize queues, adding non-value-added steps within and across the value stream.

Functional Communication

Natural communication between functional areas is seriously impaired when functional areas are established, creating delays and confusion and requiring additional external support functions to establish and communicate priorities. Except for hot jobs, work priorities are often established according to local optimization of the scheduled resources (e.g., group all like jobs together to avoid excess machine setups) and are mostly done in an office that is physically separated from the value-adding work space.

Specializing Improvement and Quality

Perhaps most damaging of all regarding the division of labor was the assumption that methods improvement and quality control could be accomplished more effectively by specialized "professional" departments (e.g., industrial engineers who "design" the work in an office away from the work area). This type of class system fails to improve flow by hiding the problems and opportunities from management, and creates a demoralizing atmosphere for workers.

Cost Accounting

Lastly, the assumption that the whole is equal to the sum of its parts gave rise to traditional cost accounting. Cost accounting is a model that states that a process is equal to the sum of its operations and that cost improvement can therefore be attained by individually improving the efficiency of functional operations. In lean the focus must be on overall system efficiency, not simply the efficiency of each part of the value stream. The idea is to design the entire system to flow value at the rate the customer requires, with the least possible resources, at the lowest total cost. When this is not understood, one part of the process may be "optimized" to produce at a low cost but may be overproducing based on what the next process can/should handle. This is also true between support operations where an improved process for one function may actually impede flow of another process, otherwise known as *suboptimizing* the value flow of the entire system.

Furthermore, focusing on reducing the cost of functional operations (e.g., the time to cut the part on the machine) often centers on the smallest part of the "time between paying and getting paid." Parts might take seconds to produce and the cycle times calculated to four decimal places. However, the parts often sit in queues or in a warehouse for months with no further advancement toward the customer and payback. No flow . . .

Today, Frederick Taylor is still heralded as the father of modern manufacturing, and undoubtedly much of his work is valuable. However, the concept of division of labor and local efficiency and its subsequent negative impact on productivity, service, and quality are not part of lean and are contrary to the concept of "flowing value." Communication between management and employees cannot be limited to one-way directives. Additionally, individual departments can no longer operate as if they were stand-alone businesses, and they must not be rewarded for undercutting the efforts of other departments in order to make their own numbers.

In a lean organization, the physical structure of the business must encourage cooperation and the free flow of value and information. Departments that should be working together must be near one another, not on different floors or in different cities. Information and material flow through operationally excellent companies occurs without delay—because these companies understand they work within a world economy where customers expect an instant response. This is the "seeking perfection" of *reducing the time between paying and getting paid.*

2.1.2.2. Seven Wastes (Muda), Fluctuation (Mura), and Overburden (Muri)

Taiichi Ohno is considered the father of the Toyota Production System (TPS). At the heart of TPS is a focus on eliminating waste (muda), reducing inconsistency or fluctuation (mura), and minimizing overburden (muri). Reducing waste, fluctuation, and overburden is most effectively addressed by proactively designing efficient and effective products and services that meet customer demand regarding cost, delivery, and quality. Applying solutions to waste, fluctuation, and overburden after the design is complete is reactive but still valuable in moving toward effective and efficient systems.

Waste (Muda)

Muda is the Japanese term for "waste," or any work the customer is not willing to pay for. This is the opposite of *value*, or what a customer is willing to pay for. All work consists of three components (see Figure 2.1.2.2-1):

1. Actual work is any activity that adds value to the product or service in the eyes of the customer

2. Auxiliary work, or incidental work, is any activity that is necessary but does not add value to the product or service in the eyes of the customer

3. Muda, or waste, is any activity that is unnecessary and does not add value to the product or service in the eyes of the customer

Ohno developed an equation for organizational capacity based on the fact that there is a separation of real work, or value-added, and waste, or non-value-added. Ohno describes that true efficiency improvement is realized when the real work is 100% and waste is 0%.

$$\text{Present capacity} = \text{Work} + \text{Waste}$$

or

$$\text{Present capacity} = \text{Work} + (\text{Waste} + \text{Auxiliary work})$$

or

$$\text{Present capacity} = \text{Value-added} + \text{Non-value-added}$$

Value-added activities are those actions that the customer determines as valuable or as adding value. "A simple test as to whether a task and its time is value-creating is to ask if the customer would judge a product less valuable if this task could be left out without affecting the product" (Marchwinski and Shook 2006, 97).

Non-value-added activities are those actions that add cost to the product/ service but provide no value in the eyes of the customer. Rework, moving material from a finished goods warehouse to a distribution center, and a clerk waiting on another clerk to finish with a customer to further process the customer through a given service being provided are examples of adding costs to the product/service

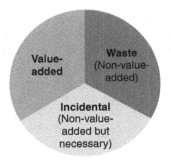

Figure 2.1.2.2-1   Breakdown of the components of work.

without providing value to the customer. In some instances, tasks like inspections may appear to be waste, but they are actually value-added activities if the customer specifically requires them to be performed. In those instances, it is important to understand what value the customer expects to receive from the inspection in order to reduce or eliminate inspection costs. In some instances, an inspection may not be required if the process can be controlled to prevent specific defects from being created or to detect them before they reach the customer.

An organization pursuing lean perfection focuses on eliminating waste and reducing auxiliary work. In order to eliminate waste from processes, it must first be identified. Ohno (1988) defined seven types of waste to be eliminated:

1. Waste of overproduction

2. Waste of time on hand (waiting)

3. Waste in transportation

4. Waste of processing itself (overprocessing)

5. Waste of stock on hand (inventory)

6. Waste of movement

7. Waste of making defective products

Overproduction was purposely selected to lead the list because it not only is a form of waste itself but also can contribute to other forms of waste (muda). Ohno considered this the root of all manufacturing evil. In the 1990s the 7 Wastes were reordered into the acronym TIM WOOD. This both changed the order of the wastes and simplified some of the terms, which required recognizing that each stated term is actually a waste. In this version the 7 Wastes are (1) transportation, (2) inventory, (3) motion, (4) waiting, (5) overproduction, (6) overprocessing, and (7) defects.

Overproduction

Overproduction is producing more than what is needed, just in case. It is making a product or providing a service well in excess of demand. In simple terms, it is defined as making things that don't sell. Overproduction results in large batch manufacturing and services and incurs additional costs such as building and warehouse maintenance, excess workers and machines, excess parts and materials, and so on. Overproduction is a root cause of the other forms of waste, such as motion where operators are making products or performing services nobody ordered, inventory for storage of finished goods and parts, and movement of materials to storage for large batches. In a push batch system, overproduction is a consequence of unplanned variability and a lack of reliability in equipment and systems, and a result of production quota systems. Moving to producing based on customer demand managed by takt time can reduce overproduction. Overproduction can be seen in the excess inventory of automobiles that extends past the normal lots and into the dirt parking areas. It can be seen as e-mail boxes full of e-mails addressed to "To," which implies an action is needed from the receiver, when a "CC" would be sufficient to inform. In service it can be seen as service providers waiting to deliver without customers prepared to receive.

Waiting

Waiting, by processes and people, appears as idle machines and idle workers standing by to perform their work. Unbalanced steps cause waiting and work-in-process (WIP) in the processes. Approvals, handoffs, and inspection cause non-value-added waiting in the process. Waiting results in delays and increases *lead time*, the time between a customer placing an order and receiving the product or service. Waiting is often the largest waste in lead-time calculations. Idle machines and people reveal waiting waste in the process and for people. Leveling process steps overall and then aligning them such that one ongoing step is the incoming step—or, "my outbox is your inbox"—will reduce waiting.

Transportation

Transportation other than a postal or package delivery is, for the most part, a form of waste. Excess walking or transport and handling due to poor layout results in both a delay to complete the work and damaged material. Transportation between facilities is also a form of waste. Colocating suppliers or locating them on the operations floor helps remove the delay in production and provide rapid communication on the quality of the product. Long order times, high transportation costs, and damage are signs of transportation waste. Considering the entire product cycle as one continuous flow with the steps located with the least possible distance can reduce transportation waste.

Overprocessing

Overprocessing occurs when more work or processing is performed than necessary to satisfy customer demand or requirements. Producing a part to higher tolerances than required, which is sometimes considered "gold-plating," adds cost and delays delivery. Unnecessary approvals, inspections to ensure quality, and handoffs all contribute to delaying delivery and increasing defects. A process to touch up solder joints can harm surrounding components. In one example, the screens for instrument clusters were being rejected for slight scratches that were not visible once the screens were installed in the shaded dashboards. The rejection, in turn, delayed delivery of the finished vehicles. Multiple entries of the same data across multiple forms when first visiting a doctor's office, registering at a hospital, or filling out forms online creates overprocessing that wastes time and is more prone to defects due to multiple entries and fatigue from performing a redundant process. Checking one more time just in case is a clear sign of overprocessing waste. Including features that are confirmed as valuable in the eyes of the customer and producing products or providing services that don't exceed customer demand reduce overprocessing.

Inventory

Inventory is the keeping of unneeded raw materials, parts, WIP, and finished product. Inventory is directly related to two other forms of waste, overproduction and waiting. Inventory occurs when the flow of value (product or service) is limited and not aligned with the takt time of the customer (pull). This is typically the result of a *push*-type system, where work is scheduled irrespective of the needs of the downstream processes or customer demand. Inventory can hide defects, as in the famous, or infamous, example by a motorcycle manufacturer whose long-term production parts on conveyors across the ceiling were discovered to be defective. Callers placed on hold by a call center, stacks of forms waiting to be completed or processed, and material housed on production floors and in storage facilities are signs of inventory waste. Maintaining inventory where necessary to respond to variability through the use of safety buffers in production and at the level required for rapid delivery based on customer demand can reduce excess inventory.

Movement

Movement is the ergonomic motion of people and resources in both the immediate work area and the prescribed work area. It can be seen in having to jump between multiple screens where programming could have the value-added entries on a single screen. It can be seen in having to stand and move across a workbench to perform assembly versus having the parts and tools readily at hand. It can be seen in a naval technician's having to walk endlessly about an aircraft carrier to gather parts and materials from assigned storage places on the carrier. A spaghetti diagram can show movement waste. Efficiently designed systems and ergonomically designed work areas will reduce non-value-added movement and steps. Movement is directly related to workplace ergonomics, where poor ergonomic workstations can adversely affect productivity, quality, and safety as a result of strain on the operator over time.

Making Defective Product

Any aspect of the service or any manufactured part that does not conform to customer requirements is a process defect. Unclear work instructions, lack of standard work, inefficient processes, poorly maintained processes, poor materials, and so on, can all result in process defects. Designing a product or service without understanding and delivering on customer value; designing a product or service that does not meet customer needs; designing a product or service around the processes and components currently available; creating complexity in the product or service that is not considered value-added by the customer; overengineering the design or processes providing the service or product, resulting in excess cost and price as well as leading to overproduction; and failing to design a service or product where it can be most efficiently produced are all forms of defects. Defects result in other forms of waste, also known as quality costs, such as the costs of the material, time, and resources necessary to repair product or correct service issues.

Over time, many variations have been made to the 7 Wastes. One variation is the addition of an eighth waste, knowledge disconnect, by Pascal Dennis.

Knowledge Disconnect

Knowledge disconnect occurs when there is a fundamental breakdown of communication or knowledge transfer between workers and management, the company and suppliers, or an organization and its customers. This restricts the flow of knowledge, or information, within the value stream and hinders the organization's ability to take advantage of all resources within the value stream to develop and implement continuous improvement. Knowledge disconnect results in an organization's inability to capitalize on the untapped, latent potential of people's ideas and actions.

Some forms of reducing waste are readily visible, while others are hidden. The efficiency of most transactional processes is less than 10% of the time being value-added time, which means most of the effort is waste and not readily visible. Waste is actually a symptom, so once it is identified, work to find its root cause and correct it. To eliminate waste, it is important to:

- Understand the customer's perception of value
- Identify and understand the types of waste
- Apply lean tools and techniques

Fluctuation (Mura)

Fluctuation (mura) includes inconsistency and unevenness from poor planning, for example, schedule conflicts, unplanned changeovers and line and service breakdowns, and a lack of standards, which creates processes with high variability. The most errant form of inconsistencyomes from tampering, in which the process is adjusted in order to get it under control without understanding the relationship between inputs and outputs, causing further reactive adjustments that generate additional inconsistency to a point of not providing the product or service as expected. The effects of inconsistency and fluctuation are best managed with variety reduction, just-in-time, and leveling. Reducing fluctuation is key to successfully implementing the just-in-time methodology, which relies on a pull system. Reduction of WIP and defects and the use of leveling and cross training are effective methods in reducing the effects of fluctuation (mura).

Excess WIP beyond safety stock creates an opportunity to change over for longer runs and for service providers to rapidly change their focus to other customers and services, generating endless restarts. By only having what is needed, having it when and where it is needed, and providing the product and service through continuous flow can the effects of needless changeover be reduced. Leveling and use of a pull system also support continuous flow, which in turn manages inconsistency out of the process or system. Defects inherently cause scheduling inconsistency through adjusted schedules requiring additional material movement and changeovers. Cross training for multi-process handling in order to move workers across processes and service providers across service offerings, as in a service call center, can move workers from a singular role and focus to a flexible one that can readily respond to variability and inconsistency in the process. Designing for lean can ensure that variability is known and planned on the basis of the operating systems that deliver the product or service, minimizing fluctuation. The most significant effects on process value delivery are achieved by designing a process capable of delivering the required results smoothly, by designing out mura.

Overburden (Muri)

While overburden (muri) is being addressed here as the third area at the heart of TPS, it is perhaps most critical to reduce because overburden (muri) can lead to or cause waste (muda) and fluctuation (mura). Muri relates to unreasonably overburdening and overstressing processes, people, and machines. It means pushing systems and people beyond normal limits. Muri generally refers to the unreasonable work that management places on workers and machines. Strained movement, performing dangerous tasks, and working at a significantly faster than normal pace are all examples of muri. *Muri* is pushing a person or a machine beyond the normal or designed limits. For people this means stressing the body to fatigue or injury, working at a rate that is unreasonable and possibly causing defects, and working in an unsafe environment. For processes this means running machines beyond their design or expecting to handle data through data lines not built to handle the load. For machines it means running them to the point of failure. It is also crucial to ensure that the process is as flexible as necessary, without stress or muri.

2.1.2.3. Connect and Align Value Added Work Fragments

More than any other individual, Henry Ford ushered in the age of modern manufacturing by introducing several key ideas that belong in the annals of time savings. The first of these was the moving assembly line, which physically synchronized and paced all factory operations. Ford understood that queued and stored inventory was not an asset, and designed a production system that moved material from value-adding operation to value-adding operation with minimal queues. Consequently, his Model T could be produced in a fraction of the time and at a fraction of the cost of those of earlier automobile producers. With the introduction of the moving assembly line, Ford was able to reduce the selling price of his Model T from $850 to $290! Henry Ford was the first person to use the word "flow" to describe his system. So the story goes, in the 1990s Toyota used Ford's book from 1926 to train its American workers—that suggests much of what is sometimes called "Japanese manufacturing" came from Henry Ford and is still relevant today.

Ford's system was an improved working model of Frederick W. Taylor's management theories, producing unprecedented economic results for decades. But there were parts of "Fordism," as it was called, that were counter to what we know as "lean" today and are important to understand in considering how to align and connect work steps:

- Ford viewed his employees as human machines, a variable expense with eyes and hands. Quality control and problem solving were deemed to be the work of professionals, not frontline workers. The lean philosophy of "going to gemba to directly observe" suggests that if workers are not understood to be in the best position to identify what is interrupting the flow value and are not understood to have the best ideas on how to reduce or eliminate waste, then the additional lean philosophy of "people are the most valuable asset" has been misunderstood.

- Ford's assembly line was a machine that could never stop. Problems were simply passed along to the next operation or taken off the line for rework. The "leanism" that "the line should be stopped so that the line is never stopped" refers to the idea that problems must be identified, immediately, at the source so that defects are never passed along (adding waste to downstream processes) and workers can take countermeasures quickly.

- Ford's assembly line was completely inflexible, producing just one model in a single color. He understood that a model change would interrupt production flow and kill his profit machine. So when a new model was developed, he set up another dedicated line. The dedicated line concept worked well enough in an expanding market where all lines had full work, but this idea of dedicated resources becomes an anchor when demand shifts and some processes do not have full work. The concept of the dedicated line is still commonplace today in many businesses, creating huge work imbalance and resource wastes. The lean approach to making value flow suggests that processes should be designed to be as flexible as possible, so that a wide variety and quantity of products can readily flow through the process. Lean tools such as SMED (single minute exchange of dies) and poka-yoke (mistake-proofing) are used to reduce the reasons often given for process inflexibility and passing defects.

The connection and alignment of value-added work fragments is an element of standard work. The idea is to connect and align, or sequence, the steps of work in an order that eliminates waste and maximizes value. In other words, identify the least-waste way to perform a process step and organize those steps (tasks) in a sequence that completes the process according to takt time (customer demand).

2.1.2.4. Organize around Flow

So the story goes, when Taiichi Ohno went to the shop floor, his direct observation allowed him to reach an important conclusion that he would not have otherwise reached: Weeks' and months' worth of "efficiently produced" inventory was sitting idle and rusting on the shop floor—inventory that represented not only millions of dollars in investment but also millions of hours in lost time. Ohno had studied the Ford Production System and, like Ford, understood that the velocity of material and information through his factory was paramount to both customer service and profits. This revelation led Ohno to question why processes were frequently not organized to flow value.

In fact, he observed that the things that got in the way of flowing value generally also contributed to higher cost, longer lead times, and increased risk of poor quality. Concepts such as "organizing by value streams" and "continuous flow production" were developed as countermeasures to poor flow. The basis for developing these tools was to promote flow by allowing work to proceed from one value-adding step to the next as quickly as possible. Shigeo Shingo, a contemporary of Taiichi Ohno's at Toyota, is best remembered for inventing other revolutionary shop-floor countermeasures that addressed Ohno's concerns about poor flow.

"The most dangerous kind of waste is the waste we do not recognize."

—Shigeo Shingo

While Ohno provided the direction, Shingo found a way to get there. For example, Shingo's improvement methods for machine changeover identified simple methods to reduce setup times from many hours to just a few minutes (Shingo and Dillon 1985). This innovation made it practical to produce much smaller batches, which in turn freed up massive machine resources and made the factory a flexible resource. Easy changeover enabled the production of a wide variety of parts through the same machine, overcoming the problems of the dedicated line that Ford had experienced. The time between paying and getting paid was slashed by Shingo's methods, because time was not lost producing unneeded products.

Shingo's ideas eliminated the need for excess stock and made the concept of producing "only what was needed" by the next process a reality in factories that previously thought this absurd. In fact, Shingo's setup improvements make it *easy* to produce small quantities, by identifying and eliminating waste in the setup process.

Shingo was also a strong advocate of reintroducing management of quality directly into the process through concepts of quality at the source, such as poka-yoke (mistake-proofing), rather than assigning inspections to a remote function. Ohno's focus on organizing to create flow and Shingo's inventions to enable flow revolutionized manufacturing by making it possible to produce the exact amount needed and with perfect quality.

2.1.2.5. Make End-to-End Flow Visible

Management's primary role in implementing lean is to continually assess the current condition and provide appropriate support and motivation to raise the bar in terms of flowing value more effectively and efficiently. Failure to keep a watchful eye on efforts to reach "True North" (often associated with the goal of perfection, or complete elimination of waste) has caused many organizations to stumble or backslide in their lean journey. Remembering that the long-term focus of all lean improvement efforts is to develop processes capable of operating in a just-in-time manner, lean organizations strive to establish processes and use best practices that make waste, fluctuation, and overburden apparent.

Value stream mapping, also referred to as material and information flow diagramming, is a powerful graphic technique used to document and communicate the current, ideal, or recommended future state for a value stream. In a value stream exercise, teams of people "go to gemba" to understand the existing value stream flow, use common symbols to document and grasp the current condition, and work together to uncover improvement opportunities. Value stream mapping is meant to be a big-picture tool, one where people step back from individual operations and away from discrete improvement activities in order to develop a more holistic image of process flow. The thinking in value stream mapping is to concentrate on improving the "whole" rather than optimizing individual parts of the process, because the customer experiences the sum total of all the activities that occur in the value stream, and quality, cost, and delivery outcomes result from overall value stream efforts, not just a portion of the value stream.

2.1.2.6. Manage the Flow Visually

Lean organizations work to make process conditions transparent to the entire team so that conditions, good or bad, are evident to all, quickly. Visual management is the primary method used to accomplish this in operationally excellent companies. Techniques such as color coding, clear homes for materials and equipment, and improved signage and process indicators are typical in a well-developed 5S (well-organized workplace) environment. However, the power of visual systems is far greater and is derived from building a workplace that "speaks" to employees and managers, letting them know at a glance "what they need to know, when they need to know it"; it helps them communicate "what they need to share, when they need to share it." Think of visual systems as communication devices designed to make vital information available to those who need to know it, when they need to know it, in a simple, straightforward manner. Managing the flow visually is vital to promoting normal outcomes and reducing abnormal ones (Galsworth 1997, 310). When abnormalities stand out, changes can be made quickly and processes can get back on track. That thinking and more is at the heart of a visual workplace, where things are self-explaining, self-ordering, self-regulating, and self-improving (Galsworth 1997, 310).

2.1.3. MATCH RATE OF PRODUCTION TO LEVEL OF CUSTOMER DEMAND—JUST-IN-TIME

The ability to operate in a just-in-time (JIT) manner—or evolution of a process to the point where it is able to produce exactly what the customer wants, when the customer wants it, in the correct quantity—is the ultimate goal of all lean implementations. JIT is the polar opposite of overproduction, the worst of the 7 Wastes (covered in an earlier section), and implies that process improvements have successfully removed a large majority of the waste, fluctuation, and overburden inherent in traditional processes. Key best practices used to facilitate JIT processes are continuous flow, kanban, and heijunka. Organizations methodically apply lean tools to business problems in the pursuit of JIT. This involves thinking

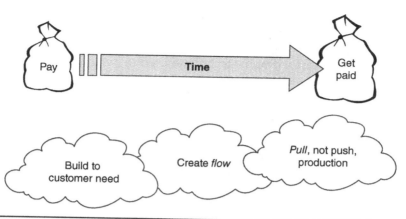

Figure 2.1.3-1   Ideal state of JIT processing.

about the application of lean tools and techniques as controlled "experiments" conducted by workers to find better ways to do work. The journey toward "True North," or perfection, becomes a series of these experiments that are conducted over time and made up of many cycles of small improvements that are systematically linked together to approach the ideal of JIT processing. Progress toward the ideal is always being measured in terms of customer value delivered and is generally related to the following outcomes: quality, cost, time, and selection.

As part of the pursuit of JIT, lean organizations seek to match rate of customer demand to rate of production, that is, to operate all processes at a pace that exactly mirrors customer requirements (see Figure 2.1.3-1). In the purest sense, lean engages workers in looking for all those things that cause a mismatch between supply and demand and provides workers with the means to address them. *Takt time*, as defined by the formula

$$\text{Takt time} = \frac{\text{Available production time}}{\text{Customer demand}}$$

refers to the production rate required to meet customer demand. Many lean tools and techniques, such as value stream mapping, continuous flow, and standardized work, cannot be successful unless there is a clear understanding of takt time. For example, to understand how much delay is apparent in a value stream, it is necessary to understand how frequently a customer requires a product. To understand how many workers are required in a department, it is necessary to understand not only how long it takes to do the work but how much work is demanded by the customer from the department.

2.1.4. SCIENTIFIC THINKING

The concept of scientific thinking falls under the Principles of Continuous Process Improvement in the Shingo Prize model and contains the components of stability, standardization, recognition of abnormality, and "go and see." Training all employees to use this thought process leads to a culture that has a common understanding, language, and approach for improving work processes. The results-based nature of scientific thinking leads to the organizational practice of clearly defined and communicated desired outcomes.

Scientific thinking is based on the *scientific method*, which is a systematic approach to collecting data and information and solving problems. In practice, this entails first creating a problem statement and then a hypothesis that will be either confirmed or proved wrong through testing. The test results are analyzed, with conclusions drawn or actions taken based on the results. This process is intended to be as objective as possible to reduce bias in the testing and in interpretation of the results.

Scientific thinking and the associated methodology have been adapted as a problem-solving tool in lean applications. Walter A. Shewhart defined an abbreviated version of the process as "hypothesis—experiment—evaluation." The concept for the Plan-Do-Check-Act (PDCA) cycle is based on the scientific method and was created by Shewhart and refined by W. Edwards Deming. One of the fundamental principles of the scientific method and PDCA is repeating the cycle to increase knowledge and continually improve the process. The discipline of using this approach by every person in the organization defines scientific thinking in lean.

Example of Scientific Method

1. Define a problem that is an opportunity for improvement

2. Observe the process and gather data and information

3. Define the proposed solution or change

4. Test or pilot the proposed solution

5. Analyze the results and data (before and after metrics)

6. Document the new process steps and ensure all affected people are trained (this step then becomes the basis for the next iteration of the PDCA cycle)

2.1.4.1. Stability

Stability is a requirement of any organization and process to ensure ongoing, consistent execution of tasks. This is exemplified in the use of stability as the base of the House of Toyota (see Figure 2.1.4.1-1). Like any house or building, an organization or process needs to have a stable foundation on which to operate. A constantly changing work environment makes process improvement difficult, if not impossible, as there is not a defined starting point or a desired state. Stability provides a foundation for problem identification and continuous process improvement.

Stability is a predecessor to achieving process flow. Many forms of waste are created due to instability of processes, and these are often viewed as inherent in the process and beyond control. Processes that allow for identification and elimination of waste can be created by applying the appropriate tools to eliminate or reduce process instability.

Standardized work is focused on stabilizing the 4 Ms—Methods, Manpower, Material, and Management—with total productive maintenance (TPM) focused on stabilizing machinery. Standardized work for managers and supervisors is an often overlooked aspect of creating organizational stability.

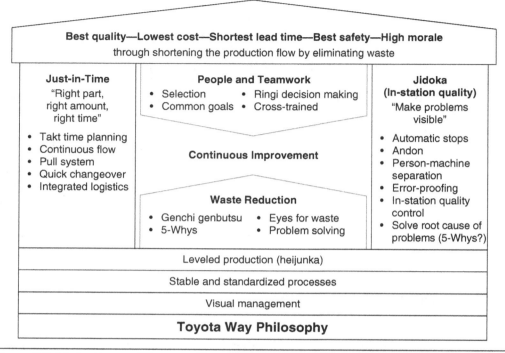

Figure 2.1.4.1-1   House of Toyota as illustrated by Liker.
Source: Adapted from Liker (2004, 33).

2.1.4.2. Standardization

Standardization applies to all processes in the organization and is a necessary first step in identifying the root cause of process variation. Standardization is one of the two daily activities at Toyota, as the term "maintenance" refers to following existing standards and maintaining the status quo. Daily management of resources requires standards, as they are used to highlight any deviation that then becomes the focus of investigation and potential improvement.

Masaaki Imai (1997) states that standardization is one of the three major kaizen activities and that it is core to building a successful lean organization and driving quality, cost, and delivery improvements. It is identified as one of the foundational elements in Imai's House of Gemba, illustrated in Figure 2.1.4.2-1. Standardization also includes translating technical and engineering requirements into work task documentation that is easy to understand and perform. Standardization builds control into the processes and is an important aspect of sustaining the gains of improvement activities by preventing a return to previous practices and results. With standardization implemented, the work itself can function as a management control mechanism, freeing up supervisors and allowing them to complete other tasks, since they no longer must monitor and control the process outputs.

Standardize is also the fourth "S" of a 5S organizational and management system. In this context, it refers to standardizing the "Sort," "Set in order," and "Shine" components so they are carried out consistently over time in accordance with the 5S procedures set on the gemba.

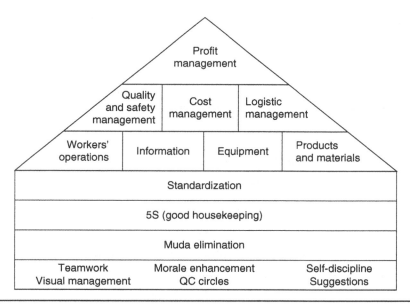

Figure 2.1.4.2-1   House of Gemba as illustrated by Imai.
Source: Adapted from Imai (1997, 20).

Standardized work is a tool for developing, confirming, and improving processes. It is commonly defined as documenting the best way to accomplish the tasks using the least amount of resources. Pascal Dennis (2007, 53), in *Lean Production Simplified*, lists three elements of standardized work:

1. Takt time

2. Work sequence—the best way to do the process?

3. In-process stock—how much inventory should there be?

Imai (1997, 54–57), in *Gemba Kaizen*, outlines nine key features of standards:

1. Represent the best, easiest, and safest way to do a job

2. Offer the best way to preserve know-how and expertise

3. Provide a way to measure performance

4. Show the relationship between cause and effect

5. Provide a basis for maintenance and improvement (maintenance means following standards)

6. Provide objectives and indicate training goals

7. Provide a basis for training

8. Create a basis for audit or diagnosis

9. Provide a means of preventing recurrence of errors and minimizing variability

There are many types of charts and forms associated with creating and documenting standard work:

- Production capacity chart
- Standardized work combination table
- Standardized work analysis chart
- Job element sheets

Benefits of Standardized Work

- Creates process stability
- Defines process boundaries (start and stop points)
- Preserves know-how and expertise
- Allows for easy identification of process deviation
- Promotes employee involvement
- Provides a baseline for improvement measurement
- Provides a basis for employee training

2.1.4.3. Recognize Abnormality

One of the keys to detecting errors in the process or deviations from the process lies in the ability to recognize abnormality. This is made easier by utilizing all of the concepts presented in the previous sections:

- Scientific thinking
- Stability
- Standardization

By instilling scientific thinking in all of the employees, creating stability of both the workforce and the equipment and standardizing the work processes, it becomes much easier to identify any deviations or abnormalities.

Through rigid adherence to the standardized work, all employees can see immediately whether there is any deviation from the defined process. If there are defects or problems, one of the first steps in investigating the issue is to determine whether the standardized work was followed exactly. If so, the process itself may have to be changed to ensure that the desired results are achieved. In this way the abnormality is a visual signal that the person needs additional training, tools, or equipment or that the process itself needs to be evaluated and changed.

2.1.4.4. Go and See

Gemba is commonly translated from Japanese to mean "real place," the place where the process actually occurs. In the context of lean, this means management needs to leave their desks and offices and go to the actual place where the processes and work are occurring and the value is added. General George S. Patton said it best: "No good decision was ever made from a swivel chair."

2.1.4.4

Perceptions, past experiences, inaccurate standards, and instincts are often used to make decisions and manage processes, but this can lead to erroneous decisions and changes that make the process more difficult and create additional waste. With direct observation, a key principle of scientific thinking, true and accurate information and data can be gathered and confirmed.

This practice is sometimes referred to as "going to gemba," indicating that the people will go to where the value-added work occurs. This is the first step in addressing any problem or issue that management has become aware of and also a method of identifying deviations and opportunities for improvement.

In *Gemba Kaizen* (Imai 1997), a kaizen consultant tells a story about the Ohno circle training method. Ohno was famous for requiring individuals to go to the gemba regularly. As part of a new engineer's training, Ohno would take the engineer to the middle of the shop floor, draw a circle on the floor with chalk, and tell the engineer to stand in the circle and observe until he returned. Typically, he would leave the person there for about an hour or two, just enough time to cause irritation. Sometimes he would go as far as to leave the person in the circle all day. Ohno wanted the engineer to remain in the circle until he or she "gained awareness." After the exercise, Ohno would review the process with the person until he or she could describe the process and identify the waste. Then he would require the individual to go and eliminate the waste now that he or she had seen it. He also did this with managers, urging them to "go to the gemba every day. And when you go, don't wear out the soles of your shoes in vain. You should come back with at least one idea for kaizen" (26). To his point, he urged accountants to go to the plant and wear out two pairs of shoes a year just by walking around and observing improvements in inventory and efficiency that resulted in reductions in costs. The "awareness" he wanted managers and support personnel to gain was to "see" with their own eyes what was occurring at the place of value. How can one manage or support a process or worker when one does not know how the process works, how the worker performs tasks, or what waste is there?

In some organizations this concept has been expanded to include planned, regular visits to specified areas of the workplace by the management team. These gemba walks typically focus on a specific area or function and include a short presentation by the workers and a review of metrics and outstanding issues. In mature lean organizations, this is a daily occurrence by all levels of management, with information being consolidated and flowing up to the facility's top management.

2.1.5. JIDOKA

Like just-in-time, jidoka is one of the two pillars in the House of Toyota. Typically translated as "autonomation," it is best defined as "automation with a human mind" (Dennis 2007, 95). In jidoka, equipment and processes are designed and operated such that work is automatically stopped if a defect is detected. In lean terms, it is the combination of automation and mistake-proofing (see Figure 2.1.5-1).

Toyota's experience with these types of devices dates back to the early twentieth century, when founder Sakichi Toyoda invented an automatic weaving machine, or loom, that would stop if any of the threads broke. Without an automatic stop, automated looms would continue to produce regardless of the broken thread, resulting in the production of defective cloth. Prior to this innovation, an operator was required to monitor the machine full-time in order to detect a problem and shut down the machine. Today, this concept of automating inspection within the process and stopping the process if problems are detected prevails throughout Toyota.

The objectives of jidoka are manyfold and include:

- Reduce costs

- Control overproduction

- Show respect for people

Reduce Costs (Productivity)

In typical manufacturing operations it is not uncommon to see one person dedicated, or assigned, to a single machine; the purpose being to monitor the process and detect problems as they occur. This approach is both expensive and marginally

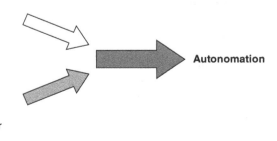

Figure 2.1.5-1   Components of autonomation.

effective—it is the rare person who can actually detect and sort out 100% of the defects. Operator-dependent detection and sorting of defects do not themselves ensure that problems are surfaced, root causes are identified, or effective corrective actions are put in place. Jidoka mechanizes the inspection into the machine and automatically stops it if problems are detected. As a result, constant human monitoring is not required, and workers are available to perform other work. This concept is called "separation of man from machine" and permits multi-process handling by a single worker. No longer tethered by the need to monitor a process and output, a single worker can perform a variety of tasks and manage multiple machines. Material handling, changeovers, and other activities can be performed while the machines produce and self-inspect the process. With jidoka in place, workers can support two, three, or more machines, and significant improvements in labor productivity will be realized.

Reduce Costs (Quality)

By definition, jidoka ensures in-station quality, where defects are detected immediately at the source. Upon detection, the process is shut down and no additional parts are produced until human intervention starts the process back up. Since notification is immediate (often via some sort of andon signal), only one defect has been produced; costs associated with inspection, sorting, rework, scrap, and warranty claims are kept low since the quantity of work-in-process is minimal.

Control Overproduction

In addition to detecting defects, jidoka devices are often designed to stop producing when a predetermined quantity has been produced. This could be the order or kanban quantity. Combined with the confidence that only good parts have been manufactured, production can be stopped automatically when the desired quantity is completed. As a result, work-in-process and raw material inventory levels can be more tightly managed.

Show Respect for People

A fundamental concept within the TPS is respect for people—respect for the work they do, how they feel, what they know, and what they need. By stopping defective processes, and with real-time identification of problems, jidoka enables workers to better understand the conditions under which the parts were made and improves their ability to identify the true root cause. With good understanding of what caused the problem, more responsible and more effective countermeasures can be designed to address the issue. Stopping the line when there is a problem increases the likelihood that workers will get appropriate support to resolve the problem—it is difficult to avoid addressing problems if line stoppages are chronic. In addition, real-time problem identification minimizes the amount of time spent on inspection, sorting, and rework and frees those resources to focus on problem solving and value-adding activities. By automating the detection, stopping the process, and communicating the problems, jidoka mechanizes the culture of "quality at the source" and empowers workers to exhibit those behaviors across the organization.

Jidoka also allows the employee to stop the production line, get to the nature of the problem, and put a fix in place so that the problem does not happen again. The steps involved in problem solving are:

1. Stopping the line

2. Understanding the nature of the defect

3. Putting a fix in place for the immediate problem

4. Uncovering the root cause

5. Error-proofing the process so mistakes will not reoccur

While it is easy to understand jidoka, it is difficult to implement it in the workplace. The following are factors to consider when implementing jidoka:

- Build trust in the workplace

- Foster a collaborative nature for problem solving

- Do not respond to mistakes with punitive measures

- Understand the basic problem-solving tools and how to apply them

- Take time to fix the problem correctly; Band-Aid fixes are not the answer

There are six key concepts that one should understand to fully implement the principle of jidoka:

1. Quality at the source

2. No defects passed forward

3. Separate man from machine

4. Multi-process handling

5. Self-detection of errors to prevent defects

6. Stop and fix

2.1.5.1. Quality at the Source

The quality management function has evolved from mere inspection to quality planning to quality management to Design for Six Sigma. However, many organizations still strongly believe in inspecting quality into product. They perform incoming inspection in the receiving of materials from suppliers, in-process inspection, final inspection, out-of-the-box audit, audit on the field, and many other non-value-added activities. While these inspections are sometimes necessary to protect the customer from receiving bad product, the idea is to eliminate the wasteful inspections across quality management processes by building in quality at the source.

The most effective way to maximize the resources of your organization is to ensure that quality (as defined by your customers) is built in to whatever product or service is produced by the people doing the work. The traditional method of having inspectors at the end of the process only results in sorting the good products from the bad. The inspector cannot change or affect the quality of the product; it cannot be inspected in. Having a separate in-process inspector catches the defect earlier in the process, but again he or she is only sorting the good from the bad. It has also been proved many times that even 100% inspection is only 80%–90% effective.

Quality at the source involves a cultural change. It requires an organization to move away from the notion that the defects will be caught by the end-of-the-line inspector. Implementing this change requires clear definition of employee expectations. One aspect of the change is employee ownership of the process and its output. This ownership typically involves the authority to optimize the process (empowerment) and the accountability that comes with the authority. However, it requires management to properly train the employee on the identification of the critical to quality attributes as well as how to use any associated test tools or equipment.

Six Elements of Quality at the Source

1. Standard work

2. Successive checks

3. Self-checks

4. Visual management

5. Poka-yoke

6. Continuous improvement

Standard Work

Throughout the value stream, there are points where critical tasks are performed that affect the end quality of the product or service. It is important for operators to know what those critical points are throughout the entire value stream. However, they cannot be expected to remember every critical task, especially in value streams where there are many control points and tasks at each process. Therefore, management must aid the worker in remembering what to inspect, how to inspect, and what to do when an error or defect is detected. This should also include how to perform a critical task to prevent an error or defect from occurring.

Management should provide documentation to the worker to reinforce the various potential quality issues associated with a given process. This documentation should be simple, not full-blown manuals or standard operating procedures (SOPs). In lean organizations, this documentation is called standard work. Manuals and SOPs can be used as a starting point from which standard work can be developed. Standard work is described in more detail in Section 2.2.6. For quality at the source to work effectively, standard work should provide information to quickly guide the worker through the quality aspects of the task and into the value-added activities. The documentation should provide the purpose; scope; applicable references; step-by-step procedure with pictorial demonstrations; flowchart in SIPOC (Supplier-Input-Process-Output-Customer) or a swim lane flowchart (cross-functional flowcharts); process controls; environmental, health, and safety conditions; metrics; and applicable records.

Documentation also provides an opportunity to standardize training of employees. This not only provides a means of training employees on how to do the job and perform key tasks, but also provides a reminder to the trainer to inform and make sure the employee understands the key potential quality issues associated with the task he or she is performing. Documentation also allows training employees on inspection methods and how to quickly perform them at each step. Training has to meet the needs of the trainee depending on his or her past education, skills, and experience. Effectiveness of the training has to be measured to address any gaps. Periodic in-process audits should be performed to review the effectiveness of processes.

Successive Checks

Often, inspections are performed at different points in the value stream. Shingo was concerned that inspections were not being performed at a time that optimizes the value stream. Shingo believed that inspections, in their current state, may not occur early enough in the process to provide the best information necessary to identify the root cause of the quality issue. Without this information, it is difficult to resolve the issue and drive improvements to prevent the issue from happening in the future.

Successive checks are checks by employees of the tasks performed by other employees upstream in the value stream. Successive checks prevent the addition of value (performing value-added work) to faulty material or information. Shingo believed that the rate of continuous improvement can be more rapid as quality feedback becomes faster. By having each employee inspect the work of the upstream employee, quality feedback can be given on a more timely basis. With successive checks, each process step performs both production and quality inspection.

Self-Checks

Self-checks are checks (or micro inspections) done by the employee performing a task according to his or her standard work. Self-checks prevent sending defective material, parts, or information forward in the process to the next process step. The inspection should be visual and fast, with the employee looking for each potential quality issue quickly and then moving on to the next process step. After all key inspections have been performed, any corrective action necessary due to a quality issue can then be initiated immediately at the point of occurrence.

While successive checks provide quick quality feedback, having the employee who performs the task check his or her own work provides even faster quality feedback. Self-checks tend to utilize poka-yoke (mistake-proofing) devices, which allows employees to assess the quality of their own work. Because they check every unit produced or service performed, employees may be able to identify the process conditions that changed, resulting in the quality issue. This insight can be used to perform a root cause analysis, immediately correct the issue, and prevent defects from occurring in the future. Because self-checks provide quality feedback faster, they are preferred to successive checks whenever possible.

While successive checks and self-checks are process-results oriented, Shingo believed that inspection prior to work (or source inspection) is the ideal method of quality control since feedback about process conditions is obtained before a process step is performed. Source inspection is intended to keep defects from occurring during the work. The addition of poka-yoke (mistake-proofing) devices into the inspection method help to evolve successive checks and self-checks into source inspections.

Visual Management

Another element of quality at the source is the development of visual aids. Visual management aids are simple tools utilized as communication aids to show work standards (examples of good and defective product) and inspection methods. One form of visual management aids is the single point lesson.

Single point lessons are commonly used to show how a task should be performed, how a product or service should be inspected, and what to look for during the inspection. Single point lessons can be created on single sheets of paper all the way up to large displays that are easily accessible to the employee performing the task (i.e., viewable while the work is being performed). The single point lesson relies heavily on photos and contains very little, if any, writing. The concept of the single point lesson is to utilize a visual picture to guide the employee through the process and make it easier to identify defects before more value is added to the product or service.

Poka-yokes (mistake-proofing devices) can be combined with visual aids to speed up the inspection process. More information on visual management (visual aids) can be found in Section 2.2.1.

Poka-Yoke

Poka-yoke is also known as mistake-proofing. In Japanese, *poka* means "inadvertent error" and *yoke* means "prevention." *Poka-yoke* means the implementation of simple, low-cost devices that either detect abnormal situations before they occur or stop the process once they occur to prevent defects (Dennis 2007, 98).

Poka-yoke devices can be used to ensure that correct process conditions are met prior to an employee performing a task. When used effectively, poka-yoke devices can make inspection systems at every step possible by reducing the time and cost of inspection to near zero. More information on poka-yoke can be found in Section 2.3.7.1.

Continuous Improvement

While Shingo supported self-check and successive check inspections, he was insistent that the true intent of the inspection is to identify quality and process issues immediately and communicate them to drive root cause analysis, prevent defects, and improve the process. His intent was not to use inspection to sort out defects.

Inspections, visual management, and poka-yoke devices are only as good as the current state of workforce knowledge. Fortunately, humans have the capacity to continuously learn. Shingo believed that these jidoka elements should evolve as we learn more about how processes can go wrong and how we can correct them and prevent defects from occurring in the future.

Traditional quality systems have relied mainly on expert knowledge to ensure that quality is inspected into a product or service before and after it is made. While using quality at the source effectively can make every employee responsible for adhering to standards of quality and productivity, it can also make those same employees responsible for creating those standards in the first place. A lean enterprise builds quality into products and services at every step in the process.

However, while improved quality is an outcome of lean transformations, lean concepts and tools seem to get all the attention. Just as tools such as 5S are credited with significant productivity improvements, quality at the source can produce significant quality improvements immediately.

Quality at the source has many other advantages, including better-informed employees, creation of a culture of customer focus, reduction in defect rework, elimination of other forms of waste (e.g., inventory due to poor quality), and most importantly the empowerment of employees.

2.1.5.2. No Defects Passed Forward

To ensure the quality, and not add additional resources to product that is defective, the operator needs to verify that the item received from the upstream process step meets all of the criteria. The operator checks the work of the person upstream (in front of him or her) to ensure that additional work is not done on a defective product. After this initial check, the operator completes his or her process step, performs the appropriate inspection, and checks to ensure the quality of the work before the product is processed further. Use of successive checks, self-checks, and source inspections is critical to this concept.

The principle of no defects passed forward is key to moving ahead with other lean concepts, such as flow and single piece manufacturing, as passing along defects would cause the downstream tasks to disrupt the process flow. This is also an integral part of just-in-time (JIT) principles, as JIT depends on the process to create defect-free products. If defects are created, the flow of the process and possibly the facility will be interrupted.

2.1.5.3. Separate Man from Machine

"Separate man from machine" (also known as man/machine separation) is a concept of a work environment where operators are able to run more than one machine at a time (see Figure 2.1.5.3-1).

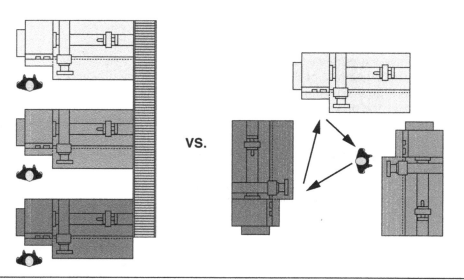

Figure 2.1.5.3–1 Example of conventional vs. man/machine separation layouts.

It is achieved by effectively combining the two lean techniques autonomation and standardized work. As previously defined, *autonomation* is the process of automating and mistake-proofing machines. By integrating automation with mistake-proofing, operators are freed up to do more value-added work. This concept is so important that Toyota made it one of the two pillars (jidoka) of the Toyota Production System.

In 1945, as Japan was recovering from World War II, American manufacturing productivity was much higher than that of the Japanese. To further complicate recovery of the Japanese auto industry, there was little demand for Japanese-made automobiles. The president of Toyota, Kiichiro Toyoda, set a vision for the company to catch up with the United States in three years in an effort to avoid total loss of the automobile industry in Japan. Because the demand for Japanese vehicles was low, Toyota could not rely on the American method of economies of scale to help lower product costs. As a result, Toyota set out on a journey of productivity improvement through waste elimination.

Taiichi Ohno moved from Toyoda Spinning and Weaving to Toyoda Motor. He implemented some of the ideas that he saw at the Spinning and Weaving plant in the automobile factory. One of those ideas was the automatically activated spinning loom. He recognized that automation was necessary to bridge the productivity gap between the Japanese auto industry and the American auto industry. He also recognized that automation alone results in waste. Therefore, he integrated mistake-proofing into the machines so that the machines would automatically detect problems or allow for operator intervention at the right time. Ohno described this combination as "automation with a human touch," which has evolved to the man/machine separation concept.

Man/machine separation is a process that happens over time. Table 2.1.5.3-1 shows four common stages that fully separate man from machine.

Table 2.1.5.3-1   Four stages of man/machine separation.

	Stage			
	Manual	**Mechanization**	**Automation**	**Autonomation**
Description	• Processes are performed manually • Typically one operator for each machine	• Machines are used to perform part of the work • Operator needed for many tasks	• Machine produces parts without operator interaction	• Machine stops when a set quantity is produced and/or a defect is detected
Issue	• Process is labor intensive	• Operator interacts frequently with machine	• Machine does not stop and will continue producing, good or defective	• Process is not standardized or balanced within the value stream
Lean tools and concepts to implement at next stage	• Value stream mapping • Continuous flow	• Load-load (operator only loads machines)	• Poka-yoke	• Standard work

2.1.5.4. Multi-Process Handling

Multi-process handling is the utilization of separation of man and machine to set up the process for an employee to operate multiple types of processes. Multi-process handling improves the efficiency, capacity, and effectiveness of people and machines. Where separation of man and machine allows a worker to operate two or more machines of the same type, multi-process handling incorporates cellular flow, where multiple processes are combined into a single operation. People can then provide oversight of a greater part of the value stream, therefore increasing utilization.

Additionally, machines can now perform multiple processes at one time. Years ago a milling machine worked on one part at a time with an operator doing die changes and overseeing the operation. Now milling machines can have three, five, or more operations, from course milling to final detail work. With the machine changing the raw billet material to the final product on its own, the operator only inserts the raw billet and removes the final product. This improves throughput, reduces defects, and maximizes machine and personnel utilization.

Of course, heavy equipment, like milling machines, is not the only type of machine to incorporate multi-process handling. Computers and cell phones have also significantly improved in this area. It used to be that computers (laptops) and cellular phones would give a brief warning before shutting down due to a depleted battery. Now they have real-time battery charge indicators and progressive warnings as the battery charge depletes, allowing users to shut them down "gracefully" and recharge or replace the battery.

Personnel can be involved in multi-process handling in two ways: (1) overseeing and doing more within a process and (2) doing more processes. This can be done in any process, from office work to manufacturing to engineering. Figure 2.1.5.4-1 shows how conventional manufacturing can be converted to a work cell layout where all three manufacturing processes are combined into multiple work cells through multi-process handling.

When a person can watch more machines with greater efficiency and effectiveness due to the machine's ability to perform more or monitor and report its

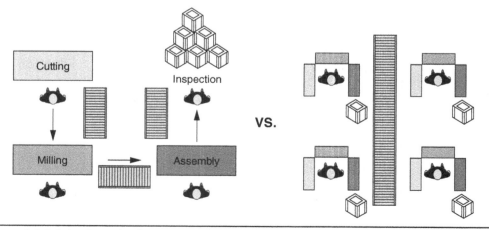

Figure 2.1.5.4-1   Example of conventional manufacturing to multi-process handling.

status, the efficiency of the operator is greater. A machine that automatically gathers components, assembles a finished product, tests the product to ensure proper assembly, and automatically offloads the finished part is an example of automated multi-process handling. Another example is a doctor's office where one employee processes many patients at the same time, moving from room to room to take the patients' vital signs and ask a few questions before the patient sees the doctor.

Personnel who perform multiple tasks or processes are also supporting multi-process handling. In a manufacturing environment, an employee may operate wave solder and surface-mount solder machines—setting up one while the other is processing. In an office environment, a person who can work shipping and receiving tasks plus provide stocking is an example. Another example is the typical "big box" home improvement store, where employees provide customers with expert advice, stock material, and help a customer check out.

For personnel, multi-process handling increases capability and capacity, reduces downtime, and increases the employee's value to the organization. Balance is needed to ensure that the employee does not do too much and that safety is not jeopardized. Multi-process handling by personnel usually leads to more employee satisfaction through accomplishment and skills enhancement.

Multi-process handling, part of jidoka, leverages Sakichi's loom invention, which reduced "defects and waiting time and raised productivity. Sakichi also raised the idea that it was okay to stop production to ferret out the root causes of defects" (Dennis 2007, 96). An organization that effectively leverages multi-process handling can reduce defects, improve utilization of equipment and personnel, and improve employee satisfaction.

2.1.5.5. Self Detection of Errors to Prevent Defects

Detection of errors is best accomplished through systemic means, mechanically for a piece of equipment. If further inspection or testing is required, quality at the source is the quickest and most economical means to find the defects and prevent disruption of flow downstream.

The term *poka-yoke* is commonly translated from Japanese as "error-proofing" or "mistake-proofing." *Poka* (inadvertent error) *yoke* (prevention) is any mechanism in a process that helps an equipment operator prevent errors. Typically, these are simple, low-cost devices that either detect abnormal conditions before they occur or, if they do occur, stop the equipment to prevent defects. Their purpose is to eliminate product defects by preventing, correcting, or drawing attention to errors as they occur. The concept was formalized, and the term adopted, by Shigeo Shingo as part of the Toyota Production System.

According to Dennis (2007, 98), in *Lean Production Simplified*, a good poka-yoke meets the following:

- Simple, with long life and low maintenance

- High reliability

- Low cost

- Designed for workplace conditions

Shigeo Shingo (1986, 101–6) defined three types of poka-yokes for detecting and preventing errors:

1. The contact method identifies product defects by testing the product's shape, size, color, or other physical attributes

2. The fixed-value (or constant number) method alerts the operator if a certain number of movements are not made

3. The motion-step (or sequence) method determines whether the defined steps of the process have been followed

For example, a jig that holds pieces for processing might be modified to only allow pieces to be held in the correct orientation, or a digital counter might track the number of spot welds on each piece to ensure that the worker executes the correct number of welds. Either the operator is alerted when a mistake is about to be made, or the poka-yoke device actually prevents the mistake from being made. In Shingo's lexicon, the former implementation would be called a warning poka-yoke, while the latter would be referred to as a control poka-yoke.

Shingo argued that errors are inevitable in any manufacturing process, but if appropriate poka-yokes are implemented, mistakes can be caught quickly and defects can be prevented. By eliminating defects at the source, the overall cost of mistakes within a company is reduced, as no further value is added to a defective product.

2.1.5.6. Stop and Fix

By utilizing the autonomation of the equipment and stopping production, the organization is able to highlight defects. Once the defect has been identified, the equipment stops until an immediate solution is found and is followed by an investigation to determine the root cause and implementation of a permanent solution to prevent a recurrence.

The basis for this principle is the Toyota philosophy that it is better to stop the whole production line to highlight and fix a single problem than to continue to manufacture products that may contain defects. At Toyota, every employee not only has the authority to "stop the line" but is expected to do so if an error or defect occurs.

While this philosophy may seem to be expensive and disruptive at the moment it occurs, the immediate improvements to the process and the elimination of the causes of the defects pay back higher returns over time. Stopping the line and implementing a permanent solution to prevent a recurrence provides the best results in the long term.

For example, in a traditional manufacturing environment, where the philosophy is that money is not being made if the machine is not running, a culture of getting the machine up and running as quickly as possible is created. These events often happen multiple times over a long period before a team of experts (engineers, management, Black Belts, etc.) is assembled to uncover the root cause and correct. Consider that this may cost 10 minutes of downtime each time an event occurs, and these 10-minute occurrences will add up over time. To continue the example, say the issue occurs three times per shift in a three-shift/five-days-per-week operation. That adds up to a total downtime of 450 minutes a week. Now add the loss of the operator time, loss of production of the machine, and the loss of expert resources for a weeklong root cause problem-solving event. The loss in defective product can also be added to this value loss. Over time, this can lead to a significant loss in value.

The lean philosophy is that production is stopped, the root cause identified, and corrective action taken to prevent a reoccurrence before production is restarted. One can easily see that 30–60 minutes of downtime to stop and fix the issue in the short term will save a significant amount of value in the long term.

2.1.6. INTEGRATE IMPROVEMENT WITH WORK

In a lean organization, all employees' work has two parts: routine work and improvement work. As the lean culture evolves and employee empowerment increases, it is natural for employees to begin to feel ownership of the processes. Part of that ownership is the responsibility to continually improve those processes. Therefore, employees need information, tools, and support to implement improvements as they identify them. The activities and approaches for continuous improvement become a part of the everyday work of every employee in an organization (*Model and Application Guidelines* 2010, 14).

Employees must evolve into process "investigators." They must continually assess the current state of their processes and identify opportunities for improvement in the pursuit of a future state that enhances value. This is true for employees at all levels of the organization (Table 2.1.6-1).

Integrating improvement with work includes much more than assigning accountability. It requires creating and maintaining standardized work that defines procedures for improvement (*Model and Application Guidelines* 2010, 14). Without integrating improvement with routine work, an organization will continue getting the same results as before (Dennis 2007, 125).

Table 2.1.6–1   Integrated improvement at different organizational levels.

Level	Responsibility
Senior leaders	Improvement of strategy-setting processes and resource allocation
Middle management	Improvement of quality systems, product/service flow, employee development, communication, training, etc.
Shop-floor (frontline) employees	Improvement of cycle times, quality, shop-floor standard work, visual management, poka-yoke, etc.

2.1.7. SEEK PERFECTION

"Complete elimination of waste is the basis of the Toyota production."

—Taiichi Ohno (1988)

Seeking perfection is oftentimes called the "True North" of lean. In other words, the end goal is to completely eliminate all wastes from processes in order to provide value to the customer without the additional costs associated with creating waste, or non-value-added activities the customer does not pay for. It is called "True North" because it is the direction in which a lean organization should always be heading. Vince Lombardi (2004), the famous Green Bay Packers head coach, said it best: "Perfection is not attainable, but if we chase perfection we can catch excellence."

A lean organization is never satisfied with anything less than perfection; therefore, those organizations will never become stagnant, as they are continually improving themselves. Organizations achieve this continuous improvement state in two ways:

1. Slow and steady (kaizen)

2. Fast and significant (kaikaku)

2.1.7.1. Incremental Continuous Improvement (Kaizen)

Kaizen is a Japanese word most commonly translated as "change for the better" or "continuous improvement." A true kaizen environment promotes continuous improvement by everyone, every day.

Historically, many organizations have viewed improvements as significant only if they have large measurable impact on process performance, and financial justification such as return on investment is evidence of their significance. Kaizen thinking promotes small, easy, low-risk, and low-cost process improvements. Most small changes require only small and quick experiments to evaluate whether the improvement idea (hypothesis) is valid.

Keeping experiments simple means many more people throughout the organization can participate in the improvement process. As a result there is much more bandwidth available to assess and implement improvement ideas. Quick and simple experimentation also means the velocity with which ideas are generated, tested, and implemented will increase. Effective kaizen execution requires hands-on, go-see, fact-based testing and evaluation of ideas.

Since kaizen improvements are small in scope, daily kaizen permits quick progression through the idea generation, testing, and evaluation phases. Consistent with the idea that we learn only when we "do" (i.e., run an experiment), a natural outcome of frequent kaizen is an organization populated with people experiencing many, many learning cycles on a daily or weekly basis. Kaizen improvements can be thought of as evolutionary in nature, as they are small modifications to the existing process.

This contrasts with the traditional methods of creating a project team, studying options, gathering information over many months, and rolling out a large project at the end. This traditional approach misses the benefits of the small incremental improvements made over time that are immediately realized with kaizen.

Figure 2.1.7.1-1 shows that the organization enjoys the benefits of smaller kaizen improvements over time from day one, whereas the traditional approach

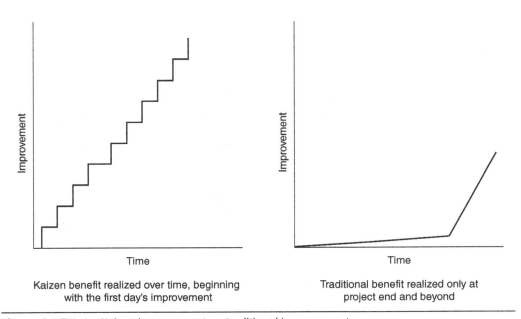

Kaizen benefit realized over time, beginning with the first day's improvement

Traditional benefit realized only at project end and beyond

Figure 2.1.7.1-1   Kaizen improvement vs. traditional improvement.

receives benefits only at the end when the project launches (assuming the project launch is successful).

While kaizen typically delivers small incremental improvements, the creation of a culture of ongoing aligned small improvements and the associated standardization often produce larger results through aggregated productivity improvement. Large long-term projects are replaced by smaller, more frequent activities that can be rapidly implemented and the benefits immediately realized as new improvements are suggested.

Paradoxically, daily kaizen activities should be driven by the concept of kaikaku. Kaikaku, discussed in the following section, describes radical or transformational change. Without a kaikaku vision of where the organization is heading, or what it aims to become, daily improvement activities lack purpose and may not have significant impact on the organization. With a clear vision of the organization's goals and objectives, kaizen activities can lead to major transformation over time.

2.1.7.2. Breakthrough Continuous Improvement (Kaikaku)

Kaikaku, typically translated as "innovation," is also described as "radical improvement," "major process redesign," and "reformation." Kaikaku changes may include major redesigns of product, part manufacturing, and facility layout or business processes. Due to its inherent magnitude of change, kaikaku innovations require radical thinking, more time to implement, extensive planning and coordination, a time commitment from people supporting them, and (often) significant financial investment. Since kaizen improvements are small incremental modifications to an established process, kaizen can be described as *evolutionary*. Due to the major rethinking related to kaikaku changes, kaikaku can be described as *revolutionary*.

Kaikaku commonly refers to a focused kaizen designed to address a particular issue over the course of a week, referred to as a "kaizen blitz" or "kaizen event." These activities are limited in scope, and any issues that arise during them are documented and may be the focus of future kaizen blitzes. Kaikaku can also connote that an entire business is radically changed, typically in the form of a project or a series of projects.

Innovation (kaikaku) without continuous improvement (kaizen) runs the risk of not being sustained (Figure 2.1.7.2-1).

Without kaizen, kaikaku improvements will deteriorate with time, as no one is responsible for constantly looking for and resolving small problems; process management and improvement is left to those who redesigned the process. With both kaizen and kaikaku, organizations will optimize their continuous improvement efforts (Figure 2.1.7.2-2).

Imai (1997, 59), in *Gemba Kaizen*, outlines an eight-step kaizen story process:

1. Selecting a theme

2. Understanding the current status and setting objectives

3. Analyzing the data thus collected to identify root causes

4. Establishing countermeasures based on the data analysis

5. Implementing countermeasures

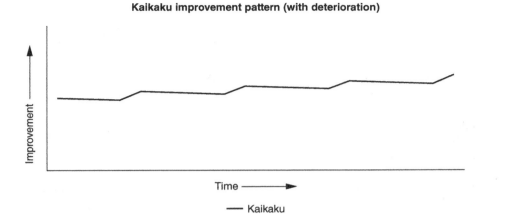

Figure 2.1.7.2-1   Kaikaku without kaizen.

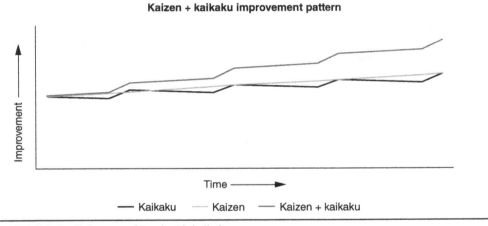

Figure 2.1.7.2-2   Kaizen combined with kaikaku.

6. Confirming the effects of the countermeasures

7. Establishing or revising standards to prevent recurrence

8. Reviewing the above processes and working on the next steps

Kaikaku is typically initiated by management, since the scope of the change and the anticipated result will impact the overall business. Kaikaku can be focused on introducing a new knowledge set, new marketing or production strategies, new approaches, new production techniques, or new equipment. Kaikaku may be triggered by external factors, such as changing market conditions, new technology, or competitors' actions.

Kaikaku can also be initiated by management when it is apparent that ongoing kaizen work is beginning to stagnate and no longer providing adequate results for the organization in relation to the effort. Kaikaku projects often result in improvements at a higher level and can also provide a new base level for continued kaizen.

REFERENCES

Dennis, Pascal. 2007. *Lean Production Simplified: A Plain-Language Guide to the World's Most Powerful Production System*. 2nd ed. New York: Productivity Press.

Galsworth, Gwendolyn D. 1997. Glossary, *Visual Systems: Harnessing the Power of the Visual Workplace*. New York: American Management Association.

Imai, Masaaki. 1997. *Gemba Kaizen: A Commonsense, Low-Cost Approach to Management*. New York: McGraw-Hill.

Liker, Jeffery. 2004. *The Toyota Way: 14 Management Principles from the World's Greatest Manufacturer*. New York: McGraw-Hill.

Lombardi, Vince, Jr. 2004. *The Lombardi Rules: 26 Lessons from Vince Lombardi—the World's Greatest Coach*. New York: McGraw-Hill.

Marchwinski, Chet, and John Shook. 2006. *Lean Lexicon*. 3rd ed. Version 3.0. Cambridge, MA: Lean Enterprise Institute.

Model and Application Guidelines: The Shingo Prize for Operational Excellence. 2010. Version 4. Logan, UT: Jon M. Huntsman School of Business, Utah State University.

Ohno, Taiichi. 1988. *Toyota Production System: Beyond Large-Scale Production*. Boca Raton, FL: CRC Press, Taylor & Francis Group.

Patton, George S. "The Official Website of General George S. Patton, Jr." http://www.generalpatton.com/quotes.

Shingo, Shigeo. 1986. *Zero Quality Control: Source Inspection and the Poka-Yoke System*. New York: Productivity Press.

Shingo, Shigeo, and Andrew P. Dillon. 1985. *A Revolution in Manufacturing: The SMED System*. New York: Productivity Press.

Taylor, Frederick Winslow. 1911. *The Principles of Scientific Management*. New York and London: Harper and Brothers.

2.2

Continuous Process Improvement Systems

To effectively practice the continuous process improvement principles, an organization must implement systems that support continuous improvement efforts throughout the entire enterprise. The purpose of continuous process improvement systems is to constantly and consistently collect and analyze information on the current state of processes and share it with employees at all levels. These systems highlight quality issues and deviations from the process standards. Making employees aware of these issues and deviations allows for the identification of areas where an improvement focus is required to continue the pursuit of perfection.

While continuous process improvement principles create a vision and strategy for organizational excellence, continuous process improvement systems provide the means of executing the vision and strategy. The key to organizational excellence is the creation of continuous process improvement systems that align the vision and strategy with the lean philosophy and "True North" (seek perfection). These systems provide clear communication channels, accountability, planning, and tracking regarding activities within an organization, along with action items for adjustments and countermeasures implemented when issues occur. Utilizing these systems effectively fosters an environment of cyclical learning and improvement.

Organizations that are successful in the lean journey achieve an alignment of principles (vision and strategy) with processes (policy and procedures) at all levels within the organization. Organizational alignment, or successful policy deployment, allows everyone in an organization to pull in a single or common direction.

It is simple physics. Forces in a single direction on an object have a cumulative impact, while forces in opposite or different directions negate the overall force on an object. Consider an organization as the object. If everyone is pulling in a common direction based on the vision, the organization will progress toward the vision at a higher rate than an organization with groups pulling in different directions (Figure 2.2-1).

When alignment is effective, the sum of individual efforts rarely adds up to the cumulative impact of the pieces as a whole. In other words, while improvement in single value streams may not appear as significant, these individual improvements will be significant to the overall organization if they are aligned in a common direction. Effectively aligning all value streams within an organization is key when pursuing the maximum value for customers (*Model and Application Guidelines* 2010, 14).

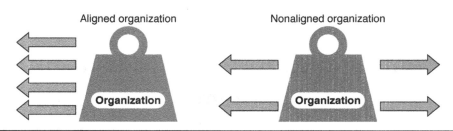

Figure 2.2-1   Aligned vs. nonaligned organization.

Continuous process improvement systems include:

1. Visual workplace

2. Lot size reduction

3. Load leveling

4. 3P (Production Process Preparation)

5. Total productive maintenance (TPM)

6. Standard work

7. Built-in feedback

8. Strategic business alignment

9. Continuous improvement process methodology

10. Quality systems

11. Corrective action system

12. Project management

13. Process design

14. Pull system

15. Knowledge transfer

With these systems in place, an organization will be able to see what and where improvements are needed.

2.2.1. VISUAL WORKPLACE*

The entire world of work—whether assembly plant, hospital, bank, airport, military depot, pharmaceutical factory, retail store, or open-pit mine—is striving to make work safer, simpler, more logical, reliable, and linked, and less costly. Central to this is the visual workplace.

The visual workplace is not a brigade of buckets and brooms or posters and signs. It is a compelling operational imperative, central to your war on waste, and

---

*©1992–2011 QMI/Visual-Lean® Institute. (Gwendolyn Galsworth) All rights reserved http://www.visualworkplace.com (Galsworth 1997).

crucial to meeting daily performance goals, vastly reduced lead times—and dramatically improved quality.

But most people do not understand the tremendous power of workplace visuality. Instead they treat it as an add-on to some other improvement effort, whether lean or six sigma. "We know what visual is. . . . Let's put up some signs and put down some lines." This is not just a mistake in thinking; it is the loss of a huge improvement opportunity.

Translating Vital Information into Visual Devices

What precisely is a visual workplace? Visual workplace is defined as:

> A visual workplace is a self-ordering, self-explaining, self-regulating, and self-improving work environment . . . where what is supposed to happen does happen, on time, every time, day or night—because of visual solutions.

This definition, which evolved over a decade of implementations, is worth a closer look. The first half—*"a visual workplace is a self-ordering, self-explaining, self-regulating, and self-improving work environment"*—describes the outcome in terms of functionality. When a workplace gets visual, it functions differently—safer, better, faster, smoother. Specifically, a visual workplace:

- Is in order, order you can see, and is able to harness that order for a business advantage

- Explains itself to anyone and everyone in it . . . sharing vital information about what to do/what not to do, how and when to do it, and how to respond if something (including yourself) goes wrong

- Is transparent . . . because it explains itself, a visual work environment can regulate itself—through high-impact/low-cost visual devices

- Acquires the ability, over time, to correct itself—to become self-improving because visual devices are constantly providing feedback on our performance and the performance of the company itself

The second half of the definition—*"where what is supposed to happen does happen, on time, every time, day or night—because of visual solutions"*—describes a broader outcome: a company that can, through visual devices, ensure the precise execution of standards—both technical and procedural standards. The result? Work is executed with precision, reliably and predictably translating perceived value (what the customer wants) into received value (what the customer buys).

A visual device is an apparatus, mechanism, item, or thing that influences, directs, limits or controls behavior by making information vital to the task-at-hand available at-a-glance, without speaking a word.

A visual workplace is made up of not hundreds—but thousands—of visual devices, created by the workforce that needs them. Added up, these devices create a language of excellence in the enterprise—a language that speaks to everyone and anyone who wants to listen.

Here are four visual devices, each sharing visual information on four aspects of day-to-day work (Figures 2.2.1-1 thru 2.2.1-4).

2.2.1

Figure 2.2.1-1   Visual device for showing status.

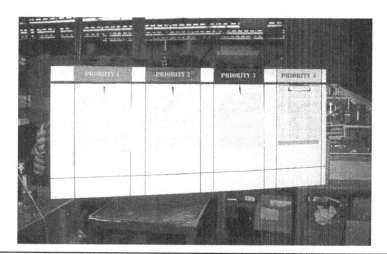

Figure 2.2.1-2   Visual device for sharing work activities.

The checkered flags in Figure 2.2.1-1 tell the supervisor and everyone else that these two extrusion machines are producing to schedule.

An area supervisor created the Figure 2.2.1-2 visual display so operators could tell—at-a-glance—what order to work on next (red is first priority).

In Figure 2.2.1-3, operators put red tape on each of these poles as a reminder not to hang wiring harnesses too low and chance damaging their delicate terminal endings.

Although the plant in Figure 2.2.1-4 has not yet gone lean, slanted green borders help forklifts pick/put pallets—while the yellow person-width border lets operators find orders more easily.

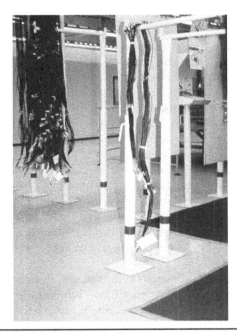

Figure 2.2.1-3   Visual device for preventing defects.

Figure 2.2.1-4   Visual device for providing ease of access.

Visual Devices: The Voice of Your Operations

In a visual workplace, information is converted into simple, commonly-understood visual devices, installed in the process of work itself—as close to the point of use as possible. The result is the transformation of a formerly mute work environment into one that speaks—clearly and precisely about how to perform error-free work safely, smoothly, reliably, and on-time.

What happens when the workplace speaks? What happens when formerly voiceless work stations, equipment, tools, machines, and material can communicate freely and precisely with us? What happens when we can know vital information—the details of work—at a glance, without speaking a word, without asking (or answering) a single question?

When a company becomes a fully-functioning visual workplace, each employee has instant on-demand access to information vital to one's own work and the enterprise is infused with intelligence you can see—intelligence that illuminates and drives the corporate intent. The result is benefits you can take to the bank.

In a visual enterprise, every section of the floor, every bench, work surface, hand tool, part, machine, rack, cabinet, and bin is equipped to make a contribution to the collective purpose that is beyond its mere existence—because now that item can visually communicate vital information to anyone and everyone who needs it as they need it. There are no exceptions.

Brilliant floor borders in this massive food manufacturer in Australia (Figure 2.2.1-5) show us the walk-lanes while alerting forklift drivers to pedestrian traffic. In a visual workplace, floors do not exist simply to walk on or hold things up. They function—showing us where it is safe to walk, where materials are, and where we are supposed to work.

Figure 2.2.1-5   Floor bordering.

Benches are not merely surfaces on which to place parts and tools. Through the *visual where*, benches tell the exact location of the "things" of work—or show us that they are missing. A simple address can even save lives, as you see in the example in Figure 2.2.1-6.

Visually highlighting the "CIS" in this drug address helps pharmacists keep dangerous mix-ups to a minimum.

Departments need not merely be a collection of furniture, things, and people. When we give them a voice through workplace visuality, they become productive allies that manage themselves and the enterprise as well. Tools are not restricted to merely helping us convert material. They can also tell us how to use them properly, when they need to be calibrated, and when they are unsafe. In a visual workplace, tools become vocal partners in the production process. And when we create equipment that speak, machines can assist in their own quick changeovers.

In the sharpening cell (Figure 2.2.1-7), operators leave dull tools in the red location on the machine face and maintenance returns them, sharpened, to the green location.

Figure 2.2.1-6   Labeling pharmaceuticals in a pharmacy.

Figure 2.2.1-7   Tooling sharpening visual workplace.

In a full-functioning visual workplace, the things of the physical workplace and the workplace itself contribute to the making of profit in ways that go far beyond their mere presence. Through visuality, they become active, sustaining partners in the process of work and day-to-day improvement.

Imagine that any employee—whether a newcomer, veteran, or temp—could safely, effectively, and efficiently run a new process in your company with merely a simple orientation because that process is visually capable . . . with vital performance information available instantly at point of use. What would that mean for your bottom line?

Go further. What if your entire enterprise—from sales and customer service through design, production, and shipping—were visually capable of responding to changes in minutes instead of days? Would that improve your competitive advantage?

And the clincher is this. Those who benefit from visual devices, more often than not, create the very devices that help them do their own work safer, better, and faster (Figure 2.2.1-8).

This scrap separator solution began as six Styrofoam cups that the assembly operator taped together so she could sort defects into groups as she found them.

Visuality is a powerful mechanism for creating an empowerment workforce and improvement that is sustainable. Consider the visual solutions you have seen so far in this section, multiply them by 100, and imagine how they would impact and benefit your own company and your own work. As you do, you begin to see the great power of information that is embedded into the process of work, visually available to everyone and anyone who needs it, as close to the point of use as possible. This is the language of your operational excellence made tangible, real, and functional.

The Problem: Information Deficits

Precisely what condition does a visual workplace address? The answer is information deficits. As every company knows, workplace information can change quickly and often—production schedules, customer requirements, engineering specifications, operational methods, tooling and fixtures, material procurement, work-in-process, and the thousand other details on which the daily life of the

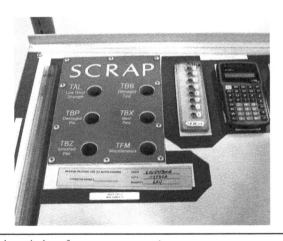

Figure 2.2.1-8   Visual workplace for a scrap separator.

enterprise depends. In any single day, literally thousands of informational transactions are required to keep work current, accurate, and timely.

Figure 2.2.1-9 shows an information-rich work area at the airport. Can you
see how this system of visual devices ensures that different planes can stop in precisely the right spot to precisely connect with the jetway and allow weary travelers
to exit the aircraft quickly and safely? The answers are built into place visually.

But what happens when this vital information is hard to access, incomplete,
inaccurate, or simply missing? What happens is this: people ask lots of questions
and lots of the same questions, repeatedly. An information-scarce workplace is the
opposite of a visual workplace. When key information is not instantly available,
the company pays for that in long lead times, late deliveries, poor quality, mistakes, accidents, low operator and managerial morale, and runaway costs.

When workplace visuality is not firmly in place, these unhappy occurrences
are chronic and unrelieved. They happen "all the time"—day in/day out, week
in/week out, year in/year out. Struggle becomes a way of life.

In the pre-visual workplace, everything and everyone are forced to exist within
a narrow definition of their capability. The physical work environment is devoid
of definition or conveyed context. There is no common purpose. It is devoid of
meaning. Attempts to improve the process of work invariably fail because even
the smallest gains disappear overnight. A pre-visual workplace has no means to
sustain them, however hard-won.

This is the unhappy state of affairs that results from *chronic deficits of information*—
unanswered questions.

Far too many offices and production floors are flooded with questions that are
asked—but many more experience a worse condition: questions that are unasked.
We say "worse" because all too often when a question is not asked, people make
stuff up. They simply make up an answer. Sometimes that works to the benefit of
the company, but all too frequently it works against it. People make stuff up and
accidents happen, material is lost, defects are produced, delivery times are missed,
and customers flee.

Working in an environment without visual information sharing is like trying
to reach a destination by driving a hundred miles without a map, on a road with
no road signs, no traffic signals, and no lines down the center of the road. You can
probably make it but you are likely to pay a terrible price.

Figure 2.2.1-9   Visual workplace at an airport.

Figure 2.2.1-10   Airport without visual workplace.

Compare the work area in Figure 2.2.1-9 with the one in Figure 2.2.1-10. What is the story it tells about the level of work that is possible here? Can you see how it is starved for information? Can you hear the questions that the lack of visuality triggers? Where do we go for the answers? Which gate area looks more like your company? What is the impact of that?

In the vast majority of companies, accurate, complete, timely, relevant information is unattainable or simply too hard to come by—and the truth is even harder to locate. That is not to say there aren't plenty of data. Data abound. Data can be found everywhere—in quality reports, SPC graphs, management briefings, in team meetings, and weekly and annual reports. Data flood the workplace.

But compiling data is a fruitless activity if those data are not translated into information and the information is not translated into meaning.

It is meaning that we are after. Without understanding the meaning of the data, we cannot make sound decisions and move the company and the people who work there forward. We cannot perform. This is the unhappy state of affairs that results from chronic deficits of information—unanswered questions.

Verbal questions are so commonplace in most companies that some people (including some managers and supervisors) sometimes think that their main job is to provide the answers—day in and day out, all the time.

Calculating the level of information deficits (missing answers) in your company is the quickest way for you to diagnose the extent to which a visual work environment is both absent and needed. You can do this by keeping track of the questions you are asked in the front of a pocket memo pad—and tracking the questions you ask on the flip side of that pad. Or you can implement the *First-Question-Is-Free Rule.*

The First Question Is Free Rule

Questions are so commonplace in most companies that some people (especially managers and supervisors) sometimes think that their main job is to provide the answers—day in and day out, all the time.

The *First-Question-Is-Free Rule* is a simple process that can minimize such endless interruptions and have a profound effect on workplace stability and reliability. And it applies on all levels of the company, whether you are the supervisor, value-add associate, marketing rep, technician, doctor, nurse—or CEO. Here's what you do:

1. When someone approaches you with a question, answer it politely and clearly. And as that person walks away, make a mental note: "That's one."

2. Then wait until you are asked that same question again, either by the same person or someone else. Again answer the question politely and clearly; and as that person walks away, make the mental note: "That's two!"

3. The first question is free. And the second time you hear that same question from the same person or anybody else, it's time for you to create a visual device—so you never ever have to answer that question again and no one ever has to ask it.

This modest approach can be highly effective in all work venues—perhaps most powerfully in such administrative areas as accounting, HR, sales, and purchasing where the level of tangible abnormalities seen on the production floor are not as noticeable. But they are there nonetheless. Making missing answers visible by noticing your questions can open huge communication possibilities in offices. Just remember, this is a tool, and not a methodology. Therefore, it cannot, alone, produce an authentic visual conversion.

As with all great visual solutions, the office device in Figure 2.2.1-11 makes it easy to imagine the endless questions that preceded it. Now all the answers are visually available at-a-glance to anyone and everyone who needs it. Great visual thinking!

A Gigantic Adherence Mechanism

Visual devices translate the thousands of informational transactions that occur every day at work into visible meaning. This visible meaning doesn't just impact performance; it creates it. Visual devices can show status (on time, process running, help needed); share work priorities (as in a work priority display board); prevent defects (from simple signage reminders to complex mistake-proofing systems); and

Figure 2.2.1-11   Fewer questions/More value add.

provide order on the plant floor (through clear borders for WIP and deliveries, along with person-width borders for easy access); and of course much more.

A visual workplace is made up of hundreds—even thousands—of such devices, created by the workforce that needs them. Added up, these devices create a language of excellence in the enterprise—a language that speaks to everyone and anyone who wants to listen.

—■-■-■—

More Visual Workplace Examples

The key to a visual workplace is that the visual devices used are easily understood and accessed by all. Think back to kindergarten days. At that age, we could not read a document on where to hang our coats, put our lunchboxes, sit for reading time, and so forth. But we could comprehend pictures, colors, and shapes. A visual workplace is much like kindergarten—simple to understand and easy to see when something is out of place (Figure 2.2.1-12).

This is not to say that employees should be treated like kindergartners. This simply means that the use of pictures, colors, shapes, and so forth, makes it easier and more efficient to quickly comprehend and react to events within a process than a spreadsheet filled with numbers, a written procedure, or no information at all. The pictures and letters on the floor rug help kindergartners remember where their spot is during activity and/or reading time.

Colors are used to quickly identify various situations of volumes, status, and so forth. Everyone can understand the stoplight concept shown in Figure 2.2.1-13.

Visual workplace can be applied anywhere, from our daily life to the sophisticated manufacturing and service workplace. An employee photo ID badge is a visual aid to ensure that outsiders do not enter an organization's work area, mingle, and cause risk to employee and information security. Most documented standard work uses pictorial work flow so that the operators can comprehend the process effectively. Incorporating a watermark feature in a document helps identify whether the document is controlled/uncontrolled, a draft, or obsolete. Inspection tags in various colors interpret product as "good," "scrap," "on hold," and so forth, thus preventing the shipping of bad products to the customer and overprocessing an already defective product.

Figure 2.2.1-12   Kindergarten classroom visual management.

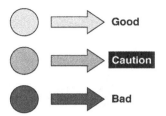

Figure 2.2.1-13 Stoplight colors green, yellow, and red indicate good, caution, and bad (red and green are used most commonly for status and volume indicators).

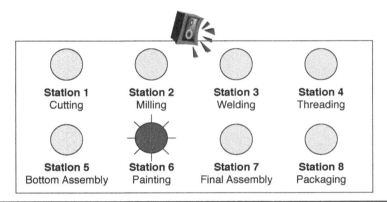

Figure 2.2.1-14 Example of an andon board.

Perhaps the most well-known type of visual workplace is the Toyota andon board (Figure 2.2.1-14). This visual display notifies the group leader, supervisor, or maintenance with a light that pinpoints the process step and sometimes includes an audible alarm when a process is stopped.

The andon board is a visual representation of production/process status. Some andon boards incorporate scrolling LED message boards that update the employee of the current production rate, total production, production variation, operational equipment efficiency, production goals, and takt time. With costs of technology dropping, large flat-screen monitors are being used more in production and service workplaces. The displays can be revised real time on the screen. Marker boards and grease boards used in emergency rooms for tracking patients are being replaced with flat-screen monitors.

Another form of visual workplace is the use of stacklights. This light is fitted to machines and has red, yellow, and green lights. Green indicates normal manufacturing with no interruption. Yellow indicates the operator needs help. Red indicates that manufacturing has stopped. The operator may signal yellow to draw attention and ask for help at any time. The line supervising personnel should provide assistance and record the incident to resolve the issue and prevent recurrence.

As stated earlier, visual management is utilized in service organizations as well. Consider the lights above admitted patients' rooms in a hospital (Figure 2.2.1-15). These lights inform hospital staff of the current status of a patient in a room. When an emergency arises, staff can get to the room quickly and do not have to spend time searching for and comprehending room numbers when tenths of a second can matter in certain situations.

Figure 2.2.1-15   Common stacklight used in hospital environments.

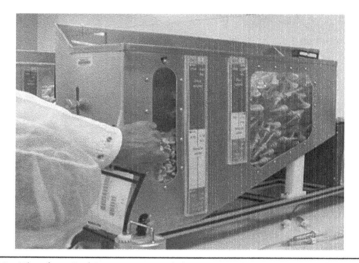

Figure 2.2.1-16   Visual control to manage work-in-process (parts) on a production line.

Material planning also uses various visual controls to display material levels of various parts in the inventory. Using the visual indicators of green, yellow, and red, the visual controls can be put in place to trigger restock of parts, material, or processes. As shown in Figures 2.2.1-16 through 2.2.1-18, visual controls can be utilized for material planning on the production line, in the warehouse, and in office areas to control reorder points and minimize inventory levels.

When a pull system is created, a kanban card is used as an effective visual indicator to trigger production of parts and components of an assembly process when they are depleted from inventory (see Section 2.2.14 to learn more about pull systems and kanban cards). Kanban cards may be used to create another visual management system in which a subassembly process will be visually alerted when to produce parts. Figure 2.2.1-19 shows how kanban cards can be used to track location of material within a manufacturing process and when safety stock needs to be replenished.

In service industries, visual management can be created to trigger when additional resources are needed in the process. Figure 2.2.1-20 shows a testing and cleaning process management board in which an additional inspector is placed in the process when work reaches a certain point or is behind customer demand.

Figure 2.2.1-17   Visual control to manage raw materials in a warehouse.

Figure 2.2.1-18   Visual control to manage office supply inventory levels.

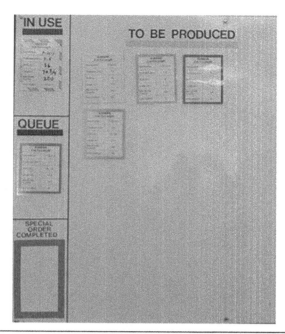

Figure 2.2.1-19 Visual management of a welding operation and steel cutting process.

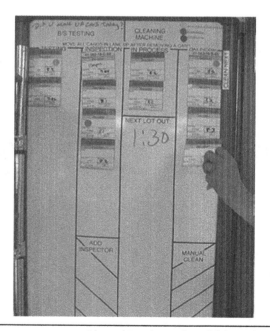

Figure 2.2.1-20 Resource management board to trigger the addition of an inspector and manual cleaning operation.

Systems like this may be utilized in the service industry to trigger the addition of a bank teller, checkout clerk, counter associate, and so forth, when a line of customers reaches a given length.

Simple color-coding techniques are used in doctor's offices, hospitals, schools, and many other places as a file management tool to reduce the time to locate files (Figure 2.2.1-21). The same color-coding technique is also used in inventory management systems to allow employees to quickly locate specific parts and supplies in a warehouse or storage space (Figure 2.2.1-22).

2.2.1

Figure 2.2.1-21 File management at a doctor's office.

	A	B	C	D	E	F
1	F-OS1217 2 Stacks 500 per stack	F-OS1316 2 Stacks 400 per stack	F-OS1319 2 Stacks 350 per stack	F-OS1314 2 Stacks 450 per stack	F-OS1321 2 Stacks 325 per stack	OPEN for Special Order
	0.8 mm × 36 in	1.0 mm × 36 in	1.1 mm × 36 3/8 in	0.9 mm × 36 3/8 in	1.2 mm × 36 3/8 in	OPEN for Special Order
2	F-OS338 2 Stacks 450 per stack	F-OS1313 2 Stacks 500 per stack	F-OS1312 2 Stacks 500 per stack	F-OS361 2 Stacks 350 per stack	F-OS657 2 Stacks 300 per stack	OPEN for Special Order
	09.mm × 36 in	0.8 mm × 37 3/8 in	0.8 mm × 36 3/8 in	1.1 mm × 36 in	1.4 mm × 36 in	OPEN for Special Order

Figure 2.2.1-22 Color coding for inventory locations in a warehouse.

A colored diagonal line can be used to quickly indicate whether a critical manual or documentation is not in its designated place (Figure 2.2.1-23). Methods like this can be deployed in maintenance areas or organizations that are regulated to maintain critical records in the event of an emergency or audit.

Equipment maintenance personnel use visual workplace to identify the status of the equipment as "up" or "down" or under preventive maintenance. They also use "lock out tag out" (LOTO) tools in high-risk areas to prevent inadvertent use of equipment that, if used, could cause a safety issue to the operator and the equipment. Hazardous areas are designated with signs that alert an employee of work hazards.

There are many manufacturing applications for visual devices. Manufacturing control valves are pictured in the correct direction for open and displayed along the valve so that employees know if the valve is mistakenly closed by anyone. Another usual application is putting limits on analog gages. This is a cut piece of paper that identifies the sector of the circle in the gage that is the operating range. This will help the operator stay within the operating range or identify when

Figure 2.2.1-23   Diagonal line identifying whether critical documents are missing.

Figure 2.2.1-24   LOTO tool.

Figure 2.2.1-25   LOTO station easily identifies where LOTO supplies are located and when they are missing.

Figure 2.2.1-26   Examples of various safety signs.

equipment requires servicing. For digital gages, audio alarms and LEDs are available that provide a similar indication.

Standard work can display visual defects to help train new inspectors and also verify during inspection. In training of employees, visual workplace employing different colored tags is used to distinguish the trainees from the skilled experts.

Visual hour-by-hour charts are used in areas where processes are expected to have a rate of output based on takt. They are specifically applicable in processes where flow has been established. These charts consist of expected output per a given period of time, or pitch. This is a good tool for employees to quickly

Table 2.2.1-1 Example of a production hour-by-hour chart.

Station: Welding Takt Time: 30 seconds			**Production Tracking Chart**				Date: 03-23-2012
Pitch	Goal pitch	Actual pitch	Variation pitch	Goal total production	Actual total	Variation total	Reason for deviation
7:30–8:30	100	80	–20	100	80	–20	10 minute start-up meeting
8:30–9:30	120	140	20	220	220		
9:30–10:30	120	100	–20	340	300	–20	Welder breakdown—power supply failure
10:30–11:30	120	20	–100	460	320	–120	Maintenance replaced power supply
11:30–12:30	120	120		580	440	–120	
12:30–1:30	120	140	20	700	560	–100	
1:30–2:30	120	60	–60	820	620	–200	Top clamp assembly part shortage
2:30–3:30	120	120		940	740	–200	

identify whether a process is operating as expected and to document reasons for deviations. Color coding (e.g., green for output met expected, and red for production not met expected) can add a level of efficiency to highlight trouble areas.

The visual workplace is limited only by the imagination. The intent is to make the comparison of actual performance with expected performance easy and accessible by all employees. The purpose is to focus on the process and highlight areas in need of focus (Mann 2010, 53).

There are challenges to the visual workplace. Employees and management must respond to the visual signal. If someone fails to respond to an alarm light, if management does not address a lost production issue, if warehouse personnel do not replenish the depleted stock, if an operator ignores a visual defect and passes it on to the next process, or if employees choose to ignore a safety display and enter the danger zone without protection, then any good visual system will have no purpose.

2.2.1.1. 5S Standards and Discipline

Behind all workplace successes and failures are the 5S's.

—Hiroyuki Hirano

5S is a phrase that refers to workplace organization and standardization. It is how we organize our areas to be free of clutter, efficient, safe, and pleasant to work in.

Table 2.2.1.1-1   The 5Ss.

Japanese	Translation	Conversion	Other*
Seiri	Organization	Sort	Sorting
Seiton	Neatness	Set in order	Simplify
Seiso	Cleaning	Shine	Sweep
Seiketsu	Standardization	Standardize	Standardize
Shitsuke	Discipline	Sustain	Self-discipline

*There are other versions of the words for 5S (some organizations have added Safety and Security).

It is considered a cornerstone for companies pursuing lean. It lays the groundwork and develops the discipline necessary to support the successful implementation of other lean concepts throughout an organization.

"5S" stands for five words in Japanese (Table 2.2.1.1-1) that begin with the letter "S" and describes the activities of workplace organization and standardization.

Explanation of Each "S"

1. Sort

The first step is to sort through the items in the work area and place them into one of three categories: (1) needed now in the work area, (2) not needed now in the work area, or (3) not needed in the work area. It is important to understand that you should keep only those items that you need now. A rule of thumb is that if you are not going to use it in the next 30 days, it should be moved out of the immediate work area. The way to perform Sort is with the 5S Red Tag Technique. Attach a red tag to the item to identify it and place it in the 5S Red Tag Holding

Area. The red tag identifies the item, who moved it, the date it was moved, and the reason it was moved (e.g., not used here, obsolete, capital item not needed, or broken). Other information can be written on the tag as needed. Make sure the red tags are easy to get and use.

The 5S Red Tag Holding Area is a temporary area where items are held until disposition is made (e.g., keep, recycle, donate, or sell). This area can also be used to get items needed by a work area. For instance, if a toolbox is red tagged and put in the 5S Red Tag Holding Area, a department that needs a toolbox can obtain that item by following the standard.

Performing Sort and 5S Red Tagging helps break the "pack-rat" mentality. People hold onto things "just in case," but what they are really doing is taking up resources that are not value-added. Holding onto things that are not needed in the immediate future takes up valuable space. Worse than that, people waste time searching for items and become frustrated because they cannot find what they need. Clearing out the clutter leaves more room to perform the value-added tasks required. Many workplaces think they need more room to do their job, but in fact the unneeded items just need to be removed. The key element here is to stay on top of 5S Red Tagging. This should not be a one-time event. This starts the discipline required for a well-run 5S system.

2. Set in Order

Next, the items that you have decided to keep need to have a specific home. Determine where these items should be located in your work area. Make it obvious where they belong. Use visual techniques such as signs, lines, labels, and color coding to help easily locate the correct items (see Section 2.2.1, "Visual Workplace"). If you use the item every day, it should be kept close to your work area. If you use it once a week, it can be placed a little farther away. If you use it only once a month, it can be kept even farther away or in another area. Set up a system for how many to have on hand, when to replenish, and who is responsible for ordering more.

Having the correct items in the correct location when you need them reduces or eliminates much of the waste in a work area. By ensuring that every appropriate item in the work area has a specific home and that it is in the right location when needed adds to good discipline. A rule of thumb for having world-class "Set in order" is that anyone in your work area can find an item in 30 seconds or less. This means that the items are clearly marked and labeled.

3. Shine

2.2.1.1

5S is much more than just cleaning. Shine is the process of inspecting while cleaning. Look for safety hazards, loose wires, poor connections, and bad hoses, basically anything that could cause a breakdown or potential problem if not attended to. Divide up the work among the team members. Decide what to clean, when to clean, how to clean, what you need to clean, and how long the cleaning and inspection should take. Remember, everybody cleans and inspects. Plan ahead so that the proper cleaning supplies are readily available. Having a portable Shine cart or station makes this easy. Clean and inspect from top to bottom and get everything in a like-new condition. Start with large items first and do the floors last. People start to take ownership and have pride of their area because of Shine. Look for ways to prevent the dirt, dust, and grime from accumulating in the first place. Replace any worn, defective, or unsafe components or equipment.

A clean work area is safer, a more pleasant place in which to work, and more efficient. It also produces better quality and impresses customers. If people resist participating in Shine by saying "I wasn't hired to clean!" remind them that they weren't hired to make a mess either.

The discipline of touching one's equipment, tools, and work area makes a person a better operator—after all, who knows the work area better? With Shine, small problems can be spotted before they become big problems, like a breakdown or safety incident.

4. Standardize

Have the teams in the work area establish the guidelines, policies, or rules for Sort, Set in order, and Shine. Many organizations pursuing 5S say that they failed at sustaining their efforts (the 5th "S"), but it's more likely that they failed at Standardize. When you standardize, you make up the rules, but then you have to follow and enforce these rules. An important element here: Don't create a rule that no one will follow.

Examples for standards might include the following:

- Sort: what information goes on the red tag, how to perform the 5S Red Tag Technique, and rules to disposition items in the 5S Red Tag Holding Area

- Set in order: where and how much inventory or supplies should be kept on hand, visual standards such as color coding

- Shine: visual standards for Shine, how should people clean and inspect, how often should cleaning and inspection be done, and what items should be cleaned and inspected

5. Sustain

The fourth and fifth "Ss" are the two functions that, without proper attention, will result in tasks being performed the "old" way.

To maintain these efforts, the team must use creative methods to share their lessons learned and to encourage the continued process of 5S. Sustaining efforts may include additional training, communication with bulletin boards or newsletters, reward and recognition, benchmarking tours, and so on. Many organizations use 5S audits to ensure that standards are not slipping back or deteriorating.

The key here is to keep the 5S efforts going and to make it part of everyone's daily work life. 5S should not be something additional or something that management tells the employees to skip because there is no time. Once the standards are in place, everyone has to support the program to make it last.

Discipline

5S is a discipline—as in "control," not as in "punishment." Having a strong 5S system will help bring the good discipline needed to build a strong, lean organization. 5S allows us to utilize other aspects of lean that need a very robust discipline, like standardized work or kanban. It sets the stage for a well-run total productive maintenance program.

5S is having a clean, neat, organized and safe workplace. It reduces waste, time spent searching for items, and stress. The foundation of a lean company, 5S sets the stage for how you want your organization to be; it is a foundation of improvement (Galsworth 1997). By employing the 5S principles you are creating a culture of lean.

2.2.2. LOT SIZE REDUCTION

In traditional mass production operations, large lots, or batches, of product are created and moved to the next process, regardless of whether the product/part/documentation is needed. At this point, the product waits in a queue as work-in-process (WIP). This is known as push production.

Push production is creating large batches of product at the maximum rate of the process, normally as a result of a forecasted customer demand. The product is then moved to the next downstream process or stored. Push production does not take into account the actual pace of work (cycle time) in the next process or actual customer demand (takt time). The traditional push production method makes it almost impossible to institute the smooth flow of work from one process to the next process, which is the trademark of lean. All we are really trying to accomplish is to get one process to make only what the next process needs, when it needs it, as the customer demands it (Rother and Shook 2009, 37).

With push production, most manufacturing and service departments find it easier to have long runs of one type of product or service scheduled in order to avoid changeovers. These longer runs of a single type of product cause lead times to expand. It becomes difficult to meet a customer's demand for a product or service that is different from the batch currently being worked. This requires organizations to create finished goods inventories to have the product on hand to meet those customers' needs when they place an order.

As previously implied, batch production causes the consumption of raw materials and parts in batches, which expands the WIP inventories for upstream processes. This can result in quality issues, because once the mass production process makes a defect, it is quickly replicated throughout the batch. Potential quality issues are another reason to reduce the batch size in order to reduce the amount of impacted WIP and inventory when a defect does occur. Additionally, with increased inventories there is a risk of not selling the finished product. This results in additional waste associated with transporting and storing the inventory. In some cases, the inventory can become obsolete and must be scrapped, another waste.

Another issue is that large batch sizes lead to an unevenness in flow of product. At times there can be more work than people or equipment (peak conditions; see Figure 2.2.2-1). At other times, there is not enough work and these same operators and equipment sit idle (valley conditions). This unevenness reduces overall efficiency, where the peaks can cause strain on employees and equipment, resulting in a reduction in safety and morale.

To reduce the strain of peak conditions, traditional mass production thinking would size the equipment, employees, inventory, and other resources for these peak conditions. This results in overall efficiency being reduced during nonpeak conditions. As these fluctuations occur with customer demand, the range and impact of the peaks and valleys increase as they move upstream to earlier processes, causing a greater impact. These fluctuations are known as mura.

To eliminate mura, fluctuation at the final product assembly should be minimized. Zero fluctuation is preferred. At Toyota, the final assembly line never

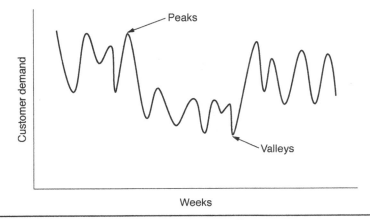

Figure 2.2.2-1 Customer demand showing peaks and valleys.

assembles the same automobile model in a batch. In other words, each automobile is a batch, or one-piece flow. The final assembly production line is leveled by making first one model, then another model, and then yet another (Ohno 1988, 126). This is known as production leveling, or heijunka (evening out the work schedule). Successful heijunka (see Section 2.2.3) is key to eliminating mura, which in turn will lead to elimination of muda and muri.

Quick changeover, setup reduction, and single minute exchange of dies (SMED) may be used to implement lot size reduction. (See Section 2.3.7.2 for more information on quick changeover/setup reduction.)

2.2.3. LOAD LEVELING

One of the benefits of reducing the lot size is to be able to level the work schedule, or load leveling. In heijunka, lot sizes are reduced, or made as small as possible. This differs from traditional mass production, where more is considered better, whether it be customer demand peaks or economies of scale. When a final assembly line produces based on smaller lot sizes, the upstream processes naturally conform to its production schedule. This forces processes to perform many more changeovers, which are generally avoided with traditional thinking. However, production leveling requires many changeovers. Changeovers must be performed quickly in order to provide the flexibility needed for the leveled production (see Section 2.3.7.2, "Quick Changeover/Setup Reduction (SMED)" for more on how this is accomplished).

Smaller lots and consistent pulling from downstream processes will result in fewer adjustments. Work can be performed evenly and the significant peaks and valleys eliminated. When looking at this from the value stream as a whole, the result is less strain on employees, equipment, suppliers, and customers. An additional benefit is a reduction in inventories needed.

Production leveling has been applied successfully across many different industries, including high- and low-volume production systems. There are three components of production leveling (Figure 2.2.3-1):

1. Total volume

2. Model sequence

3. Model volume

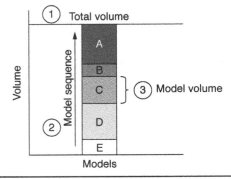

Figure 2.2.3-1   Three components of production leveling.

In production leveling, it is assumed that each of these components is held constant (unchanged based on historical customer demand over a given period of time). This is basically the same assumption used with calculating takt time. To apply production leveling, an organization must make progress by addressing customer demand, beginning with an understanding of total production volume, moving to specific details on the demand of individual product/service types (models), and ending with an evaluation of a product/service type (model) sequence of production.

Total Production Volume

The total customer demand may vary from day to day. However, there are usually predictable patterns throughout a specific time period when demand, on average, is relatively constant. The goal is to identify the patterns and time periods and then level the total production volume over each period (Figure 2.2.3-2).

Model Sequence

As the total volume of customer demand varies from day to day, so does the type of product or service. The sequence in which these product or service types are performed affects the time needed to change over the production or servicing from one type to another. Therefore, the sequence of production and servicing has an impact on the overall capacity of an organization, or the number of products and services the organization can perform within a given time period. (See Section 4.3.3.5 for more information regarding sequencing of models [product and service types].)

Model Volume

Even with a constant total production volume demand, immediate response to fluctuations in demand for individual product types can result in waste (Figure 2.2.3-3).

Similar to total production volume, product type volumes often vary from day to day. However, product types also have predictable patterns and time periods

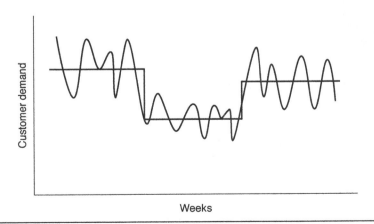

Figure 2.2.3-2   Production leveled for different time periods.

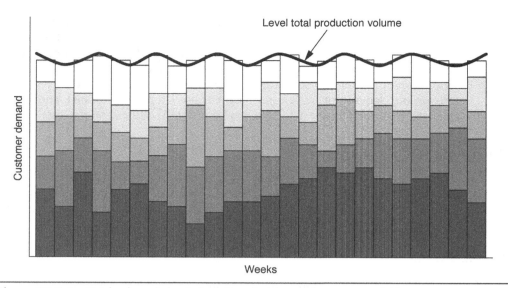

Figure 2.2.3-3 Total volume is leveled, and product type volumes are variable.

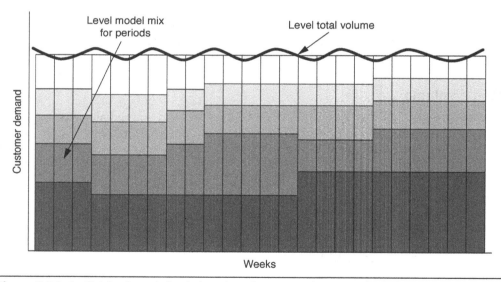

Figure 2.2.3-4 Total volume is leveled, and product type volumes are leveled over a time period.

where demand is, on average, constant. The goal is to identify the patterns and time periods and level the product type volumes over each period (Figure 2.2.3-4).

Mixed Model Production

Even with total production volume and product type volume leveled, production still results in batching. The next step is to create a mixed model production system. This requires that the demand per product type per unit of time (e.g., 5 units per hour for Product A, 15 units per hour for Product B, and 10 units per hour for Product C) and the total demand per unit of time be calculated (30 total units per hour for Products A, B, and C). There are a few different scenarios for sequence model production.

1. Equal Volumes for Each Product Type

If the demand over a given time period (month, quarter, etc.) is 20 per hour for Product A, 20 per hour for Product B, and 20 per hour for Product C, then the sequence of product type production simply alternates among the three product types.

$$\text{Takt time} = \frac{\text{Available time}}{\text{Required volume}} = \frac{60 \text{ min}}{(10 + 20 + 30)} = 1 \text{ part per minute}$$

This means that the sequence of product types would be ABCABCABCABC rather than AAABBBCCCAAA, producing each product at a rate of one per minute.

2. Different Volumes for Each Product Type

If the demand over a given time period (month, quarter, etc.) is 10 per hour for Product A, 20 per hour for Product B, and 30 per hour for Product C, then the sequence of product type production is a little more complex than simply alternating production among the three product types. Utilizing the individual product type demands and the total demand, one can calculate the repeatability number, or how often the sequence will repeat itself.

$$\text{Product A: } \frac{\text{Customer demand for product type during time period}}{\text{Total demand during time period}} = \frac{10}{60} = \frac{1}{6}$$

$$\text{Product B: } \frac{\text{Customer demand for product type during time period}}{\text{Total demand during time period}} = \frac{20}{60} = \frac{1}{3} = \frac{2}{6}$$

$$\text{Product C: } \frac{\text{Customer demand for product type during time period}}{\text{Total demand during time period}} = \frac{30}{60} = \frac{1}{2} = \frac{3}{6}$$

Determine the fraction at the least common denominator for each product type. The least common denominator will be the repeatability number. The repeatability number is the total number of "open slots" in the sequence, and the numerator is the number of "slots" in the sequence that will be filled by each product type. Beginning with the lowest-demand product, divide the denominator by the numerator. This determines the slot location of occurrence for that product type in the sequence.

Product A is 6/1, or every sixth slot. Product B is 6/2, or every third slot. In this case, slot 6 is taken, so the product must be shifted down to slot 5; the third slot from slot 5, then, is slot 2. So Product B occupies slots 2 and 5 in the sequence. Finally, Product C fills the remaining slots.

Product type	C	B	C	C	B	A
Sequence slot	1	2	3	4	5	6

2.2.3

Mixed model production allows for a reduction in inventory levels as well. For instance, during large batch production, Product A inventory is consumed while a large batch of Product B is produced (Figure 2.2.3-5). However, the application of mixed model production by reducing lot sizes results in reduced levels of inventory needed for customer consumption during production of another product type.

Mixed model production forms the basis of the heijunka box. A *heijunka box* is a production scheduling tool that visually lets production know when, what, and how many of a product to build. The scheduler loads the box with withdrawal kanbans based on that day's order (Figure 2.2.3-6). The rows and columns of the heijunka box correspond to the products/services the plant or department provides (rows) and the pitch (columns). The *pitch* is the interval in which the product/service is required to be finished and the next product/service is required to begin.

Heijunka easily translates to nonproduction environments, such as accounting, engineering, maintenance, and quality, and products are service oriented, such as processing paperwork, servicing equipment (e.g., automotive oil-change shops), or assisting customers (e.g., call center). The fundamental concepts and steps to production leveling and mixed model production remain the same.

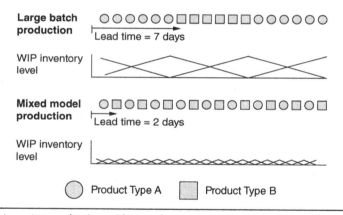

Figure 2.2.3-5 Inventory reduction with mixed model production.

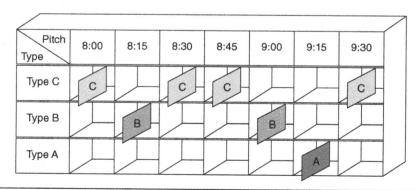

Figure 2.2.3-6 Example of a heijunka box.

2.2.4. 3P PRODUCTION PROCESS PREPARATION

Production Process Preparation (3P) is a process designed to minimize waste by evaluating the true requirements and function of a production or process design. It is a disciplined method for designing a lean process or redesigning an existing process when the design or demand changes. 3P consists of examining the process, developing a number of alternatives for each process step, and evaluating these against criteria set by a cross-functional team. The team mocks up the process to test various assumptions and alternatives to prove that they work before equipment is designed and ordered.

3P introduces a process that drives an organization's development to achieve common shared goals in the pursuit of creating and improving products, services, and products through lean transformation. It requires input, facts, and hands-on examples from all areas of the organization. 3P should be performed by a cross-functional team composed of representatives from sales, marketing, engineering, purchasing, manufacturing, quality, and safety. The team must realize up front that 3P is difficult, because it challenges everyone to justify every idea and concept. The mind-set should include the fact that there are no existing barriers, such as the way things have always been done, organization monuments (or those things that cannot be moved), or subject matter experts on a given technology.

3P helps eliminate waste, reduce costs, improve quality, drive continuous improvement, and improve an organization's capabilities. It is perfect for performing an early assessment on new products and processes in the design/concept phase and for supporting the budgeting process.

3P is broken down into two fundamental types: design and right-sized equipment. This section focuses on the design 3P, and Section 2.3.7.4 focuses on right-sized equipment.

Steps to a Design 3P

1. Break down the product/process into parts/steps
2. Determine the function(s) of each part/step
3. Determine key words for each function (hold, lift, remove, connect, twist, etc.)
4. Find examples in nature that perform those same key actions or work functions
5. Sketch and post examples
6. Sketch the background concept
7. Combine ideas and create new designs
8. Combine designs and sketch (7 ideas quickly—brainstorming)
9. Complete process at a glance by sketching and listing tools, fixtures, and gauges needed
10. Construct prototypes of each design (trystorming)
11. Test each design against the true requirements
12. Select the best designs based on the criteria
13. Refine the best designs and reassess against the criteria

14. Select the top design

15. Design the product/process

2.2.5. TOTAL PRODUCTIVE MAINTENANCE (INCLUDING PREDICTIVE)

Total productive maintenance (TPM) is a lean maintenance strategy for maximizing equipment reliability. In the 1950s, equipment maintenance was not practiced to be preventive and predominantly involved just the act of repairing a piece of equipment after it broke down (breakdown maintenance). Factory managers eventually realized the importance of preventing equipment breakdowns in order to boost productivity. Thus, systems for subjecting equipment to scheduled maintenance activities in order to prevent unforeseen breakdowns (preventive maintenance) became popular. Under this scheme, equipment maintenance was the sole responsibility of technical personnel.

In the 1970s, the concept of "productive maintenance" emerged, rolling into one system the following: preventive maintenance, equipment reliability engineering, equipment maintainability engineering, and equipment engineering economics. Under this system, the technical or engineering group still had the main responsibility for equipment maintenance.

The concept of "true" TPM, wherein everyone from the operator to top management owns equipment maintenance, came about a little later. TPM embraces various disciplines to create a manufacturing environment where everyone feels responsible for keeping the equipment running and productive. Under TPM, operators no longer limit themselves to simply using the machine and calling the technician when a breakdown occurs. Operators can inspect, clean, lubricate, adjust, and even perform simple calibrations on their respective equipment. This frees the technical workforce for higher-level preventive maintenance activities that require more of their technical expertise.

Management should be interested in data concerning equipment uptime, utilization, and efficiency. In short, everyone understands that zero breakdowns, maximum productivity, and zero defects are goals shared by everyone under TPM.

TPM focuses on the entire equipment life cycle by coordinating all departments and involving all employees in group activities, from the design, through production, to the end of its useful life. TPM fosters an environment where improvement efforts in safety, quality, cost, delivery, and creativity are encouraged through employee participation.

TPM requires the mastery of four basic maintenance techniques:

1. *Preventive maintenance.* Preventing breakdowns from happening through regular checks and inspections

2. *Corrective maintenance.* Improving or modifying equipment to prevent breakdowns or make maintenance easier

3. *Maintenance prevention.* Designing or installing equipment that needs little or no maintenance

4. *Breakdown maintenance.* Repairing after breakdowns occur, planned repairs and unplanned repairs

In order to sustain a world-class TPM system, there must be a solid infrastructure. Any world-class TPM system must have certain elements, including, but not limited to, the following:

- Maintenance infrastructure
- Maintenance goals and objectives
- Data collection system (overall equipment effectiveness)
- Training and education
- Work flow and controls
- Preventive maintenance
- Operational involvement (autonomous maintenance)
- Computerized maintenance management software system utilization
- Spare parts management
- Predictive maintenance
- Reliability centered maintenance
- Continuous improvement

Overall Equipment Effectiveness

The key metric for TPM is overall equipment effectiveness (OEE). OEE is maximized by reducing equipment breakdowns, improving throughput and quality, reducing inventory, and reducing overall lead times, while lowering operating costs.

To understand the current situation and measure the effectiveness of any improvement activity, you need a baseline measurement of OEE.

$$OEE = Availability \times Performance\ efficiency \times Quality\ rate$$

Availability is sometimes referred to as uptime or machine utilization. Availability is used to track the unscheduled downtime losses with the machine. The availability rate is equal to the actual run time (equipment scheduled and operating) divided by the net operating time (scheduled run time). It is critical to note that scheduled run time is not based on calendar time (i.e., it does not include planned downtime for activities such as preventive maintenance or when the equipment is not needed for production).

$$Availability = \frac{Operating\ time}{Net\ available\ time}$$

Performance efficiency reflects whether equipment is running at full capacity (or speed) for individual products. Performance is used to track the speed losses with the machine. The performance rate is the actual output divided by the targeted output. This can also be calculated based on the ideal time it takes to produce the actual number of parts made divided by the actual operating time. The two major categories affecting performance rate are (1) idling and minor stoppages and (2) reduced speed.

$$\text{Performance efficiency} = \frac{\text{Actual output}}{\text{Target output}} = \frac{(\text{Ideal cycle time} \times \text{Total parts run})}{\text{Operating time}}$$

Quality rate is the ratio of first-run good parts. The quality rate tracks the quality losses with the machine and is equal to good output (no defects) divided by actual output. The two major categories affecting quality rate are (1) scrap and rework and (2) start-up losses.

$$\text{Quality rate} = \frac{(\text{Total parts run} - \text{Total defects})}{\text{Total parts run}}$$

Visually, this can be depicted in a waterfall chart (Figure 2.2.5-1).

OEE is broken down into different losses. The loss of availability is a downtime loss. The loss of performance is a speed loss. The loss of quality is a quality loss. A TPM program includes activities to get rid of the Six Big Losses (Figure 2.2.5-2 and Table 2.2.5-1) that drain productivity.

While downtime is a common measure, other types of data may be useful to collect:

- Mean time to repair (MTTR)—the average time taken for repairs

- Mean time between failures (MTBF)—the average time between breakdowns

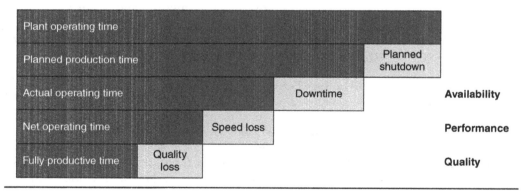

Figure 2.2.5-1 OEE waterfall chart.

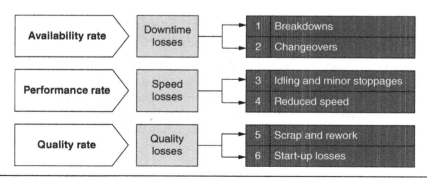

Figure 2.2.5-2 OEE loss categories.

Table 2.2.5-1   The Six Big Losses of OEE.

Loss	Description
Breakdowns	A breakdown is a mechanical failure that either stops production or causes production to be stopped while repairs are made.
Changeovers	A changeover is a tooling or setup change that causes production to be stopped. This category can include periodic tests that must be performed for quality or process capability. For calculating OEE, changeover spans the time between the end of the initial production run and the start of the subsequent production run.
Idling and minor stoppages	Idling is analogous to a car stopped at a stoplight. The line is ready to run, but is producing no product due to outside forces such as lack of raw material. Minor stoppages are machine faults that can be corrected in less than a minute.
Reduced speed	Speed reduction losses occur when the line does not run at the standard rate due to it being intentionally slowed for one reason or another; slowing may also be due to problems with machine functionality that do not result in complete breakdown.
Scrap and rework	Scrap and rework losses result from manufacturing product that does not conform to customer standards.
Start-up losses	Start-up losses occur while making a change, for example, a color change in a plastic operation. The machine is running but is not yet manufacturing salable product.

The early signs of a breakdown, here called hidden failures and minor failures, are anomalies that do not cause any function loss but whose detection helps prevent breakdowns and improves our understanding of our equipment. Minor anomalies often fail to attract our attention. For example, when driving, we might ignore a strange noise in the car's motor, as long as the car is running well. We might wait for the breakdown before responding. TPM means listening and watching for anomalies and taking action before the breakdown. These losses can be expressed in what is commonly known as the machine loss pyramid (Figure 2.2.5-3).

Production Example

Let's look at an example in a manufacturing environment, where we will examine a 10-hour shift in an injection molding process, calculate the shift's OEE, and pinpoint areas for problem solving.

Step 1: The first calculation is the availability rate. This is determined by the following formula:

Availability rate = Actual run time ÷ Net operating time (scheduled run time)

In this case the net operating time is eight hours, or 480 minutes (the press is not scheduled for two hours during the shift for lunch and breaks). The actual time is only 420 minutes because the shift reported a 30-minute breakdown and three 10-minute changeovers. Therefore, the availability rate is:

Availability rate = 420 minutes ÷ 480 minutes = $\boxed{87.5\%}$

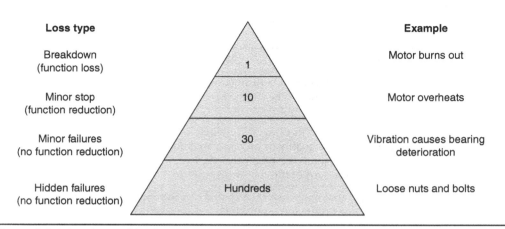

Loss type		Example
Breakdown (function loss)	1	Motor burns out
Minor stop (function reduction)	10	Motor overheats
Minor failures (no function reduction)	30	Vibration causes bearing deterioration
Hidden failures (no function reduction)	Hundreds	Loose nuts and bolts

Figure 2.2.5-3 The machine loss pyramid.

Step 2: The second calculation is the performance rate of the injection molding process. This is determined by the following formula:

$$\text{Performance rate} = \text{Actual output} \div \text{Target output}$$

First we calculate our target output. Our machine is rated at 140 parts per minute. Therefore,

$$\text{Target output} = 140 \text{ parts per minute} \times 420 \text{ minutes} = 58{,}800 \text{ parts}$$

However, the two items that affect performance rate are idling/minor stopping and reduced speeds. Due to the condition of the injection molding process, the shift has been able to produce only 100 parts per minute from this cutting operation and had minor stops that collectively accounted for 30 minutes of lost production. Therefore,

$$\text{Actual output} = 100 \text{ parts per minute} \times (420 - 30 \text{ minutes}) = 39{,}000 \text{ parts}$$
$$\text{Performance rate} = 39{,}000 \text{ parts} \div 58{,}800 \text{ parts} = \boxed{66.3\%}$$

Step 3: The final calculation is the quality rate. This is determined by the following formula:

$$\text{Quality rate} = \text{Good output} \div \text{Actual output}$$

Good output is the amount of product that passes through the process without requiring scrap or rework. The injection molding process reports losses due to both scrap/rework and start-up losses. On our product, a dimension went out of spec for a period of one hour without correction, resulting in 6000 pieces being scrapped (100 pieces per minute × 60 minutes). In addition, it took 15 minutes for the machine to warm up and begin producing acceptable product after the three changeovers, resulting in 4500 pieces during the day that were either scrapped or reworked (15 minutes/setup × 100 pieces/minute × 3 setups). Therefore:

$$\text{Quality rate} = (39{,}000 - 6{,}000 - 4{,}500 \text{ parts}) \div 39{,}000 \text{ parts} = \boxed{73.1\%}$$

Calculate OEE and analyze:

OEE = 87.5% (availability) × 66.3% (performance) × 73.1% (quality) × 100 = 42.4%

Analyzing the breakdown of the OEE figure and comparing it with industry and benchmark data indicate performance can readily be improved. Likely areas in which to focus improvement efforts include improving the performance rate by applying a TPM program to the press or improving the quality rate by applying mistake-proofing.

Nonproduction Example

OEE is also applicable in service environments. For example, consider a typical shift for a clerk at the Department of Motor Vehicles.

The availability rate for an eight-hour period may be affected by downtime due to breakdowns and changeovers similar to a manufacturing environment. For a clerk operation, the breakdown may be due to equipment malfunctions with the computer system. A changeover could occur when clerks switch out due to lunch or breaks or when a clerk switches from processing a customer requesting a license renewal to a customer getting a new license for a new vehicle.

The performance rate can also be monitored. Idling and minor stops can occur when customers come to the window and clerks cannot immediately respond to their requests because the clerks have misplaced a form or the license plate tags supply is empty. Similarly, reduced speed losses occur due to lack of training or knowledge capability issues. For example, it might take a new clerk 10 minutes per transaction, whereas the average experienced clerk could process the same requests in 6 minutes.

The quality rate can be monitored by checking how many requests are completed without follow-ups by the customer.

The following are some facts to better understand OEE:

- Baseline OEE measures are typically less than 50%

- World-class TPM companies can expect OEE measures of 85%

- TPM programs cannot be implemented overnight; it takes at least two years for an organization to implement an effective TPM program

- Typically, breakdown maintenance is 10 times more expensive than TPM

Implementing TPM

The first step in implementing a TPM program is to pilot TPM on one critical machine, in a cell, or on a small group of machines. When OEE results show improvement it is much easier to obtain buy-in to the project and spread the program to other pieces of equipment.

Eighty percent of equipment downtime is caused by improper lubrication (over- or underlubrication or wrong lubrication) or contamination (chips, dust, dirt, etc.). Therefore, any TPM activity should focus on ensuring correct lubrication as well as reducing or eliminating contamination. Production team members should be involved in checking, reporting, and, where possible, correcting hidden failures and minor stoppages. Check sheets should be developed for each piece of equipment, and a system should be in place to track and make visible the conditions (see Section 2.2.1, "Visual Workplace"). All employees and all functions should be involved in TPM activities, as all have different roles to play.

Operators

- Prevent deterioration through regular inspections
- Correct deterioration through regular cleaning of equipment
- Measure deterioration through data collection
- Participate in team activities as equipment experts
- Assist in maintenance activities

Maintenance Personnel

- Planned maintenance activities to reduce disruption to production
- Preventive maintenance through scheduled checks and adjustments
- Training in TPM and OEE principles for operators and supervisors
- Design of equipment—helping eliminate design weaknesses
- Root cause analysis—helping understand root causes of downtime
- Participate in team activities as maintenance resource

Engineers

- Early equipment management—designing for maintainability and life cycle
- Root cause analysis—helping understand root causes of downtime
- Participate in team activities as engineering resource
- Prevent contamination at equipment design stage

Managers and Supervisors

- Root cause analysis—helping understand root causes of downtime
- Participate in team activities—offering leadership and direction
- Training—provide facilitation and development
- Accountability—to ensure data collection and worksheets completed

A good way of kicking off any TPM program is to hold a TPM kaizen event. This will encourage teamwork and is an opportunity to educate and train team members on the principles of TPM.

The following are short-term goals of a TPM kaizen:

- Create daily operator preventive maintenance inspection
- Develop/Enhance a preventive maintenance activity list
- Clean-to-inspect and repair equipment issues
- Develop equipment critical spare parts list

- Develop understanding of OEE
- Use 5S, setup reduction, and root cause analysis to solve problems

The following are long-term objectives of a TPM kaizen:

- Improve OEE (capacity) to >85%
- Create enthusiasm/Change culture
- Improve quality by reducing variability
- Incorporate preventive/predictive maintenance
- Dramatically improve manufacturing effectiveness
- Increase capacity and reduce lead times

It is important to communicate the positive effects of a well-deployed TPM program:

- Improves safety
- Improves quality
- Increases equipment productivity
- Reduces energy costs
- Reduces maintenance costs

A successful TPM program will often include other lean systems and tools. Table 2.2.5-2 identifies some common lean systems and tools and how they can be included with a TPM program.

Table 2.2.5–2   Other lean tools implemented during the TPM process.

Lean system or practice	Description of TPM use
5S	Cleaning the equipment. Sorting the necessary tools for machine operation and maintenance. 5S provides a good foundation for TPM.
Visual workplace	Organize tools with shadow boards. Organize gauges with color coding and highlight optimal operating ranges. Highlight lubrication points. Communication board with all key information for the TPM program on the equipment.
Pareto chart	Organize the losses into the Six Big Losses categories to create focus on the areas causing greatest inefficiencies. Use additional details on the Pareto chart. Be specific on the station, part, instrument, etc., causing the loss. For example, instead of a general "machine failure" category, use "Station 3" or "Station 3 Back Cylinder failure."
Root cause and corrective action	Using the information from the Pareto chart, drive to root cause of the issue causing the loss and implement corrective action to eliminate the cause.
Standard work	Create TPM check sheets, data collection forms, 5S checklists, and maintenance logs. Create standard work that shows the operator how to perform various TPM activities.

2.2.5

2.2.6. STANDARD WORK

Standard work is "a precise description of each work activity, specifying cycle time, takt time, the work sequence of specific tasks and the minimum inventory of parts on hand needed to conduct the activity. All jobs are organized around human motion to create an efficient sequence without waste. Work organized in such a way is called standard(ized) work. The three elements that make up standard work are takt time, working sequence, and standard in-process stock" (Dennis 2007).

The purpose of standard work is to provide a baseline for improvement. All processes possess waste. Standard work helps define the process, which is the steps and action to reach a defined goal (Dennis 2007). This means that standard work will be dynamic and change as processes are modified and waste is removed.

Standard work can be generated proactively and reactively. When generated proactively, it establishes the bases for performing tasks and activities to obtain a desired result. These results directly link to product and process quality, cost, schedule, execution, cycle time, and customer satisfaction. Process and product quality are normalized to ensure that the materials, setup, consumables, and so on, used to perform the work produce the desired output within the desired goals (i.e., the standard work). Improvements in quality and cycle time and reductions in waste (e.g., elimination of excess movement, scrap, and rework) can be realized.

Standard work can be applied to product- or service-related work. Standard work is established through analysis, observation, and employee involvement. Observation is recommended to ensure that all tasks/activities, constraints, normal wait states (e.g., cure time), and so on, are considered, because there is a high probability that some things will be overlooked if only analysis is performed. Employees are involved because the people closest to the work understand it best. With takt time analysis (see Sections 2.3.1.4 and 4.3.2.1), experience, and observation, the standard work definition can be made robust.

It is easy to see, especially in the context of this book, how standard work applies to product (i.e., hardware, software, consumer goods). The relationship between standard work and service may be harder to identify but it is very similar to the relationship between standard work and product. For example, standard work for a customer service representative includes the following:

- Computer and applicable programs

- Estimates and average takt time

- Key attributes to collect (e.g., customer name, problem category, phone, address, and dissatisfaction level)

- Key discussion points (e.g., explain how long to resolve problem and why, provide additional resources such as website and reference number to get status)

It should be noted that employees may be resistant to the establishment of standard work. Common objections and responses are noted in Table 2.2.6-1. This information will help management anticipate the resistance and overcome the barriers. Use of quality and management tools, such as the Benefits and Barriers Exercise (Tague 2005) or the Buy-In and Barriers Assessment Tool (Maio 2010), can help identify those most likely to be resistant and can help management overcome the

Table 2.2.6-1 Reasons for resistance to standard work.

Objection	Responses
1. If I do it faster, I'll just get more work.	You'll be doing it better, so there is less rework. You're more of an asset. You're going to be here eight hours, so you might as well make it productive and easier.
2. If I do it faster, they'll get rid of people.	We're not looking to get rid of people; we're looking to alleviate some of the workload and stress levels. This will make us more valuable to the company.
3. I've been doing it this way for 15 years.	Great! You'll be able to see the benefits that are created. Things have changed from the way we did it 15 years ago. You can teach an old dog new tricks.
4. Are you trying to tell me that I don't know how to do my job?	We are trying to find a way to do it faster, better, and easier.
5. If I show everyone else how to do it, I'll lose my importance (or job security).	Now you'll have someone to back you up when you are on vacation, so you don't come back to a mountain of work.
6. Why do I have to do it this way?	If you can think of a better way, show us.
7. This will never work in our department.	You'll never know unless you try. If you can think of a better way, show us.
8. Every day is different, "it depends . . ."	We know it depends; we are trying to streamline 65% of your day so you can react to the unexpected 35% much easier.
9. This stuff doesn't work. This is another flavor of the month. We've already done this before.	We have saved money from these types of events and it will pay off in our profit sharing.

Source: Alukal and Manos 2006.

resistance. Both tools assess the potential barriers through analysis and/or team involvement and use a process like the following:

1. Communicate the change
2. Identify the benefits
3. Identify the barriers
4. Identify how to capitalize on the benefits
5. Identify the methods to mitigate the barriers
6. Get buy-in/agreement to steps 4 and 5
7. Implement the change
8. Communicate the results
9. Celebrate success

As noted in item 8 in Table 2.2.6-1, recognize that variances do occur and be prepared to address them. "All manner of problems and abnormalities occur . . . every day . . . Whenever a giving problem arises, management must solve it and make sure it will not recur" (Imai 1997, 33). Masaaki Imai recognized that problems do occur and solutions become new standard work or updates to existing standard work. Knowing that variances may occur at your company and communicating them will help obtain buy-in.

Benefits of standard work include the following:

- Process stability—stability means repeatability
- Clear stop and start points for each process
- Organizational learning
- Audit and problem solving
- Employee involvement and poka-yoke
- Kaizen
- Training (Dennis 2007, 51–52)

Three charts are utilized to create standard work: production capacity chart, standardized work combination table, and standardized work analysis chart (Dennis 2007).

Production Capacity Chart

The production capacity chart (Figure 2.2.6-1) is used to determine the capacity of machines/humans in a process. Its purpose is to identify bottlenecks within the process. It is based on the capacity calculation:

$$\text{Capacity} = \frac{\text{Operational time per shift}}{\left(\text{Process time} + \dfrac{\text{Setup time}}{\text{Interval}}\right)}$$

Standardized Work Combination Table

The standardized work combination table (Figure 2.2.6-2) shows the work elements and their sequence. Each element is broken down into individual times, including operator and machine. The table may include the interactions between the operator and the machine or other operators and machines.

This table is commonly used to analyze the value-added times versus the non-value-added times during each process step. This provides another visual representation for assessing the process and identifying areas for improvement. It often highlights idle areas of an operator that can be filled with another value-added work element.

Standardized Work Analysis Chart

The standardized work analysis chart (Figure 2.2.6-3) can be used as rationalization of a process layout. It provides a visual aid to an employee in training. The chart should include the work/cell layout, process steps, and times. It is also a good chart to highlight quality and safety items and define standardized

Part name	Titanium screw		Model	LN42		Process Capacity Sheet			Section			Department 100		Approved	Checked	Checked	Prepared
Part number	03-11-28-365		Qty	1					Working hr/shift			480 minutes					

			Basic time (sec)				Setup			Per piece			
Process no.	Name of process	Machine no.	Manual work	Auto transfer	Completion time	Exchange quantity of tool	Exchange time for tool	Exchange for one-piece	Total	Process capacity (pcs/shift)	Remarks		
1	Head forming	1	5.0	40.0	45.0	300.0	150.0	0.5	45.5	633			
2	Threads	2	6.0	15.0	21.0	500.0	120.0	0.2	21.2	1358			
3	Deburring	Op 1	30.0		30.0				30.0	960			
4													
5													
6													

Figure 2.2.6-1 Example of production (process) capacity chart.

2.2.6

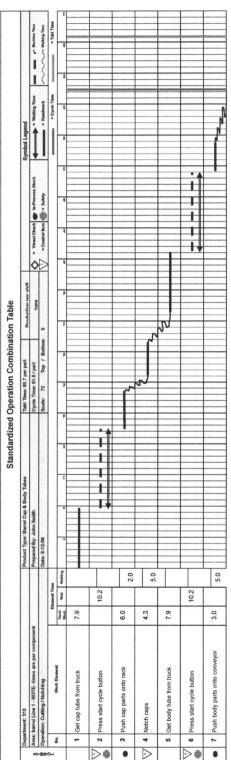

Figure 2.2.6–2 Example of standardized work (operation) combination table.

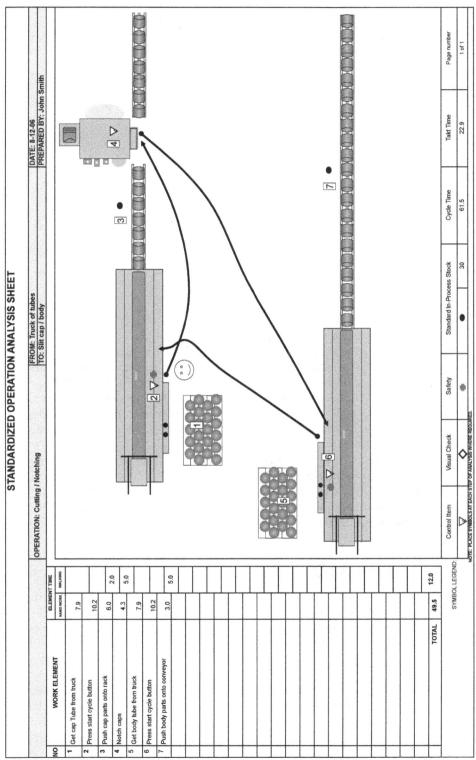

Figure 2.2.6-3 Example of a standardized work analysis chart.

2.2.6

Job element sheet				
Department:	RUN	Operation:	Prepared by:	Page 1 of 1
No.	Operation sequence	Key points	Inspection/ measurement/test	Illustrations

Figure 2.2.6-4 Example of a job element sheet.

work-in-process (WIP). It looks much like the spaghetti diagram, with additional information for the employee.

Another form of standard work is the single point lesson (Figure 2.2.6-4), also known as the job element sheet. A *job element* is defined as the "minimum action or group of actions required to advance a process" (Dennis 2007, 57). A *single point lesson* is a one-page form that defines the actions of an element (process step), gives the rationale of performing the process step, and provides pictures and photos that visualize key points of the process step, and a revision for updating (Dennis 2007).

When defining and implementing standard work, "keep things simple, clear, and engaging! Involve the right people/functions within the organization" (Maio 2010, 24). By engaging the employees, communicating the benefits of standard work, understanding and addressing employee concerns, and involving the right people, success is easier to obtain.

2.2.7. BUILT-IN FEEDBACK

All processes have suppliers and customers; these may be internal or external. The goal of the process is to produce quality products the first time, within budget and schedule. However, for various reasons, variations occur in process execution and product quality. Thus, feedback loops—especially those built into the process that produces the product—provide valuable information to assess product quality.

There are two primary types of feedback loops associated with two types of operations (open-loop and closed-loop). The two primary types of feedback loops are (1) those within the process producing the product (internal) and (2) those from outside the process (external). According to Dennis (2007, 100), Toyota referred to

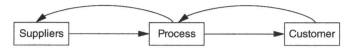

Figure 2.2.7-1 A typical feedback loop.

the internal process feedback loop as "in the zone," where each supervisor (or process owner) is "encouraged to think like a small business owner with suppliers and customers." External feedback loops provide information from downstream operations or customers. A typical feedback loop is shown in Figure 2.2.7-1.

Internal feedback loops provide information on critical to quality (CTQ) attributes to those producing the product. This type of feedback loop provides all information (good and bad) on the CTQ attributes, including defects (bad) and acceptance (good) rates, classifications, and process performance parameters. This information can be used proactively and reactively. Proactive use includes the monitoring of process or machine performance settings; parameters and statistical methods (charting, analysis, etc.) to monitor performance; and CTQ attributes to prevent defects, downtime, or excessive wear. Identifying and correcting a defect (nonconformance or noncompliance) is reactive use of a feedback loop. Note that a defect, when identified in the process that produced it, requires a reactive response and is a good example of quality at the source (see Section 2.1.5.1).

External feedback loops are reactive because the customer (internal or external) identifies the problem. These types of defects are commonly referred to as "escapes," as they escaped detection in the area where produced. Although reactive, external feedback loops are extremely important to the company or process owner to facilitate fixing the root cause to prevent recurrence.

As noted earlier, there are also open- and closed-loop operations; a good explanation of the differences between the two types of operations follows. This information is useful when analyzing the type of feedback loop, establishing the CTQ, and establishing standard work (see Section 2.2.6.) for feedback proactive and reactive actions.

> Consider the experience of folding and flying paper airplanes, hoping that they would fly straight and true to their targets. Once launched, those planes went where they went. Consider the enthusiasts flying model planes controlled by radio or wires. When the wind blows them off course, the operator adjusts the rudder and ailerons, and the craft is soon back on course.
>
> This difference in operation is known as open loop versus closed loop. The difference is the use of feedback to continually monitor the discrepancy between objectives and reality and making changes to reduce the gap. In closed-loop processes and operations, the output affects inputs to keep the output close to target. This feedback loop must have sensitivity to the objective and should be tied directly to key controlling inputs. It must be monitored continuously so that the need for adjustments—sometimes major, sometimes minor—is recognized. (Okes and Westcott 2006, 133)

Feedback loops are foundational requirements of lean. They provide information to monitor, assess, fix, and improve process performance; eliminate waste; and maintain or improve product quality.

2.2.8. STRATEGIC BUSINESS ASSESSMENT

A company must measure and report meaningful performance on a regular basis in order to assess the operational results toward a strategic set of objectives.

Assessing business performance is of critical importance to an organization's strategic and fiscal well-being. The balanced scorecard concept has gained a tremendous following, along with the more recent concept of "alignment," because the strategic leaders must know what is going on within the organization and in the surrounding business environment (Kaplan and Norton 1996).

When designed and implemented effectively, strategic business assessment through performance measurement provides the following benefits:

- It supports the organization's strategic plan by providing leaders with tangible indicators and goals that are relevant to their daily activities and those of the management team

- It provides executive management with sufficient and timely information about the effectiveness and efficiency of operations *before* significant financial impacts are experienced

- It creates a work environment that supports and rewards coordination and cooperation among and between departments and key functional areas in order to attain desired results

- It clarifies management and staff roles and responsibilities as they relate to driving expected performance and outcomes

- It drives change by focusing resources and shaping behaviors toward specific and tangible expectations and results

- It establishes a mechanism for assigning and enforcing accountability and for recognizing and rewarding outstanding performance

Whether the vehicle used for strategic business assessment is called the balanced scorecard, key performance indicators, or a dashboard report card, they all serve to satisfy an organization's need and desire for strategic assessment, enhanced reporting, increased control, and accountability.

The *balanced scorecard* is basically a report card on the core business processes and functions that focuses on three key components, or perspectives, of performance:

1. Historical-state performance information (baseline/trends)

2. Current-state performance levels

3. Future-state performance goals/targets

Setting measures is a process of first identifying what is important and to whom. Much has been written about the Voice of the Customer. New articles are now exploring the concepts of Voice of the Process, Voice of the Employee, and Voice of the Industry. These "voices" are nothing more than distillations of requirements demanded of the company from different stakeholders.

These inputs are the basis for establishing the balanced scorecard. The four or, at most, five major target measures are simply summary metrics of numerous sets of data gathered from within the divisions of the organization and surrounding suppliers, partners, and customers. They constitute a report card for the organization. The original four categories identified by Kaplan and Norton (1996, 44) are:

- Customers

- Financial

- Internal

- Innovation and learning

The internal measures are the ones most identified for "alignment" with the organizational goals established during strategic planning activities. These generally equate to the following areas:

- Cost effectiveness

- Staff productivity

- Process efficiency

- Cycle time

These measures are important only inasmuch as they specifically relate to meeting the major requirements of your customers.

Before proceeding it is important to note what a report card is and what it is not. A *report card* is a management tool intended to provide all levels of management and staff with an enhanced ability to assess and monitor performance, establish and maintain accountability and responsibility, reward superior results, identify operational deficiencies, and encourage appropriate behavior and actions toward common goals. It is not a replacement for other meaningful and necessary reporting mechanisms such as monthly financial statements or departmental-level operating reports. It is also not a panacea for a company's fiscal problems. A report card, in and of itself, will not be effective unless it is designed, implemented, and supported in an effective and consistent manner.

Using Organizational Data for Strategic Business Assessment

Figure 2.2.8-1 is a useful model for aligning strategic goals with the operational measures that are rolled up through organizational functions to the four critical measures recommended by Kaplan and Norton (1996). The figure illustrates the top-down flow of priorities, the operational level of working measures related to process performance, and the resultant summary of data back up through the management chain for effective strategic assessment.

The senior executive leads the company vision and goal setting. Involving others in setting assessment measures will strongly increase commitment and

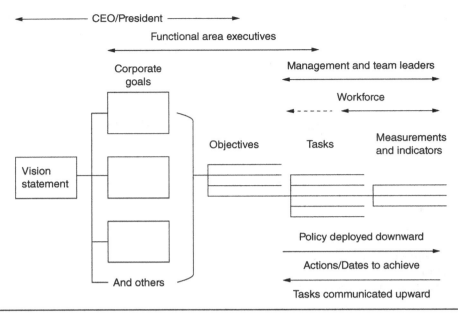

Figure 2.2.8–1 Aligning organizational goals and operational measures.
Source: Adapted from Duffy and Moran (2008, 18).

loyalty to company goals. Measure what truly indicates the effectiveness of the required outcomes as identified by the customers of the process, whether internal or external.

These measures come in many different forms, some of which may be:

- Hourly
- Daily
- Weekly
- Monthly
- Quarterly
- Yearly

For these measures to be useful, they must be quantitative and believable by those held accountable for their generation and application. Use evidence-based data to track the performance you wish to target. Once senior management sets the company strategic plan, identify targets for each major outcome required by customers, stockholders, employees, regulators, and the industry. This set of targets drives the measures with which business is assessed. The current term for these measures is the "balanced scorecard." These indicators are crucial for the operational and strategic competitiveness of your company.

Table 2.2.8-1 is a compilation of indicators generated through business activity that provide supporting data for assessing the soundness of your business strategy. It suggests how to use organizational measures for strategic business assessment.

Table 2.2.8-1 Measures useful for strategic and tactical business assessment.

Hourly	Daily	Weekly	Monthly	Quarterly	Semiyearly/ Yearly
Observation listening	*Wall Street Journal*	Key performance output variables	Internal indicators	Internal indicators	Industry
Tone of ongoing operations	Market	Key performance input variables	Financials	Auditors	Board
	Executive assistants	Financials	Customers	HR climate	Regulatory
	Direct reports	Major customers	Employees	Financials	Financial
	Employee health: • physical • mental • spiritual • social	Major competitors	Competition trends	Industry	
			Middle management	Innovation, R&D	

2.2.9. CONTINUOUS IMPROVEMENT PROCESS METHODOLOGY

Improvements tend to be continual rather than continuous. In a continual approach, the improvements are incremental (i.e., the actions are monitored for stability and sustainability for a period before further improvements are driven). It is important to first hold the gains before kick-starting further improvements. This will help us understand the difference between actual improvement and noise, and any chaos surrounding the process. In reality, improvements do not happen "continuously," or nonstop.

Practitioners have traditionally used the word "continuous improvement." ISO 9001 corrected the usage to "continual" in the 2000 version (see Figure 2.3.5.4-1 in Section 2.3.5.4). Incremental improvement is often referred to as "kaizen" in lean manufacturing.

There are many methodologies of continual improvement: Shewhart's Plan-Do-Check-Act; Deming's modified Plan-Do-Study-Act; Six Sigma's Define-Measure-Analyze-Improve-Control, Define-Measure-Analyze-Design-Verify; and Juran's Quality Trilogy (Figure 2.2.9-1). The fundamentals are similar in all methodologies. It comes down to a structured approach to improvement.

2.2.9

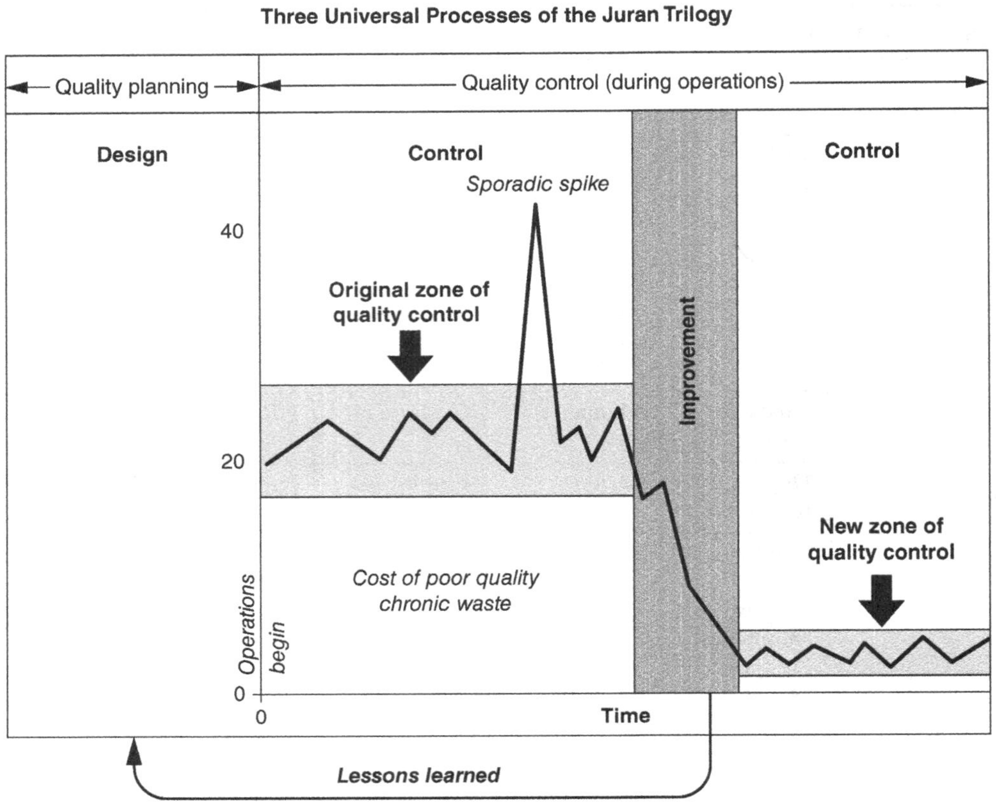

Three Universal Processes of the Juran Trilogy

Figure 2.2.9-1 Juran's Quality Trilogy.

It is common for people to jump right into solving a problem or making an improvement. This may be due to a lack of training in planning and execution of improvement or a sense of urgency or sheer impatience. Whatever the reason, this "shoot from the hip" approach rarely produces sustainable improvements. Management should be wary of these approaches, as they not only create a short-term illusion of improvement but also create chronic issues.

Without defining the problem or the improvement opportunity, it is not possible to determine whether an improvement has occurred. Similarly, without a measure or metric, improvement cannot be quantified. If a proper statistical and analytical approach is not used, the improvement cannot be confirmed with an adequate confidence level. Without controls in place, improvements will not be sustainable.

Having said that, there are occasions where a "just do it" approach is appropriate. This may be acceptable for simple improvements such as the following:

- Relocating the granite surface table from the corner of the room to the middle of the inspection room so that all four sides have better access

- Alphabetizing files for quick retrievability

- Assigning different ringtones for calls from home, calls from the office, calls from friends, and emergency calls

Quick and swift action is used to contain the situation. Safety, environmental, and health-related risks have to be immediately addressed. There may not be time to wait until the fully structured improvement is finished. In these cases, use known best practices and address the situation immediately, before the impact widens.

There are situations where breakthrough improvement is more appropriate than continual improvement (often an incremental approach). Breakthrough improvement is also structured and systematic; however, the duration in achieving the results is rapid. When the organization is lagging behind its competitors in product development or is significantly low in yield, throughput, and productivity, incremental improvement is not appropriate, as the market share will be lost while the improvement is incrementally made over a long period of time (see Section 2.3.5.4 for more on breakthrough improvement techniques).

Breakthrough improvement is also used when the team has exhausted all possibilities through incremental improvement. After a certain stage, it may become more expensive to invest in the improvement effort, as the returns do not make a good business case. This is another situation when the team might explore breakthrough improvement techniques. Lean enterprises use kaizen blitz events to perform breakthrough improvements. Breakthrough improvement is also accomplished through Six Sigma and/or reengineering methodologies.

In order to implement continual improvement, there needs to be the following:

- Management support

- Employee participation and involvement

- Infrastructure for managing the improvement

- Management oversight to review progress made

- Reward and recognition to motivate employee participation and reinforce disciplined approach

Management support can be achieved by tying improvement opportunities to the strategic direction of the organization, to critical business needs, and to the bottom line. Annual management review and quarterly performance review may be used to highlight the improvement opportunity through data collection,

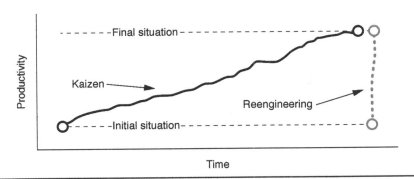

Figure 2.2.9-2 The concept of continuous improvement versus reengineering.

Source: Adapted from Santos, Wysk, and Torres (2006, 3).

organization, presentation, and statistical analysis. The future state should be identified up front so that management knows what to expect when the improvement is successful. An organization's culture often dictates employee participation and involvement.

If the management were rewarding a quick fix and firefighting, it is highly unlikely that employees would be interested in a structured approach to improvement. Management has to show interest and attention by offering time during the meetings to review the progress made and recognize the efforts. This oversight assures the improvement team that the effort matters.

The infrastructure may include project management, a measurement and reporting system, tools, equipment required to accomplish the improvement, and knowledge management. Employees need to be trained on the overall approach to continual improvement and the quality improvement tools that will be used for driving improvement. Employee reward and recognition help motivate employees. Organizations use a nomination process to identify the best-performing team by quarter. Teams are reviewed using a set of criteria that reinforce values.

There are three formal approaches to continual improvement commonly used in organizations:

1. Plan-Do-Check-Act

2. Define-Measure-Analyze-Improve-Control

3. Problem-solving storyboards

2.2.9.1. PDCA

Plan-Do-Check-Act (PDCA) is an improvement cycle methodology that evolved from 1939 to 1993, from Shewhart to Deming, and was adapted by Ishikawa (1985, 56–61) during the Japanese Quality Circle movement. A variation of this model is Plan-Do-Study-Act (PDSA).

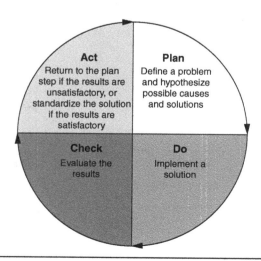

Figure 2.2.9.1-1 The PDCA cycle of improvement.

The model is a simple circle divided into four quadrants named "Plan," "Do," "Check," and "Act." The improvement team brainstorms the activities that the four quadrants should encompass in the context of the problem at hand and populates these activities into the quadrants. Quality gurus like Deming and Ishikawa provided a foundation of this model to build on.

The initial PDCA cycle was created to assist with solving shop-floor problems and preventing recurrence of the problems. The 7 Quality Tools were used along with the PDCA model. The model is robust and has many applications, including product design and development, service offering, educational curriculum, and healthcare. Regardless of the application, the activities can be mapped to PDCA. This forces a disciplined approach to program management and provides the team members with a big-picture view of what needs to be accomplished and where they are in the quadrant.

Ishikawa later modified the PDCA model to incorporate additions to the "Plan" and "Do" steps (Figure 2.2.9.1-2).

At the "Plan" stage, the process or problem selected for improvement is described, and improvement goals and objectives are defined. The current process, which is resulting in the problem situation, is described through process mapping. Quality tools are used to analyze the problem and identify the root causes. A cross-functional team develops a solution and an action plan.

At the "Do" stage, the team implements the solution. At the "Check" stage, the team evaluates the effects of the implementation. At the "Act" stage, the team decides whether to continue the cycle by going back to the "Plan" stage or standardize the learning to ensure sustainability of the actions and potential deployment to other areas.

Deming differentiates his PDSA model (Figure 2.2.9.1-3) from the Japanese PDCA as more of a plan for management. The "Study" step of PDSA intends to compare the results with the initial predictions as process learning. The improvement team is encouraged to develop a checklist using the PDCA/PDSA model.

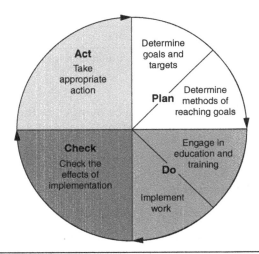

Figure 2.2.9.1-2 Ishikawa's modified PDCA cycle of improvement.

Source: Adapted from Moen and Norman (2010, 26).

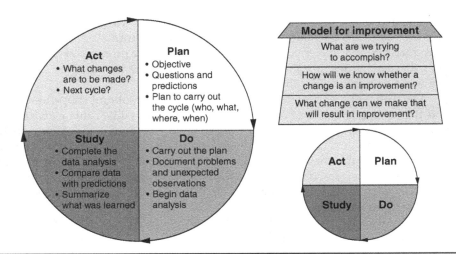

Figure 2.2.9.1–3   Deming's modified PDSA Cycle.

Source: Adapted from Moen and Norman (2010, 27).

Table 2.2.9.1–1   Comparison of improvement methodologies.

PDCA/PDSA	DMAIC	8 Discipline approach
Plan	Define	Identify the problem; use team approach
Do	Measure	Describe the problem
		Interim containment
Check/Study	Analyze	Define root cause
	Improve	Develop solutions
Act	Control	Implement solutions
		Prevent recurrence
		Congratulate the team

The PDCA and PDSA models can be mapped to the Six Sigma DMAIC methodology and the 8 Discipline approach of the Automotive Industry Action Group (AIAG) (Table 2.2.9.1-1).

PDCA is meant to be applied as a cycle: continually testing your hypothesis, learning, and trying a new way of operating. Continuing the PDCA cycle has two important unsaid components:

1. It's OK to make a mistake—but a very measured mistake

2. It's OK to try new things—but learn and be surgical in the approach

2.2.9.2. DMAIC

DMAIC, pronounced "dee-mai-yak," is a structured and systematic methodology used by Six Sigma professionals for improvement and problem solving. DMAIC methodology involves five steps: Define, Measure, Analyze, Improve, and Control.

At a high level, DMAIC can be outlined as shown in Table 2.2.9.2-1. A more detailed RDMAIC worksheet can be developed to assist the continuous improvement team at each stage.

Recognize

- Ask the team how the problem was identified, how the data were verified, and whether the problem was diagnosed adequately.

- Can this problem be resolved by assigning it to an individual or will it require a cross-functional team approach?

- Does the team understand the urgency and impact of the problem?

Table 2.2.9.2-1 DMAIC methodology.

Define	The improvement project's purpose, scope, and boundaries are defined. The improvement team works on current-state mapping, developing process flow, understanding stakeholder feedback, and translating Voice of the Customer in the form of needs and expectations (key quality characteristics or critical to quality characteristics).
Measure	The improvement team collects background data, historical performance of the process, and possible defects. The team uses statistical and analytical tools to analyze and validate the data and to calculate the current defect level (also known as process sigma). The measurement system is also validated. At this stage, the team revisits the need for the improvement project. It is not uncommon for a full-blown project to be initiated at the direction of high-profile executives, only for them to realize later that the problem is not as significant as initially perceived. The measure stage provides justification of the project and the project's financial viability is scrutinized. For this reason, some organizations practice a step prior to Define called "Recognize." This step uses prioritization techniques, financial viability, customer needs, and urgency to identify candidates for the DMAIC problem solving or process improvement.
Analyze	The team develops a focused problem statement. This is often a refined version of the statement developed at the Define stage. Using statistical and analytical tools, root causes for the problem or the improvement are identified. The cause-and-effect relationship is explored.
Improve	The team creates possible solutions for the root causes and develops plans. Typically, the solutions are piloted in a small scale to review the effectiveness before expanding to wider implementation.
Control	The team plans for full-scale implementation by developing documentation and process guidelines (standard work, visual management, poka-yoke, etc.). Implementation teams are trained. Process controls and monitoring are established. Globalize the learning across the organization (lessons learned, knowledge transfer, etc.). If applicable, kick-start a plan to further refine the process for further improvement.

Define

- Has the team identified project objectives, scope, and boundaries?
- Have the project team members been assigned?
- Has the problem statement been developed?
- Has the team identified the process owner, the team champion, the team leader and the subject matter expert?
- Have the roles and responsibilities been clearly defined for the team?
- Has a detailed project plan been developed and communicated with the team?

Measure

- Have the critical to quality (CTQ) attributes for the project been identified by capturing Voice of the Customer (VOC)?
- Have the measurement source and the integrity of the data been verified and validated?
- Is the measurement system capable?

Analyze

- Has a root cause analysis been done?
- Were appropriate tools used for the root cause analysis?
- Has the root cause been verified by running a confirmation experiment?

Improve

- Has a list of possible solutions been developed?
- Do the solutions prevent recurrence of the problem?
- Are the solutions practically feasible and cost effective?
- Are solutions prioritized according to key attributes?
- Can the solutions be developed and deployed within the project timeline?
- Are there any major changes to the organization management system based on the proposed solution?
- Are there any changes to major infrastructure?

Control

- Has the action plan been verified for effectiveness?
- Have the action plans been documented?
- Has the necessary training been provided?

- Have actions been measured and monitored to ensure adequate controls?

- Are the controls effective enough to prevent the system returning to status quo?

- Has globalization of the implementation been done?

2.2.9.3. Problem Solving Storyboards

Storyboarding is a concept that has many applications, such as development of new ideas or a new process, investigation of a problem or accident/disaster situation, or identification of an interrelationship. This is a useful tool in lean manufacturing for developing future-state value stream mapping, kaizen, and so on.

Storyboarding uses brainstorming and mind mapping/idea mapping techniques to generate ideas from team members. The topics for the discussion are brainstormed. Team members are encouraged to engage in creative thinking without judgment. Once the inputs are collected, they are arranged in the storyboard in a sequence that makes meaningful interpretation.

For a problem-solving storyboard, the topics typically include the following:

- Problem statement (Pareto chart, control chart, is/is not analysis)

- Why the problem happened (5-Whys, cause and effect, etc.)

- Plausible solutions (prioritization matrix)

- Pilot solutions

- Confirmation

- Mistake-proofing

- Implementation/Wider deployment

- Data sources, pictures, diagrams, and flowcharts are supported where applicable

While problem solving can occur anywhere, most organizations have problem-solving events where a team is assembled in a meeting room and the tools are "walked" through. However, the point of the problem-solving storyboard is to perform the problem-solving process where the problem occurs, often on the shop floor. This is why the problem-solving storyboard is usually mapped out on a sheet of A3-sized paper (see Section 3.3.1).

Once the topics are adequately brainstormed (team members have exhausted all ideas, and all redundancy has been removed), the team assembles the ideas and documents the data/graphs, along with topics to complete the "story." An important point to emphasize is that this approach does not need any sophisticated computer application, making it less intimidating and more inviting to shop-floor employees. Upon completion of the problem solving, the storyboard can be displayed to serve as a knowledge sharing tool for other employees and provide a sense of accomplishment for the team, thus improving team members' morale.

Examples of various A3 problem-solving storyboards are found in Figures 2.2.9.3-1 through 2.2.9.3-3.

2.2.9.3

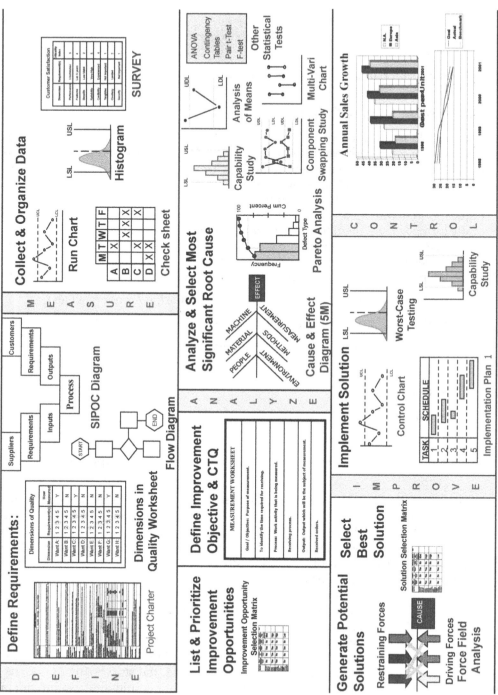

Figure 2.2.9.3-1 Examples of problem-solving storyboard based on DMAIC structure.

Team: _____   Date: _____

**5 Principles for
Problem Solving**

Step 1 | Problem Statement

1-A | Problem Definition (Problem side)

What:

When:

Where:

Why:

How:

How many:

1-B | Problem Definition (Clarifying/Pinpointing facts)

2-A | Identify Root Cause (Question and answer analysis)

Problem (1)	Why (2)	Why (3)	Why (4)	Why (5)
	Occurrence (hard side)			
	Non-creation (soft side)			

2-B | Identify Root Cause (Summary)

Root cause statement/illustration

Step 3 | Corrective Countermeasure(s)

Identify temporary and permanent

	Who	When

Step 4 | Confirm Countermeasure(s)

	Who	When

Step 5 | Feedback/Feedforward

	Who	When

2.2.9.3

Figure 2.2.9.3-2 Simplified example of problem-solving storyboard (A3 format).

2.2.9.3

Title: What change or improvement are you talking about?

Owner/Date

1. Background: What are you talking about and why?

What is the purpose, the business reason for choosing this issue?

What specific performance measure needs to be improved?

What is the strategic, operational, historical, or organizational context of the situation?

2. Current Conditions: Where do things stand now?

What is the problem or need—the gap in performance?

What is happening now versus what you want or what needs to be happening?

Have you been to the gemba?

What facts or data indicate there is a problem?

What specific conditions indicate that you have a problem or need?

Where and how much? Can you break the problem into smaller pieces?

→ Show facts and processes visually using charts, graphs, maps, etc.

3. Goal: What specific outcome is required?

What specific improvement(s) in performance do you need to achieve?

→ Show visually how much, by when, and with what impact.

→ Don't state a countermeasure as a goal!

4. Analysis: Why does the problem or need exist?

What do the specifics of the issues in work processes (location, patterns, trends, factors) indicate about why the performance gap or need exists?

What conditions or occurrences are preventing you from achieving the goals?

Why do they exist? What is (are) their cause(s)?

→ Use the simplest problem-analysis tool that will suffice to show cause-and-effect down to root cause—from 5-Whys to 7 QC tools (fishbones, analysis trees, Pareto charts) to more sophisticated SPC, Six Sigma, and other tools as needed.

→ Test the cause-and-effect logic by asking "why?" downward and stating "therefore" upward.

5. Recommendations: What do you propose and why?

What are the options for addressing the gaps and improving performance in the current situation?

→ Always start with two or three alternatives to evaluate.

How do they compare in effectiveness, feasibility, and potential disruption?

What are their relative costs and benefits?

Which do you recommend and why?

→ Show how your proposed actions will address the specific causes of the gaps or constraints you identified in your analysis. The link should be clear and explicit!

6. Plan: How will you implement? (4Ws, 1H)

What will be the main actions and outcomes in the implementation process and in what sequence?

What support and resources will be required?

Who will be responsible for what, when, and how much?

How will you measure effectiveness?

When will progress be reviewed and by whom?

→ Use a Gantt chart (or similar diagram) to display actions, steps, outcomes, timelines, and roles.

7. Follow-up: How will you ensure ongoing PDCA?

How and when will you know if plans have been followed and the actions have had the impact planned and needed?

How will you know if you meet your targets?

How will you know if you reduced the gap in performance?

What related issues or unintended consequences do you anticipate?

What contingencies can you anticipate?

What processes will you use to enable, ensure, and sustain success?

How will you share your learnings with other areas?

Figure 2.2.9.3-3   Example of a detailed A3 from *Managing to Learn*.

Source: Adapted from Shook (2008).

2.2.10. QUALITY SYSTEMS

Many organizations have some sort of quality system in place. Whether this system is required by the customer (ISO 9001), the industry (the automobile industry's Society of Automotive Engineers [SAE]), or the federal government (the Food and Drug Administration's [FDA] current good manufacturing practices [cGMPs] and the Code of Federal Regulations [CFR]), an organization inherently must ensure that customer requirements are being met—product or service.

With lean catching on in more organizations, there has been some resistance to completely accepting lean as a quality system. Make no mistake—lean is a culture and not a system. This does not mean that lean is incompatible with various quality system structures. In fact, a lean culture actually complements any quality system and, in most cases, makes adhering to quality standards much easier.

2.2.10.1. ISO and Other Standards

For the most part, all standards have some sort of basic structure and principles. Take ISO 9001, for example. The following are eight management principles of ISO 9001:

1. Customer-focused organization
2. Leadership
3. Involvement of people
4. Process approach
5. System approach
6. Continual improvement
7. Factual approach to decision making
8. Mutually beneficial supplier relationships

If these eight principles were given without identifying them as coming from ISO, a lean practitioner would think that the list is about lean.

Another argument is that lean is about eliminating waste, while standards tend to require much documentation to comply and is therefore counterintuitive to lean. Examine the seven areas often examined during an FDA audit:

1. Management
2. Design controls
3. Corrective and preventive actions
4. Production and process controls
5. Equipment and facility controls
6. Records, documents, and change controls
7. Material controls

Most, if not all, of the principles, systems, techniques, and practices discussed in this book positively impact each of those areas. More often than not, organizations actually create waste through redundant documentation in an effort to comply with a quality standard while also practicing lean. This often causes problems during an audit when the redundant documentation does not match up. For example, the shop floor may be working off a standard work that tells them to do it one way, and a standard operating procedure (SOP) up in an office says it should be performed another way. The practicing will continue for those organizations until they realize that applying lean thinking to their existing quality system will eliminate the waste and improve the system's compliance with standards. Too often an organization creates functional silos by separating the quality function from the lean culture. A well-deployed lean initiative will comply with any quality standard.

Simply ask the question, "What is the least-waste way to comply with (insert standard)?"

2.2.11. CORRECTIVE ACTION SYSTEM

To be successful on the lean journey and implement a continuous improvement system is to have a process that ensures that corrective actions are taken when problems occur. Therefore, a corrective action system is needed to drive to the root cause of issues and formally implement corrections to those issues.

2.2.11.1. Root Cause Analysis

Root cause analysis (RCA) is a methodology used to analyze a problem and put a solution in place so that the problem does not happen again. The goal of RCA is to determine and address the root cause of the problem.

"Every defect is a treasure, if the company can uncover its cause and work to prevent it across the corporation."
—Kiichiro Toyoda, founder of Toyota

Problems in an organization can be uncovered from many sources:

- Noncompliances from internal audits, second-party audits, or third-party audits

- Customer complaints, customer returns, warranty issues, and field failures

- Negative trends in key process indicators

- Failure to achieve a stated goal or objective

- Internal failures such as scrap, rework, or reprocessing

- Material nonconformances found during receiving inspection, in-process inspection, and final inspection

- Poor supplier performance

Each one of these examples is a reason to dig for the underlying cause, or root cause, so that a solution can be put in place to rectify the system and prevent its occurrence or recurrence. The methodology is the cornerstone of continual improvement.

Problem solving and RCA are at the heart of the corrective and preventive action (CAPA) process. The difference between corrective action and preventive action is the timing of the problem. If the problem has already happened, the request is called a corrective action, and RCA focuses on the root cause that allowed the problem to happen in the first place. If the problem has not yet happened but is likely to happen, the request is called a preventive action, and RCA focuses on the root cause that could potentially allow the problem to happen.

RCA is also conducted in failure analysis, incident analysis, or near misses to investigate the root cause of failures or incidents or determine the underlying weakness in a system that could lead to a problem.

"Houston, we have a problem."
—Jim Lovell, Astronaut, Apollo 13

2.2.11.1

The general methodology for performing RCA is:

1. Define and document the problem/potential problem.

2. Understand the nature of the problem. This is done in a team setting with subject matter experts.

3. Collect and analyze data to establish the cause-and-effect relationship. This step may be iterative until the data support the hypothesis of cause and effect.

4. Determine the root cause(s).

5. Establish a corrective action plan to eliminate the root cause(s).

6. Implement the corrective action plan.

7. Evaluate the effects of implementation to determine whether the plan was effective and solved the problem. This step may be iterative; the objective evidence collected must prove that the root cause of the problem was eliminated.

Some of the RCA methodologies in use are the following:

- 8 Discipline (8D) methodology

- 5-Whys

- Six Sigma—DMAIC (Define, Measure, Analyze, Improve, Control)

- Drill Deep and Wide (DDW) by Ford

The RCA methodology follows the general Plan-Do-Check-Act (PDCA) approach. RCA utilizes the basic tools of quality for arriving at the root cause, such as the SIPOC (Supplier-Input-Process-Output-Customer) diagram, process map, brainstorming, nominal group technique, cause-and-effect diagram, histogram, Pareto chart, bar chart, and scatterplot. Depending on the complexity of the problem, sophisticated analysis tools such as analysis of variance (ANOVA), regression, and design of experiments (DOE) can be used to uncover significant factors affecting a relationship.

Some techniques used to uncover the root cause are the following:

- Value-added and non-value-added analysis

- Comparison of the as-is processes and the should-be processes

- Failure mode and effects analysis (FMEA)

- Change analysis (evaluating changes made that could potentially affect the outcome)

- Barrier analysis (errors in prevention—why did the inspection fail to capture the defect?)

- Prediction analysis (why did the organization fail to predict the problem?)

See Section 2.3.3 for root cause analysis techniques and practices.

2.2.11.1

2.2.12. PROJECT MANAGEMENT

Project management is concerned with the planning, control, monitoring, and review of projects. In the context of problem solving, complex problems are often handled using a project management approach, where a specific problem is dealt with as a project. It has a specific beginning and end—encompassing all activities starting with the Define phase of identifying a problem, putting a team in place, and ending with the project closeout after successful implementation of the solution to address the root cause. It is an essential discipline of getting things done.

General Requirements for Project Management

- Creating a project charter
- Project planning
  - Creating a Gantt chart and a work breakdown structure (WBS)
  - Program evaluation and review technique (PERT)/critical path method (CPM)
- Communicating project status
- Evaluating project results

Project Charter

A *project charter* is a document that outlines the expectations and deliverables between upper management and the team. It is a must and needs to be created before a project can start. It contains signatures of upper management and the project manager, denoting authority to start work on the project.

A project charter typically contains the following:

- Project description
- Project scope (in scope and out of scope)
- Business objectives; success criteria and deliverables
- Resources and risks
- High-level timeline showing milestones
- Budget

Project Planning

Project planning encompasses the identification of activities to drive the project from beginning to end. Tools such as a Gantt chart and a WBS are used, respectively, to develop a timeline of activities and to detail each task into smaller activities that can be assigned to an individual or group. The activities in the WBS can be further linked to resource requirements needed for completion. Both the Gantt and the WBS are useful tracking tools that the project manager uses to ensure that the project is progressing according to schedule and within budget.

2.2.12

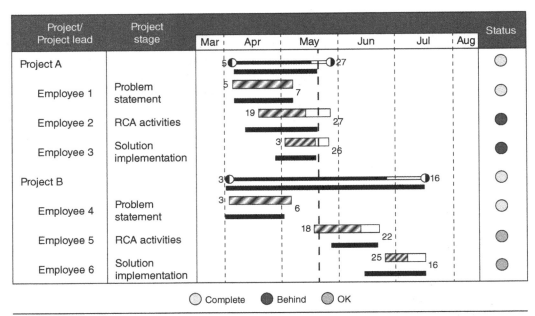

Figure 2.2.12–1   Example of a Gantt chart with visual management incorporated.

Gantt Chart

A *Gantt chart* (Figure 2.2.12-1) is a horizontal bar chart that graphically represents the WBS activities and provides an overview of all the activities and dependencies of a project. A Gantt chart is used as a project monitoring and communication tool for the team and upper management. Since the activities are linked to dependencies and resources, it is also used to evaluate whether the project is progressing to plan.

Program Evaluation and Review Technique (PERT) Chart

Network modeling is another form of addressing project scheduling. The program evaluation and review technique (PERT) chart (Figure 2.2.12-2) is an example of network modeling and is different from the Gantt chart in that it does not show a timeline but shows dependencies and time estimates for the activities.

A *node* is a circle on the graph that designates the beginning or ending of an arc. An *arc* is the arrow that begins at one node and ends at another node. The arrowhead denotes the direction of the ending point. The PERT chart flows from left to right. Precedence is indicated at each node: All the arrowheads that lead to the node must be completed before a new arc can begin. The expected time for the activity is denoted above the arrow.

Time estimates for each activity are provided in three values: optimistic, most likely or expected, and pessimistic. Expected time is calculated using the formula:

$$\text{Expected time} = \frac{[\text{Optimistic} + (4 \times \text{Most likely}) + \text{Pessimistic}]}{6}$$

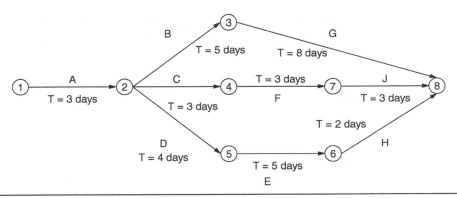

Figure 2.2.12-2 Example of a PERT chart.

Critical Path Method (CPM)

Critical path method (CPM) is similar to PERT, but where PERT is event oriented, CPM is activity oriented. The critical path determines the total time required for a project. To identify the critical path in a project, slack time is calculated for all the activities. Slack time indicates that if an activity is not on the critical path, speeding up or slowing down will not impact the total project time.

Slack time is calculated as follows: The earliest start time and finish time for each activity are calculated and then the latest start time and finish time are calculated. The difference between the latest finish and the earliest finish indicates the slack time for that activity. The *critical path* is the path through the network where the activities have zero slack. Activities on the critical path that are delayed will delay the entire project.

Communication

Effective and timely communication regarding project status is one of the keys to success. Communication must be both top down from management to the team and bottom up from the team to management. A communication plan provides a guide for identifying what must be communicated to whom as well as a roadmap for keeping them informed on the technical and other aspects of the project.

Within lean organizations, communication is commonly achieved with the use of an A3 project report (see Section 3.3.1 for additional information on A3 reports).

Project Results

At the completion of a project, the results must be evaluated and compared against what was predicted at the start of the project. Project results are evaluated by comparing the benefits of a given project against the investment and costs.

The following are steps for calculating project results:

1. Identify the associated costs

2. Identify the revenue/savings benefits

3. Map out the projected timeline for the expected costs and benefits

4. Evaluate the return on investment, net present value, and payback period

Return on investment (ROI) is the ratio comparing expected income with expected cost. It is most often expressed as a percentage.

$$ROI = (Income/Cost) \times 100$$

Net present value (NPV) is the current value of an amount to be received in the future.

$$NPV = A / (1 + i)n$$

A = The amount to be received n years in the future

i = Annual interest rate

Payback period is the length of time it takes for the cash inflows (financial benefits) to equal the cash outflows (costs/investment).

$$Payback\ period = Investment/Financial\ benefit$$

2.2.13. PROCESS DESIGN

Lean thinking follows a holistic approach to process design that involves many areas and considers a variety of factors. Unlike the traditional approach, processes in a lean environment are never developed in isolation—they include active involvement from suppliers and representatives from all affected areas of the organization. The focus throughout the design process is to meet or exceed customer needs without adding activities or costs that do not add value.

SIPOC

One of the most valuable tools used in designing and improving processes in a lean environment is Supplier-Input-Process-Output-Customer (SIPOC) charting. SIPOC offers a very basic approach to process development based on understanding the customer's needs and studying how the linkages throughout the operation create the associated product or service to meet those needs. SIPOC forces reflection on the interactions that occur internally in, as well as externally to, the organization, highlighting the need for the organization to serve internal customers in order to satisfy its external customers.

The SIPOC process (Figure 2.2.13-1) begins with identifying who receives or is affected by the output of the process (i.e., the customers). Once the customers are identified, clarifying the outputs of the process, including the specific requirements that the customers deem important, becomes easier.

The next step involves defining the inputs to the process and the associated requirements necessary to develop or maintain the characteristics related to customer requirements. The requirements are communicated to suppliers, which in

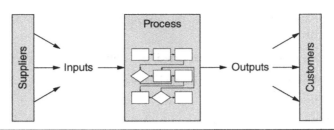

Figure 2.2.13-1   SIPOC diagram.

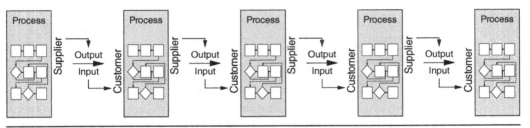

Figure 2.2.13-2   SIPOC and the linking of processes.

many cases are areas internal to the organization that provide materials and information for the process.

After analyzing and understanding the suppliers, inputs, outputs, and customers (including the requirements at each stage), the process is developed, identifying the steps needed to convert the inputs to outputs in an efficient and customer-focused manner.

Figure 2.2.13-2 presents a simple example of the linkage of processes throughout a typical organization. Each process converts inputs provided by suppliers into outputs for customers, who, in turn, do the same for one or more other processes. A process often has several different suppliers and customers, which can make gaining an understanding of the total process fairly difficult. SIPOC, however, simplifies the process by providing a structured approach to increase knowledge of the company's overall system, an absolute necessity for effective process design.

One of the most important benefits of using SIPOC to develop processes is recognizing that nothing in an organization is done in isolation. In one way or another, everyone serves either the customer or someone else who does. By providing a structured method to understand who serves whom, a SIPOC chart can greatly improve the design of processes.

Process Stability

The initial focus in the design and implementation of a lean process is stability. A stable process is one that is predictable (i.e., has a consistent amount of variation) in terms of cost, quality, and cycle time. Alternatively, without stability in a process, quality suffers, costs cannot be accurately determined, and planning becomes very difficult.

To achieve stability in a process, the following conditions, as a minimum, must occur (see Figure 2.2.13-3):

- Process steps are clearly defined and consistently followed (the method)
- People involved in the process have achieved minimum levels of training and qualification (the people)
- Various tooling and equipment used in the process are designed and maintained in a consistent manner (the machinery)
- Measurement equipment is properly used, maintained, and calibrated at regular intervals (the measurements)
- Materials and components used in the process are of consistent quality (the materials)

All of these elements contribute variability to the process. Effective process design includes implementing methods to minimize the variation caused by each of these elements to help the process achieve stability quickly.

A process will always contain variation. When the process is stable, however, this variation becomes predictable within limits determined by the process average and standard deviation (Figure 2.2.13-4).

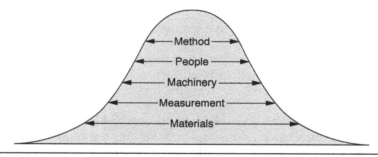

Figure 2.2.13-3 Contributors to variation.

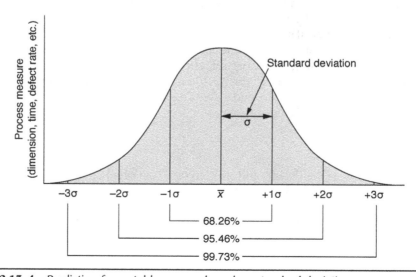

Figure 2.2.13-4 Prediction for a stable process based on standard deviation.

In Figure 2.2.13-4, $\bar{x}$ is the average of one measure of the process output (e.g., a given dimension, cost, or process time). Using basic control charting formulas, the standard deviation can be estimated fairly quickly to determine the spread of the measured result (e.g., 68.26% of the process output falls within one standard deviation of the average).

It is important to note that a stable process does not necessarily deliver its output on time or produce at a desired level of quality. It does, however, provide a predictable level of performance, which is a prerequisite to achieving a sustained level of quality, cost, and delivery.

Process Capability

As mentioned earlier, process stability, although important, does not tell anything about the capability to meet targets for quality, costs, or cycle times. *Process capability* (C_{pk}) is a measure that describes how well a process can meet a given target. It is calculated as a ratio of target specification to process spread (or the amount of variation in the process). In simple terms, process capability represents a comparison of the Voice of the Customer (VOC) with the Voice of the Process (VOP). The higher the result, the more capable the process is of meeting customer needs.

Process capability generally uses 3σ as the measure of process spread, or 99.73% of its output. Therefore, as shown in Figure 2.2.13-4, a process capability of 1.00 means that the process can be expected to produce within specifications 99.73% of the time.

Table 2.2.13-1 presents very basic information concerning process capability related to expected acceptable output from a process. It should be noted, however, that other factors should be taken into account when using capability measures in real-world applications. Six sigma methodology includes a process shift of 1.5 sigma in process capability calculation, which results in a lower yield (higher percent defective) than presented in Table 2.2.13-1.

Process Capacity

For planning purposes, it is critical to understand the capacity of a process; and to understand the capacity of a process, it is critical to have standardized work ("Method" in Figure 2.2.13-3). If a process is unstable, it is not repeatable or predictable, making planning very difficult, if not impossible.

Table 2.2.13-1   Translation of process capability measure.

Process capability (C_{pk})	Sigma level	Expected process yield	Expected defective
0.33	1	68.25%	31.75%
0.67	2	95.46%	4.54%
1.00	3	99.73%	0.27%
1.33	4	99.994%	0.006%

Standard work enables labor times to be clearly understood and, when combined with predictable machine times, allows process capability to be calculated fairly easily. And whether in a lean environment or not, determining process capacity is vital for planning, costing, and improving areas in the process.

A *process capacity sheet* is a commonly used lean tool to calculate and understand the capacity of the equipment in a particular work area. The sheet (Table 2.2.13-2) provides the theoretical capacity based on the following inputs:

- Machine time per piece

- Manual time per piece (operator time performed while the machine is not producing product)

- Total cycle time per piece (calculated as machine time per piece + manual time per piece)

- Number of pieces before a tool change is needed

- Time required to perform a tool change

- Tool change time per piece (calculated as time to perform tool change / number of pieces before a tool change is needed)

- Available time per shift (reported in units similar to the other time-related measures)

Using this information, process capacity is calculated as:

$$\text{Capacity} = \text{Available time per shift} / (\text{Total cycle time per piece} + \text{Tool change time per piece})$$

In addition to the costing and planning benefits, understanding theoretical process capacity (based on the calculation) provides valuable information regarding when a process is not performing as expected. A particular process step that is not able to produce to its theoretical capacity identifies where problem-solving efforts should be focused. Correcting the situation may involve additional training, improved material quality, better equipment maintenance, or a number of other corrective actions.

Table 2.2.13-2 Example of process capacity sheet.

Process step	Description	Machine time (sec)	Manual time (sec)	Total cycle time per piece (sec)	Pieces per change	Time per change (sec)	Change time per piece (sec)	Total time per piece (sec)	Shift time (sec)	Capacity (pieces)
1	Drill holes	15	3	18	200	60	0.3	18.3	27612	1509
2	Turn face	12	3	15	100	50	0.5	15.5	27612	1781
3	Injection mold	32	5	37	250	110	0.44	37.44	27612	738

An additional benefit of understanding process capacity is related to takt time. If the capacity calculation shows that the process is not able to keep up with its takt time, something will need to change or customer satisfaction will suffer.

Other Factors

There are several other factors to keep in mind when applying lean thinking to the development or improvement of processes, including streamlined layout, one-piece flow, and quality at the source. The move toward improved quality, reduced cost, and shorter cycle times requires a systems-thinking mind-set with a constant focus on improving flow of materials and information and reducing activities that do not add value.

Streamlining the layout of a process to improve the flow of materials and information is a critical focus of lean thinking. Developing a spaghetti diagram (Figure 2.2.13-5) to show the movement of people and materials through a process is one of the most basic ways to understand the flow and see where improvements can be made.

Companies often serve customers through a complex series of processes that work together to produce products and services. The interaction of processes and process steps can be thought of as a series of gears (as shown in Figure 2.2.13-6) that must turn at a precise speed to keep the system working effectively. If one gear gets out of sync with the others, the system can break down under the pressure.

Thinking of the company in this manner helps prioritize improvement efforts toward the *gear*, or process, interfering with the system's overall flow. It also improves the ability to think at the system level and determine which factors to consider when developing or improving processes.

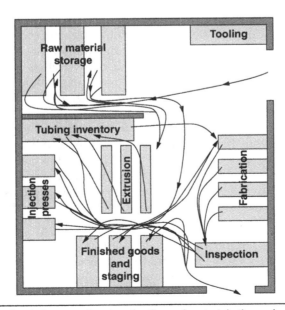

Figure 2.2.13-5 Spaghetti diagram showing the flow of materials through an operation.

2.2.13

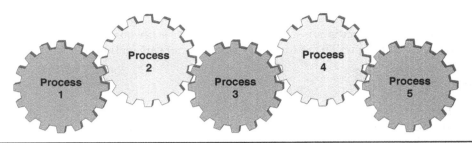

Figure 2.2.13-6 The organization as a series of processes working together to serve customers.

Lean thinking requires an intimate knowledge of the company's processes, systems, and customers in order to make the trade-off decisions necessary to serve customers well. For example, some processes are well suited to one-piece flow, while others require inventory buffers to keep the system running effectively. Although some decisions can make an individual process operate more efficiently in isolation, lean thinking helps us understand whether they benefit the overall system as well.

2.2.14. PULL SYSTEM

Pull systems are an integral part of lean manufacturing, yet they are frequently misunderstood and considered difficult to implement. A *pull system* is one in which processes are based on customer demand. The concept is that each process manufactures each component in line with another department to build a final part to the exact expectation of delivery to the customer.

In traditional manufacturing, a *push system* of production, in which products are pushed along the production stream and finally outward, has historically been the norm. With a push system, manufacturers mass-produce ahead of time, estimating and anticipating demand. Operating under this system frequently resulted in overproduction, excess inventory, and costly delays and waiting. When the demand isn't there, idle inventory sits around consuming space and resources. In addition, unrealized demand also requires costly marketing campaigns to create an artificial demand.

Pull is one of the three elements of just-in-time, the others being standard work and takt time. The pull system enables the production of what is needed, based on a signal of what has just been "sold." The downstream process/customer "pulls" the needed product/service from the producer. This "customer pull" is a signal to the producer that the product/service has been used/consumed by the customer. The pull system links accurate information with the process to minimize overproduction. Three primary elements distinguish pull from push:

1. Defined: A defined agreement with specified limits pertaining to volume of product, model mix, and the sequence of model mix between the two parties (supplier and customer).

2. Dedicated: Items that are shared between the two parties must be dedicated to them. This includes resources, locations, storage, containers, and a common reference time (takt time).

3. Controlled: Simple control methods, which are visually apparent and physically constraining, maintain the defined agreement. (Liker and Meier 2006, 94)

There is no defined agreement between the supplier and the customer regarding the quantity of work to be supplied in a push system. The supplier works at his or her own pace and completes work according to his or her own schedule. This material is then delivered to the customer, regardless of whether it was requested. Material is placed where there is an opening, since locations are not defined and dedicated. There is no clear way to understand what to control or how to control it because there is no definition or dedication. Of course, some element of control happens through expediting, changing the schedule, and moving resources, but this only leads to additional waste and variation.

There are three basic types of pull systems:

1. Replenishment (supermarket) pull

2. Sequential pull

3. Mixed pull system with elements of the other two

Supermarket Pull System

In a supermarket pull system (Figure 2.2.14-1), each process has a store, or supermarket, that holds an amount of each product it produces. Each process simply produces to replenish what is withdrawn from its supermarket.

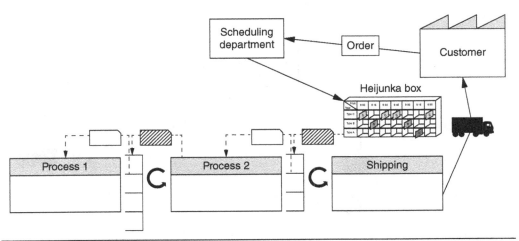

Figure 2.2.14-1 Example of a supermarket pull system.
Source: Adapted from Marchwinski and Shook (2006, 76).

Sequential Pull System

A sequential pull system (Figure 2.2.14-2) may be used when there are too many part numbers to hold inventory of each in a supermarket. Products are essentially made to order while overall system inventory is minimized.

Mixed Pull System

The supermarket and sequential pull systems may be used together in a mixed system (Figure 2.2.14-3). A mixed system may be appropriate when the 80/20 rule applies, with a small percentage of part numbers (perhaps 20%) accounting for the majority (perhaps 80%) of daily production volume.

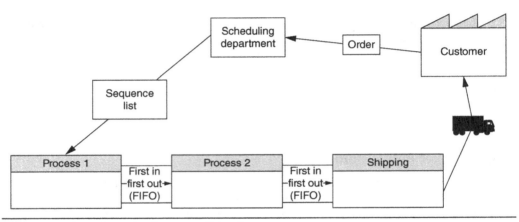

Figure 2.2.14-2   Example of a sequential pull system.
Source: Adapted from Marchwinski and Shook (2006, 77).

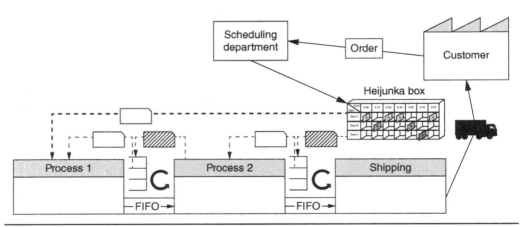

Figure 2.2.14-3   Example of a mixed pull system.
Source: Adapted from Marchwinski and Shook (2006, 77).

In all three cases, the following are important technical elements for systems to succeed:

- Flowing product in small batches (approaching one-piece flow where possible)

- Pacing the processes to takt time (to stop overproduction)

- Signaling replenishment via a kanban signal

- Leveling of product mix and quantity over time

The pull process focuses on eliminating wasteful activity during the production process, placing materials at point of use (rather than all in the warehouse), and establishing a regular drumbeat replenishment process.

Using a pull system in a supply chain has significant advantages. Pull systems are an economical way to:

- Simplify communications

- Reduce inventory

- Shorten and control lead times

- Reduce work-in-process

- Reduce order turnaround time

- Increase customer satisfaction

- Improve cash flow

- Reduce cycle time

Even though pull systems have many benefits, they may not be practical in every situation. A key component in making this decision is continuity of supply coupled with demand stability. Businesses should choose the appropriate replenishment method for the appropriate demand. Pull systems are more difficult to apply on items with irregular or sporadic demand. Since pull systems are based on replenishment, ongoing demand has to be assumed.

Pull systems can be a very efficient and cost-effective stock control tool. They are not without issues and require close management (and a willing and able supplier partner). However, when used effectively they can make a real difference in simplifying inventory management.

2.2.15. KNOWLEDGE TRANSFER

Knowledge management "involves transforming data into information, the acquisition or creation of knowledge, as well as processes and technology employed in identifying, categorizing, storing, retrieving, disseminating, and using information and knowledge for the purposes of improving decisions and plans" (Okes and Westcott 2006, 606). In other words, knowledge is the result of analyzing and using data

2.2.15

and information. Knowledge can be the result of analysis or experience. Undocumented knowledge is sometimes referred to as "gray-beard" or "tribal" knowledge, referring to understanding gained through experience or trial and error.

Knowledge transfer differs slightly from knowledge management in that knowledge transfer focuses on capturing and communicating knowledge not only for decisions and plans but for documentation, process baselines, and training—for example, when performing observations when developing standard work (see Section 2.2.6), validation plans and procedures, or process or machine setup. Consider a flow soldering process with a process setup that identifies wave height, temperature, and conveyor speed. For a specific product with a multiple layer printed wiring board with a large ground plane, the circuit board needs to be preheated to reduce the potential for defects. When the process technician runs the flow solder machine, the error (defect) rate is low, but when others run the machine, the rate is much higher. This is an example of knowledge transfer failure: The process technician "in the know" did not transfer that knowledge to others. This results in rework, which translates into waste.

According to Dennis (2007, 124), there are nine wastes of knowledge:

1. Handoff
2. Useless information
3. Discarded knowledge
4. Wishful thinking
5. Waiting
6. Misalignment
7. Communication barriers
8. Inadequate checking
9. Wrong tool

Understanding these types of wastes and working with employees to capture and communicate knowledge support the lean goal of waste elimination. "*Tacit knowledge* consists of all the difficult to articulate 'know how' and expert techniques and processes that are part of an individual's and/or organization's expertise" (Okes and Westcott 2006, 200)—the unwritten or unrecorded knowledge that can be lost. "Explicit knowledge is the captured and recorded tools that are codified and can be transmitted between individuals" (Okes and Westcott 2006, 200).

Examples of knowledge waste, based on tacit and explicit knowledge, are provided in Table 2.2.15-1.

The capture and transfer of data and information to create knowledge are necessary to ensure process stability and product quality. Gaining buy-in to transform tacit knowledge to explicit knowledge is key to long-term sustainment and improvement.

Table 2.2.15-1   Examples of knowledge waste.

Knowledge waste	Examples
Handoff	• Storytelling exemplifies the loss of tacit knowledge. Tell a short story—just a few sentences—to a person and then have this person do this with someone else. Do this with 5–10 people, with the last person telling you. By the time you get the story it will have changed significantly. If this knowledge (the story) was explicit (written) and passed on, the story would not change.
Useless information	• Presentations (e.g., Microsoft PowerPoint slides) that are in paragraph form versus bullet format (i.e., single lines) make it hard to pick out the key points from the clutter. Caution should be used, though, to ensure that key points are not communicated verbally, thus becoming tacit knowledge and being at risk of loss. • Excessive written instructions, procedures, and policies versus pictorial data—a picture is worth a thousand words
Discarded knowledge	• Unused explicit knowledge—note reviewing and implementing a change to a document (knowingly ignoring instructions—see the discussion of resistance to standard work in Section 2.2.6)
Wishful thinking	• Hoping for things to get better or change without communication, effort, etc.
Waiting	• Excessive approvals (lack of empowerment) • System downtime (breakage, no preventive maintenance) • Upstream (internal or external supplier) delays or errors (rework)
Misalignment	• Employees (or leadership) not supporting company vision or goals • Resistance to change
Communication barriers	• Unwillingness on management's part to be open to bad news • Personnel availability • Cultural, language, or technology failures
Inadequate checking	• Improper quality at the source • Inadequate time to perform checks
Wrong tool	• Improper documentation • Inadequate tool availability—causing improvisation

REFERENCES

Alukal, G., and A. Manos. 2006. *Lean Kaizen: A Simplified Approach to Process Improvement.* Milwaukee, WI: ASQ Quality Press.

Dennis, Pascal. 2007. *Lean Production Simplified: A Plain-Language Guide to the World's Most Powerful Production System.* 2nd ed. New York: Productivity Press.

Duffy, Grace L., and John W. Moran. 2008. *Executive Focus: Your Life and Career.* Milwaukee, WI: ASQ Quality Press.

Galsworth, Gwendolyn. 1997. *Visual Systems*. New York: AMACOM.

Imai, Masaaki. 1997. *Gemba Kaizen: A Commonsense, Low-Cost Approach to Management*. New York: McGraw-Hill.

Ishikawa, Kaoru. 1985. *What Is Total Quality Control? The Japanese Way*. Englewood Cliffs, NJ: Prentice-Hall, 56–61.

Kaplan, R. S., and D. Norton. 1996. "The Balanced Scorecard." *Harvard Business Review* 74 (November-December).

Liker, Jeffrey, and David Meier. 2006. *The Toyota Way Fieldbook*. New York: McGraw-Hill.

Maio, M. 2010. *Quality Improvement Made Simple . . . and Fast!* Milwaukee, WI: ASQ Quality Press.

Mann, David. 2010. *Creating a Lean Culture*. 2nd ed. Boca Raton, FL: CRC Press.

Marchwinski, Chet, and John Shook. 2006. *Lean Lexicon*. 3rd ed. Version 3.0. Cambridge, MA: Lean Enterprise Institute.

Model and Application Guidelines: The Shingo Prize for Operational Excellence. 2010. Version 4. Logan, UT: Jon M. Huntsman School of Business, Utah State University.

Moen, Ronald D., and Clifford L. Norman. 2010. "Circling Back." ASQ *Quality Progress*, November, 22–28.

Ohno, Taiichi. 1988. *Toyota Production System: Beyond Large-Scale Production*. Boca Raton, FL: CRC Press, Taylor & Francis Group.

Okes, D., and R. Westcott. 2006. *The Certified Quality Manager Handbook*. Milwaukee, WI: ASQ Quality Press.

Rother, Mike, and John Shook. 2009. *Learning to See*. Version 1.4. Cambridge, MA: Lean Enterprise Institute.

Shook, John. 2008. *Managing to Learn*. Cambridge, MA: Lean Enterprise Institute.

Tague, N. 2005. *The Quality Toolbox*. 2nd ed. Milwaukee, WI: ASQ Quality Press.

2.3

Continuous Process Improvement Techniques & Practices

Improvements require studying and observing a system or processes and then changing the way the work is performed for the better, or least-waste way. In order to acquire knowledge about the work system and work processes, a continuous improvement system should be in place to monitor and identify areas that require improvement. Decisions for improvements must be based on data. This is called management by fact, or management by data.

In order to manage by fact, information and data must be collected, and there must be confidence in the data and information gathered. This section presents techniques and practices for analyzing the current state of a work system/process and improving it. The data gathering and analysis allow the team to develop the ability to improve the process using data from the continuous improvement system rather than relying on guesswork, experience (gut feel), or opinion.

There are techniques and practices for not only gathering and analyzing the data but also implementing improvements to the work systems/processes to achieve results that can be tracked and monitored by the continuous improvement systems. The various continuous process improvement techniques and practices are divided into the following nine categories:

1. Work flow analysis
2. Data collection and presentation
3. Identify root cause
4. Presenting variation data
5. Product and service design
6. Organizing for improvement
7. Countermeasure activities
8. Supply processes external
9. Supply processes internal

2.3.1. WORK FLOW ANALYSIS

In order to understand work flow analysis, one needs to understand what a system and process are. In the context of lean, a *system* is anything that has interacting, interrelated, or interdependent processes. A *process* is a sequence of linked

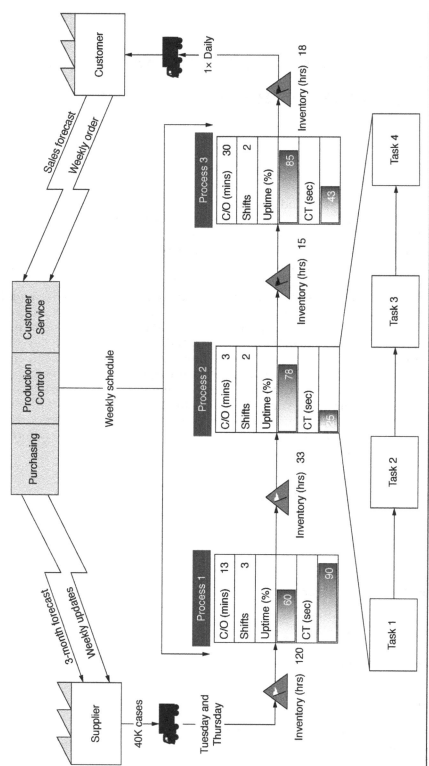

Figure 2.3.1–1 Value stream map system broken down into processes and tasks.

activities, or tasks, with the purpose of producing a product or performing a service for a customer (internal or external). A process is commonly associated with work. However, since a system is a structure of repeatable processes, a system can be associated with flow—in other words, how well processes are linked together to achieve an expected outcome (product or service).

With the contexts of a system and process understood, work flow should now be clearer. *Work flow* is the ability, or rate, at which work is processed through a system. It can be stated as the measure of how well the processes within a system are linked and work together. *Work flow analysis*, then, is the evaluation of flow in a system and how the efficiency and effectiveness of the flow can be improved.

There are several points to remember with work flow analysis:

- There is no standard that defines the correct way to model a system

- The perspective of the person describing a view of a system should always be considered

- A system can be modeled from the top down or the bottom up

This section reviews four ways to evaluate work flow within an organization:

1. Flowcharts
2. Flow analysis charts
3. Value stream mapping
4. Takt time analysis

2.3.1.1. Flowcharting

A *flowchart* is a visual representation of a sequentially ordered set of tasks (Tague 2004, 255–57). A flowchart can be constructed very easily by assembling a group of individuals with knowledge of the process being charted. The participants enumerate a list of tasks, place each task on a small piece of paper, and organize them sequentially. The resulting collection of sequentially ordered activities is the foundation of a flowchart.

There is no flowchart standard. The National Institute of Standards in the United States has developed a set of suggested ways to document organizational activities, called the IDEF Standard. While the IDEF models are well developed, they are not widely used. Flowcharts can be as simple (Figure 2.3.1.1-1) or as detailed (Figure 2.3.1.1-2) as needed for the team for evaluation purposes.

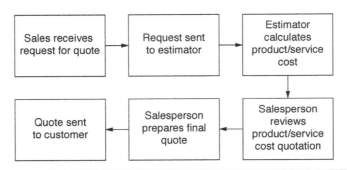

Figure 2.3.1.1-1   High-level flowchart for a request-for-quote process.

2.3.1.1

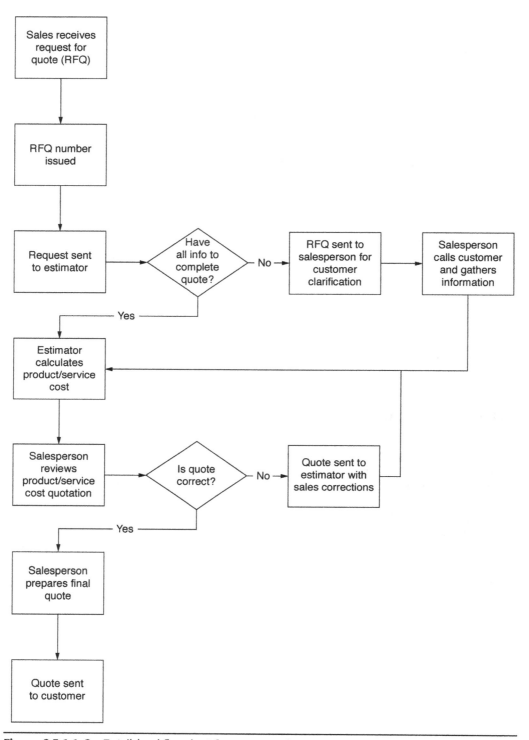

Figure 2.3.1.1-2   Detail-level flowchart for a request-for-quote process.

A flowchart can include practically anything that is relevant to the process, for example, various process inputs and outputs, decision points, personnel, times, and metrics. The versatility of the flowchart allows for its use on any process. This includes, but is not limited to, manufacturing processes, manufacturing support processes, service processes, project plans, and transactions.

A flowchart can be used for describing how a process is performed, identifying areas for process improvements, communicating with others such as training or cross-functional teams, planning a process or project, and documenting a process.

The following is a basic procedure for creating a flowchart within a team setting (ASQ):

1. Define the process to be diagrammed.

2. Discuss and decide on the boundaries of your process: Where or when does the process start? Where or when does it end? Discuss and decide on the level of detail to be included in the diagram.

3. Brainstorm the activities that take place. Write each on a card or sticky note. Sequence is not important at this point, although thinking in sequence may help people remember all the steps.

4. Arrange the activities in proper sequence.

5. When all activities are included and everyone agrees that the sequence is correct, draw arrows to show the flow of the process.

6. Review the flowchart with others involved in the process (workers, supervisors, suppliers, customers) to see if they agree that the process is drawn accurately.

2.3.1.2. Flow Analysis Charts

Shigeo Shingo (2005, 5) defined five distinct process elements that are critical in the examination of production efficiency, specifically the flow of raw materials into products:

1. Processing—the processing element is used to represent a physical change in the material or the quality of a work item

2. Inspection—the inspection element is used to make a comparison to a standard

3. Transportation—the transportation element is used when a work item is moved from one location to another

Delay is a period of time in which no processing, inspection, or transportation occurs. Shingo defined two delay elements:

1. Process delay—the process delay element is used to represent the delay of an entire production lot while the previous lot is processed, inspected, or moved (the three previous process elements)

2. Lot delay—the lot delay element is used to represent the situation where one piece is processed while the other pieces of the lot wait to be inspected or transported

These five elements can be documented in a visual map of the process. A typical flow analysis chart, or analytical process chart, employs the sequential arrangement of these five elements that communicate the work flow through the process. Shingo used the following symbols for each element:

○	Processing
◆	Inspection
●	Transportation
▼	Process delay
✡	Lot delay
▲	Storage (Optional)

All processes can be analyzed using the five elements and an analytical process chart, as shown in Figures 2.3.1.2-1 and 2.3.1.2-2.

As with the flowchart, there is no standard method of creating an analytical process chart. They can be as simple or as detailed as needed for the team during process evaluation.

2.3.1.3. Value Stream Mapping

In order to map a value stream, one must first understand what a value stream is. As defined by Mike Rother and John Shook (2009, 1) in *Learning to See*:

> A value stream is all the actions (both value-added and nonvalue-added) currently required to bring a product through the main flows essential to every product: (1) the production flow from raw material into the arms of the customer, and (2) the design flow from concept to launch.

Value stream mapping is simply an illustration of the sequential activities that take place within a value stream. At each step of the map the practitioner evaluates whether value is being created and whether one or more of the wastes exist. The purpose of the value stream map is to identify those activities that add value and those that create waste, with the latter being targets for elimination. Every organization strives for value streams that add only value and have eliminated all waste.

The following are benefits of value stream mapping:

- It allows visualization of the big picture (more than just a single process) to see the flow of product, service, and information. Other quantitative tools and flow diagrams do not provide the same information at that level.

- It allows visualization of waste and the sources of that waste.

- It provides a foundation for all levels and functions to discuss the value stream and its processes.

- It allows for factual-based decisions about the flow of the process.
- It lays the foundation for creating an improvement strategy and implementation plan for the value stream.
- It shows the relationship between information and product flows.

	Process	Injection mold 43	**Manuf. pcs.**	800
	Part name	2 x 4 block (red)	**Part #**	02-04-R
	Material	ABS	**Pcs./Set**	1
	Inspector	#2	**Date of inspection**	2012-5-14

Pieces	Dist.	Time	Symbol	Process (place)	Operator	Machine	Tools, jigs, etc.	Storage	Operating conditions, development, etc.
			▲	Warehouse				Stack on floor	
50 kg	80 m		●	To hopper	Molder	Hopper 2			
24.5 g		1 hr	▲		Molder			In hopper	
24.5 g	3 m		●	To dryer	Molder	Dryer 43			
24.5 g		4 hrs	○	Drying	Molder				80–90°C
24.5 g	3 m		●	To inj. mold	Molder	Inj. mold 43			
24.5 g		1 min	○	Molding	Molder				Barrel temp. 250°C Hold time 13 sec. Cool time 30 sec.
8 pcs.	10 m		●	To de-flash	Molder				
8 pcs.		6 min	✡		Operator			Tote	
8 pcs.		1 min	○	Flash removal	Operator	De-flasher			
8 pcs.	1m		●	To inspection	Operator				
800 pcs.		8 min	▼		Inspector			Bulk bag	
800 pcs.		5 min	◆	Inspection	Inspector		Magnifier		Dimensional and visual inspection requirements

Figure 2.3.1.2-1 Analytical process chart for a LEGO block manufacturing process.

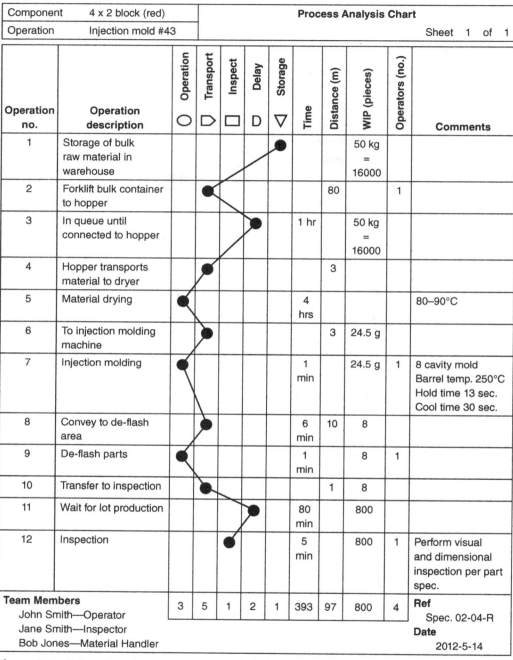

Component	4 x 2 block (red)						Process Analysis Chart			
Operation	Injection mold #43								Sheet 1 of 1	

Operation no.	Operation description	Operation ○	Transport ▷	Inspect ▢	Delay D	Storage ▽	Time	Distance (m)	WIP (pieces)	Operators (no.)	Comments
1	Storage of bulk raw material in warehouse					●			50 kg = 16000		
2	Forklift bulk container to hopper		●					80		1	
3	In queue until connected to hopper				●		1 hr		50 kg = 16000		
4	Hopper transports material to dryer		●					3			
5	Material drying	●					4 hrs				80–90°C
6	To injection molding machine		●					3	24.5 g		
7	Injection molding	●					1 min		24.5 g	1	8 cavity mold Barrel temp. 250°C Hold time 13 sec. Cool time 30 sec.
8	Convey to de-flash area		●				6 min	10	8		
9	De-flash parts	●					1 min		8	1	
10	Transfer to inspection		●					1	8		
11	Wait for lot production				●		80 min		800		
12	Inspection			●			5 min		800	1	Perform visual and dimensional inspection per part spec.
Team Members John Smith—Operator Jane Smith—Inspector Bob Jones—Material Handler		3	5	1	2	1	393	97	800	4	**Ref** Spec. 02-04-R **Date** 2012-5-14

Figure 2.3.1.2-2 Alternate example of an analytical process chart for a LEGO block manufacturing process.

Value Stream Mapping Steps

In the simplest of terms, the value stream process consists of the steps in Figure 2.3.1.3-1.

Value stream mapping follows the Plan-Do-Check-Act (PDCA) cycle of improvement methodology. The intent is to map the current state of the value stream, plan a future-state value stream with action items to get there, implement the action items, and then check the new current state of the value stream and act accordingly with countermeasures to achieve a new future state. This cycle continues throughout the lean journey. But first, one must know what to map.

Product or Service Family

It is often difficult to determine what value streams are present within an organization. This is why it is a good first step to understand what product families exist within an organization. A *product family* is a group of products or services that share similar processes, steps, and equipment. One way to determine the product/service families within an organization is to use a product family matrix (Figure 2.3.1.3-2).

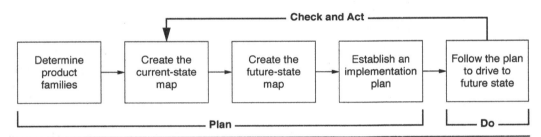

Figure 2.3.1.3-1 The process of value stream mapping.

		Process steps and equipment									
		1	2	3	4	5	6	7	8	9	10
	A	X	X	X		X	X	X		X	X
	B	X		X		X	X	X		X	
Products or services	C	X	X	X		X		X			X
	D	X	X		X				X		X
	E	X	X		X	X			X		X
	F		X		X	X					X
	G	X	X	X	X						
	H	X	X	X	X	X					
	I		X	X	X	X					

Figure 2.3.1.3-2 Example of a product family matrix.

Those products or services that share a large number of processes, steps, and equipment are grouped together into a value stream.

Current State

The value stream map can be considered a flowchart on steroids. While a flowchart is a simple visualization of a process, the value stream map is a bigger picture of the flow of a given product/service throughout the entire organization. Before beginning to map the process, it is important to plan how the process will be mapped. The following are considerations for value stream mapping:

1. Collect information while walking the value stream. Common practice is to use a cross-functional team of individuals who operate within the value stream, including the value stream owner and supporting functions at various levels. Each individual should carry an A3-sized piece of paper and document the value stream and information while walking the product/service flow and information flow, from beginning to end of the value stream.

2. It is common practice to begin at the shipping end of the value stream, closest to the customer. This helps keep a customer focus throughout the entire value stream.

3. Obtain all information directly from the value stream through observations, time study, inventory counting, and so on. Bring a stopwatch and physically count work-in-process (WIP). Do not rely on standard times and inventory levels established for the existing financial system, as this information is typically inaccurate.

4. Draw the value stream manually during the mapping exercise. The team does not need to waste time while one plots on a computer and everyone else waits. Each person draws the value stream at the value stream. It is common practice to use butcher paper, markers, and sticky notes on a wall for the entire team to participate in constructing the value stream for discussion and clarifications. Things can sometimes be overlooked by a team, but a number of individuals performing the same task will likely catch information missed by a group.

The common mapping format is for material flow on the bottom from left to right and information flow at the top from right to left (Figure 2.3.1.3-3).

The following are examples of information commonly gathered during the value stream mapping of the current state:

*   Cycle time
*   Changeover time
*   Number of people
*   Uptime/Downtime
*   WIP

- Inventory
- Packaging size
- Scrap/Defect rate
- Total operating time (minus breaks)
- Value-added time vs. non-value-added time
- Lead time
- Number of changeovers

A number of these pieces of information (Figures 2.3.1.3-4 and 2.3.1.3-5) are metrics associated with lean. Specific definitions can be found in the glossary or in the representative areas of this book.

Future State

With the current state of the value stream now mapped, it is time to look at what improvements are needed. Therefore, the lean value stream needs to be

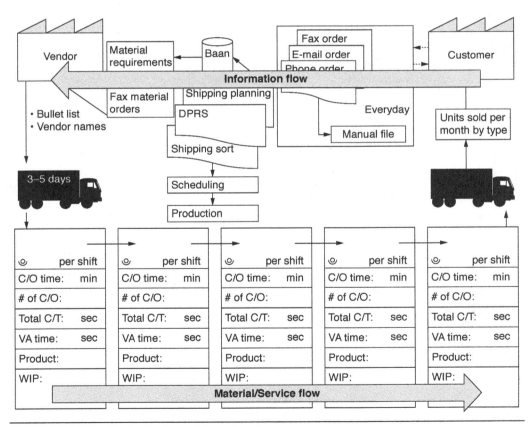

Figure 2.3.1.3-3 Basic structure of the value stream map.

2.3.1.3

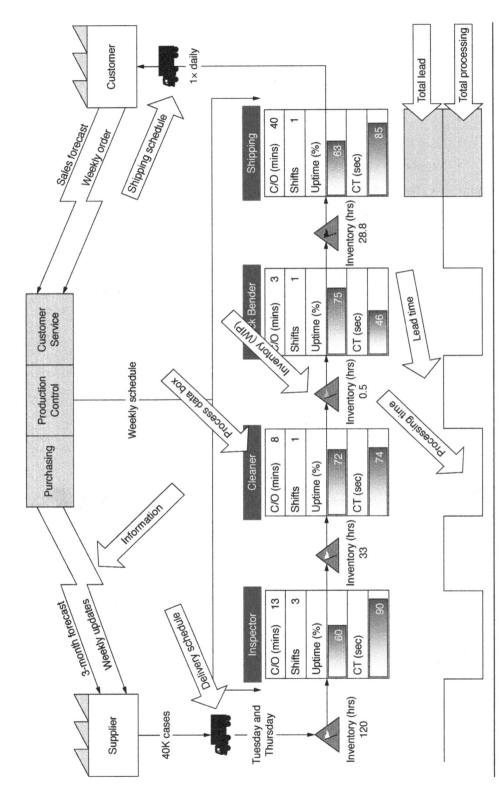

Figure 2.3.1.3-4 Value stream map components.

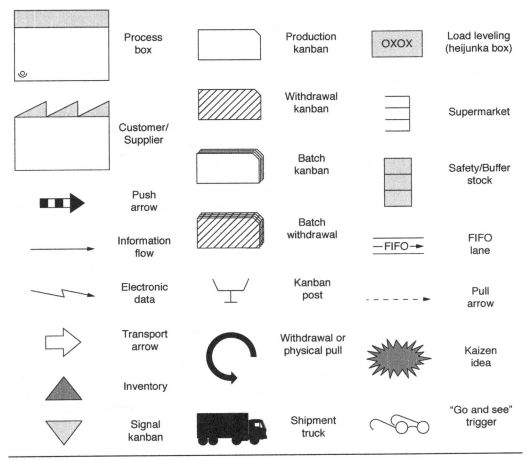

Figure 2.3.1.3-5 Common value stream mapping icons.

understood. Rother and Shook (2009, 38–48) offer the following seven guidelines in *Learning to See*:

1. Produce to the takt time

2. Create continuous flow wherever possible

3. Use supermarket pull systems to control production where continuous flow does not extend upstream

4. Send the customer schedule to only one production process (the pacemaker process)

5. Level the product/service mix evenly over time at the pacemaker process

6. Level the production volume by creating an "initial pull," releasing and withdrawing small, consistent increments of work at the pacemaker process

7. Develop the ability to make "every part every day" in processes upstream of the pacemaker process

The intent is to brainstorm ideas for improving the current-state value stream and then reconstruct the value stream with the improvements in place (i.e., the future-state value stream map).

Establish and Implement a Plan

Considering that some value streams are complex and large, Rother and Shook (2009) suggest breaking down the value stream into smaller, more manageable loops. Once the loops are identified, start looking at each loop and create an action plan (i.e., countermeasures) to reach the future-state value stream goal. It is also suggested that these plans be reviewed and revised yearly. Reconstruction of the current-state value stream map may be triggered when most of the countermeasures have been implemented. As a rule of thumb, a new current-state value stream map should be created when about 80% of the improvements (countermeasures) have been implemented.

In addition to the plan, value stream metrics should be established and monitored to verify performance improvement of the value stream. Rother and Shook (2009, 89) suggest that the measures adhere to the following principles:

1. Encourage desired behavior by those performing the work (adding the value)

2. Provide information to management to make decisions

3. Principle 1 takes precedence over principle 2

Keep value stream mapping in perspective; it is simply a tool to visually show the current flow of product/service and information in the organization and to guide everyone in the organization through the analysis of the process to improve the flows and design improved value streams.

2.3.1.4. Takt Time Analysis

Takt is the German word for "pace" or "rhythm," like the beat an orchestra conductor uses to regulate the speed of the musicians' playing. Takt time, often referred to by lean practitioners as the heartbeat of the process, is a measure of customer demand (see Section 4.3.2.1 for more detail on the calculation of takt time). Takt time is calculated as:

$$\text{Takt time} = \frac{\text{Available work time}}{\text{Customer demand}} \quad \text{(over a given period of time)}$$

Takt time predates the theory of constraints and was developed as a manufacturing flow tool in the 1930s and adapted by Toyota as a manufacturing management tool in the 1950s. The primary purpose of takt time is to serve as a management tool to indicate, at a glance, whether the value stream or process is meeting customer demand at any given time. It also serves as a tool to align upstream processes with downstream processes in a value stream with the customer demand requirements.

The intent of takt time analysis is to take a good look at an organization's products or services through the eyes of the customer (i.e., customer demand rate). The idea is to match the value stream's process time (cycle time) with takt time (or customer demand) as closely as possible.

The analysis is performed by comparing various segments of the value stream and organization with takt time and identifying areas of focus for optimization to takt time. Takt times of individual products, services, and processes can be compared to identify issues with production leveling, load leveling, and various forms of waste. Figure 2.3.1.4-1 is an example of takt time analysis by processes in a value stream. Process C needs to make countermeasures in order to reduce cycle time and meet takt time, and Processes A and B may be combined to reduce the risk of overproduction. Table 2.3.1.4-1 is an example of a takt time analysis by service type to identify areas for production leveling in a mixed model production schedule.

The purpose of performing a takt time analysis is to balance the work within a process, or line balancing. Line balancing is used to ensure continuous work flow through the process. Originally, line balancing terminology was used, as lean was focused on manufacturing environments that had production lines. As lean grew beyond manufacturing, the use of the line balance was applied to service processes. In short, the goal of line balancing is to ensure that the workload through a process is balanced, with faster steps "feeding" or being "fed" by slower processes—eliminating backups and excess inventory.

Although line balancing can be performed independently, combining it with other lean tools, like takt time analysis, process flow, and value stream mapping, provides the best benefit. To perform line balancing, one must understand the total

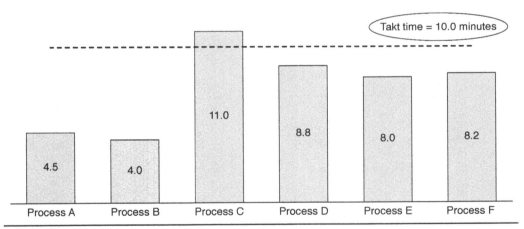

Figure 2.3.1.4-1 Takt time analysis of processes in a value stream.

Table 2.3.1.4-1 Takt time analysis of services in an organization.

Service type	Takt time (minutes)	Cycle time (minutes)
Service A	18	13
Service B	20	10
Service C	6	5
Service D	12	3
Service E	3	4

time each process step takes. Total time for each step should include the time from when the "product" reaches that step to the time it leaves that process step. This can be a manufacturing process step (e.g., component placement) or a service process step (e.g., hotel check-in). Since total time includes waste (muda) like waiting, as noted earlier, the partnering of load leveling with other lean tools eliminates waste within the overall process and within each individual process step.

A quick line balancing assessment was performed on a process with five steps, as shown in Figure 2.3.1.4-2. This figure shows the original process and the times (measured through observation using a stopwatch) to perform each step within the process. Figure 2.3.1.4-3 shows the same assessment in bar chart format.

The organization decided to increase throughput, so it added a second station for process step 3, allowing two products to be produced in 30 minutes. This can be accomplished because process steps 1, 2, 4, and 5 take five minutes for processing. With the addition of a second process step 3, each one receives an input and provides an output every 10 minutes. Figure 2.3.1.4-4 shows the results of the line

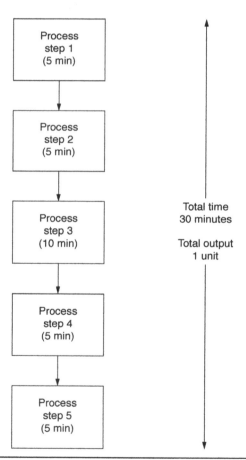

Figure 2.3.1.4–2   Line balancing example: current state.

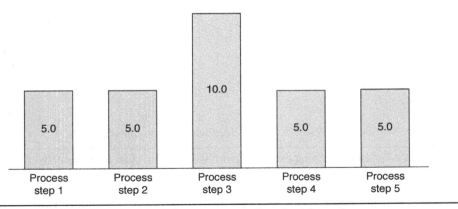

Figure 2.3.1.4-3   Line balancing example: current state (bar chart format).

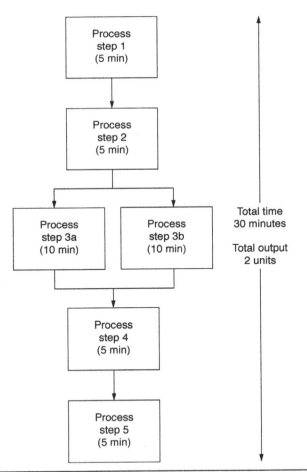

Figure 2.3.1.4-4   Line balancing example: future state option 1.

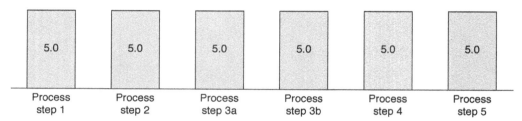

Note: Process step 3 time was divided by the number of operators to equal 5 minutes.

Figure 2.3.1.4-5 Line balancing example: future state option 1 (bar chart format).

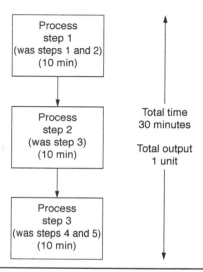

Figure 2.3.1.4-6 Line balancing example: future state option 2.

balancing analysis and the associated process changes. Figure 2.3.1.4-5 shows the same results in bar chart format.

In the next example, the organization decided to keep output levels the same but reduce the area (footprint) and the number of personnel needed to process the work in order to allow the personnel to do other work. To accomplish this goal, the organization combined steps 1 and 2 and steps 4 and 5; thus, all process steps now take 10 minutes. This move reduced the steps from five to three, reduced work-in-process, and reduced the area footprint (reduction of input and output shelving, operation process space, etc.). Figure 2.3.1.4-6 shows the result. Figure 2.3.1.4-7 shows the same results in bar chart format.

Line balancing analysis can be performed with more detail by adding in takt time, number of operators, and waste (or non-value-added work content). Figure 2.3.1.4-8 is an example of the original process with the detail added to the bar chart.

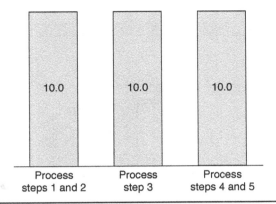

Figure 2.3.1.4-7   Line balancing example: future state option 2 (bar chart format).

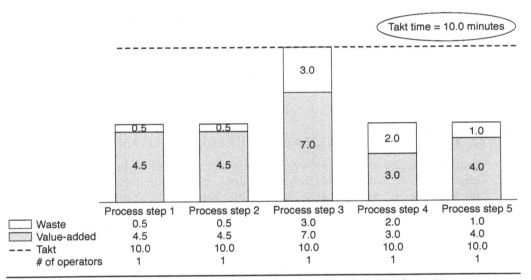

Figure 2.3.1.4-8   Line balancing example: current state (modified bar chart format).

The ideal state for a level loaded process is one in which all processes are as close to takt time as possible, with little or no waste time, and stacked in a sequence where the downstream process is slightly faster than the process preceding it (Figure 2.3.1.4-9). This scenario creates a natural pull where the downstream process must pull from the upstream processes.

Line balancing analysis helps improve work flow. Depending on the organizational goals, line balancing can reduce the process footprint and in-process work, free up personnel (see Figure 2.3.1.4-6), and increase output (see Figure 2.3.1.4-4). Line balancing analysis is performed through observation, motion studies, or process flow analysis. While a powerful tool on its own, load leveling can be combined with other lean tools to have a greater impact on reducing waste (muda).

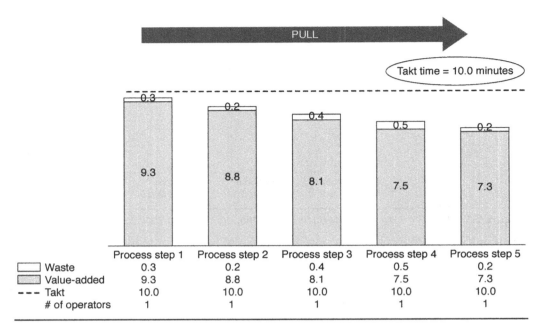

Figure 2.3.1.4-9 Line balancing example: ideal state (modified bar chart format).

2.3.2. DATA COLLECTION AND PRESENTATION

Proper organization of the data is critical if they are to be helpful in continuous improvement. Rational subgrouping allows the sample data to be collected and presented in a manner that will reveal the sources of variation. Data from each subgroup need to be collected from a small area so that homogenous conditions reside within the subgroup. Data collected and presented in such a manner can potentially reveal variations from two sources: within subgroup and across subgroup. We would like to treat the within-subgroup variation as noise so that we can look for any signals between subgroups over time.

Example: A department has five punch presses, each of which has five cavities, that make Product A. Data can be collected in any of the following ways:

1. Select one sample from each press on the hour to create a subgroup size of five

2. Select five samples (one from each cavity) within each press

3. Select five samples within each cavity in each press

If method one is chosen, we are looking at the variation of the five presses from one hour to the next. If method two is chosen, we are looking at the variation within each press. If method three is chosen, we are looking at the variation within each cavity of a press. Proper subgrouping of the data is critical to process improvement efforts. When subgroups are not rationally created, useful information may not be obtained.

A variety of basic statistical tools are available to help in understanding the process, where problems are occurring, and which problems are trivial and which are significant. Histograms, Pareto charts, and check sheets are some basic tools that can be used by any team member to better understand what is occurring within a process.

2.3.2.1. Histograms

A *histogram* is a bar graph that provides a picture of the shape and spread of the data gathered by showing the frequency of the measurements or occurrences. A histogram can be constructed whenever quantitative (continuous) data or qualitative (categorical) data are involved. The measurement scales are shown on the *x* axis, and the frequency in each interval is shown on the *y* axis. The height of the bars in each interval is represented by the frequency of observations within that interval.

Histogram Statistics

A histogram and accompanying data allow for the following statistics to be calculated:

- *Mean:* The arithmetic average of all the values. This is the sum of all the data in the data set divided by the number of observations in the data set.

- *Minimum:* The smallest number in the data set.

- *Maximum:* The biggest number in the data set.

- *Standard deviation:* The amount of variation or dispersion there is from the "average." A small standard deviation value indicates that data are clustered together, while a large value indicates that data are spread apart.

- *Bin width:* The *x* axis distance between the left and right edges of each bin in the histogram.

- *Number of classes:* The number of bins in the histogram.

- *Skewness:* Is the histogram symmetrical? If so, skewness is zero. If the left-hand tail is longer, skewness is negative. If the right-hand tail is longer, skewness is positive.

- *Kurtosis:* A measure of the peak of a distribution. The standard normal curve has a kurtosis of zero. Positive kurtosis indicates a "peaked" distribution, and negative kurtosis indicates a "flat" distribution.

Histogram Interpretation

The shape of a histogram will vary depending on the choice of the size of the intervals. Once constructed, the histogram will show the pattern of variation in the data. Histograms show shape, skewness, and modes.

Shape

The shape of the distribution conveys important information such as the probability distribution of the data. The normal curve (Figure 2.3.2.1-1), with its bell shape, means the data collected from the process under study have a normal distribution,

2.3.2.1

2.3.2.1

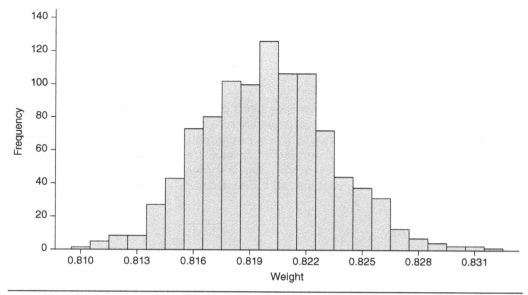

Figure 2.3.2.1-1 Histogram with a normal distribution.

which is the desired shape. If we know that the data fit into the normal distribution, we can use the probability tables from the standard normal distribution to make predictions about the data.

Symmetry (Skewness)

The skewed curve tells us that the distribution is not symmetrical. Positive skewed, or right skewed, data are so named because the "tail" of the distribution points to the right, while with negative skewed data, the distribution's tail points to the left (Figure 2.3.2.1-2). Real estate prices are usually skewed, since you may have a number of homes sold below or above the average selling price in a suburb. It is for this reason that the median statistic would be a better predictor than the mean.

Modes

The *mode* is the value that occurs most frequently in a set of data. It is found by simply counting the number of times each value occurs in a data set. A distribution with one such high point, such as a normal distribution, is called unimodal. A distribution that has two modes is called bimodal (Figure 2.3.2.1-3) and indicates that one may have collected data from a mixed population. For example, data could have been collected from two different machines making the same product. If this is the case, data need to be collected on each of the machines separately. Having more than two modes means that the distribution is multimodal and that stratification of the data might be a probable cause.

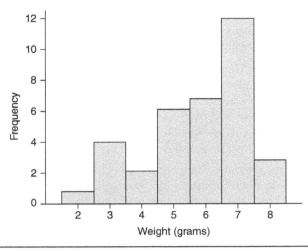

Figure 2.3.2.1-2 Histogram with negatively skewed data.

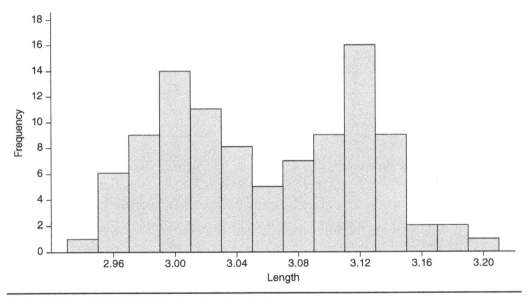

Figure 2.3.2.1-3 Histogram with a bimodal distribution.

Constructing a Histogram

The following steps are involved in constructing a histogram:

1. Identify a characteristic of a product for which data need to be collected. For example, consider the volume of a bottle of detergent.

2. Determine the sample size, ideally about 100 data points or 100 bottles.

3. Select the samples and record the measurement value. In this case, the volume of detergent in each bottle sampled is recorded. Record the value on a tabular sheet in time order.

2.3.2.1

4. Find the range of the data set. This is done by studying the tabular sheet to find the highest and lowest volumes. If the heaviest volume is 156.3 oz and the lowest is 150 oz, then the range is 6.3 oz.

5. Decide on how many bins you will need for your histogram. Too few or too many will make interpretation of the data difficult. For continuous data as in the example, it often depends on the precision of the measurement instrument and of the equipment. For categorical data, it is simply the number of categories being used. In this example, seven bins should be used since the range is 6.3.

6. For continuous data, determine the width of each bin. Make sure the numbers do not overlap. In this example, the bins will have increments of 0.9 oz. Since the lowest value is 150 oz, the widths of the bins are as follows:

Bin size	Count
150–150.9	1111
151–151.9	1111111111
152–152.9	111111111111111111
153–153.9	1111111111111111111111111111111111111
154–154.9	111111111111111111
155–155.9	11111111111
156–156.9	11111

7. Post the data on the check sheet. Each value recorded on the tabular sheet becomes a talley mark on the check sheet.

8. Construct the histogram by using the information on the check sheet.

9. Record other information in the legend such as shift, operator, machine, and product name.

10. Calculate the histogram statistics from the 100 values in the data set.

11. Interpret the shape, symmetry, and mode of the histogram.

2.3.2.2. Pareto Charts

Italian economist Vilfredo Pareto was interested in finding out the distribution of wealth in his country. Accordingly, he collected data and showed that the wealth was unevenly distributed, with about 80% of the wealth in the hands of about 20% of the people. Dr. Joseph Juran applied the same principle to business situations, and it became known as the Pareto principle. The Pareto principle states that a few errors or defects account for most of the problems—or 80% of the effects are the result of 20% of the causes—and is the basis for the Pareto chart. The Pareto principle is also known as the 80/20 rule or the law of the vital few. The significance of the Pareto principle is that it helps an organization specify causes of most of the process issues, or the vital few.

A visual representation of the Pareto principle, the *Pareto chart* is a simple graphical technique for rank-ordering data from the most important to the least important. Data are displayed in a format to compare the relative significance of events, costs, or any other measure. By distinguishing the significant errors and defects from those of lesser importance, organizations can leverage maximum improvement by focusing attention on a few of the causes rather than all of the causes.

It is a tool commonly used in problem solving. In the "Define" phase of the DMAIC structure, it can be used to identify those significant few problems so people can target them for process improvement and narrow the scope of the problem to focus the team. In the "Measure" phase of the DMAIC structure, it can be used as a drill-down tool to get to the most likely cause of a problem, to provide a basis for action.

As organizations conduct their business, data can be generated and collected from many sources, such as errors, defects, lead time, customer complaints, causes for rework, scrap, customer returns, and field failures. A common example is where 80% of sales volume or sales revenue comes from 20% of the customers. Capturing data on these measures of an organization's processes and creating a Pareto chart can help identify different classes or types of problems. It also graphically displays the results so that the significant few problems emerge from the general background and enable sound business decisions.

Constructing a Pareto Chart

Following are common steps for constructing a Pareto chart:

1. Decide on what data to collect—for example, a quality measure of a process such as customer returns, scrap, or lead times or a productivity/ efficiency measure such as downtime causes.

2. Create a preliminary list of categories. For example, if selecting customer returns, the category may be "Reason for customer return." If selecting scrap or rework/reprocessing, the category may be "Cause for scrap or rework/reprocessing."

3. Decide on a time frame for data collection. Should it be one year, six months, or some other measure? Decide who will collect the data and how the data will be collected. If needed, a check sheet can be created to capture the raw data and the source of data identified.

4. Collect the data for the desired time frame. Tally the occurrences in each problem category.

5. Create a table to calculate the values for the Pareto chart using the data (Table 2.3.2.2-1).

6. Enter the different categories in the first column.

7. Enter the frequency of occurrence against that category in the second column.

2.3.2.2

Table 2.3.2.2-1   Example of a Pareto data table.

Category	Frequency of occurrence (high to low)	Individual percentage	Cumulative percentage
Grand total			

Table 2.3.2.2-2   Example of a Pareto data table.

Accidents by department	Frequency of occurrence (high to low)	Individual percentage	Cumulative percentage
Plating	245	27.1	27.1
Heat-treat	196	21.7	48.8
Assembly	160	17.7	66.6
Grinding	127	14.1	80.6
Testing	82	9.1	89.7
Stockroom	50	5.5	95.2
Receiving	31	3.4	98.7
Accounting	12	1.3	100.0
Grand total	**903**		**100.0**

8. Once the first two columns are completed as shown in Table 2.3.2.2-2, compute the grand totals. The grand total equals the sum of the frequency of occurrence in all the categories. Enter this value at the bottom of column two.

9. Compute the individual percentage for each category. Individual percentage equals the frequency of occurrence divided by the grand total and multiplied by 100. Enter this value against each category in column three. This value represents the individual percentage contribution of that category to all the problems.

10. Calculate the cumulative percentage. The cumulative percentage for the first category is the same as the individual percentage. The cumulative percentage for the second category is the total of the individual percentages for the first two categories, and so on. Once the cumulative percentage has been computed, the Pareto chart can be drawn.

11. Draw a horizontal *x* axis and two vertical *y* axes. Mark the left *y* axis in increments from 0 to the grand total and label the axis "Frequency." Mark the right *y* axis in increments from 0 to 100 and label the axis "Percent."

12. Construct the Pareto chart starting on the left with the highest-frequency category and ending with the lowest frequency. The height of each bar should correspond to the frequency of occurrences for that category.

13. Label the bars with the category name under the horizontal *x* axis.

14. Place a dot in the chart that corresponds to the cumulative percentage value shown on the right axis for each of the categories. Connect the dots with a line showing the cumulative percentage total reached with the addition of each problem category. The line should end at the 100% mark on the right axis.

15. Title the chart and include a brief synopsis of the data collection and source data.

Example of a Pareto Chart

A company collected data on the number of accidents in the various departments for a one year period (Figure 2.3.2.2-1).

The Pareto chart shows that the plating department has the highest number of accidents, with an individual contribution of 27.1%. Plating, heat-treat, assembly, and grinding combined contribute to 80.6% of the accidents.

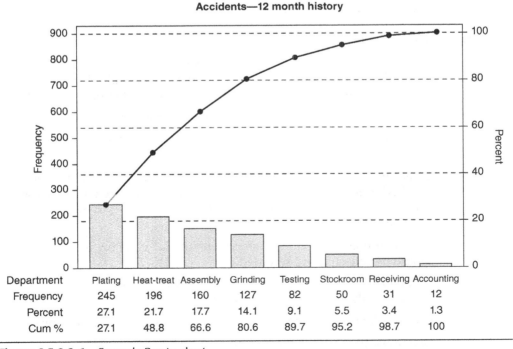

Department	Plating	Heat-treat	Assembly	Grinding	Testing	Stockroom	Receiving	Accounting
Frequency	245	196	160	127	82	50	31	12
Percent	27.1	21.7	17.7	14.1	9.1	5.5	3.4	1.3
Cum %	27.1	48.8	66.6	80.6	89.7	95.2	98.7	100

Figure 2.3.2.2-1 Example Pareto chart.

2.3.2.3. Check Sheets

Data can be collected in many ways. One method is the use of check sheets. Check sheets allow people to collect and record data on a real-time basis at the location of the data source. The check sheet is typically used for data on locations. This can be anything from defect locations on a product to injuries on a body location to locations in a facility where injuries or other events occur. Like the Pareto chart, the check sheet attempts to narrow down occurrences or root causes to the vital few areas of needed focus.

In order to collect data, a check sheet needs to be set up. To set up a check sheet you must decide on the type of data you want to collect and the time frame required for collecting the data. It captures the data at the source and is an input to process improvement tools such as Pareto charts and histograms.

Data are recorded on a check sheet by placing a tick mark; for example, "III" or "XXX" indicates three instances for that location during the observation. Once the check sheet is completed, it is read by observing the number of tick marks on the sheet against each location.

Check sheets can be used for any of the following:

- To categorize observations. Observations can be categorized and the frequency of occurrence captured under each category.

- To show the location of an occurrence—such as a measles chart. This type of check sheet is known as a pictogram (see Section 2.3.4.2, "Concentration Diagrams").

- To record inspection data. The check sheet is segmented into measurement intervals and the actual measurements are recorded as tick marks in the appropriate interval.

Constructing a Check Sheet

1. Decide what data to collect and why they need to be collected. What question will be answered by collecting these data? Who will collect the data? Select the appropriate data to be collected that will address the purpose.

2. Decide on the frequency, timing, and location for collecting the data.

3. Construct a form to collect the appropriate data. A table or picture may be used.

4. Create an operational definition for the data to be collected. In other words, define the categories, defect types, locations, and so on, that will help the person gathering the data determine the category where a tick mark should be placed.

5. Provide training to the person recording the data on how the data should be collected and recorded.

6. Let people know what is going on, and how the data will be used, in the area where the data collection is taking place.

7. Keep the data honest; do not discard data that disagree with the hypothesis.

8. Determine how the data will be analyzed.

9. Do not punish or blame people for what the data reveal. If you penalize individuals, subsequent data collection efforts may not be successful.

Example of a Check Sheet

A high school wanted to collect data on errors that occur on an essay test administered to students. A check sheet was constructed and data gathered (Table 2.3.2.3-1).

Example of a Pictogram (Concentration Diagram)

A car service center identified the location of rust on car doors by having a picture of the car door and marking the location of the rust for every car it serviced. "X" marks the location of the rust. At the end of the study, the pictogram identified areas where the service center will have to provide rust prevention. The pictogram (Figure 2.3.2.3-1) indicates that rust on the bottom of the door is a problem. There is no rust on the other areas of the car door.

Histograms, Pareto charts, and check sheets are all tools utilized in root cause problem solving. Each of these tools can be used for defining an issue or determining the significant root causes of a particular problem.

2.3.2.3

Table 2.3.2.3-1   Example of a check sheet for errors on an essay test.

Error	April				Total
	Week 1	Week 2	Week 3	Week 4	
Spelling	11	1111	1111111	11	15
Punctuation	1111111	111	111	111	16
Grammar	11111	111111	111111	111111	23
Formatting	111	111	111	111	12
Font	1	11	1111	1	8
Total	18	18	23	15	74

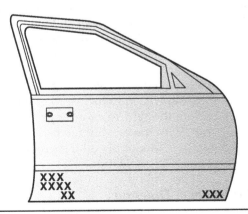

Figure 2.3.2.3-1   Example of a check sheet (pictogram) of rust location occurrences on a car door at a service center.

2.3.3. IDENTIFY ROOT CAUSE

What is often called a problem is really only the "failure mode" or a symptom of a failure of an output to a process. This manifests itself in a product or service not meeting requirements. The effect of this failure, if left unresolved, can have unintended consequences and carries with it an inherent risk to the organization. Traditionally, the output of a process is checked to determine whether it meets requirements. However, the true (root) cause lies in the inputs to the process or the design of the process. If the inputs are known to have a significant effect on the output, it will be easy to proactively control the input so that the output will always meet requirements. Also, if the design of the process is significantly impacting the output, the process can be redesigned or a poka-yoke can be implemented to prevent an issue from occurring.

The root cause of a problem, therefore, lies in the input(s) and process itself. Efficiently identifying the root cause can only be done in a structured and systematic manner, using various tools and techniques. A variety of industries, such as manufacturing, medical devices, pharmaceuticals, hospitals, transportation, and banking, perform root cause analysis to drive improvement efforts.

Fixing audit noncompliances also requires identifying the root cause, creating an action plan to address the root cause, implementing the plan, and effectively closing out the corrective action or preventive action request. Root cause analysis digs below the surface, looking beyond the symptoms to find the root cause that led to the undesired effect. Once the root cause has been identified, putting in the proper controls ensures that the problem will not reoccur.

2.3.3.1. Cause and Effect Diagrams (Fishbone)

Causes are the conditions that create the failure mode or problem. The failure mode manifests itself as an effect that is undesirable. Failure modes commonly have more than one potential root cause. Therefore, it is essential to identify all the potential root causes for a particular failure mode in order to collect more data and drive to the root cause for the particular issue. A cause-and-effect (CE) diagram is a tool used to identify the many potential causes for an effect, or the problem.

Professor Kaoru Ishikawa is the father of the CE diagram. He first used it in the shipyards to show the relationship of causes to a problem or event. The CE diagram has since become a basic quality tool used in conjunction with other analytical tools to solve problems.

CE diagrams are also called Ishikawa diagrams or fishbone diagrams because the resultant causes are shown on branches that, when completed, resemble the skeleton of a fish. Factors thought to cause a problem or results in an event are grouped into categories, with the head of the fish depicting the problem or event. The goal of a CE diagram is to identify all the probable causes and then select the most likely ones for further investigation.

Constructing a CE (Fishbone) Diagram

1. Create a team of individuals who are familiar with the process, problem, and other functions (e.g., engineering and maintenance if equipment related).

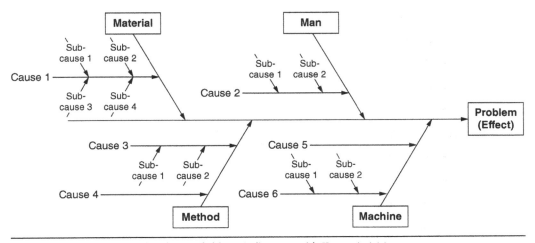

Figure 2.3.3.1-1   Example of a CE (fishbone) diagram with Toyota's 4 Ms.

2. Define the problem (effect). Place the effect in the extreme right-hand corner and draw an arrow with the head pointing to the effect.

3. Brainstorm and list all the possible causes that may contribute to the problem.

4. Group the causes into categories and give each category a name.

5. Begin constructing the diagram by drawing lines, or the bones of the fish. Title the bones with the names of the categories.

6. Assign the group of causes that you have brainstormed and position these to feed into the related category. The completed diagram is known as the CE (fishbone) diagram (Figure 2.3.3.1-1).

7. Circle any potential root causes on the CE diagram. The team can then gather data to verify the most likely root cause(s).

While the standard structure of the diagram represents a fishbone, the number and types of categories to group the potential causes are unlimited. Toyota looks at processes in terms of the 4Ms:

- Man
- Machine
- Material
- Method

Variations to this include the addition of Measurement and Mother Nature for the 6Ms, and Management and Maintenance for the 8Ms. Service industries typically use some variation of the 8Ps, or:

- Product (service)
- Place
- People

- Process
- Promotion
- Productivity
- Price
- Physical evidence

Or even the 4Ss:

- Suppliers
- Systems
- Surroundings
- Skills

The fishbone diagram is often used in conjunction with the 5-Whys. As potential causes are identified, the 5-Whys tool is used to drive to a deeper understanding of the cause and eventually reach the root cause.

2.3.3.2. 5-Whys

The 5-Whys method of analysis is used to arrive at the root causes of a problem. This is done by simply asking the question, "Why does this problem exist?" or "Why did this event occur?" five times and driving to a more detailed level with each "why" to arrive at the root cause of the problem. At this time, the questioning is stopped.

Some teams are unsure of when to stop, or they stop when they find a person is at fault and put in a fix saying "training" is needed. This is not usually correct, because more often than not the root cause lies with a system or process. In other words, something failed in the system or the process to allow the error to happen or be missed by the employee.

The process is called 5-Whys because one can usually arrive at the root cause by asking "why" about five times.

In the example shown in Table 2.3.3.2-1, "why?" needed to be asked only four times in order to arrive at the root cause. Also note that employees were not "retrained" but trained after a root cause was identified and corrected with a change in the system. The training only occurred for the system change and not prematurely as an employee error.

The 5-Whys analysis is a good tool for solving any process issue. The analysis has been used for determining root causes of low employee satisfaction, injuries, information technology glitches, low customer satisfaction, product defects, and process inefficiencies.

2.3.3.3. Failure Mode and Effects Analysis

The concept of failure mode and effects analysis (FMEA) has been practiced for a long time. The idea behind identifying the failure modes in the system, design, and process was first used by the US military in the 1940s with changes on how the overall risks are weighted, categorized, and calculated. The Military Standard MIL-STD-1629A (now obsolete) was a formal document used by the aerospace and defense industries to conduct an FMEA.

Table 2.3.3.2-1 Example of 5-Whys.

Why	Level of problem	Corresponding level of countermeasure
Original problem	Centrality of the keyway was out of specification	Rework and correct centrality issue
Why was it out of specification?	Because the incorrect grinding wheel was used	Replace with correct grinding wheel
Why was the incorrect grinding wheel installed?	Because that was the grinding wheel issued by the stockroom to the setup person for installation	*Train employees on modified system*
Why did the stockroom issue the incorrect grinding wheel?	Because the incorrect grinding wheel was stored in the location assigned by the computer system for the correct grinding wheel	
Why was the incorrect grinding wheel in the location intended for the correct grinding wheel?	Because an experimental wheel from an offshore vendor was being tested as a less expensive alternative, and the computer system assigned it to the same location based on the component part number	Assign a separate location for experimental parts in the system that is not based on component part numbers

In 1993, Chrysler, Ford, and General Motors, with input from several technical professionals, created a document that included the FMEA that encompassed Design FMEAs and Process FMEAs. This document became part of the QS9000, now TS 16949, standard for expectations from automotive-tier-level suppliers. This document, currently in its third edition, has been revised with significant input from the SAEJ1739 workgroup and other automotive products–related organizations.

AIAG (2001) describes an FMEA as a systematic group of activities intended to:

- Recognize and evaluate the potential failure of a product/process and the effects of that failure,

- Identify actions that could eliminate or reduce the chance of the potential failure occurring, and

- Document the entire process.

The purpose of an FMEA is to:

- Understand the opportunity for failure and impact of risks in a product or process design,

- Prioritize the risk,

- And take actions to eliminate or reduce the impact of risks.

The FMEA is a preventive tool typically used at the front end of new product or process development. Successful product/process development requires anticipating the failure mode and taking actions to eliminate or reduce failure during deployment and the life cycle. The product/process design team needs to periodically review and update the failure modes. During the early stages of product/process development, the team identifies the risk using existing data from similar processes, knowledge, and experience. As the product/process is deployed, new unforeseen risks and failures may show up. Hence, reviewing the FMEA on a continual basis ensures sustainable success. The FMEA is a good starting point for solving issues with a current product, service, or process.

The FMEA needs to be formally documented and revision controlled and should be part of the existing quality management system (QMS). In a well-designed QMS, the FMEA is linked to quality function deployment (QFD) in the design and process Houses of Quality and linked to a control plan in the production House of Quality (see Section 2.3.5.2, "Quality Function Deployment").

The FMEA is not just confined to manufacturing applications. It has been successfully used in service/transactional processes, software devolvement, and the medical field.

Although, in principle, the FMEA is conducted to address the potential failures in product design and process design, it has been identified separately as Design FMEA and Process FMEA.

The primary objective of Design FMEA is to uncover potential failures associated with the product that could cause the following:

- Product malfunctions resulting in safety and regulatory violations

- Shortened product life resulting in economic loss to the organization or society

The Design FMEA should be created at the planning stage; developed at the design stage; and reviewed at the design, qualification, and limited production stages before the final document is released.

The primary objective of the Process FMEA is to uncover potential failures associated with the process that could cause the following:

- Reduced product quality resulting in low process yield

- Reduced process reliability resulting in customer dissatisfaction

- Safety or environmental hazards resulting in industrial/government violations

Constructing an FMEA

Assemble a cross-functional team of people with diverse knowledge about the process, product, service, and customer needs. Functions often included are design, engineering, manufacturing, quality, testing, reliability, maintenance, purchasing (and suppliers), sales, marketing (and customers), and customer service. It is important to have a process expert's presence in Design FMEA as well as design experts in Process FMEA. The team is typically 5 to 7 individuals, for effective interaction. If additional experts are needed to provide input on safety, regulatory, and legal issues, an extended team can be created.

Identify the scope of the FMEA. Is it for concept, system, design, process, or service? What are the boundaries? How detailed should it be? After answering these first questions, the team will be ready to construct the FMEA. Constructing the FMEA generally follows the steps identified in Table 2.3.3.3-1.

Table 2.3.3.3-1 Steps to construct an FMEA.

Step	Design FMEA	Process FMEA
Review the design/process	Use a schematics diagram and/or a functional block diagram to identify each of the main components of the design and determine the function or functions of those components and the interfaces between them. Make sure all components defined in the scope of the Design FMEA are reviewed. Some components may have more than one function.	Use flowcharts to identify the scope and to make sure every team member understands it in detail. It is also recommended that the team perform a walkthrough of the process and understand the process steps firsthand.
Brainstorm potential failure modes	A potential failure mode represents any manner in which the product component could fail to perform its intended function or functions.	A potential failure mode represents any manner in which the process step could fail to perform its intended function or functions.
List potential effects of failure	Both the potential effects at interim (local) and the end effects are identified. The effect is the ability of the component to perform its intended function due to the failure mode.	Both the potential effects at interim (local) and the end effects are identified. The effect is the impact on the process outcome and product quality due to the failure mode.
Assign severity rating (S)	The severity rating corresponds to each effect the failure mode can cause. Typically the scale is 1–10, although other scales can be defined. Higher severity is rated at the upper end of the scale, and lower severity at the low end of the scale.	
List potential causes	For every failure mode, list possible cause(s). Use team tools like brainstorming, cause and effect, multivoting, 5-Whys, etc. Where applicable, use pilot experiment, past data, and expert knowledge.	
Assign occurrence rating (O)	The occurrence rating corresponds to the likelihood that the cause will occur or the frequency with which the cause will occur. Typically the scale is 1–10. Higher occurrence is rated at the upper end of the scale, and lower occurrence at the low end of the scale.	
Identify current controls	For each cause, current process controls are identified. Controls can be of different types. They may detect the failure or prevent the failure from happening. The controls range anywhere from work instructions to AQL sampling, statistical process control, alarms, mistake-proofing fixture, etc.	
Assign detection rating (D)	The detection rating corresponds to the ability to detect the occurrence of the failure mode. Typically the scale is 1–10. Higher detect ability is rated at the low end of the scale, and lower detect ability at the high end of the scale.	

(continued)

2.3.3.3

Table 2.3.3.3-1   Steps to construct an FMEA. *(continued)*

Step	Design FMEA	Process FMEA
Calculate risk priority number (RPN)	Product of severity (S), occurrence (O), and detection (D). $$S \times O \times D = RPN$$ Criticality is also important in some industries. Severity × Occurrence = Criticality	
Develop action plan	Actual plan may contain tasks to improve the current controls or reduce the frequency for the occurrence of the cause. In order to reduce the severity, the team may have to consider redesigning the product or process. Assign realistic completion date, responsibility for tasks.	
Take action	Most FMEAs fall apart during this step due to lack of management support, conflicting priorities, lack of resources, and lack of team leadership. The actions have to be implemented and results should be validated. Building a prototype and testing the action or piloting the process on a small scale before mass producing are recommended.	
Recalculate the RPN	After all actions have been taken, bring the team back and objectively recalculate the RPN. Use objective evidence like customer feedback, reliability test, warranty return rate, yield tracking, etc., to reassess the score.	
Periodically review and update new risks	Carefully evaluate the customer feedback, warranty analysis, internal nonconformance report, ongoing reliability test reports, etc., to explore new risks and update the FMEA as needed. Keep the FMEA as a living document.	

Successful FMEA implementation requires a leadership and management commitment. Once the initial risk priority number (RPN) scores are tabulated, the team may decide on a cutoff score. For most organizations, a cutoff score is standardized. The cutoff score of one organization may not be directly applicable to another. Too low of a cutoff score can result in using many resources to eliminate or reduce several risks. Too high of a cutoff score can result in not addressing important risks. Management needs to review and agree on a score. Additionally, rating scales and cutoff scores for Design FMEAs and Process FMEAs may be different. Depending on the level of detail, an FMEA may be anywhere from a couple of pages to hundreds of pages. Once an initial FMEA has been constructed and mitigation has been determined for higher-risk items, the mitigations will be implemented. It is a good practice to revisit the FMEA and update it once the mitigation is completed to reevaluate the risk and verify all high-risk items are completed. Figure 2.3.3.3-1 provides a single page from an FMEA as an example with mitigation implemented.

2.3.4. PRESENTING VARIATION DATA

Variation is associated with muri (see Section 2.1.2.2), or the waste caused by variations. Variation is a critical measure of process behavior without which any judgment on how a process has performed over time and a prediction as to where the

FMEA type: Process/Equip.
Tracking no.: FMEA-P0256
FMEA date: 5/12/2012

Process Failure Mode and Effects Analysis

Description: CNC Center—machining operation for titanium screw

Entry no.	Process step or object name	Function	Failure mode	Cause	Effect	PSC	Current control (prevention)	Current control (detection)	Detection	Occurrence	Severity	RPN	Risk mitigation needed
134	CNC machining center	Machine parts from rod stock (main spindle, cut off, back spindle, face mill)	Does not machine parts from rod stock	Main chuck failure	Downtime (major)		Preventive maintenance	Operator detection @ CNC	5	1	3	15	
135				Back chuck failure	Downtime (major)		Preventive maintenance	Operator detection @ CNC	5	1	3	15	
136				Main spindle slide failure	Downtime (catastrophic)		Preventive maintenance	Operator detection @ CNC	5	1	5	25	
137				Spindle toggle failure	Downtime (catastrophic)			Operator detection @ CNC	5	1	5	25	Preventive maintenance
138				Program failure	Downtime (major)		Controlled program	Operator detection @ CNC	5	1	3	15	Operator verification during setup
140				CNC battery failure	Downtime (minor)		1) Spare parts (tool crib) 2) Preventive maintenance	1) Operator detection @ CNC 2) Machine alarm (CNC)	5	2	2	20	
141		Lubricate, remove chips, and cool work and tools during machining operation	MP system high pressure coolant failure	High pressure pump failure	Downtime (catastrophic)			1) Operator detection @ CNC 2) Machine alarm (CNC)	5	1	5	25	1) High pressure pump alarm (CNC) 2) Preventive maintenance
142				Operator technique error—no or low coolant level	Downtime (minor)			1) Operator detection @ CNC 2) Machine alarm (CNC)	5	2	2	20	1) Standard work 2) Shift check 3) Visual management at sight glass
143				Operator technique error—coolant at incorrect concentration	Downtime (minor)			1) Operator detection @ CNC 2) Machine alarm (CNC)	5	2	2	20	1) Standard work 2) Shift check 3) Fluid concentration matrix

Figure 2.3.3.3–1 Example of a process FMEA.

2.3.4

Table 2.3.4-1 Examples of various analysis tools compared with variation and audience types.

Type/Nature of variation	Statistical/Analytical/ Graphical tool	Target audience
Product measurements	Histogram, dot plots	Shop-floor employees, management
	Normal distribution curve, box plot	Technicians, Six Sigma Green Belts
	Normal probability plot, interval plot, stem and leaf charts	Six Sigma Green Belts, Black Belts
Process measurements	Run chart	Shop-floor employees, management
	Control charts—I-MR, X bar-R charts	Technicians, Six Sigma Green Belts
	Multivariate charts; advanced control charts—CUSUM, EWMA, T-Squared	Black Belts and Master Black Belts, statisticians
Components of variation	Pareto of % variation by variable	All
Equipment variation	Gage run chart, Gage repeatability and reproducibility chart	Six Sigma Green Belts, Black Belts

2.3.4.1

process is heading are meaningless. Variation can be measured in the process by performing repetitive measurements of the same product or process parameter or by taking periodic measurements of products coming off a manufacturing line or process parameter over time. Knowing variation can result in a better understanding of "precision" of the measurement equipment, inherent process variation (control limits in statistical process control charts), short- and long-term process capability, batch-to-batch material variation, and other components of variation. While measuring and analyzing variation is fundamental to process improvement, it is also important that the variation be presented in a way that the team members and management can understand and identify what and how to improve.

As Shewhart and Deming remind us, we need to recognize common cause variation from special cause variation. Without the right analysis and presentation, we may overreact and tamper with a process that is already stable. Table 2.3.4-1 provides examples of different analysis tools.

Successful lean implementation depends on understanding process variation. This understanding is key to monitoring the stability and predictability of a process. Without having the ability to predict the process's behavior, the organization will remain in reactive mode, correcting the issues and situations rather than proactively anticipating and preventing problems. Any waste reduction gained through traditional lean tools can be undone by not having a stable, predictable process.

2.3.4.1. Statistical Process Control Charts

Statistical process control (SPC) is a powerful tool for monitoring, studying, and understanding process behavior and improving performance over time. The tool uses probability concepts to identify and detect special causes responsible for impacting process stability. An SPC chart monitors both changes in variation and shift in

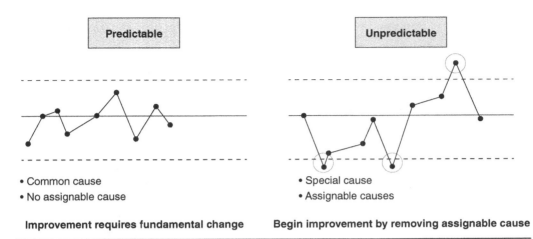

Figure 2.3.4.1-1   Common causes versus special causes.

average. Factors that cause variation in the process can be classified as common or special causes. Figure 2.3.4.1-1 provides a visual differentiation between common and special causes as seen on an SPC chart. SPC forms the foundation for estimating capability indices of the process in relation to whether it meets requirements.

Common causes are inherent to the process design. They are an effect of equipment capability, process capability, process recipes (equipment settings), natural lot-to-lot material variation, fixture variation, measurement system variation, and so on. Common cause variation can be reduced by process redesign or optimization techniques.

Special causes can be from an extended list of possible sources. Anything outside normal operating conditions can potentially be a special cause. A supplier that makes a process change that results in significantly different material properties is an example of a special cause situation. Training a new person at a drive-up window can be considered a special cause. Figure 2.3.4.1-2 explains many other special causes.

Charts to monitor variable (quantitative) and attribute (qualitative) data can aid in identifying process variation. Variable SPC charts (Figure 2.3.4.1-3) monitor shifts in average in the X-bar chart (average chart) or X chart (individual chart) and monitor variation in the range or standard deviation chart (R or S). Attribute charts like the p chart and the np chart monitor shift in the proportion (%) defective product/service. C charts and U charts monitor the number of defects per units.

Statistical rules for identification of special causes, known as Western Electric Rules, are as follows:

- 1 point more than 3 standard deviations from centerline

- 9 points in a row on same side of centerline

- 6 points in a row, all increasing or all decreasing

- 14 points in a row, alternating up and down

- 2 out of 3 points more than 2 standard deviations from centerline (same side)

- 4 out of 5 points more than 1 standard deviation from centerline (same side)

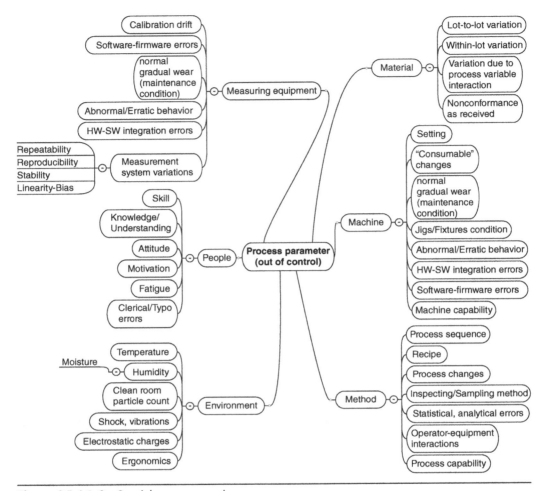

Figure 2.3.4.1–2 Special causes mapping.

- 15 points in a row within 1 standard deviation of centerline (either side)
- 8 points in a row more than 1 standard deviation from centerline (either side)

Anytime one of these situations occurs, a special cause is likely the case. While the Western Electric Rules are standard, organizations can create their own rules specific for a given process.

Identification of Customer and Process Critical Characteristics

What to monitor for process stability is a fundamental question. First, assemble a team consisting of product line management, account management, research and development (R&D), quality, manufacturing engineering, and customer representation. Where customer representation is not practical, the quality department, marketing, sales, or account management should provide support on behalf of

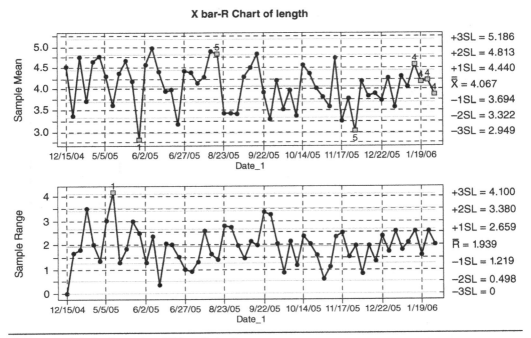

Figure 2.3.4.1-3 Example of X bar-R chart.

the customer. This team is assigned with identification of critical to quality (CTQ) characteristics.

For the same product line, assemble a second team for the purpose of critical to process parameter (CTP) identification related to the CTQs. Include manufacturing, quality, equipment, and production engineers, and invite R&D engineers where applicable. It is beneficial to segregate CTQ team members from R&D, quality, and manufacturing engineering from the CTQ team in the CTP identification exercise.

The team assigned the task of identifying CTQ characteristics should use resources like Voice of the Customer (VOC) tables, customer surveys, scorecards, market needs, engineering specifications, historical failure data from comparable legacy products, and contracts to identify basic and perceived requirements and delighters for the product. The team should further brainstorm any new expectations for the product. This exercise will yield CTQ characteristics that are both qualitative and quantitative.

Next, the team assigned CTP identification starts a brainstorming discussion. The inputs come from a combination of historical product knowledge, experience with the product, quality tools like cause-and-effect diagrams, and statistical methods like correlation and design of experiments. The output should be a set of CTPs for each CTQ. Once the relationship is established, the information can be presented in the form of a CTQ tree (Figure 2.3.4.1-4) to provide traceability of the CTP all the way to VOC.

The team should explore the degree of relationship between CTP and CTQ with a relationship matrix. This will be useful for the process improvement team

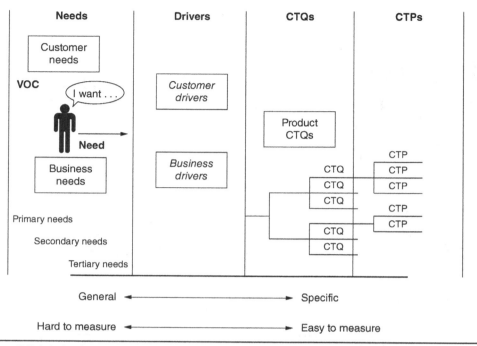

Figure 2.3.4.1-4 CTQ tree.

to work on the appropriate CTP based on the degree of relationship and resolve any process issues.

These CTPs are identified as items for controlling process stability and variation. A baseline study is usually conducted to establish control limits. The control limits are established using the process variation. In order to conduct the study, 100 individual data points are collected at regular intervals. For high-volume manufacturing or service, the data are collected as sample subgroups at equal intervals. The sample subgroup size may vary depending on production rates, number of cavities for an injection molding process, number of work cells, number of people performing a process, and so on. Typical subgroup size is 4 or 5 samples, and around 25 subgroups are sampled to establish control limits.

The baseline study is arranged by time sequence of collected data and charted as either an Individual–Moving Range chart or an X Bar-R chart, depending on how the data are collected. Control limits are calculated using the baseline data and compared on the chart as the upper control limit (UCL) and the lower control limit (LCL). Data points violating the Western Electric Rules are evaluated for special causes. Once the special causes are eliminated from the data set, and given that there are enough data to make a statistical analysis, the control limits are recalculated and set as the baseline. The variation representative of the baseline control limits is the common cause variation of the process.

The process is monitored against the control limits, and Western Electric Rules are applied for any violation as the process continues. The violations to the rules are the suspected special causes. The special causes are investigated and promptly resolved to ensure continued stability of the process. Once the process is stable, capability indices (C_p, C_{pk}) are calculated to estimate whether the current process variation is well within the process specification (C_p), and the process is centered to the specification (C_{pk}). (See Section 2.3.5.6 for additional information on C_p and C_{pk} calculations.)

The special cause elimination and process centering are performed using root cause analysis, 7 Quality Tools, design of experiments, and so on. In summary, SPC is an important fundamental tool for driving continuous process improvement.

2.3.4.2. Scatter and Concentration Diagrams

Suppose that the problem has been defined by using Pareto diagrams and pinpointing the focus area. Additionally, the process has been analyzed through the use of process flow diagrams, histograms, and SPC charts. The process is defined as in control, but the results are not optimal. There is still too much common cause variation in the process, or it just is not operating at the wanted level (i.e., average). To find out what is causing the process to behave as it does, a cause-and-effect diagram has been constructed. Now that all the possible causes of the problem have been defined, how are they responsible for the variation determined? For example, is the process yield affected more by time, temperature, or pressure? For service, an example would be, Is the process yield affected more by an employee or work center equipment? One method of determining the impact of process variables is to use a scatter diagram.

Scatter Diagram

A *scatter diagram* is a simple, visual, and easy to use graphical analysis tool for exploring the relationship between two variables. Quality management professionals unanimously agree with the application and benefit of this tool, and it is recognized as one of the 7 Quality Tools required for problem solving and improvement.

A scatter diagram is created by plotting the independent variable on the x axis and the dependent variable on the y axis. Unless a cause-and-effect diagram is done prior to the application of this tool, a user may not know which variable is independent and which one is dependent. For the purpose of exploring the presence of a relationship, this does not matter. However, if we have to know the nature of the relationship, knowing which of the two variables is independent is important.

To perform an analysis using a scatter diagram, the user collects data from a variable pair for which a relationship needs to be explored, for example, oven temperature versus material hardness, chemical concentration versus conductivity, customer call volume versus customer satisfaction, or a nation's gross domestic product versus its literacy rate. The pattern of the data is visually observed to determine whether a relationship exists. A strong relationship is identified by the formation of a thin cluster across the graph, appearing to form a line. Statistical analyses like correlation coefficient and regression are used to further confirm the relationship and predict Y values for a given X value.

To explore whether a relationship exists between variables from the plotted graph and simple math:

1. Collect data of X and Y for which a relationship may exist ($X_1, Y_1, X_2, Y_2 \ldots X_n, Y_n$).

2. Draw a simple X Y graph by plotting the collected data.

3. Look for any obvious relationship in the graph; a relationship is often displayed as a cluster of points appearing to form a line. Lines formed that are not straight are analyzed through statistical techniques like regression.

4. If the relationship is not visually obvious, consult a statistical expert for additional analysis.

Figure 2.3.4.2-1 provides an example of a scatter diagram based on the data provided in Table 2.3.4.2-1.

A number of different correlations can be visually identified on a scatter diagram. Figure 2.3.4.2-2 shows the most common correlations.

Graph A in the figure shows a strong positive correlation between X and Y: As X increases, so will Y. Graph B shows a potential positive correlation where an increase in X will result in a slight increase in Y. Graph C is an example of no correlation between X and Y. Graph D shows a possible negative correlation: As X increases, Y will decrease slightly. Graph E shows a strong negative correlation; therefore, as X increases, Y will decrease.

Users have to exercise caution in interpreting the scatter diagram. Visual indication of a relationship between two variables does not necessarily mean a cause-and-effect relationship. Both variables may be influenced by a new, third

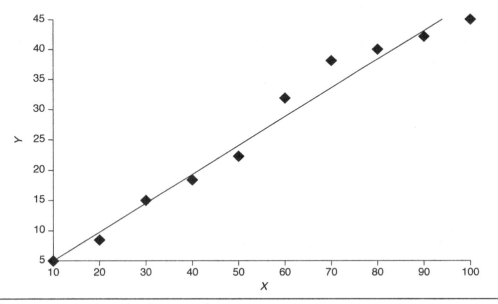

Figure 2.3.4.2-1   Example of a scatter diagram.

Table 2.3.4.2-1 Scatter diagram data.

X	Y
10	5
20	8
30	15
40	18
50	22
60	32
70	38
80	40
90	42
100	45

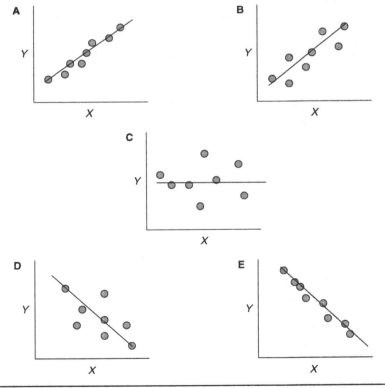

Figure 2.3.4.2-2 Correlation examples from a scatter diagram.

variable. For more complex situations, the scatter diagram has to be completed with other complementary statistical and analytical techniques and human judgment.

There are also some practical issues that may result in not recognizing a pattern. If the collected data did not cover an adequate range, resolution of an axis is not properly graphed, and the data are stratified. A mixture of data sources may also have an impact.

Concentration Diagram

The *concentration diagram* is a simple visual tool used to identify patterns and localization of defects in parts, products, building location, and so on. It is much like the check sheet but uses a picture (pictogram) to document locations. The concentration diagram has a combined advantage of being both a data collection sheet and a tool used for analysis. Identified patterns provide clues to contain the issues and correct and prevent the root cause of the problem. This diagram can be easily generated by taking a picture or image of the object and marking the location of the defects.

If the part or product has different types of defects, it will be important to define the defect and allocate a legend to distinguish one defect type from another. The definition of the defect will help train inspectors and analysts and will help build consistency. If the occurrence of the events, errors, or defects is time-dependent, different colors may be used to identify different time periods.

The following are steps for creating a concentration diagram:

1. Obtain an image of the part, product, process map, or layout to be analyzed for defect/error/event concentration.

2. Document the operational definitions for the event to be observed and the description of the defect or the error to be collected.

3. Provide legends to identify the defects or occurrence by type. Also provide color differentiations for different times when the defects have to be collected.

4. Train the inspector or the experimenter to consistently document the defect when it occurs.

5. Run the experiment for a time period that captures the variable and time dependencies adequately.

6. Once the experimenter has collected the necessary data, bring the improvement team together to review the concentration and pattern with a critical eye and collect the team's interpretations. This is often required, as the experimenter could be evolving with his or her own perceptions during the data collection. The extended team provides objectivity and validation to the interpretation.

7. Use additional analysis tools to narrow down the source and cause of the defect/error.

The following variable dependencies may be important to an analyst:

- Comparing equipment
- Within equipment—semiconductor ovens often have multiple chambers
- Between employees (with names decoded)

The following time dependencies may be important for the analyst:

- Three shifts
- Start and finish of the work shift
- Before and after improvement action

Figure 2.3.4.2-3 shows an example of a concentration diagram for documenting defects that occur during a toy car manufacturing process across two shifts. What can be gathered from the data collected is that the loose wheel defects may be the result of an operator issue since each shift's defects occur on one wheel, but different wheels for each shift. It can also be determined that the scratched paint defect may be an equipment issue since defects on both shifts occur at the same locations (with the exception of the two separate occurrences from each shift in a different location being considered as special cause). Concentration diagrams can also be used to show the location of documentation defects on forms (Figure 2.3.4.2-4), possibly resulting in a redesign of the form to prevent these errors from occurring in the future.

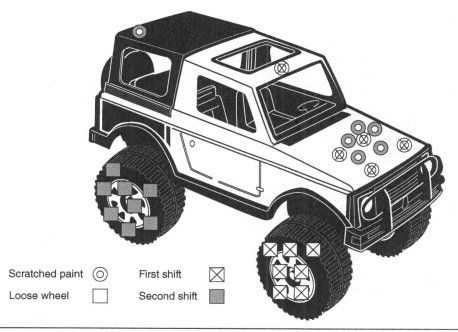

Scratched paint	◎	First shift	⊠
Loose wheel	☐	Second shift	■

Figure 2.3.4.2-3   Example of a concentration diagram.

2.3.4.2

Form **1040EZ**	**Income Tax Return for Single and Joint Filers With No Dependents** (99)	**2011**	OMB No. 1545-0074

Your first name and initial	Last name	Your social security number

If a joint return, spouse's first name and initial	Last name	Spouse's social security number

Home address (number and street). If you have a P.O. box, see instructions.	Apt. no.	⊠ Make sure the SSN(s) above are correct.

City, town or post office, state, and ZIP code. If you have a foreign address, also complete spaces below (see instructions).

Presidential Election Campaign
Check here if you, or your spouse if filing jointly, want $3 to go to this fund. Checking a box below will not change your tax or refund. ☐ You ☐ Spouse

Foreign country name	Foreign province/county	Foreign postal code

Income
Attach Form(s) W-2 here.

Enclose, but do not attach, any payment.

1	Wages, salaries, and tips. This should be shown in box 1 of your Form(s) W-2. Attach your Form(s) W-2.	1
2	Taxable interest. If the total is over $1,500, you cannot use Form 1040EZ.	2
3	Unemployment compensation and Alaska Permanent Fund dividends (see instructions).	3
4	Add lines 1, 2, and 3. This is your **adjusted gross income.**	4
5	If someone can claim you (or your spouse if a joint return) as a dependent, check the applicable box(es) below and enter the amount from the worksheet on back. ☐ You ☐ Spouse If no one can claim you (or your spouse if a joint return), enter $9,500 if **single;** $19,000 if **married filing jointly.** See back for explanation.	5
6	Subtract line 5 from line 4. If line 5 is larger than line 4, enter -0-. This is your **taxable income.**	6

Payments, Credits, and Tax

7	Federal income tax withheld from Form(s) W-2 and 1099.	7
8a	**Earned income credit (EIC)** (see instructions).	8a
b	Nontaxable combat pay election. 8b	
9	Add lines 7 and 8a. These are your **total payments and credits.**	9
10	**Tax.** Use the amount on **line 6 above** to find your tax in the tax table in the instructions. Then, enter the tax from the table on this line.	10

Refund
Have it directly deposited! See instructions and fill in 11b, 11c, and 11d or Form 8888.

11a	If line 9 is larger than line 10, subtract line 10 from line 9. This is your **refund.** If Form 8888 is attached, check here ⊠ ☐	11a
⊠ b	Routing number	⊠ c Type: ☐ Checking ☐ Savings
⊠ d	Account number	

Amount You Owe

12	If line 10 is larger than line 9, subtract line 9 from line 10. This is the **amount you owe.** For details on how to pay, see instructions.	12

Third Party Designee
Do you want to allow another person to discuss this return with the IRS (see instructions)? ☐ **Yes.** Complete below. ☐ **No**

Designee's name ⊠	Phone no. ⊠	Personal identification number (PIN) ⊠

Sign Here
Joint return? See instructions.
Keep a copy for your records.

Under penalties of perjury, I declare that I have examined this return and, to the best of my knowledge and belief, it is true, correct, and accurately lists all amounts and sources of income I received during the tax year. Declaration of preparer (other than the taxpayer) is based on all information of which the preparer has any knowledge.

Your signature	Date	Your occupation	Daytime phone number
Spouse's signature. If a joint return, **both** must sign.	Date	Spouse's occupation	If the IRS sent you an Identity Protection PIN, enter it here (see inst.)

Paid Preparer Use Only

Print/Type preparer's name	Preparer's signature	Date	Check ☐ if self-employed	PTIN
Firm's name ⊠			Firm's EIN ⊠	
Firm's address ⊠			Phone no.	

For Disclosure, Privacy Act, and Paperwork Reduction Act Notice, see instructions. | Cat. No. 11329W | Form **1040EZ** (2011)

◎ Incorrect entry   ★ Missed entry

Figure 2.3.4.2–4 Example of the 1040EZ tax form showing where certain types of documentation errors occur.

2.3.5. PRODUCT AND SERVICE DESIGN

Lean design, also called Design for Lean (DfL) or Design for Lean Six Sigma (DfLSS), begins with defining customer value by capturing the Voice of the Customer (VOC). Generally stated, VOC wants products or services that have traits that are better, faster, and cheaper. The VOCs are developed into critical to quality (CTQ) features that are quantified with a target and minimum and maximum value. Capturing and confirming customer value does not begin and end in marketing or with customer-supplied blueprints. Customer and supplier interaction and feedback occur through multiple rapid prototyping events in design development and with participation and confirmation of the value of the design attributes selected in each Design for X (DFX) function.

Another clear distinction of lean design is that it provides designs that holistically meet design requirements in 50%–75% less time when compared to traditional design processes and at 10%–50% lower costs. Lean design/DfLSS was applied in developing the Advanced Launch System (ALS). The mission was to develop the ALS design, production, and operations at 10% of the cost of current systems. This was not a 10% reduction, but 10% of the cost of current systems (90% reduction).

The product and service development life cycle in lean design relies on a "leaned" out design process that utilizes integrated design teams composed of customers, suppliers, sales and marketing, product and service design, operations, and service and warranty. Concepts such as concurrent design, rapid prototyping, and DFX are essential elements of lean design.

An example of more efficient applications of a design process within lean design is engineering changes. Engineering changes are those changes that affect any function, design element or product, process, or service function or part related to DFX. In traditional use of engineering changes, 6–12 functional areas have approval authority to sign off on any change. This delays communication of changes in both the traditional paper systems and the automated systems and actively engages resources that don't need to be consumed.

The intent of lean design is to ensure that each function is aware of changes so that it can adjust its portion of the design or process, such as operations or testing. In lean design, by using the conflicting and complementary functions of the roof of the House of Quality in quality function deployment (QFD), the design team can improve the engineering change process. Using the roof of the House of Quality as a check sheet, project and design teams can indicate which functions should have approval authority for conflicting or complementary functions of specified elements of the product or service design and which elements simply need to be communicated. This can be done at the beginning of the design process as part of the project plan. Figure 2.3.5-1 shows the difference between concurrent engineering and traditional engineering over the course of the product development life cycle.

Figure 2.3.5-2 shows an example of design changes and total product development as a function of time for an American automobile versus a Japanese automobile. Tools like concurrent engineering and QFD can significantly reduce design changes post product release, resulting in savings in life-cycle cost.

2.3.5

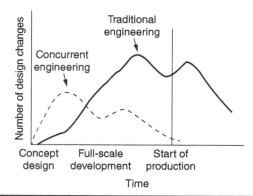

Figure 2.3.5–1 Product development life cycle showing concurrent engineering versus traditional engineering.

Source: Adapted from Chapman, Bahill, and Wymore (1992).

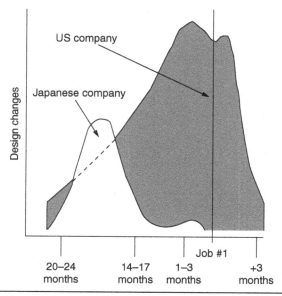

Figure 2.3.5–2 Fewer design changes and reduced product development time for the Japanese automobile.

Source: Adapted from Hauser and Clausing (1988).

2.3.5.1. Concurrent Engineering

The following is an extreme representation of traditional product development. The basic process is one of functional silos where each function operates fairly independently in getting through its tasks, throws the design over the wall to the next silo, and then moves on to the next project. This is thought to create a stream-line flow. However, without joint communication up front, much rework occurs in both product and process design and well into the late release of the design into production. You can see this manifested in transactional services with multiple screen queries to get to a decision point versus one screen with the decision data, or in manufacturing with archaic test equipment and processes due to receiving the "final final" requirements after the product is already released to manufacturing.

Concurrent engineering utilizes an integrated design team composed of customers, suppliers, sales and marketing, product and service design, operations, and service and warranty throughout the product or service development cycle. A concurrent engineering team reviews requirements, matches process capability with design needs, and jointly manages each project through a series of design gates to ensure efficient and effective progress. The main focus of the concurrent engineering team is fit, form, and function of the design; manufacturability; and assembly. This requires more work up front, which is initially resisted, but much less rework overall throughout product development. After several product development cycles and high-level prototyping, the organization sees the overall benefit of concurrent engineering and further reduces the cost of development.

Design for excellence (DFE) applies concurrent engineering evolved with Design for X (DFX) methodologies, rapid prototyping, and product development continuous flow (PDCF). (DFX methodologies are covered in Section 2.3.5.4, "Design for Product Life Cycle [DFx]—Cradle to Cradle.") Rapid prototyping is utilized much deeper and faster with smaller portions of the design rapidly reviewed multiple times with the customer or a customer focus group. Computer-aided design (CAD) and electronic communication, rather than complete physical models, are used at the early stages. PDCF considers the design process a continuous flow of ideas with an output of products and services of which the customer sees value. In PDCF, ideas generated are saved for future designs, rapid prototyping generates other new ideas captured for later development, improvements in operations are actively generated, and product disposal is proactively managed with a focus on lean and green concepts.

DFE meets the needs of the customer as defined by customer value and includes benefits such as:

- Reuse of design, software modules, processes, parts, and components

- Development of robust designs and processes

- Increase in concepts to consider

- Simpler designs and processes

- Rapid prototyping of designs

- Design for green, or reduced impact on society after the product's or service's life cycle is complete

- Rapid prototyping of operations and service processes

- Designing lean into manufacturing and support processes (i.e., considering the entire value stream), which results in:

    - Shorter production time

    - Shorter time to deliver a service

    - Fewer production and service steps with fewer handoffs

- Standard part use

- Modular part use

- Wider supplier base to draw on

- Ergonomically designed processes

- Mistake-proofing designs and processes

- Lower overall cost

- Shorter development time

Some organizations make the mistake of taking the term "concurrent engineering" literally. They believe that engineering, or product design, occurs in parallel with full manufacturing or service line setup, implementation, and sale of the final product. This literal interpretation results in a worse scenario than traditional engineering: Production and service equipment is ordered, built, and installed at the same time that design changes are being made to the end product, resulting in changes in the equipment and process designs during the implementation stage. This often results in higher overall cost of the development of the product/service. This also increases the risk of sending product and services with significant issues to the customer, resulting in long-term service and warranty issues in the future. Make no mistake—concurrent engineering means that all functions work in parallel during the concept and design phases to address issues in a "virtual" environment rather than a live environment. There is still the proverbial wall that the design is thrown over; however, all functions are doing the throwing and catching.

2.3.5.2. Quality Function Deployment

Quality function deployment (QFD) is a product/service development tool that provides a structured and systematic approach to capturing a customer's stated requirements, implied requirements, and foreseen expectations. QFD translates these requirements into how-to technical requirements phase by phase, from planning to customer delivery. While the tool is typically used for designing new products and services, it is equally useful for redesigning existing products and services.

Translating customer requirements into technical requirements is not always a straightforward activity. There are bound to be conflicting requirements, so trade-offs may be required in some instances. Risk needs to be evaluated and managed. Organizations may need to go above and beyond meeting customer requirements and benchmark themselves against competitors and best in class.

The input to the process is the Voice of the Customer (VOC), but there are also other listening posts. Input may be received through customer focus groups, surveys, and face-to-face interviews. There are some lagging indicators that are hard to ignore: customer satisfaction and dissatisfaction metrics. These may also include failure rates at different points in the product life cycle, such as during the reliability and qualification stages of development and field failures upon product deployment. The QFD process requires putting together a cross-functional team that has knowledge of customer expectations (basic, performance, and delighters). The first order of business is for the QFD program manager to identify all plausible inputs to the process and assign responsibility for collection and validation.

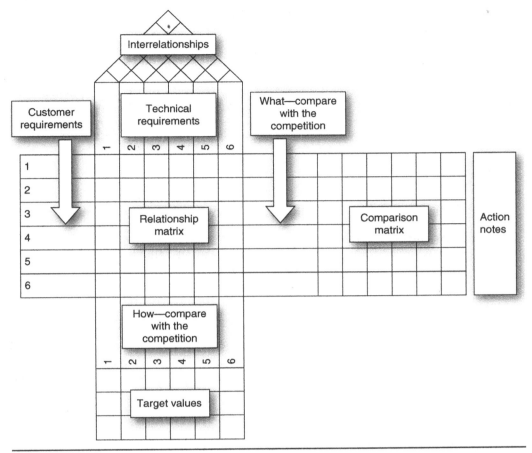

Figure 2.3.5.2-1 House of Quality.

Before we go too far into the process, let us first explore all compartments of the QFD (also known as the "House of Quality"). A QFD matrix consists of many compartments, each of which has a purpose. A map of the various parts of the QFD is shown in Figure 2.3.5.2-1.

Left Wing

The left wing of the house is where customer requirements are captured. Often, customer requirements are received at mixed levels of need. Customer needs can be classified as primary, secondary, or tertiary. A *primary need* is at a high level, whether the customer is referring to quality, reliability, cost, or regulatory compliance. A *tertiary need* is a specific requirement telling the organization what it should do. A *secondary need* is in between. Also, customers tend to advise "how to" rather than "what" they want. It is the responsibility of the organization to capture the input and work back to what the customer wants. For example, a customer might say that the hard-copy final inspection test reports should reach him or her by carrier within three business days from shipment. He or she may not be aware that the organization has electronic data transfer capability to send the inspection data to the customer's server once the product is barcode scanned for shipment. This could be a customer delighter! In this case, the organization captures "Test data availability within 3 business days" as a "what" and educates the customer on the organization infrastructure and technology.

This section also includes a 1–5 Likert scale, reflecting the importance of the requirements from the customer and market perspective. Regulatory, statutory, and legal requirements are excluded from weighting, as these are nonnegotiable to do business in certain market conditions.

Attic

The "how" technical requirements are established in response to the customer requirements and placed in the technical requirements section of the attic. Symbols are used to visually indicate the target design criteria for the requirement. The down arrow (↓) and up arrow (↑) on the top line in this section indicate which is better. A circle (o) indicates that achieving a target value is better. The technical requirements corresponding to achieving the "what" customer requirements are derived through product/service knowledge expertise, experiments, a published body of knowledge, and so on. It is likely that there will be three to five "hows" for every "what." One can assume that if we do not group the "what" at the primary level, we will end up with scores of "how." Hence, the primary needs are maintained at a manageable 8–10 items for logistical reasons. This does not mean that the users drop important customer requirements to make the QFD process manageable. Rather, users are encouraged to split the QFD into manageable modules or use a bigger QFD.

Living Room

The living room is the relationship matrix of "what" and "how" and displays the interrelation between the technical requirements and the customer requirements. The most common symbols are a circle (significant), a square (moderate), and a triangle (least). To reflect the relationship between a "what" and a "how," values of 9, 5, or 1 are assigned in the matrix area.

The weighted total for "how" is obtained by multiplying the "importance" value in the customer requirements section by values assigned to the symbols in the relationship matrix. These values are displayed as a Pareto chart to identify the "hows" that will become the "what" for the next cascaded "design" house. This continues cascading through the subsequent houses all the way to the Manufacturing or Service House (Figure 2.3.5.2-2).

Right Wing

The benchmarking area, or "What—compare with the competition" section, is not shown on all QFD matrices due to the difficulty of obtaining such data. These data may be indirectly obtained by the customer by ranking the organization relative to competitors without divulging who is ahead of whom. Most customers are comfortable with this approach. These data may also be obtained from competitor websites, data sheets, industry journals, third-party organizations, and so on. In this area, the organization plots comparisons with the competition for the "what"

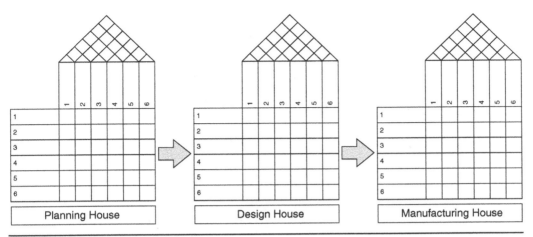

Figure 2.3.5.2-2 Sequence of QFD matrices for product, part, and process planning.

customer requirements. This information also makes this document proprietary for some organizations.

Basement

Like the benchmarking area of the house, the "How—compare with the competition" section is not shown on all QFD matrices due to the difficulty of obtaining such data. This basement compartment comparing the "how" between competitors is even more challenging. Typically, organizations purchase the product and reverse engineer it to figure out the "how" comparison. For mechanically and/or electrically assembled products, this is sometimes, but not always, possible. For example, highly complex processes are used to manufacture semiconductors. These are almost impossible to reverse engineer, as the chemicals are applied at a certain temperature at a certain time to a certain thickness on top of one another. This area of the basement plots comparisons with the competition for the technical requirements. The "target values" section of the basement is used to list the target values for the technical requirements.

Roof

The roof of the house shows the interrelationships between the technical requirements. A positive correlation indicates that both technical requirements can be improved at the same time without conflicts. A negative correlation indicates that improving one of the technical requirements will worsen the other. This is where product development should use trade-off analysis and the first principle of physics to innovate breakthrough ideas to achieve both the "how" and the "what" of the desired values.

For example, how do you achieve a faster, fuel-efficient vehicle that is also strong and robust to impacts from all directions? Common sense says that the lighter the vehicle, the faster it will go and the less fuel it will burn. But common sense also says that a lighter vehicle can collapse in a road accident and fail safety ratings. If the team can develop an innovative design that creates a stronger body with lightweight material, the conflict can be resolved. The design team should

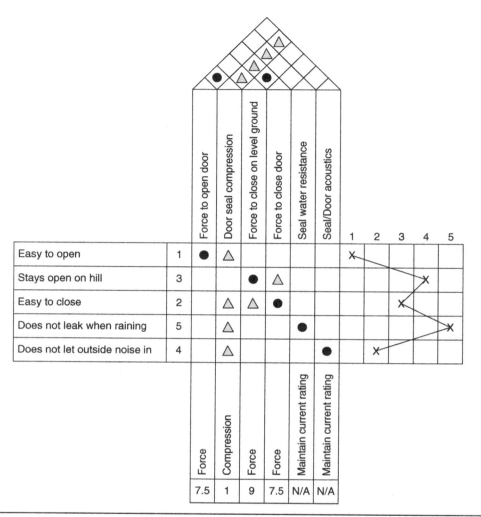

Figure 2.3.5.2-3   Example of a simplified QFD matrix for a car door.

achieve these goals without exceeding the price target. This is where the trade-off comes in. An expensive vehicle cannot succeed in many market segments, and too cheap of a vehicle will not attract any market and will erode an organization's profit margin.

The completed matrix can provide a database of useful information for product development, serve as a basis for planning product or process improvements, and suggest opportunities for new or revised product or process introductions. Figure 2.3.5.2-3 shows an example of a completed QFD matrix.

Practical Challenges

While QFD is an extremely disciplined approach, it is often time consuming to the product development process. In practice, it will be difficult to get traction from a product development team to sit through multiple sessions developing the house and cascading from "what" to "how" and "how" to "what" to the Production House.

The facilitator should watch out for team members assigning unusually high relationship numbers in order to move certain predetermined "hows" to the next level, as this defeats the purpose of prioritizing the requirements.

It is important to separate the brainstorming sessions, which figure out the "hows" that are meant to be creative, from the judgment or critical review sessions (assigning relationship significance). Combining them can tire out the participants and thus create low quality of interaction and inputs. Although a specific purpose is being fulfilled while going through the cascade of matrices, the most important thing to remember is that the true value is in the cross-functional discussions that occur.

The most difficult part, perhaps, for those not using QFD and concurrent engineering, beyond the overall less competitive traditional engineering process, is the number of changes that occur after the release of the design to production.

2.3.5.3. Product or Process Benchmarking

Benchmarking of process, product, and service is looking for best practices that could be used in the development, operations, and warranty for your processes, product, and services. The natural direction to benchmark would be with the organization's direct competitors. While it is natural to want to see how the competition does what it does, it is unlikely that you could capture such data. More importantly, even though it may be a leap for your company, it would be a look backward to what has been done instead of the looking-forward approach that is desired in benchmarking. Benchmarking seeks to look to processes, products, and services that leap beyond the organization and its competitors' best practices. However, when looking where to benchmark for potential quick improvements, consider benchmarking across your processes, facilities, or offices and potential current best practices of competitors' processes, which can be more readily accessed through trade shows.

The next step is to benchmark leaders across industries for their best processes. In benchmarking, mirroring a benchmark company is not an objective. To go beyond the benchmark company with best-practice processes, which may include looking across industries, is an objective—perhaps a call center for one, logistics for another, product development for another, lean manufacturing for another, and designing for green for another. The other benefit of reaching beyond the competition is that the door is more open to share best practices such as in the open house sessions of Malcolm Baldrige National Quality Award winners.

2.3.5.4. Design for Product Life Cycle (DFx)—Cradle to Cradle

The product life cycle can be simplified to four main steps:

1. Concept

2. Full-scale development

3. Start of production

4. Recycling

A focus on Design for X (DFX) at each step provides highly competitive and fully integrated designs, efficient processes, and retirement of a product considered lean and green throughout development, production, and disposal.

The market is getting very competitive, and profit margins are eroding. Customers expect high performance and a reliable product, and they expect it at a very competitive cost and in a shorter time. Conventional continual improvement methodologies, however useful, take longer to realize the benefits. Breakthrough improvement (Figure 2.3.5.4-1) like the design for excellence (DFE) strategy and DFX methodologies is used where a significant improvement has to be made in a shorter duration and with a higher level of focus.

DFE applies DFX, where "X" stands for effective design methods applied in cost, manufacturability, assembly, testing, performance, quality, reliability, maintainability, environment, recyclability, safety, time to market, and supply chain.

All applications of DFX begin with capturing and anticipating customer/market needs and building attributes like usability, interoperability, scalability, compatibility, maintainability, flexibility, and modularity into the product on top of high performance and reliability. This is achieved by customer value analysis, Voice of the Customer (VOC) analysis, quality function deployment (QFD), and TRIZ (theory of inventive problem solving).

DFX methodology and related tools help:

- Simplify product architecture and design
- Reduce the number of parts
- Improve reliability and maintainability
- Standardize and utilize common parts and materials
- Design for ease of fabrication
- Design within process capabilities of in-house and suppliers
- Mistake-proof product design and assembly
- Develop features for intermediate testing
- Incorporate customer delight features
- Reduce overall life-cycle cost

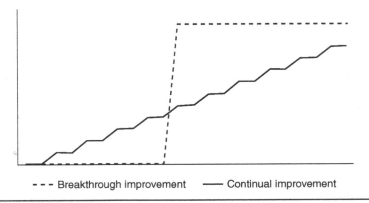

- - - Breakthrough improvement   —— Continual improvement

Figure 2.3.5.4-1   Breakthrough improvement.

Design functions and methodologies in lean design fall under the umbrella term "Design for X (DFX)" and include the following:

- Design for Assembly (DFA)
- Design for Cost (DFC)
- Design for Disassembly (DFD)
- Design for Green (DFG)
- Design for Installation (DFI)
- Design for Logistics (DFL)
- Design for Manufacturing (DFM)
- Design for Poka-Yoke or Mistake-Proofing (DFP)
- Design for Quality (DFQ)
- Design for Reliability (DFR)
- Design for Reuse (DFU)
- Design for Safety (DFS)
- Design for Test (DFT)
- Design for Warranty and Service (DFW)

Life-cycle cost is an important competitive factor. It is important to not only conceive innovative breakthrough products but also develop the products free from defects at all stages of the product life cycle. As seen in Figure 2.3.5.4-2, the cost significantly increases as the defects are detected on the customer's end, including loss of customer confidence.

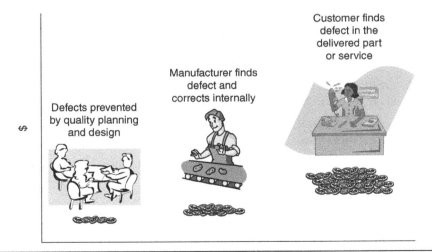

Figure 2.3.5.4–2   Product life cycle.

Source: Concept adapted from Campanella (1999).

Some of the DFX definitions follow.

Design for Cost involves designing products with improved value. *Value*, as defined, is the ratio of function to cost. Value can therefore be increased by either improving the function or reducing the cost. This is done by adding more customer-delight features for the same product cost or reducing the product cost by switching to lower-cost parts and a more efficient value stream (less complex process, logistics, waste reduction) and performing concurrent engineering.

Design for Manufacturing involves the simplification of product design to improve the efficiencies of manufacturing the product and reduce design-related defects related to the manufacturing process. This is documented as guidelines for manufacturing design, also known as manufacturing design rules (see Section 2.3.5.6, "Design for Manufacturability").

Design for Assembly involves designing for ease of assembly and testing, designing for efficient joining and fastening of matting parts, designing modular products, designing for automation, mistake-proofing product design for assembly errors (poka-yoke), and, most importantly, designing within process and equipment capabilities. This is documented as guidelines for manufacturing design, also known as manufacturing design rules.

Design for Reliability is designing product to meet customer/market life expectation, achieving failures in time (FIT)/mean time between failures (MTBF)/mean time to failure (MTTF) targets under the required customer system environmental conditions with low or no deterioration in performance. This is obtained by designing reliable parts from proven suppliers, robust manufacturing and/or assembly processes, failure mode and effects analysis (FMEA), fault tree analysis, and extensive due diligence in tests and review across all stages of the development cycle.

Design for Green involves applying lean and green methods and practices throughout development, production, and disposal by eliminating the 8 Green Wastes:

1. Water: usage for production, usage by employees, and waste water

2. Electricity: created by both non-renewable resources (i.e., gas, coal, nuclear, petroleum-based fuels) and renewable resources (i.e., wind, hydroelectric, geothermal, solar, bio-fuels)

3. Gas: natural, propane, methane, etc.

4. Earth material: soil and earth, plants, and non-preprocessed raw materials (salt, coal, crude oil, bauxite, lead, etc.)

5. Emissions: smoke, water vapor, heated air, gaseous toxins, residual gases from processes, etc.

6. Product use: waste from product discard after use, product packaging, containers for product shipping, etc.

7. Raw material: like traditional waste from production scrap that is excess material discarded for no further use by the organization.

8. Byproducts: solid waste toxins, processed materials not usable by the organization, bio-hazardous waste, etc. (Vincent 2009, 19)

The following are goals of lean to green:

- Minimizing the use of nonrenewable resources
- Maximizing the value usage of nonrenewable resources when they must be used
- Maximizing the value usage of renewable resources
- Maximizing the value use of materials
- Maximizing the reuse of scrap raw materials
- Minimizing total byproducts
- Maximizing byproducts that can be used
- Minimizing the creation of toxic byproducts or those byproducts that cannot be used
- Minimizing the use of product materials and packaging (including shipping materials)
- Maximizing the reuse of product materials and packaging after use

DFX Tools

Several engineering, quality, and analytical tools are used for effective DFX implementation. Product development will use a comprehensive list of tools, such as:

- Finite element analysis
- Statistical tolerancing
- Design failure mode and effects analysis (DFMEA) and process failure mode and effects analysis (PFMEA)
- Monte Carlo simulation
- Electrical circuit modeling
- Function cost analysis
- Process capability studies
- Manufacturing design rules
- FIT rate/reliability modeling tools
- Supplier capability
- Value stream mapping
- Quality function deployment
- Robust design of experiment
- Highly accelerated life testing (HALT)/highly accelerated stress screen (HASS) testing

- Measurement system analysis
- Mistake-proofing
- Standardization
- Cycle time reduction
- Ergonomics
- Pugh concept
- Design margin/test to failure
- Process hazards review
- Integration testing

DFX Tools Interactions

These tools are used at different stages of product development. The tools are not exclusive to any specific DFX activity. Typically more than one tool is used in combination to achieve the overall benefits of a DFX activity. For example, Design for Cost will use statistical tolerancing to improve interchangeability for stack-up tolerances, FMEA for reducing risks of failure modes, manufacturing design rules, value stream mapping, standardization, and function cost analysis. Similarly, DFX activities are interrelated to one another. For example, Design for Cost implementation heavily depends on Design for Manufacturing, Assembly, Reliability, Quality, and Supply Chain.

DFX Tools versus Design for Product Life Cycle—Cradle to Grave (Potential Applications)

DFX tools are also well connected to the typical product development process. Following are examples of DFX tools that can potentially be used for various gate review deliverables.

Opportunity Assessment Stage Gate (Concept Step)

- Competitive assessment—perceptual map
- Customer analysis—customer value analysis, Voice of the Customer (VOC) table, QFD
- Risk analysis—Monte Carlo simulation, sensitive analysis
- Target cost analysis—function cost analysis, value engineering, activity-based costing

Planning Stage Gate (Concept Step)

- Hardware/Software/Firmware requirements—VOC, QFD, design rules
- Reliability and qualification requirements, reliability analysis, qualification strategy—VOC, QFD, HALT/HASS, FIT analysis
- Verification strategy and environment—VOC, QFD
- Validation strategy and environment—VOC, QFD, HALT/HASS

- Environmental, health, and safety (EH&S) requirements—VOC, QFD, process hazards review, ergonomics review

- Product data requirements list—QFD

- Risk analysis—Monte Carlo simulation, DFMEA, PFMEA

- Business process requirements—value stream mapping, cycle time reduction

- Sourcing strategy—supplier capability

- Key components identification—QFD, CTQ tree, DFMEA

- Configuration management planning—supplier capability, concurrent engineering

- Component cost targets—function cost analysis, value engineering

- Supplier qualification plan—supplier capability

- Key components/subsystems and volume forecasts—supplier capability

Designing Stage Gate (Full Scale Development Step)

- Architecture (design)—federal enterprise architecture (FEA), electrical circuit modeling, DFMEA, Pugh selection

- Design tolerance analysis—statistical tolerancing, Monte Carlo simulation

- Test specification—manufacturing design rules (testability)

- Component specifications—manufacturing design rules, standardization

- Part drawings—mistake-proofing, manufacturing design rules, standardization

- Product user manuals—mistake-proofing, flowchart simplification

- Assembly drawings—manufacturing design rules

- Process flow diagrams—value stream mapping

- Work instructions—process hazards review, mistake-proofing, standardization

- Inspection and test criteria—PFMEA-control plan

- Manufacturing test definition—manufacturing design rules (testability)

- Manufacturing process design documentation—manufacturing design rules, design of experiments (DOE), C_{pk}

- Tooling and fixture documentation—manufacturing design rules

- Manufacturing travelers—mistake-proofing

- Equipment capability—Gauge R&R Analysis, measurement systems analysis (MSA)

- Cost analysis—function cost analysis, value engineering

- Design FMEA
- Process FMEA
- Hazard analysis, environmental impacts
- Inspection and test development—PFMEA/Control plan

Verification and Validation Stage Gate (Full Scale Development Step)

- Electrical and mechanical stress analysis—FEA, stress-testing
- Vibration analysis
- FIT rate analysis
- Component reliability allocations/requirements—FIT, reliability modeling, apportionment
- Design margin/Test to failure

Manufacturing Stage Gate (Start of Production Step)

- Yield assessment—Process capability—C_p, C_{pk}
- Control plans—PFMEA (input)
- Surveillance plans—FIT, reliability modeling
- Continuous improvement plans—value stream mapping, process capability, MSA

End of Life Stage Gate (Recycling Step)

- Risk assessment—DFMEA, PFMEA
- Logistics—value stream mapping
- Continuity of products on the field—parts standardization, Design for Environment
- Lean and green

Rolling out a DFX strategy requires a mission, charter, program management, deliverables, timeline, and so on. There should be a knowledge management infrastructure, for example, SharePoint, with DFX training material, related articles, publications, procedures, formats, real project examples, and best practices. Subject matter experts (SMEs) for various DFX should be identified. If there are no local experts, external experts should be hired as consultants to train select internal candidates. These SMEs will help monitor product development and act as mentors for employees.

Metrics to measure the effectiveness of DFX implementation should be established and monitored by product line management. DFX implementation should also leverage existing corporate initiatives like Lean Enterprise for tools such as value stream mapping, cycle time reduction, and standardization. There should be an integrated approach, otherwise two factions within the organization could be created that compete for resources rather than create synergy. Like any other major initiative, successful DFX implementation requires visible senior management commitment and teamwork from employees at all levels.

2.3.5.5. Variety Reduction—Product and Component

Variety reduction includes understanding and designing to the known capability of the process in meeting the expectations of the customer's requirements (C_p and C_{pk}), designing at an optimum economic value based on the quality loss function, and utilizing tolerance stacking in the overall design. In the design state, variety reduction focuses on understanding the capability of available processes and building the design without allowance for the variety. In operations, variety reduction focuses on the continuous improvement of the existing processes with a focus on reducing the variety of process inputs and outputs. Improved operational variety provides more flexibility in design.

C_p and C_{pk}

The purpose of a capability study is to determine whether a process is capable of meeting the specifications as determined by the Voice of the Customer (VOC). Process capability is measured using many indices; however, C_p and C_{pk} are the focus here. The higher the value of the index, the more capable the process is to meet the VOC.

C_p provides a quick assessment as to whether the overall spread of the process can meet the tightness of the specification or requirements provided by the customer. The formula for the process capability index C_p is:

$$C_p = \frac{(USL - LSL)}{6s}$$

where

$$USL = \text{Upper specification limit}$$

$$LSL = \text{Lower specification limit}$$

$$s = \text{Standard deviation of the sample population}$$

C_{pk} provides a clear assessment as to whether the overall spread of the process currently meets the tightness of the specification or requirements provided by the customer. The formula for the process capability index C_{pk} is:

$$C_{pk} = \text{Min} \frac{(USL - \overline{X})}{3s}, \frac{(\overline{X} - LSL)}{3s}$$

where $\overline{x}$ = Average

As C_p increases, the capability to meet specifications increases (Figure 2.3.5.5-1). A C_p of less than one consumes more of the specification than allowed; the process variance is wider than the specification. A C_p of 1.00 covers approximately 100% of the specification. A C_p of 1.33 utilizes 75% of the specification. A C_p of 2.00 represents a six sigma process and consumes only 50% of the allowable variance of the specification. Product components and service steps should be developed to different levels of capability (Table 2.3.5.5-1).

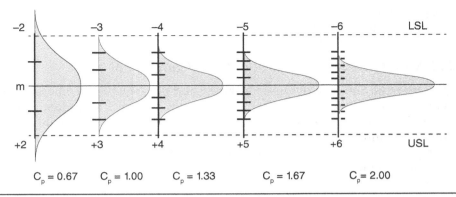

Figure 2.3.5.5-1 Effect of C_p against specification limits.

Table 2.3.5.5-1 Correlation of C_p with sigma levels.

C_p value	Represents	Means
<1.0	<3 sigma	Process is not capable
1–1.5	3–4.5 sigma	Process is capable but can be improved
1.5–1.67	4.5–5 sigma	Should be a minimum requirement for all new processes
1.67–2	5–6 sigma	World-class process

Quality Loss Function

Developed by Genichi Taguchi, the *quality loss function* (Figure 2.3.5.5-2) illustrates and puts into practice the concept that the less variability you have in a process or part, the less costly it will be to produce the product. It is a quadratic function that lies on top of the distribution curve of the process, and each specification limit is compared with the customer specifications. Essentially, we can reduce costs by reducing variation. Typical loss analysis states that a loss is not incurred unless the part does not meet specification, at which point a loss occurs. In practice, the closer the output lays next to the specification, the more costly it is to produce the part due to hidden factory costs, including rework, defects, additional processing, and delays.

Tolerance Stacking

Tolerance stacking takes into consideration two main themes: (1) not all components of a design are equally critical and (2) most products and services rely on many parts or steps.

Determining the allowable variability or tightness needed for certain components and their functions is critical to planning the design of the product or service process. For example, the fixtures that hold a pacemaker together (screws, snaps, and welds) could handle a larger degree of variability compared to other components in relation to the criticality of their functions. The components that mechanically provide a charge when needed should have a very low degree of variability.

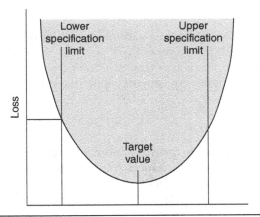

Figure 2.3.5.5-2 Quality loss function.

The software that interacts with readings and determines when to send a charge should have a very low degree of variability with respect to sending signals.

Tolerance stacking considers the variability of each part or process step's cycle time for a service and allows for common cause variation due to normal behavior in the process so that components match in assembly and the process cycle times do not overlap in operations or services.

2.3.5.6. Design for Manufacturability

Design for Manufacturing (DFM) involves simplifying the design and reducing the number of parts, standardizing and using common parts and materials, designing for ease of fabrication, designing for parts orientation and handling, minimizing flexible parts and interconnections that are prone to damage, and, most importantly, designing within process and equipment capabilities. This is documented as guidelines for manufacturing design, aka manufacturing design rules. DFM involves designing products while keeping in mind the ease and capability of manufacturing both in-house and at outsourced/supplier locations. DFM adheres to the following mistake-proofing principles:

- Elimination: The possibility of error is eliminated by redesigning the product or process so that the task or part is no longer necessary

- Replacement: To improve reliability, simply substitute an unpredictable process with a more reliable process

- Prevention: Design engineers should design the product or process so that it is impossible to make a mistake

- Facilitation: Utilizing specific methods and grouping steps will make the assembly process easier to perform

- Detection: Errors are detected before they move to the next processing step so that the user can quickly correct the problem

- Mitigation: The principle of attempting to decrease the effects of errors

Some strategies to achieve DFM are laid out in the following sections.

Simplification of the Design

Simplification means designing assembly and parts that are well within the manufacturing capability to meet C_p, $C_{pk} \geq 1.33$. Ease of assembly helps reduce the assembly cycle time. The designers obtain equipment capability, parameters, design rules, and supplier equipment capability and take these into consideration during the design.

Reduction of Number of Parts

By integrating the parts to provide more functions per part, the overall product cost decreases. This also reduces the inventory cost and administration cost involved in sourcing multiple parts. An example is designing a screw whose head has a built-in washer, eliminating the need for a separate screw and washer.

Standardization

By incorporating common parts across various product lines, the need for designing, manufacturing, procuring, and storing unique parts is significantly reduced, saving the organization significant material and inventory costs. Standardization also includes designing fasteners that require the same torque throughout multiple fastening points. Having different fasteners requires different torque and different torque drivers, and thus it is an opportunity for assembly operators to mix up the torque and make mistakes.

Ease of Fabrication

Parts are designed so that the subsequent manufacturing operations are performed with ease, lesser yield loss, and improved throughput yield. The design of the product helps mounting in the equipment, ensures that the correct amount of material is available to the machine and that the material can withstand manufacturing pressures without yielding or breaking, and ensures that the parts remain stable during manufacturing.

Designing Parts with Orientation, Nonsymmetric Profile

Designing parts with nonsymmetric profiles allows them to be easily oriented for subsequent operations. The orientation tasks are opportunities for errors and require mistake-proofing. This helps reduce confusion during manufacturing and prevents assembly errors and reworks, for example, dowel pins, hole position in unequal distance, contour with nonsymmetry.

Transportation and Storage

Designing parts that are easily handled during transportation and storage should be considered. Products can be accommodated in commercially available storage systems, for example, semiconductor wafers that fit in a cassette box and parts that can be gravity fed into assembly rather than assembled by pick and place. Even if the part were to be assembled by pick and place, parts geometry allows robots to pick.

Automatic Assembly Inspection

Designing parts that help automatic assembly inspection through placement of a serial number or part identification number and laser marking helps traceability. This also helps during the assembly process for nonconformance management and configuration management.

2.3.6. ORGANIZING FOR IMPROVEMENT

There are two aspects of an improvement organization. The first is the improvement organization itself centered on the lean champions and steering committee. The second aspect is the improvement structure itself made up of five levels of kaizen from individual to supply chain.

Many organizations, including Toyota, have found that implementing and sustaining lean requires full-time expert facilitators. They are the repository of expertise and should have general responsibility for lean momentum. This function is often referred to as the Lean Promotion Office (LPO) or the Kaizen Promotion Office (KPO). The purpose of this office is to provide the resources for continuous improvement.

The LPO and KPO can motivate people, collect resources, find external resources for education and implementation, and take on rapid improvement projects. The LPO and KPO can also make connections between different parts of the organization that may be pursuing independent or uncoordinated improvement activities. The LPO is a facilitating office, not a doing function.

Lean improvement needs to be organized on five levels in most, if not all, organizations on a lean journey. The following sections discuss levels of improvement, in order of increasing scope and depth.

Individual (Point Kaizen)

At the individual workstation level, there are always opportunities to reduce waste—workplace organization, inventory and tool location, work sequence, ergonomics, poka-yoke, and on and on. The team leader has an important role to play here—encouraging, facilitating, and recognizing achievement and bringing individual improvements to the attention of others.

Work Teams (Mini Kaizen)

Work teams or groups that work in a cell or on a line segment undertake improvement projects affecting their collective work area. Examples include work flows, cell layout, line balancing, 5S, and quality improvements. These initiatives may be done on the fly or may be part of a one- to two-day mini kaizen.

Kaizen Blitz

A kaizen blitz is an event carried out in a local area, but it involves more time and outsiders. These events address more complex issues than what the work team

2.3.6.1

can comfortably handle. For many companies, blitz teams are the prime engine for improvement. For this type of improvement, the team forms for the specific purpose of the event and disbands thereafter.

Flow Kaizen

Flow kaizen teams typically work across a full-value stream, taking weeks to months for a project. They are the prime engines for creating future states. Their targets are those set out in a future state and action plane activity. These teams are usually led by a project manager, often assisted by a champion, and sometimes mentored by consultants. The team comprises multidisciplinary and cross-functional members. Flow kaizen projects usually address process issues, system issues, and organizational issues.

Supply Chain Kaizen

Supply chain project teams comprise part-time representatives from participating companies within the value stream. They are focused on optimizing the entire value stream so that all within the supply chain can benefit from improvement. These teams usually have a project manager, typically from the original equipment manufacturer (OEM) company, and are supported by champions and consultants.

When you first start with improvements you may find it difficult to differentiate among short-, medium-, and long-term goals. It is best to just start and sort things out as you go. Here are a few guidelines to help you along the way:

- Manage each improvement with a single person

- Manage improvements visually in a single location

- Manage each improvement with a single schedule

- Hold review sessions weekly

- Avoid long projects (greater than 90 days)

Each organization needs to find its own style of improvement process and establish a standard method for everyone to follow.

2.3.6.1. Kaizen Blitz Events

Kaizen is a Japanese term that literally means "to break apart and put back together in a better way." It is commonly referred to as continuous improvement.

The term "kaizen blitz" refers to a team approach to quickly tear down and rebuild a process to function more efficiently. However, "kaizen" is commonly used for all types of continuous improvement.

Kaizen events fill the gaps between the individual, local improvement initiatives, and bigger initiatives such as value stream improvement. They are essential for getting cross-functional and multilevel teams involved in a lean transformation. In that respect, kaizen events have a dual role—to make improvements and to teach and communicate.

The kaizen principles from a lean perspective are composed of the following:

- Define value as perceived by the customer
- Identify the value stream
- Eliminate waste
- Create flow
- Establish pull where flow is not possible
- Pursue perfection (Womack and Jones 2003, 16–26)

Kaizen is much more than an event; it is a philosophy, a mind-set, and, for break-through performance, a critical vehicle to achieve strategic objectives and execute value stream/process improvements. Kaizen principles are a comprehensive way of approaching the continual improvement of an organization's processes. Applying kaizen principles is the mind-set of a continually improving organization. Kaizen thinking, or a kaizen mind-set, consists of the following elements:

- Kaizen is everyone's job
- "Go to the gemba," observe, and document reality
- Emphasis on problem awareness
- Use of problem-solving tools
- Bias for action
- Standardization once improvement has been achieved
- Focus on improving both process and results
- Applies to any aspect of the work
- Continual improvement to achieve higher standards by involving and engaging the workforce

A kaizen event follows a systematic methodology for implementing rapid change through elimination of waste. The methodology is based on the Plan-Do-Check-Act (PDCA) cycle and can be defined as:

1. Plan—establish the goals for the targeted process and identify the required changes (improvements) to achieve the goals
2. Do—implement the changes
3. Check—assess whether and how the executed plan delivered the intended results
4. Act—depending on the results from the prior step, standardize and stabilize the improvements to sustain them, or begin the cycle again

The kaizen event has become a popular tool for implementing lean at many companies. It is typically structured as a five-day event, starting with training on Monday, analysis and problem solving on Tuesday, implementation and experimenting on Wednesday and Thursday, and presenting the results on Friday.

2.3.6.1

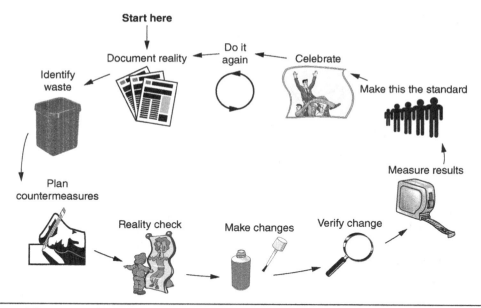

Figure 2.3.6.1-1   Kaizen in 10 steps.

Figure 2.3.6.1-1 is an example of the PDCA philosophy for kaizen expanded into a simple 10-step process.

There are two basic levels of kaizen: flow kaizen and process kaizen.

Flow Kaizen

Flow kaizen is about value stream improvement, getting flow going, and should be a major concern of senior management. Flow kaizen is performed on the material and information flow of an overall value stream.

Process Kaizen

Process kaizen is about the elimination of waste, with focus on a specific process or subprocess, which should be more the responsibility of the front line. Process kaizen in a mature lean organization is driven significantly by daily kaizen activities.

Most kaizen events are focused on internal processes. But there is another, growing opportunity: the customer-focused kaizen event. Here the focus shifts to solving the customer's problems or improving the customer's effectiveness.

Kaizen Pitfalls

A successful kaizen event requires a great deal of both preparation and follow-up. From years of experience, here are 10 mistakes to avoid during a kaizen:

1. *Lack of a charter.* A charter establishes the framework of the kaizen. It determines the problem statement, relevant background information, time frame, team members, resources involved, and how the improvement will be measured. Without a charter, the kaizen could take a very different direction.

2. *Lack of identification of critical success factors.* For a successful kaizen, the elements that are critical to the process need to be identified. How to determine the success of this kaizen needs to be defined and measured. This allows for verification of the effectiveness of action items and countermeasures. Without measurement, the kaizen can go on and on.

3. *Scope is too large.* The size of the scope or the amount tackled within the kaizen is important for getting things done. If the scope is too large, improvements may not be implemented.

4. *Kaizen event not linked to business plan (organizational strategy).* Kaizens should be aligned to meet an organization's goals. It can be wasteful to improve processes that are not part of the plan, since resources to perform kaizens are limited.

5. *Poor team selection.* The team members on the kaizen are the brainpower and manpower behind the improvement. Picking the team members should be an important part of planning the kaizen. People's skill sets, individuals' expertise or knowledge, individuals within and outside the process, and who will provide the learning should be considered.

6. *Striving for perfection.* The kaizen will take a very long time if the team tries to implement a perfect solution. Perfection is elusive. Call the kaizen complete if 80% of the goal is accomplished. The new state can be improved once the initial improvements have been verified as successful.

7. *Poor follow-through.* In some kaizens, it can be difficult to complete all the items within the time frame. Failure to follow through on these can undermine the team's efforts. Good follow-through is necessary to ensure the improvements that are made are maintained to prevent backsliding.

8. *Not presenting results.* Failure to present the results after the kaizen can cause the team to feel unappreciated. It also restricts learning throughout the organization, as another area with a similar situation could benefit from knowing how this team solved the problem.

9. *Lack of visibility for nonparticipants.* Getting buy-in from those not participating on the team is important for sustaining the improvement. Team members are involved in creating and implementing the solution. Those who are not involved need to be aware of the improvements the team is making. If they are not made aware, they will naturally resist the improvement.

10. *Lack of management commitment.* Management must not only support the kaizen but actively participate. Kaizens are as much a learning opportunity as anything else in the organization. Management must ensure the team has everything it needs to be successful, and when the team is successful, management must recognize the accomplishment.

The kaizen event has become the cornerstone of lean implementation for many companies. They want to use the lean toolkit to quickly drive change in the

2.3.6.1

organization and achieve aggressive metrics. Some organizations track the number of events held to judge the level of lean activity and the dollars saved in order to impress the board of directors with the benefits of lean. The primary purpose of kaizen events is to develop lean leadership and problem-solving skills of employees. Certainly, a side benefit is to improve the business indicators, but it is not the driver.

2.3.7. COUNTERMEASURE ACTIVITIES

Lean companies like Toyota do not consider any of the tools or practices, such as kanbans or single minute exchange of dies (SMED), which so many outsiders have observed and copied, as fundamental to lean. They use them merely as temporary responses to specific problems until a better approach is found or conditions change. They're referred to as "countermeasures," rather than "solutions," because the latter would imply a permanent resolution to a problem.

Toyota calls the improvements countermeasures (rather than the ubiquitous "solutions") because it implies that (1) we are countering a specific problem, and (2) it is what we will use until we discover a better countermeasure. The countermeasures address the root cause(s) while conforming to the lean principles.

Countermeasures are the actions taken to reduce or eliminate the root causes of problems that are preventing you from reaching your goals. Countermeasures are typically identified by team members for the purpose of eliminating waste (muda), unevenness (mura), and/or unreasonableness (muri). Countermeasures are also taken when a problem pops up.

Every countermeasure must be tested to determine whether it is consistent with lean and improves the situation. Countermeasures are part of a robust thinking process called Plan-Do-Check-Act (PDCA). If the countermeasure does not effectively eliminate the root cause, another countermeasure is needed. Countermeasures must be prioritized; not every countermeasure can and should be executed.

Here are some countermeasures that will be discussed in the next sections:

- *Mistake- and error-proofing (poka-yoke):* Mistake-proofing is the use of process design features to facilitate correct actions, prevent simple errors, or mitigate the negative impact of errors. *Poka-yoke* is Japanese slang for "mistake-proofing," a term coined by Shigeo Shingo.

- *Quick changeover/setup reduction:* Quick changeover or setup reduction is a process for changing over production equipment from one part number to another in as little time as possible. The overall goal is to reduce the time devoted to setup/changeover so that more time is available to produce a wider variety of products.

- *One-piece flow:* One-piece flow refers to the concept of moving one work piece at a time between operations within a work cell. The goals of one-piece flow are to make one part at a time, to make that part correctly all the time, and to produce without unplanned interruptions and lengthy queue times.

- *Right-sized equipment:* Right-sized equipment is highly capable, easy to maintain (therefore available to produce whenever needed), quick to change over, easy to move, and designed to be installed in small increments of capacity to facilitate capital and labor linearity.

- *Cellular flow:* Cellular flow manufacturing is the linking of manual and machine operations into the most efficient combination of resources to maximize value-added content while minimizing waste. The most efficient combination implies the concept of line balancing. When processes are balanced, the product flows continuously, parts movement is minimized, wait time between operations is reduced, inventory is reduced, and productivity increases.

- *Sensible automation:* Sensible automation, or jidoka as it is referred to in lean, gives equipment the ability to distinguish good parts from bad parts autonomously, without being monitored by an operator. An essential component of jidoka is the stoppage of work to fix problems as they occur. This leads to improvements in the process that build in quality by eliminating the root causes of defects.

- *Material signals (kanban):* Kanban is a Japanese word that means "sign" or "signboard." At its core, kanban is a replenishment system that orders new material only after consumption of existing material.

- *Source inspection:* Source inspection is a quality inspection that the buyer performs at the vendor's location before the material is received or shipped. Source inspection means the work is reviewed before it is passed on to the next station. It is used to identify, correct, and contain a problem before it enters into the value stream.

Over the years, lean companies have developed a robust set of tools and practices that they use as countermeasures, but many tools have changed or have even been eliminated as improvements are made.

2.3.7.1. Mistake and Error Proofing (Poka Yoke)

Poka-yoke is Japanese for "without mistake," or to avoid (yokeru) inadvertent errors (poka). It respects the intelligence of workers by taking the judgment out of repetitive tasks or actions where errors are likely to occur by designing error prevention into products or processes. It supports the Toyota Production System (TPS) concept of "zero defects." It becomes a critical countermeasure as companies approach one-piece flow, because a defect can "stop the line" when inventory has been significantly reduced.

The ultimate goal of mistake-proofing is to eliminate the causes of errors that result in defects. To understand poka-yoke thinking, let's begin by distinguishing between an error (mistake) and a defect. An error occurs when a worker deviates from a standard process. For example, the process says to lock the part into the fixture before rotating it, but the worker forgets to lock it in. The worker has made an error (mistake).

A defect occurs when a part or product does not meet specifications or customer expectations. In the example, if the worker rotates the part after forgetting to lock it into the fixture and the part falls on the floor and is damaged, the part is now defective. Please note that defects are caused by errors, but not all errors will become defects. Therefore, errors and defects are not the same thing. Poka-yoke assumes errors can be prevented by exposing the sources of defects.

Three components define a poka-yoke device:

1. 100% inspection

2. Rapid feedback

3. Low cost and simple

100% Inspection

The 100% inspection component requires that actual parts or products be checked against the standard every time a part or product is made, 100% of the time, at the point where the error could occur. The goal in doing this is to ensure that real-time information about the process is available so that workers will know immediately if an error has been made and can make a correction, before it becomes a defect. Sometimes this component is referred to as "source inspection," or a method of inspection that catches errors and provides feedback before additional processing is done. This type of inspection is the most powerful from the viewpoint of TPS, because it gives the people doing the work the right information at the right time to minimize the chances of defects occurring. Source inspection is more beneficial than other traditional inspection types such as judgment inspections or informative inspections. In a judgment inspection, an inspector at the end of the line determines whether items are defective. Informative inspections include successive inspections, where the employee at the next operation checks the work of the prior operation, and self-inspections, where an operator checks his or her own parts for defects. Note that self-inspection is useful only if it results in problem-solving and error-proofing activities when defects are found.

Rapid Feedback

The second component, rapid feedback, is necessary whenever an error occurs in order to minimize the risk of defect creation and to allow associates to immediately call for help or make process corrections to get back on track. This component dictates that poka-yoke devices be placed as close to the source of an error as possible to provide real-time feedback.

Low Cost and Simple

The third component suggests that poka-yoke devices need not be expensive or complex. In fact, some of the most elegant poka-yoke devices are made with very little cash and a bit of creativity. Figure 2.3.7.1-1 shows an example; by placing the cardboard template in front of several rows of parts bins, the operator cannot pick parts from the incorrect bin.

Types of Poka-Yoke

There are two types of poka-yoke devices:

1. Prevent devices

2. Detect devices

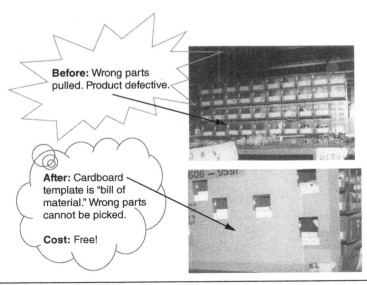

Before: Wrong parts pulled. Product defective.

After: Cardboard template is "bill of material." Wrong parts cannot be picked.

Cost: Free!

Figure 2.3.7.1-1   Example of a prevent device for poka-yoke.

Prevent Device

The more powerful of the two poka-yoke devices is the prevent device, or a poka-yoke that prevents an error from being made. The cardboard part template in Figure 2.3.7.1-1 is an example of this type of device, because the worker is prevented from reaching into the incorrect bins when the device is in place. Another example is a fixture where the shape of the part has been cut into the fixture, and thus the part can only be inserted in the correct orientation.

Detect Device

A detect poka-yoke detects a mistake as soon as possible after it is made and prevents the mistake from being passed on to the next operation. Figure 2.3.7.1-2 shows a detect poka-yoke where the switch-holding fixture also serves as a check fixture for correct wiring. If the switch is not wired correctly, it cannot be released from the fixture, and bad parts cannot be passed to the customer at the next production step.

Obviously a prevent device is always preferable to a detect device. However, this may not always be possible and/or practical. The next best choice is a detect device.

2.3.7.2. Quick Changeover/Setup Reduction (SMED)

Quick changeover, also referred to as setup reduction or single minute exchange of dies (SMED), is a technique that can significantly reduce the time taken to switch from producing one product to producing another. "Single minute" reflects Shigeo Shingo's (creator of the SMED concept) thinking that changeovers and set-ups should take less than 10 minutes (a single digit). A closely related concept is one-touch exchange of die (OTED), which suggests that changeovers can occur in less than one minute!

Switch is sometimes miswired to terminal block.

Detect devise that catches assembly error before removal from assembly fixture.

Cost: $500.00

Continuity tester swings over terminal block. Won't release if wiring is wrong.

Figure 2.3.7.1–2   Example of a detect device for poka-yoke.

The concept of quick changeover/SMED is important because long change-overs create bottlenecks, drive up lot sizes, and reduce flexibility to provide a broad selection of products to customers. Traditionally, companies adhering to "economic order quantities" (EOQ) formulas endorsed making large amounts to amortize the cost of long setups, but lean considers this thinking fundamentally wrong because it penalizes customers. Quick changeover/SMED also acknowledges the hidden costs of producing large amounts of inventory, for example, the cost of storing excess material, counting it, moving it around, and scrapping it.

Setup time is the key metric for quick changeover/SMED. *Setup time* is the total elapsed time from the *last* piece of one product made from one process to the first *good* piece of the next product produced by another process. This definition may be different from what many people traditionally know as setup time. For example, if the first piece off the machine must be checked by the quality control department, and the operator walks the piece over to the department and it sits for one hour before someone is available to check it, then the walk time, the waiting time, the time to check the part, and the time to walk it back to the machine operator must be included in the total changeover time. The overall goal of quick changeover/SMED is to reduce the time devoted to setup/changeover so that more time is available to set up and produce a wider variety of products/services.

The key steps for reducing setup time are:

1. Go see and document the current condition for setups

2. Separate internal and external setup steps

3. Convert internal steps to external steps wherever possible

4. Improve internal steps

5. Document and standardize the setup method

6. Train workers in the new method and hold them accountable for following it

7. Be on the lookout for additional ways to cut setup time and perform problem solving whenever the standard cannot be followed, costs are rising, quality problems are exposed, or customer conditions change

- Preparation—30%

- Mounting and removing—5%

- Measures, settings, and calibration—15%

- Trial runs and adjustments—50%

Figure 2.3.7.2-1   Breakdown of typical changeover time components.

Figure 2.3.7.2-1 shows the typical breakdown of changeover time components.

The best way to begin reducing changeover time is to "go see" how the process is done today. Using a video camera to film a setup/changeover provides documentation of all the steps and makes it easy to break them down to understand which are valuable, which take the most time, and which are the best candidates for improvement. The use of the video camera is not to replace the step of the team observing the process firsthand. The video camera should be used as an aid to catch things the team did not initially notice during observation and for timing of steps.

The next step after watching the setup is to understand which aspects of a setup are internal and which are external. Internal setup activities occur while the process is stopped. For example, tooling is removed and new tooling is installed on a CNC machine while it is stopped. External activities are steps that are done while the process is still running. An example might be bringing the stock for the next job to the machine while the current job is still running, or gathering the CNC tooling at the point of the machine where it will be changed (to reduce walking time) before the machine is shut down for the changeover.

A key goal for setups and changeovers is to reduce or eliminate all the activities that are handled internally to the setup, and handle as much of the setup as possible externally. This means the process is stopped as little as possible and can continue to create value.

Often first changeover improvements are simple workplace organization efforts. 5S is a great place to start quick changeover/SMED, making sure all the tools, machines, materials, supplies, setup sheets, and information needed are accessible and well organized.

Other early SMED improvement efforts focus on reducing the amount of internal setup time by identifying steps that can be done while the prior job is still running, such as getting materials and documentation, heating dies, and presetting tooling.

Once as many steps are externalized as possible, the focus should be on improving those setup steps that must remain internal. Typically this will involve focusing on drivers of operator motion, for example, fastening and unfastening bolts. Another key to reducing internal setup time is standardization. For example, does the operator have to spend a lot of time getting things square or the right height because plating and/or bolting patterns are not standardized? The following are some things to look into when focusing on improving internal setup times:

- Eliminate bolts

- Eliminate adjustments

2.3.7.2

- Standardize tools
- Standardize tool positions
- Standardize programs (e.g., machine programming such as CNCs, injection molding)
- Use setup teams

Finally, it is important to develop standardized work for setups. Once a standard for quick changeover/SMED is established, it should be documented like any other standardized work. This will spell out the conditions necessary for success and help ensure that time, quality, safety, and cost expectations are consistent for changeovers. Once setup standards are determined, employees are trained and held accountable for following the standards. As Figure 2.3.7.2-2 identifies, the four steps for reducing setups are (1) making the process stable, (2) making it standard, (3) making it easy, and (4) making it stick.

As with all other lean countermeasures, the assumption with setup reduction is that experiments will continue and standards will change as better ways are discovered and proved through worker involvement. Remember, the best setup is no setup, and lean organizations keep chipping away at changeover times to create capacity, cut lot sizes, improve flexibility, and increase operational availability. As Dr. Shingo noted, the vast majority of changeover time can be eliminated by continuing to apply the PDCA process to changeover activities. Operators experienced in setups and skilled in problem identification and problem solving will be able to point to more ways to reduce setups.

2.3.7.3. One Piece Flow

One-piece, or single-piece, flow is "a situation in which products proceed, one complete product at a time, through various operations in design, order-tasking, and production, without interruptions, backflows, or scrap" (Womack and Jones 2003, 352). This does not mean that only one product is produced at a time; rather,

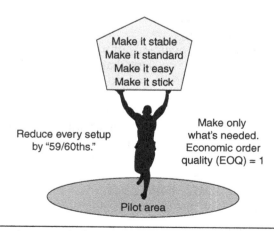

Figure 2.3.7.2-2 Four steps to reducing setups.

only one operation is performed at a time on any single product. It also has considerations for line balancing (takt, cycle, and lead times).

Consider the following process examples (machine and human):

- A printed circuit board population process has several operations (see Figure 2.3.7.3-1 for a simplified process flow). During this overall process of circuit board population, only one piece flows through each of the operations, achieving one-piece flow.

- The supplier purchase-order placement process also has several operations. To achieve one-piece flow, the purchasing agent performs one operation at a time, from part request to order placement.

Using the example in Figure 2.3.7.3-1, it is possible for several circuit boards to be in work at once depending on the machine configuration. Using the basic process and assuming the machine "picks" and "places" all the parts in one station, lead bending occurs in another, and clinching in yet another, it is possible for three pieces to be in work at once. This still achieves one-piece flow, as only one piece is at each station at a time.

Like the circuit board population example, the purchasing example has many operations (e.g., identify commodity, identify preferred/approved suppliers,

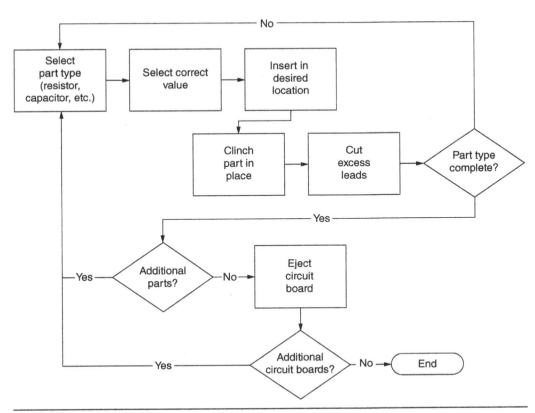

Figure 2.3.7.3-1 Simplified printed circuit board population process flow.

develop purchase order package, request quotation, review quotations, place order, and close order upon receipt of parts) within the process that can result in several purchase orders being worked at one time, but only one purchase order should be in any one operation at a time.

According to Levionson and Rerick (2002, 128), one-piece processing "also promotes inventory reductions" through reduction in takt and cycle times, rework reduction through sensible automation (see Section 2.3.7.6), and built-in feedback (see Section 2.2.7).

2.3.7.4. Right Sized Equipment

Cellular flow (see Section 2.3.7.5) and right-sized equipment are directly related. The primary goal of right-sized equipment is to ensure that equipment and tools are efficiently and effectively utilized to maximum extent. This goal, in conjunction with other lean enterprise methods and principles, ensures that equipment and tools are correct for current and planned build rates. "[Taiichi] Ohno and his associates achieved continuous flow in low-volume production ... by 'right-sizing' (miniaturizing) machines so that processing steps of different types (say, molding, painting, and assembly) could be conducted immediately adjacent to each other" (Womack and Jones 2003, 23).

Other benefits of right-sized equipment include:

- Reduced inventory through reduction of batch processing

- Reduced capital investment through analysis of need

- Improved cycle time by having the equipment and tools necessary to do the work

- Reduced and streamlined floor space requirements

- Lower inventory carrying costs

- Support for just-in-time processing

- Lower setup and teardown time and effort

- Waste reduction through shorter wait times and reduced movement

Implementation of right-sized equipment is done through a process (Figure 2.3.7.4-1) that ensures alignment with company goals and strategy, customer needs (demand or "pull"), and environment (business) change. The personnel performing this analysis will do the following:

1. Identify and review the products being produced for process requirements, test requirements, and so on.

2. Determine the current or planned production rates so that capacity analysis can be performed to ensure that the equipment assessed can support demand while having a high utilization rate that provides for required maintenance based on predicted equipment reliability.

3. Determine the equipment required to produce the product.

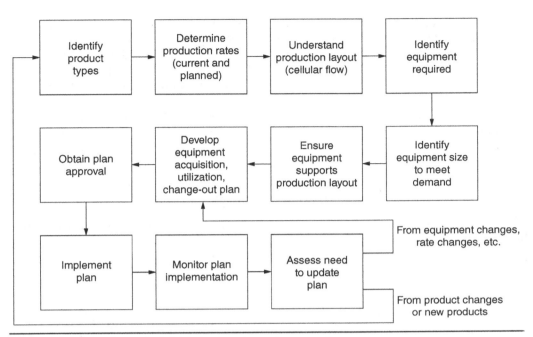

Figure 2.3.7.4-1 Suggested right–sized equipment process flow.

4–5. Given items 1–3, determine what equipment can be or should be used to support product build, test, inspection, and so on. As part of sensible automation (see Section 2.3.7.6):

   – Determine what processes can be automated versus those that require human knowledge and touch to ensure product quality.

   – Assess equipment complexity against employee skills to identify gaps and develop mitigation plans.

6. Review the production layout to assess available flow space for equipment and locations that support cellular flow and drive reductions in movement and other wastes.

7. Develop a plan for review by employees and management, provide cost benefit analysis, implement a schedule based on approval, and understand capitalization versus expense and align equipment to these two categories. Prioritize equipment needs according to return on investment analysis. Be prepared to answer questions. Ensure expectations for approval are consistent with company goals and budget.

8. Schedule time to present the plan to stakeholders. Move forward based on approval, schedule, and changes.

9–11. Implement, monitor, and update the plan as needed and approved. With the authority provided by management, make adjustments to the plan or update and present for approval of changes.

"As you right-size your tools, it will become apparent that a large fraction of your people and tools can be dedicated to specific product families" (Womack and Jones 2003, 256). This statement—proved over and over through lean enterprise/ manufacturing—ties the process of analyzing and right-sizing equipment to reductions in waste, improvements in product quality and cycle time, and higher utilization of people and machines.

Right Sizing Equipment 3P is one type of the 3P Production Process Preparation process (see Section 2.2.4). The focus should be on creating a machine or work cell that does not currently exist or is a complicated cell. The steps to a Right Sizing Equipment 3P are as follows:

1. Define the purpose with at least one measurement of performance and target.

2. List and review each process step using flowcharts, a spaghetti diagram, a fishbone diagram, and so on.

3. Clarify the scope (single machine, work cell, size of batch, etc.).

4. Gather representative parts (or documents for service).

5. Begin the "process at a glance" sheet (Figure 2.3.7.4-2) for each component/step, including material sketch, process method, gage method, tools required, jig/fixture/hanedashi (auto-eject mechanisms), and machine.

Step no.				
Concept no.				
Sketch				
Tools				
Fixtures				
Gages				
Comments				

Figure 2.3.7.4–2 "Process at a glance" sheet.

6. Complete seven ways for each process, including process method, gage method, tools required, and jig/fixture/hanedashi needed. Go back to nature by identifying key action words such as "hole," "coat," "remove," "lift," "attach," and so on. Find seven examples of each key word found in nature and look at how nature accomplishes this. This is an aid for brainstorming purposes.

7. Post and group examples.

8. Generate seven ideas for the machine, work cell, or process from a combination of the previous ideas for each action word.

9. Complete "process at a glance" sheets, including fixtures, poka-yoke, and gages for each of the ideas. Create one sheet for each of the seven ideas.

10. Select the three best designs using criteria set by the team (Table 2.3.7.4-1).

11. Construct prototypes of the three best machines, work cells, or processes.

12. Simulate the three best designs (trystorming).

13. Build in poka-yoke/hanedashi devices as needed.

14. Update "process at a glance" sheets.

15. Select top design.

16. Begin equipment specification.

Table 2.3.7.4-1   Example of right-sized equipment criteria for selection.

Criteria	Description	Rating scale
1-by-1	Equipment or process processes only one item at a time (one-piece flow)	One-piece flow = 5 Small batch = 3 Large batch = 1
City/Mall store shaped	Equipment or work cell stations should have a footprint that is narrow and deep like a city store. It should also be ergonomically short (maximum height of 5 ft.) Narrow and deep	Narrow and deep = 5 Requires reaching = 3 Requires walking = 1
Sidewalk shop	Operations should be like shopping from the sidewalk (operation in the front and supported in the back only) Support from back Work from front	Complete separation = 5 Some operations on the side = 3 No separation = 1

(continued)

2.3.7.4

Table 2.3.7.4-1   Example of right-sized equipment criteria for selection. *(continued)*

Criteria	Description	Rating scale
Part sizing	Equipment should be as narrow as possible; width should be as close as possible to the widest dimension of a single part	Close to part dimensions = 5 Twice as wide as part = 3 >3× as wide as part = 1
Takt speed	Equipment or work cell cycle time (manual + auto time) should be no faster than the target takt time of the product/service it's intended for	Cycle time is takt time = 5 Cycle faster than takt = 3 Cycle slower than takt = 1
Self-contained	Equipment should be completely self-contained; it should be easily moved on an immediate basis and easy to hook up and operate (e.g., single electric line)	Self-contained = 5 Multiple modules = 1
Load-load	Operates on a load-load basis, where the operator only loads the equipment (incorporates auto-eject features)	All load-load = 5 Some load-load = 3 No load-load = 1
Fast setup	Changeovers (COs) are nonexistent or occur in less than takt time, and the first part is always good	CO time < takt = 5 CO time about 2× takt = 3 CO time > 3× takt = 1
Safe and clean	Equipment should be safe and ergonomic for the employee, well-guarded, and easy to keep clean in less than 60 sec/shift	Clean-ability < 60 sec = 5 Clean-ability < 120 sec = 3 Clean-ability > 180 sec = 1
Easy operation	Correct operating conditions and steps should be visual; all controls should be in the front or at point of use (POUS)	POUS and visual = 5 No POUS or visual = 1
Easy maintenance	Equipment should be easy to maintain by operator (max. 60 sec/shift), maintenance department (max. 60 min/yr), and total productive maintenance (TPM) initiated	TPM part of design = 5 Not easily maintained = 1
Reconfiguring	Equipment should consist of mostly standardized modules that can be easily reused in other machines	Standard components = 5 Special components = 1
Poka-yoke	Equipment should not rely on the operator to make a choice where the equipment will auto-eject rejected product to a reject bin away from the operator, does not allow misloading, etc.	Poka-yoke = 5 No poka-yoke = 1
Development	Equipment should be simple and not require long development, build, or install time	Immediate = 5 Long lead time = 1

2.3.7.5. Cellular Flow

Typically a flow arrangement or work cell is set up for products, activities, or parts that share similar processing steps. Completing a part-quantity-process chart (Figure 2.3.7.5-1) is a great way to examine groups of products or parts and determine whether they can be combined and produced in a cellular flow arrangement.

Figure 2.3.7.5-1 shows that three of the four parts go through the gauge step (part C1 skips this step), but all four parts go through the wire and inspect steps. Notice that part D1 takes much longer to produce than the other three. The figure also shows the relative frequency of the parts. All of these data together can help suggest which parts are easily or reasonably combined and produced in a flow cell environment. For example, parts A1, B1, and C1 could easily be built in the same work cell. It may be difficult to produce D1 in the same work cell, even though it shares similar operations, because of the significant differences in cycle times for the gauge and wire steps for this product. This can also apply for service operations for different types of services.

Once a set of items has been defined for the cellular flow arrangement, the next step is to calculate the takt time for the cell so that the cell can be designed and staffed to operate at the customer's demand rate. In other words, in setting up a flow arrangement it is necessary to understand how fast things have to flow to meet customer demand; the cellular design has to support that rate.

With takt time information in hand, the next step is to develop a compact layout for the flow arrangement. Often a U-cell design (Figures 2.3.7.5-2 and 2.3.7.5-3) is used, with process steps arranged, in order, in a horseshoe shape. The beginning of the work area is across from the end of the work area, a' ''e opening of the 'U.' This arrangement facilitates flow and communication ; little room for inventory to accumulate. It also provides balance work across workers (see Section 2.2.6, "Standard

The next step is to divide up the work routine so that cell can accomplish his or her assigned set of tasks withir workers are assigned tasks that take longer than takt tim

Part	Quantity	Cycle time in minutes		
Process		Gauge	Wire	Inspect
A1	25	20	14	15
B1	20	30	20	14
C1	15		20	10
D1	5	200	100	3
Etc.				
Exclude wide variations. Identify product mix and average cycle time.				

Figure 2.3.7.5–1   Example of part–quantity–process chart.

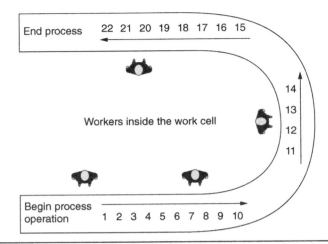

Everything the workers need to perform the work is placed in the order used, where needed

Figure 2.3.7.5-2 Example of a U-shaped cell layout.

Figure 2.3.7.5-3 Photo of a U-shaped cell layout.

requirement will not be met. If workers are given work content with very different work times, it will result in some workers waiting and other workers with inventory pileups. And if workers are all assigned tasks that can be completed in less than takt time, there is a tendency to overproduce. The goal is to have the right amount of people assigned to the work area to meet customer demand at a steady, reasonable pace.

The next step in creating cellular flow is to determine how much inventory is necessary to maintain the flow. In the best case, the only inventory in the process would be the work pieces employees are actually working on. However, some process conditions may dictate that additional inventory be held in the layout to accommodate flow interruptions and/or resupply issues. A case where raw material can be supplied to the work area only twice per day by the warehouse is an example where a standard amount of inventory (and space) will need to be held in the work cell in order for flow to be maintained. Another example of standard work-in-process (WIP) is a step where glue has to dry before the next step can be performed. Instead of the worker waiting for the glue to dry, extra WIP pieces can be inserted between the work steps to allow the next process to always have a piece with dry glue available to work on.

Good cellular flow requires a material and/or information conveyance plan documenting how and when materials will be brought to and taken away from the work area. This plan will affect space requirements, the workers' ability to work at takt rate, lead times, the frequency of feedback on quality or problems, and so on. A key thought in developing material conveyance plans is to make every effort to allow workers to stay focused on value-added work and not on moving or resupplying materials. These activities should be assigned to a specific material-handling function or lead people/supervisors in the area.

In a continuous flow environment, workers are expected to communicate and help one another in order to meet takt time. In the best case, workers have been cross trained to perform all jobs in the work area, thus increasing flexibility and improving the area's ability to quickly respond to changes in demand. In the best cellular flow arrangements, workers switch jobs frequently throughout the shift, perhaps every 1–2 hours. This has many benefits: It keeps employees practiced in every aspect of the job on a regular basis, it provides relief from repetitive motion and mental strain, and it means many sets of eyes are looking for improvement opportunities in all areas, every day. It also makes it easier to rebalance work should a worker call in sick or have to attend a meeting.

To maintain takt time, a cellular flow process must institute measurements and feedback mechanisms capable of alerting workers and supervisors to problems very quickly. The idea is to recognize immediately when countermeasures need to be taken to get back on track. Tools such as output charts and andon lights are visual management examples of how this is done in some processes. An example of a production output chart is shown in Figure 2.3.7.5-4. Using this type of form, employees track production output against goals every hour and can comment on reasons they are ahead or behind.

As parts of the value stream are moved into cellular flow, additional opportunities will become apparent and wastes may be exposed as process changes are made. The goal is to keep cycles of improvement going until true one-piece flow is attained. Even then, further improvements will still be possible based on workers' knowledge and creativity or as process or product conditions change.

Lean always seeks to move more and more of the value stream into continuous flow. The idea is to employ lean thinking and countermeasures to keep chipping away at the value stream in order to reduce or eliminate any breaks in the flow.

- What is the reasonable target by hour?
- What problems prevent that target from being achieved?
- Are there trends by hour, day, or week?

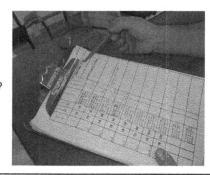

Figure 2.3.7.5-4 Example of a production output chart.

2.3.7.6. Sensible Automation

Sensible automation has two primary functions: (1) automation of machines and (2) automating the right portions of the process. Automation of machines "means imparting human intelligence to machines" (Levionson and Rerick 2002, 17). Automating the right portions of the process means changing to machine processing versus human processing where practical.

"An *autonomated* machine is therefore one that can distinguish between normal and abnormal conditions. It does not require continuous operator attention and a single worker can therefore handle several machines" (Levionson and Rerick 2002, 17). Essentially this means the machine will stop when a problem occurs or a defect is detected, reducing rework (muda). Examples of machine automation are as follows:

- Automatic detection of wear versus periodic inspection for wear (Levionson and Rerick 2002)

- Automatic collection of data (with warnings or stoppage for trends or out-of-control points—e.g., Western Electric Rules—for process variation)

- Machine changeover of dies, parameters, and so on, based on product worked (i.e., automated adjustment of flow solder machine parameters based on product part number)

"If an abnormal condition stops an automated workstation (machine) the operator shouldn't simply fix it and restart it. It could be a chronic problem that people must keep correcting" (Levionson and Rerick 2002, 17). The root cause of the problem is determined to prevent recurrence, reducing operator involvement in the future and positively impacting processing time.

"Involve the right people/functions within the organization" (Maio 2010, 24) when determining what processes or portions of the process can be automated. Employees closest to the process have tacit knowledge (see Section 2.2.15) that can help in automation analysis and decision making. Consider the cellular layout, one-piece flow, and right-sized equipment when analyzing process (or portion of) automation. The analysis should consider the return on investment (ROI), special processes, the ability to detect problems, available technology, and the impact on employee and customer satisfaction.

According to Imler (2006, 11), ROI can be "calculated as reduced costs in terms of:

- Reduced new product development cycle-time

- Reduced new product development costs

- Reduced new product testing and clinical study costs

- Reduced post market launch costs

- Reduced service, warranty, and field corrective action costs

- Improved margins"

Additionally, when related to sensible automation, ROI calculations include:

- Defect reduction projections

- Changeover time reductions

- Maximization of employee utilization

- Reductions in downtime (it is easier to fix something that has wear than something that is broken)

Sensible automation works with managing flow visually to alert employees to machine problems. However, just because a machine is stopped does not mean there is a defect. "When we see a machine that is stopped, we need to know why. Is it stopped because of scheduled down-time? changeover and setup? quality problems? machine breakdown? preventive repair?" (Imai 1997, 97). When possible, different visual indicators should be used for defects and breakage versus planned downtime (changeover, preventive maintenance, etc.). The use of audible signals, in addition to visual signals, for machine breakage or defect detection should be considered when implementing sensible automation.

Sensible automation can have a significant ROI. It is also known as jidoka and "was pioneered by Sakichi Toyoda at the turn of the twentieth century when he invented automatic looms that stopped if a thread broke. This permitted one operator to oversee many machines with no risk of producing vast amounts of defective cloth" (Womack and Jones 2003, 231). Clearly, jidoka maximizes employee utilization and eliminates waste (muda).

2.3.7.7. Material Signals (Kanban)

It is important to distinguish between kanban and pull. They are related but too often confounded. With pull, production is based on consumption at the successive process. In other words, there needs to be a demand "pull" from a downstream process to initiate production at the feeding process.

So how are pull and kanban related? Pull is the scheduling principle; kanban is one mechanism where pull can be created. At its core, kanban is a replenishment system that orders, or triggers, new material production to begin only after consumption of existing material. The word "kanban" is derived from the Japanese *kamban*, which literally means "signboard." It is a signaling device that gives authorization and instructions for the production or withdrawal (conveyance) of items in a pull system. Ordering is not based on a forecast that may have been made months ago, but is visually "ordered" by means of a signboard. In this way, kanban aligns inventory and orders with actual current usage.

The kanban system was developed more than 20 years ago by Taiichi Ohno to achieve the following objectives:

- Reducing costs by eliminating waste/scrap

- Try to create work sites that can respond to changes quickly

- Facilitate the methods of achieving and assuring quality control

- Design work sites according to human dignity, mutual trust and support, and allowing workers to reach their maximum potential (Singh 1995, 630–31)

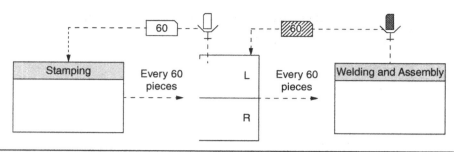

Figure 2.3.7.7-1   Example of production and withdrawal kanbans.
Source: Adapted from Marchwinski and Shook (2006, 76).

The premise of kanban is to create visual indicators to allow the operators to determine how much of a product to run and when to stop or change over. Operators then produce product based on actual usage rather than forecasted usage. They only produce new product to replace the product consumed by its consumer(s), and they only produce product based on visual signals sent by its customer(s).

There are two main types of kanbans: production kanbans and move kanbans. Production kanbans give the signal to build. Move kanbans, or withdrawal kanbans (Figure 2.3.7.7-1), give the signal to move product or material.

Each organization must define, apply, and follow its own set of kanban rules (policies and procedures). Here are some of the major rules that should be considered when setting up a kanban system:

- Never move or produce parts without a kanban.

- Never produce more parts than kanbans available. Kanbans are used to control inventory for many reasons. Producing parts without a kanban will create waste.

- Never move more parts than kanbans available. Storage locations are usually established with a set level of inventory in mind. Moving extra boxes could result in unnecessary overflow at the storage location.

- No one is permitted to send information other than that on a kanban. A kanban will signal what to build, when to build it, and how much to build. Communicating information other than this will violate one of the other rules.

- Do not send defective product to the next operation. This is a basic lean manufacturing concept, but it also applies to kanban systems. As the amount of inventory will be low, passing on bad parts could lead to many types of waste, especially waste of defects.

To ensure success when implementing a kanban system, everyone must be trained on the proper use, and the importance of discipline must be emphasized. Establish rules and ensure that everyone in the organization understands them. This way it will be obvious to anyone in the company when something is out of place.

To determine the amount of kanban signals (bins, cards, etc.) and the frequency of kanban withdrawals requires some analysis. Keep the following general rule in mind when thinking about the number of kanbans:

$$y = \frac{DT(1 + x)}{C}$$

where

y = Number of kanbans

D = Demand per unit of time

T = Lead time

C = Container capacity

x = Buffer, or safety factor

For example, suppose that hourly demand is 200 units, lead time is 12 hours, and the container capacity is 144 units. Assume that there is variation in lead time or demand, so a safety factor may be set to 15%:

$$y = ((200 \times 12) \times (1 + .15)) / 144 = 20 \text{ kanban cards}$$

How many hours' worth of demand will 20 cards represent?

$$(20 \text{ cards} \times 144 \text{ units}) = 2880 \text{ units}$$

$$2880 / 200 \text{ units per hour} = 14.4 \text{ hours' worth of material}$$

There are numerous ways to set up kanban visual signals. An organization may use common types of visual signals, or it may be creative and come up with something specific for the facility. The following are examples of some of the most common types of visual signals (see Section 2.2.1 for more examples in visual workplace):

- Kanban cards are most commonly thought of when discussing kanban, as Toyota used these when it introduced its kanban scheduling system.

- Look-see uses floor markings or signs that tell you at a glance when to replenish an item. The use of color gives the visual signal at a glance.

- Kanban boards are a variation of kanban cards. The board simply uses magnets, plastic chips, or colored washers as signals. Each object represents a container or production item.

- Two-card kanban systems work well in situations where product rotation is important. The cards signal the product location and age. This type of system is typically used for large items where flow racks are not used.

- Faxbans are a variation of the kanban card system. In this type of system, used in large plants or when off-site warehouses or vendors are involved, a fax—or more often these days, an e-mail—is sent when it's time to replenish products.

- Electronic kanban is the high-tech version of the faxban. The electronic kanban automatically transmits requirements or allows suppliers to access the customer's inventory status and ship replacement material.

A kanban is an effective way of reducing muda (waste) and mura (unevenness), and to eliminate muri (overburden—overload). Kanban scheduling also results in the following benefits:

- Reduces inventory
- Improves flow
- Prevents overproduction
- Places control at the operations level
- Improves responsiveness to changes in demand
- Minimizes risk of having obsolete inventory

Finally, fluctuating or exceptional demand will kill a kanban system stone dead unless it is seen coming. To make the kanban system work, a smoothed daily production rate is essential. Where the schedule is not level, quite significant buffer inventories between the various stages may be idle for lengthy periods, waiting to be pulled.

Notice also that the number of kanbans depends on demand. This means that when demand changes, the number of kanbans should change. When takt time changes, kanbans will often have to change. Kanbans don't replace the need for proper production planning completely.

2.3.7.8. Source Inspection

Inspection, as defined in the ASQ Quality Glossary, is "measuring, examining, testing and gauging one or more characteristics of a product or service and comparing the results with specified requirements to determine whether conformity is achieved for each characteristic" (ASQ 2010). Source inspection serves this purpose but assigns company representatives to perform the work at the supplier's facility. Source inspection has several advantages and approaches, including:

- Monitoring of supplier processes and product
- Reduced company inventory and/or floor space
- Ensuring the product meets requirements before being received by the company
- Enables dock-to-stock or drop-shipment-to-place-of-need options
- Reduced costs

Source inspection needs are analyzed by a quality representative of the company with special consideration of supplier product criticality to end product; costs; return on investment; the ability of the company to verify supplier product; the end goal of performing source inspection; and the overall desired activities, tasks, and results. Source inspection can be tailored based on the depth of supplier oversight and the product being procured. Tailoring includes the type of company representative, frequency of source inspection, detail of source inspection role and activities performed, shipment options, and so on. Source inspection needs to be communicated and agreed to by the supplier and the company.

The company representative performing source inspection needs to be a contract service provider—acting as an agent of the company—or a company employee. The type of representative is determined by supplier location, product criticality to the company's end product, skills needed for the implemented source inspection, frequency of source inspection, and type of source inspection performed. If the supplier is not located near a company representative or location, the company will usually outsource this role to a supplier or source inspection service. If company personnel do not possess the required skill set or certifications (e.g., special processes like welding), this increases the need to outsource the source inspection activity.

Source inspection oversight activities and tasks are determined based on the criticality of the product procured. Activities and tasks may be as simple as a final inspection and authorization to ship (i.e., shipment documentation sign-off) to full-time (or near full-time) onsite company representation to monitor processes, change control, supplier test and inspection, and critical to quality (CTQ) attributes and to witness the performance of tests or inspections or independent verification and validation.

Source inspection can reduce company costs through reducing the need for additional or specialized test or inspection equipment, receiving inspection, supplier product transfer directly to stock, point-of-use, or drop shipment (reduced movement and shipping cost). These advantages can also reduce warehousing or company production floor space when partnered with a just-in-time material schedule approach.

For more information on inspection types, see Section 2.1.5.1, "Quality at the Source."

2.3.8. SUPPLY PROCESSES EXTERNAL

Womack and Jones (2003) explain in *Lean Thinking* that it is rare for an organization to have more than one-third of its internal processes account for total cost and lead time to get its products to the customer. Therefore, it can be determined that a majority of savings comes from processes external to the organization. At some point along the lean journey, an organization gets to a position where its suppliers and customers need to be involved in order to continue applying lean to internal operations. The next logical step for an organization is to begin building its supplier relations. As Womack and Jones further explain, building these relationships can be done by simply taking what the organization has learned along its lean journey and transferring this knowledge to its suppliers. The organization must convince its suppliers to take the same steps it took along its lean journey.

2.3.8.1. Supplier Managed Inventory

The traditional method of supplying an internal process with an outside supplier consists of the manufacturer placing an order with the supplier. With traditional manufacturing, the supplier normally does not have any prior notification of the order or a schedule from the manufacturer in order to be prepared with inventory ahead of the order. Therefore, the supplier creates inventory, or safety stock, as a cushion against uncertainty from the manufacturer. Additionally, the

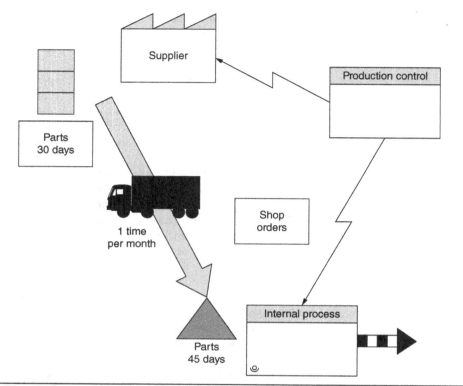

Figure 2.3.8.1-1 Traditional supply chain.

manufacturer carries a safety stock of the same parts to create a buffer against delivery delays or supply shortages. These traditional methods result in higher levels of inventory within the entire value stream. This added inventory causes the same problems that are realized with internal processes (e.g., decreased responsiveness and hidden quality issues), but they are multiplied due to the disconnect between supplier and manufacturer. The traditional supply chain (value stream) is shown graphically in Figure 2.3.8.1-1.

Through relationship building with the supplier, a value stream can be converted to utilize a supplier managed inventory system. Supplier managed inventory is a value stream concept in which the manufacturer, or buyer of the supplied item(s), provides information to its supplier(s) of the item(s) and the supplier takes on the responsibility for maintaining the inventory, often at the manufacturer's facility.

Suppliers often have more experience with and control of the logistical processes involved with the supply chain. Supplier managed inventory empowers the supplier to make decisions on how to distribute goods across its various customers' locations. This can result in the supplier having the ability to increase customer service, reduce transportation waste, and reduce inventory levels. The end result may be lowered prices of the goods it makes, which is beneficial to the manufacturer. This can be accomplished by strengthening the supplier relationship and allowing increased access to information to the actual demand of the manufacturer. A possible new value stream is shown graphically in Figure 2.3.8.1-2.

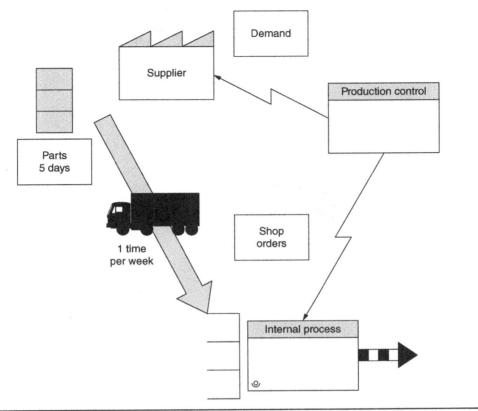

Figure 2.3.8.1–2 Example of supplier managed inventory.

Figure 2.3.8.1-2 shows just one example of a supplier managed inventory. Notice the information between production control and the supplier. Orders are no longer part of the information transferred between the supplier and the manufacturer, but demand (increases and decreases) is communicated. The most common type of supplier managed inventory is vending (soda and snack) machines.

Figure 2.3.8.1-3 provides another example of supplier managed inventory based on customer pitch. The safety stock at the supplier has been removed. This is because the supplier now has access to inventory information at the first-in, first-out (FIFO) points at the manufacturer, whereas before the supplier could view only its internal inventory. Additionally, the delivery route has been expanded to include additional customers of the supplier to create a "milk run" to reduce transportation waste.

Supplier managed inventory also provides flexibility in the value stream, meaning the inventory can be managed not only by FIFO but also by other lean methods such as supermarkets with a kanban. The combinations of potential delivery configurations, lean inventory management methods, and customers/ suppliers are endless. As the value stream continues to become leaner and the rate of product flow increases, the number of deliveries to a manufacturer can potentially increase to multiple shipments from a single supplier each day!

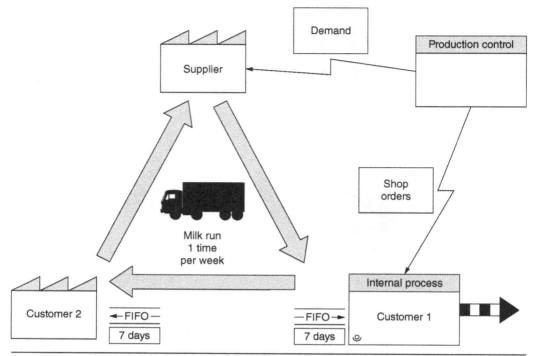

Figure 2.3.8.1-3   Example of supplier managed inventory based on customer pitch.

2.3.8.2. Cross-Docking

For suppliers dealing with large volumes, multiple deliveries to customers may be logistically easier to design. However, more often than not, suppliers are low volume. Therefore, multiple shipments per day is economically infeasible. Volumes, distances, and geographies of suppliers and customers must be considered when optimizing the value stream. Otherwise, forcing a supplier to adhere to a specific delivery schedule based on the manufacturer's demand, without consideration of the supplier's other customers, may create a suboptimization for the supplier and another customer. A solution used in these instances is cross-docking.

Cross-docking was first used by the US trucking industry in the 1930s. Since then, cross-docking has expanded to the US military and large-volume retailers. It is typically used in the less than truckload (LTL) industry, where a shipment directly from a supplier to a customer does not completely fill a delivery truck or other mode of transportation.

Cross-docking is a method of distribution that includes the unloading of large volumes of materials from incoming suppliers, breaking these down into smaller sizes, and then loading these materials directly onto smaller outbound delivery modes of transportation. Cross-docking consists of little or no storage in between the receiving and shipping of material. Sometimes, cross-docking incorporates sorting, consolidating, and storing shipments from different suppliers to convert large volumes into smaller volumes that are right-sized to the demand levels of the customers. This may be done to change type of conveyance (e.g., method of material transfer to the customer), to sort material intended for different customer

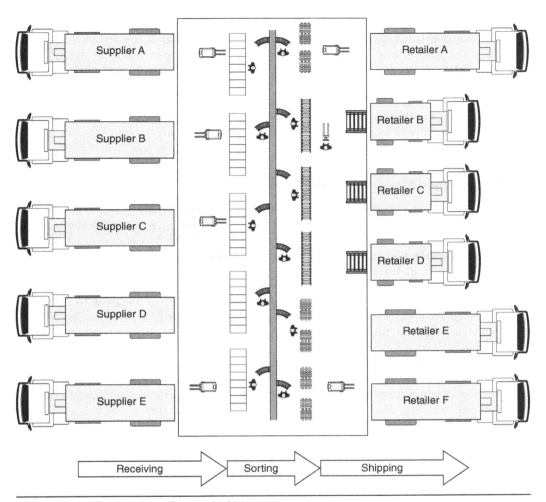

Figure 2.3.8.2-1   Example of cross-docking.

locations, or to combine material from different suppliers into modes of transportation for the same customer location. An example of a cross-dock center is shown in Figure 2.3.8.2-1.

Cross-docking is heavily contingent on communication among suppliers, cross-docking centers, and customers. This is why it is essential for manufacturers to build strong supplier/customer relationships.

Wal-Mart is the most famous example of the cross-docking method. Wal-Mart has a number of large distribution centers within structured regions. Each distribution center contains the inventories for the stores within the region. Wal-Mart takes wholesale shipments (truckloads of a single product) from suppliers and breaks them down to smaller store inventory-level shipments (pallets or partial pallets). These smaller inventories are mixed with other products and loaded onto trucks that deliver the inventory to the stores.

Amazon.com is another example of the cross-docking method. However, Amazon has taken this method a step further by adding in other lean tools, such as visual workplace, to reduce the waste of the cross-docking process (e.g., incorrect shipments). Amazon has an automated system that takes an online order, pulls the goods from warehouse positions, and conveys them to designated "bins." When an entire order is completed (all items in a designated bin), a visual device either notifies the shipping operator that the order is ready or places the bin on a conveyor that transports the order to packaging/shipping. From that point, the operator places the order in a box and sends it out for delivery. This is also an example of an order picking system. (Order picking systems are discussed further in Section 2.3.9.2.)

2.3.8.3. Supplier Assessment and Feedback

Part of building a strong relationship with a supplier is communication of not only the manufacturer's requirements but also the end customer's requirements. The baseline of this relationship is the supplier assessment. An assessment is a tool that helps a manufacturer view the supplier's organization, including the supply chain value stream, in the eyes of the manufacturer (customer). It can be performed using anything from a questionnaire to a formal on-site audit. The traditional purpose of the assessment from the quality function perspective has been to evaluate how well the supplier complies with the customer's quality system requirements. However, because this is a lean guidebook, we will discuss the assessment from a lean perspective.

The assessment's purpose is to act as a method of communication between the supplier and the manufacturer during an early lean partnership, and to act as a method of evaluation for continuous improvement opportunities in more mature lean partnerships. The lean supplier assessment concentrates on the value stream. The assessment may incorporate tools the manufacturer is already experienced in using, such as value stream mapping, spaghetti charting, takt time analysis, and flowcharting, to assess the opportunities the supplier has for continuous improvement of the value stream.

The other key point of the assessment is the feedback, or the communication of the assessment findings to the supplier. Feedback provides an opportunity for the manufacturer to begin a partnership with the supplier by not only pointing out opportunities for improvement but offering the manufacturer's expertise with lean to help "teach" the supplier how to implement lean within its organization. This is the beginning of supplier development.

2.3.8.4. Supplier Development

Usually, the assessment finds that current and/or new suppliers are not the perfect supplier. A majority of the time, the perfect supplier does not exist. Therefore, manufacturers find themselves settling for a less than desirable supplier. This does not mean that the manufacturer gives up on its lean journey. This is where the manufacturer must take it upon itself to aid the suppliers in improvement. Depending on the relationship with the supplier, improvements and knowledge sharing can impact the supplier's capabilities in technology, logistics, operations, administration, scheduling, and quality. Therefore, *supplier development* can be defined as the process by which manufacturers collaborate with suppliers to improve and/or expand the supplier's capabilities.

In today's global economy, a manufacturer's competitiveness is continually more dependent on processes outside the organization than those internal to the organization. Success now relies more on the performance of the full value stream, or supply chain. Therefore, supplier relationships and development are becoming increasingly important.

2.3.8.5. Supplier Benchmarking

According to Camp (1995, 15), in *Business Process Benchmarking*, benchmarking is:

> The search for and implementation of best practices. Benchmarking's primary objective is to understand those practices that will provide a competitive advantage. Target setting is secondary.

Benchmarking data can be descriptive or quantitative. Descriptive data are how something is done. This can be analyzing a process flow, understanding a method, or identifying inputs and outputs. Simply, this is the assessment of a SIPOC (Supplier, Inputs, Process, Outputs, Customer). Quantitative data are a measure or metric. They involve converting benchmark measures into operational measures to see where the performance levels are.

A number of things can be benchmarked: products and services, business processes, and performance measures. Benchmarking products and services helps evaluate features and functions desired by customers. Benchmarking business processes provides the basis for improving internal business processes. Benchmarking performance measures allows for the establishment and validation of objectives that steer the organization.

Benchmarking can be internal, competitive, functional, or generic. *Internal benchmarking* is the comparison among similar processes within one's organization. Considering that a supplier relationship is strong, this can be a comparison of similar processes between the supplier and the manufacturer. *Competitive benchmarking* is a comparison with direct competitors. A strong supplier relationship allows for this type of benchmarking to be slightly easier than traditional means. The supplier relationship provides the open communication and information sharing that is necessary to directly or indirectly compare suppliers and customers external to the specific supplier-manufacturer value stream through lessons learned from dealings with other suppliers and customers. *Functional benchmarking* compares methods of similar functions across industries. Sometimes, a manufacturer's supplier may be a supplier to industries outside the manufacturer's industry. This can create networking points to gain contacts for additional benchmarking opportunities. Finally, *generic benchmarking* is a comparison with companies that have world-class or innovative processes and performance measures. The supplier may be able to help an organization gain access to these benchmarking opportunities.

Benchmarking can be strategic or tactical. Tactical benchmarking is used to understand processes, practices, and performance levels at the tactical level (or at lower organizational levels). Tactical benchmarking is equivalent to what is performed during the supplier assessment and feedback. This begins to open the communication channels between the supplier and the manufacturer and strengthen the supplier relationship. Eventually, this can create a supplier-manufacturer partnership that expands benchmarking to the strategic level. This is where the supplier and the manufacturer focus on competitive strengths and weaknesses of both entities to create opportunities for broad organizational improvements. Strengths of one organization can be exploited to overcome the weaknesses of the other organization, or strengths may be combined to create breakthrough opportunities for both organizations. The end result should be a strategic improvement of the entire supply chain to optimize the flow of products, services, and information throughout the entire value stream.

2.3.8.6. Logistics

Logistics is a business concept that came about in the 1950s as suppliers began experiencing increasing complexity with shipping products as markets continued to expand globally. *Logistics* is the management of the flow of product and services from the point of origin through the point of consumption to meet customer demand requirements. Logistics integrates methods of information transfer, modes of transportation, management of inventory, organization of warehousing, movement of products and services, packaging of goods and services, and securing products and information. The purpose of logistics is to manage the complexity of these integrated components for optimizing the value of the end product or service by reducing waste in the supply chain. Simply put, it is:

- Having the right product or service,
- In the correct quantity,
- At the time the customer demands it,
- Where the customer needs it,
- For the price the customer wants to pay for it,
- In the condition or quality the customer requires,
- To the customer who asks for it.

When extending lean throughout the value stream, beyond the four walls of the organization, one must be careful not to fall into the trap of suboptimization. In *The Toyota Way*, Liker (2004, 40) identifies the principle of "respecting your extended network of partners and suppliers by challenging them and helping them improve." While reducing waste within the supply chain (between the organization and its suppliers) results in savings beyond what is realized within the organization's four walls, this could be accomplished at the expense of the supplier (suboptimizing). The end result is an increased cost of the supplied items. Liker describes what happened with Ford in the 1990s when it made changes that resulted in massive increases in logistical costs. While inside the assembly plant inventories were reduced and space was utilized for additional production, the changes that Ford made led to the logistics firm renting warehouse facilities near the plants, resulting in increased logistical costs. The result was a supply chain that had more waste than the original and was caused by Ford not working with the supplier and the logistics firm on a compromised logistics plan based on a common vision.

Logistics is only a larger version of what occurs within an organization. Within the organization, functional silos exist prior to the lean journey. Over time, these groups become less siloed and begin to work together to reduce waste throughout the entire value stream. The same is true for logistics. The only difference is that the silos are more significant due to separate companies rather than separate departments within the same company.

2.3.9. SUPPLY PROCESSES INTERNAL

Internal supply processes provide parts and assemblies from upstream operations (or external suppliers) to the operation where the materials are needed and when they are needed. This includes material handling, warehousing, and planning and scheduling. Internal supply processes are discussed in the sections regarding pull systems and kanban.

2.3.9.1. Material Handling

Material handling is the movement of materials and parts from one location to another. Internal material handling is any movement of materials and parts from one operation (upstream) to another (downstream). While movement in lean is considered waste, we are really only talking about unnecessary or excessive movement. It is understood that some movement is necessary to produce product. This includes movement of finished goods to the shipping area for final packaging and shipment to the customer, or movement of parts and materials from the receiving dock to the point of use.

Material handling can be performed by personnel assigned to the activity or by employees producing the product. Although, those producing the product usually only move material from one operation to another within the work cell. Because of these constraints, implementation of systems such as visual workplace, lot size reduction, load leveling, and pull systems is key to reducing the waste with material handling.

In a traditional material handling function, an organization has a designated storage area for materials, and someone transfers that material to the point of use as needed (Figure 2.3.9.1-1).

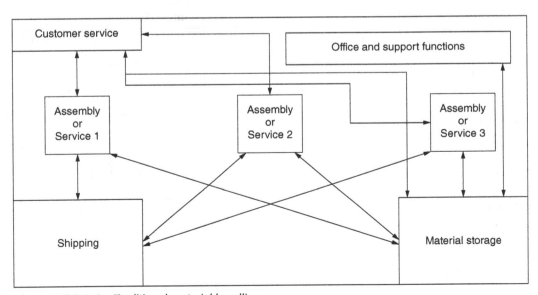

Figure 2.3.9.1-1 Traditional material handling.

Traditional material handling results in much wasted transportation. While it may make sense that the materials are consolidated, the transportation waste is dependent on who is transferring the material and the distance the material is transferred.

Yasuhiro Monden (1998, 207), in *Toyota Production System*, states that 30%–40% of processing costs and 80%–90% of processing time is spent on material handling. He describes some simple rules for material handling.

Utilize First-In, First-Out (FIFO)

First-in, first-out (FIFO) is where material or work-in-process (WIP) that is placed first in inventory/storage is the first to be taken out and used. This prevents new parts from being used before older parts and prevents inventory from becoming obsolete or expiring prior to use.

Set Up a System for Easy Handling

For an organization to operate efficiently and effectively, improvement of the material handling process is crucial. Monden describes the use of a material handling index of liveliness (Table 2.3.9.1-1).

The index is calculated by classifying the number of tasks required into varying levels of activity, such as bulk, smaller grouping, raised platform, mobile cart, and moving. Then the total number of activity levels is divided by the total number of process steps. An example of the analysis is performed in Figure 2.3.9.1-2.

The index allows for analyzing material handling activity and helps determine the best method of transferring the material. If the index of liveliness is less

Table 2.3.9.1-1   Material handling index of liveliness.

Classification	Index of liveliness	Number of required tasks	Variety of required tasks				Condition
			Group	Raise	Lift up	Carry	
Bulk	0	4	Yes	Yes	Yes	Yes	Left in bulk at the point of use
Distributed in a box or smaller batch	1	3	—	Yes	Yes	Yes	Placed in a smaller container or smaller groups
In box with raised platform	2	2	—	—	Yes	Yes	Raised by platforms, pallets, or lifts
On a cart	3	1	—	—	—	Yes	Set on a cart with wheels
Moving	4	0	—	—	—	—	Transported by conveyor, chute, and indexing trays

Source: Monden (1998, 209).

2.3.9.1

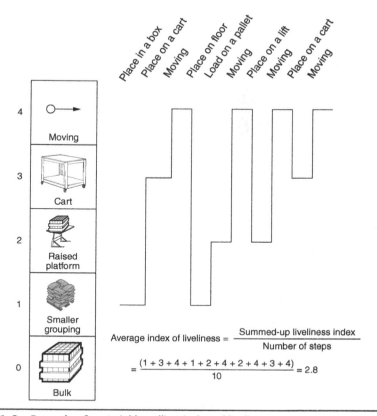

Figure 2.3.9.1-2   Example of material handling index of liveliness.

than 0.5, then pallets, carts, carriers, and containers should be used instead of placing items at the point of use in bulk. If the average index is greater than 1.3, then
pallets, carts, carriers, and containers should be used even more widely. In the
example in Figure 2.3.9.1-2, an index of 2.8 implies that many smaller conveyance
methods should be used.

Consider Inventory Space as Part of the Manufacturing/Service Area

Since parts, materials, tools, and other items take up a significant amount of space,
it is important to place them where there is ease of access without disrupting flow.
These items can be organized a number of ways, such as by process, similarity of
items, frequency of use, and so on. Methods of conveyance figure into point-of-use
storage. Various methods can be used to get the material close to the processes and
the point of use.

A milk run is an example of material conveyance to get the necessary items
closer to the point of use in smaller quantities (Figure 2.3.9.1-3). A milk run is
created by splitting bulk inventory into smaller quantities based on pitch, takt,
and cycle times and distributing them to the processes that need them. Different
items for different processes can be distributed based on a like pitch to different
processes.

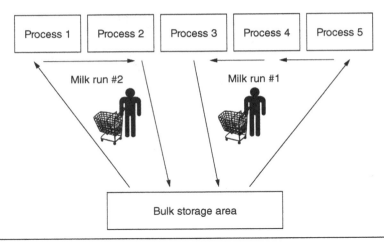

Figure 2.3.9.1–3 Example of an internal milk run.

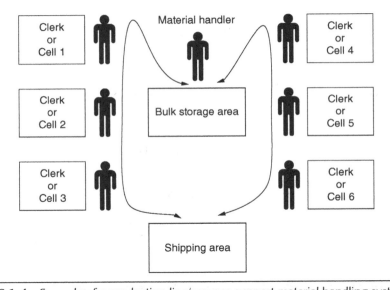

Figure 2.3.9.1–4 Example of a production line/process support material handling system.

Similarly, for multiple cells or processes, a local central material storage area is defined, and a dedicated material handling support person distributes material as the different cells or processes require them (Figure 2.3.9.1-4). This can be thought of in terms of mail distribution in a large organization, where an individual delivers mail to different areas as it is received in the mail room.

2.3.9.2. Warehousing

Some level of warehousing, or inventory, is needed in all systems ("push" and "pull"). Warehousing may be receiving, in-process, or shipment.

Receiving warehousing is performed to account for necessary staging. Staging includes, but is not limited to, acceptance of external (to the process or company) materials, raw materials storage for transfer to the point of use prior to immediate need, and the segregation of chemicals or hazardous materials prior to transfer to smaller point-of-use containers.

In-process warehousing is performed to provide appropriate staging for line balancing. This is done to ensure that downstream processes have the materials and parts necessary to produce product based on demand (takt, cycle, and lead times).

Shipment warehousing is performed to maximize shipping methods. For example, it would be cost prohibitive for a large automobile manufacturer to ship each vehicle individually (even if built in a total "pull" system).

The goal is to minimize warehousing to the level necessary to support product build and customer demand and not "push" material into the warehouse system. Benefits of minimal warehousing include the following:

- Reduces inventory

- Increases company cash flow

- Supports process demand

- Requires analysis of processing, times (takt, cycle, lead), and planning (product) in support of continual improvement

A number of lean systems, techniques, and practices may be integrated into the warehouse, such as pull systems, visual workplace, and cellular flow. As discussed in Section 2.3.8.2, an order picking system is a method of integrating automation and visual workplace with the warehouse. Think of an order picking system as tables in a restaurant, with each table having a small stand with a designated number. When the waitstaff take orders, they record the table number where the order was taken. When the order is complete, a number stand is placed on the order tray and the waitperson takes the order directly to the corresponding numbered table.

Order picking systems can be like the Amazon.com warehouse example, or another example might involve huge warehouses with forklifts going to different designated inventory locations to pick the order. For example, as an order barcode is scanned, the inventory control system illuminates the lights in an aisle and the aisle position so the forklift operator knows exactly where to go to pick up the material, parts, and components to complete the order. Specifically, this is known as a pick-to-light system.

It can be estimated that 50% of warehouse costs are associated with order picking. Given that order picking is labor intensive, it is also full of non-value-added transportation and operator waiting during the travel. Therefore, optimization of the order picking route is critical to reducing the waste within the warehouse operation. There are three methods of order picking to reduce some of the transportation waste: transversal, midpoint, and largest gap.

Transversal Order Picking

The transversal order picking method (Figure 2.3.9.2-1) starts with the order picker at the location the order was provided. The order picker moves up one aisle and down the next until every necessary aisle is traveled. This method is the simplest, but not the most optimal for waste reduction. Often, this is a starting point in which to create an order picking system that is designed to the organization's needs. If the warehouse frequently encounters storage location discrepancies, this method is optimal until the discrepancies are corrected.

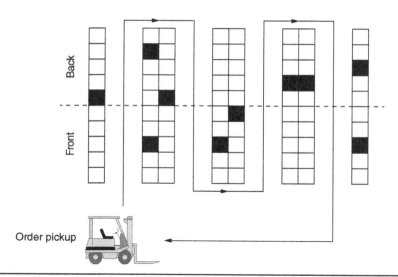

Figure 2.3.9.2-1   Transversal order picking method.

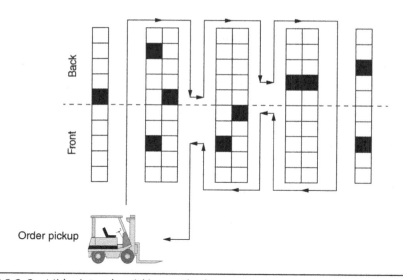

Figure 2.3.9.2-2   Midpoint order picking method.

Midpoint Order Picking

The midpoint order picking method (Figure 2.3.9.2-2) starts with the order picker at the location the order was provided and traveling along the first aisle. If the order requires picking at a point in the next aisle, the order picker will enter the first aisle only as deep as halfway and then exit the aisle in the same direction. This method is slightly more complicated, but still not the most optimal for waste reduction. Often, this is a next step after the transversal method is ready to be improved.

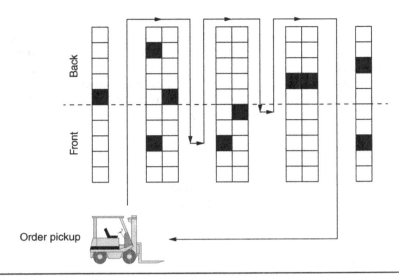

Figure 2.3.9.2-3   Largest gap order picking method.

Largest Gap Order Picking

The largest gap order picking method (Figure 2.3.9.2-3) starts with the order picker at the location the order was provided and traveling along the first aisle. If the order requires picking at a point in the next aisle, the order picker will enter only as deep as the item (even crossing the halfway point of the aisle), exit the aisle in the same way that the picker entered, and then move to the next item location.

2.3.9.3. Planning and Scheduling

Planning and scheduling starts with understanding the material requirements demand (final product back through individual parts), analyzing needed materials, identifying lead times, understanding the internal cycle times, and accounting for delivery time to customers. It starts with the customer's need time (demand) and applies delivery and internal and supplier processing/delivery times to identify purchase order needs to ensure that the material is available for processing, preferably in support of just-in-time (JIT) requirements (see Section 2.1.3).

Although material resource planning (MRP) systems are still prevalent today, they are based on a push rather than pull approach to manufacturing. This means that parts are purchased, provided to manufacturing, and built to assembly or end product (i.e., the item delivered to the external customer) based on a schedule that does not consider customer need or demand. Push systems create undue inventory (waste), while pull systems recognize some inventory is needed to meet customer demand and process product; pull systems ensure that excessive inventory is not purchased, held, or scrapped (due to not being needed). MRP systems can be utilized by pull systems, especially to help with back-off logic analysis and determination, upstream demand notification, and interfacing with purchasing and other systems.

Scheduling is the result of planning. After the planning process is completed (analyzing the demand, processing times, and delivery times), a schedule is developed to meet the demands. The schedule takes the customer demand and applies the back-off logic from product end-state to piece/part procurement identified during the planning, to ensure that all material is obtained when necessary. For internal scheduling, it is assumed that upstream processes and supplier materials will be available when and where needed.

REFERENCES

AIAG. 2001. *Potential Failure Mode and Effects Analysis*. 3rd ed.

ASQ. "Flowchart." http://asq.org/learn-about-quality/process-analysis-tools/overview/flowchart.html.

ASQ. "Quality Glossary." Accessed February 19, 2011. http://asq.org/glossary/i.html.

Camp, Robert C. 1995. *Business Process Benchmarking: Finding and Implementing Best Practices*. Milwaukee, WI: ASQC Quality Press.

Campanella, Jack. 1999. *Principles of Quality Cost: Principles, Implementation and Use*. 3rd ed. Milwaukee, WI: ASQ Quality Press.

Chapman, William, A. Terry Bahill, and A. Wayne Wymore. 1992. *Engineering Modeling and Design*. Boca Raton, FL: CRC Press, Taylor & Francis Group.

Hauser, J. R., and D. Clausing. 1988. "The House of Quality." *Harvard Business Review*, May-June.

Imai, Masaaki. 1997. *Gemba Kaizen: A Commonsense, Low-Cost Approach to Management*. New York: McGraw-Hill.

Imler, K. 2006. *Get It Right. A Guide to Strategic Quality Systems*. Milwaukee, WI: ASQ Quality Press.

Liker, Jeffery. 2004. *The Toyota Way: 14 Management Principles from the World's Greatest Manufacturer*. New York: McGraw-Hill.

Levionson, W., and R. Rerick. 2002. *Lean Enterprise: A Synergistic Approach to Minimizing Waste*. Milwaukee, WI: ASQ Quality Press.

Maio, M. 2010. *Quality Improvement Made Simple . . . and Fast!* Milwaukee, WI: ASQ Quality Press.

Marchwinski, Chet, and John Shook. 2006. *Lean Lexicon*. 3rd ed. Version 3.0. Cambridge, MA: Lean Enterprise Institute.

Monden, Yasuhiro. 1998. *Toyota Production System: An Integrated Approach to Just-in-Time*. 3rd ed. Norcross, GA: Institute of Industrial Engineers.

Rother, Mike, and John Shook. 1999. *Learning to See: Value Stream Mapping to Add Value and Eliminate MUDA*. Cambridge, MA: Lean Enterprise Institute.

Santos, Javier, Richard A. Wysk, and Jose M. Torres. 2006. *Improving Production with Lean Thinking*. Hoboken, NJ: John Wiley & Sons.

Shingo, Shigeo. 2005. *A Study of the Toyota Production System*. Translated by Andrew Dillon. Boca Raton, FL: CRC Press, Taylor & Francis Group.

Singh, Nanua. 1995. *Systems Approach to Computer-Integrated Design and Manufacturing*. New York: John Wiley & Sons.

Tague, Nancy. 2004. *The Quality Toolbox*. 2nd ed. Milwaukee, WI: ASQ Quality Press.

Vincent, Chad. 2009. "Back in Circulation." *ASQ Quality Progress*, March.

Womack, James P., and Daniel T. Jones. 2003. *Lean Thinking: Banish Waste and Create Wealth in Your Corporation*. 2nd ed. New York: Free Press.

Module 3
Consistent Lean Enterprise Culture

3.1. Principles of Consistent Lean Enterprise Culture

3.2. Processes for Developing Consistent Lean Enterprise Culture

3.3. Consistent Enterprise Culture Techniques & Practices

The key to the Toyota Way and what makes Toyota stand out is not any of the individual elements . . . But what is important is having all the elements together as a system. It must be practiced every day in a very consistent manner, not in spurts.

—Taiichi Ohno

Knowing the tools will only get you part of the way there. Any company can copy the tools forged by Toyota; it is the culture of the organization that makes it stand above its competitors. This module will lead you through the principles, processes, techniques, and practices of a lean culture.

Thinking through these rubrics will solidify that lean is not just about the tools. These topics focus on the people part of lean, from how we think to how we align our organization.

3.1

Principles of Consistent Lean
Enterprise Culture

Systemic thinking is an approach to managing and improving organizations that focuses on the value stream as a whole rather than the individual components. Systemic thinking views the organization as a continually evolving system in which components work together to achieve the goal of serving customers through its products or services. Although this appears to be a simple concept and very similar to traditional business thinking, it is actually very complex and requires a level of individual transformation to fully understand.

3.1.1. SYSTEMIC THINKING

If you try to take a cat apart to see how it works, the first thing you have in your hand is a nonworking cat.

—Douglas Adams, *Salmon of Doubt: Hitchhiking the Galaxy One More Time*

What matters more to a business: the performance of individuals or the performance of the company as a whole? Although it is obvious that the performance of the company is more important, the way many businesses are organized and managed emphasizes just the opposite.

A holistic approach to managing and improving organizations, systems thinking rejects the reductionist approach that breaks down the organization into individually managed components—or functions—often with separate measures and conflicting goals, and focuses the efforts of everyone, regardless of function, on achieving the objectives of the value stream or the company as a whole.

Systems thinkers recognize that the organization achieves its objectives through a series of complex interactions between people and teams that work together to benefit the company as a whole. It is critical to improve these interactions, but only from the standpoint that they contribute to the company's objectives. Objectives are set at the company or value stream level because optimizing the system sometimes requires the performance of certain individuals or teams to appear suboptimized—especially when looking at performance in isolation. Because of this, management focus is at the value stream level rather than on the individual components (process steps, functions, etc.), as shown in Figure 3.1.1-1.

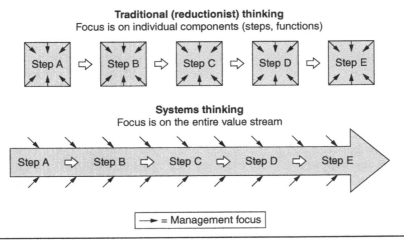

Figure 3.1.1-1 Management focus—traditional thinking versus systems thinking.

The value of systemic thinking comes from understanding how the components work with one another to accomplish the system's fundamental purpose (serving customers) and make the organization successful.

As an example of how prevalent the reduction approach is in business today, it is common practice to measure and reward procurement professionals for reducing the price of incoming materials. In response to this, there is often a tendency to focus solely on price, with little regard to the quality or delivery of materials purchased. The result may be reduced material costs, but the corresponding effect on production and warranty costs, teamwork, and customer satisfaction can easily raise the total costs for the operation. In effect, this type of behavior makes people think that a component of the system—procurement—is more important than the overall system.

As demonstrated in the previous example, reward systems often force people to focus efforts on improving their own functions while virtually ignoring the overall system. People do not intentionally work against the system. Even when they recognize that meeting personal objectives causes problems for others, they do it to survive. If they don't actively pursue their goals, at best they won't receive a bonus, and at worst they can lose their jobs. This is a major reason that batching occurs within manufacturing operations even when it causes problems downstream in the process. Batching is a natural way to improve individual efficiency because it is often easier and quicker to produce as much output as possible with a single setup. Unfortunately, downstream processes can end up waiting for work or become buried in work when the upstream process finishes a batch.

Lean naturally drives the organization toward a systemic-thinking mind-set because of the focus on improving flow and reducing waste throughout the value stream. The mapping process brings together representatives from the various areas—the components—who work together to improve the overall system. It is very common during a mapping session for people to become aware of the problems they cause others in the value stream. By concentrating the improvement effort on the overall system and studying the handoffs between individuals and teams, lean naturally drives the organization toward systems thinking.

3.1.1.1. Part-Whole Relationships Are Clear and Explicit through Holistic Thinking

Holistic thinking enables people within the organization to better understand and improve the system. In *Lean Production Simplified: A Plain Language Guide to the World's Most Powerful Production System*, Pascal Dennis (2007) emphasizes that understanding the system requires understanding its purpose, its interdependencies, and its interactions. A system's purpose describes the value it provides to customers, or its reason for existence. The interdependencies are the relationships that exist between components throughout the value stream (i.e., the internal customers and suppliers), and the interactions are the handoffs between components.

In systems thinking, the focus becomes the value stream, and how each person's role supports the value stream's efforts to provide value to customers. People are clear that their job responsibilities include serving others inside the company and continually working to understand the needs of those they serve. When people become systems thinkers, it is much more evident when a proposed improvement in one area causes problems for others. Functionally focused leaders and conflicting objectives are removed as people begin to understand how their role supports others and fits into the overall system.

Perhaps the most significant characteristic of a systems-thinking organization that separates it from a traditional organization is the idea that the needs of the value stream are primary, and functional or departmental needs are secondary.

A holistic systems-thinking view of the organization is depicted in Figure 3.1.1.1-1. Since the functions would not exist without the value streams, the sole purpose of the functions is to serve the value streams. Although skills matter in this type of environment, functions do not.

The philosophy of value stream first and function second applies regardless of the type of business. In manufacturing, for example, product development, manufacturing engineering, production planning, and procurement all exist to serve the value stream, whose goal is to provide products to customers. In an oil exploration and production company, geology, geophysics, drilling, and reservoir

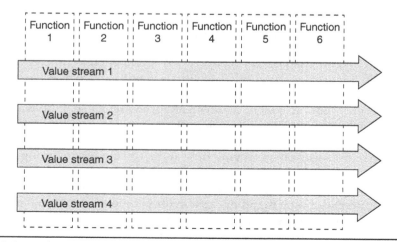

Figure 3.1.1.1-1 The systems-thinking organization.

engineering exist solely to enable the value stream to produce oil to deliver to markets. In a retail business, procurement, marketing, information technology, and human resources all exist to support the salespeoples' efforts to serve customers effectively.

Although a loosely based functional organization can be maintained to ensure that the skills of individuals continue to develop, care must be exercised to ensure that the environment does not degrade into a functional organization. Also, although growth and promotion within the function are much more limited in a systems-thinking environment than in a traditional organization, growth shifts to the value stream, and the better one understands and serves the entire stream, the more potential for growth that individual has.

Lean thinking naturally increases understanding of the relationships between people and functions through the value stream mapping process. By documenting the flow of materials and information through the system, people more clearly understand how the work they do supports others, and ultimately helps achieve the company's goals. The improvement process never ends, because the broadened understanding of the system and the increased level of communication between people help make changes in the external environment more evident. In the end, the value stream becomes more flexible and responsive to changes in the world.

3.1.1.2. The Organization Evolves as Necessary to Accommodate Future Conditions through Dynamic Thinking

In a systems-thinking environment, the organization is always looking out for its customers. People understand customers intimately and work to stay ahead of their needs by continually developing better ways to provide value. Dynamic thinking recognizes that nothing is permanent, meaning that solutions that work today will not necessarily work tomorrow. In reality, "solutions" are often nothing more than fixes that work given today's situation. As the environment changes, what worked in the past will not necessarily work today. Toyota has refrained from using the term "solution," opting instead to refer to fixes as "countermeasures."

Organizations are complex, and so are the problems they face. Dynamic thinking recognizes the complexity and approaches problems from the perspective of multiple issues rather than a single root cause. Improvement results from identifying causes and implementing countermeasures to address the issues identified, given the company's current environment.

Since dynamic thinkers believe that the world is in constant change, and that what is acceptable today may not be acceptable tomorrow, continual learning is critical. Teams must learn about themselves, their processes, and the external environment, and how the interactions among these three components lead to problems and opportunities for improvement.

Getting to the root causes of a problem can be extremely difficult. Often, people look only to current factors to find the cause of a problem when, in fact, the causes can be the result of interactions and decisions that occurred well in the past.

The Plan-Do-Check-Act (PDCA) cycle, presented in Section 2.2.9.1, facilitates dynamic thinking by continually comparing the desired target with current conditions and making appropriate adjustments, either when studying problems or when making improvements. Where traditional thinking often underthinks or overthinks a problem, PDCA continually helps improve understanding by encouraging experimentation and studying results.

Developing dynamic thinking skills does not come easily to most people, but without people with these skills, the organization has little chance to evolve along with its environment and remain competitive. The level of creativity required and the ability to look at a situation from a variety of angles are generally not developed or rewarded in Western cultures. Because of this, coaching is often required to help people develop a sustained ability to apply dynamic thinking in everyday situations.

A coach or sensei will regularly challenge and remind a student to question assumptions and fight the urge to jump to a solution when faced with a problem. Besides regular discussions between a coach and a student, documenting the thought process on an A3 is very effective for developing dynamic thinking skills.

Developed by Toyota, the A3 (a term used to describe information displayed in an 11 × 17 format) is, in effect, a storyboard (see Section 2.2.9.3, "Problem Solving Storyboards") of the PDCA cycle, including the thought process used to address a problem. When the A3 is used as a tool to develop dynamic thinking, the coach can see what the student was thinking throughout the process and constantly challenge assumptions made at every step. A3s are written and rewritten throughout the problem-solving process as the student, through active inquiry from the coach, changes his or her thought process and learns more about the situation.

From the coach's perspective, the objective is not to resolve a specific problem but to develop the student's dynamic thinking skills.

3.1.1.3. Closed-Loop Thinking to Assure Effective Feedback of Organizational Learning

Closed-loop thinking is like many aspects of lean: easy to understand but surprisingly difficult to execute consistently. In essence, closed-loop thinking starts with identifying a problem, getting to the root cause, revising and communicating standardized work to reflect the solution, and making sure the solution stays in place. Without this last step, the loop remains open, with a high likelihood of the problem reappearing.

Deming's PDCA Cycle

Probably the most widely known example of closed-loop thinking is the Deming PDCA wheel, shown in Figure 3.1.1.3-1: Plan, Do, Check (or Reflect), Act (or Adjust) (see Section 2.2.9.1, "PDCA").

When unexpected variation occurs in a process—an interruption, delay, defect, or any type of glitch—the closed-loop thinker's approach is to capture information about the glitch right when it occurs and then use problem solving to understand what caused the problem. If warranted, continue with the following steps to eliminate the cause so that the problem does not reoccur.

For example, in Deming's terms, you make a *plan* to eliminate the cause. Next, you execute, or *do*, your plan. After you've taken the steps to do your plan, you *check* (or reflect on, or study) the outcome: What did you learn from this trial? Did your solution work as expected, eliminating the problem and improving the process as your plan predicted? If not, you need to *act*, to adjust your approach. With

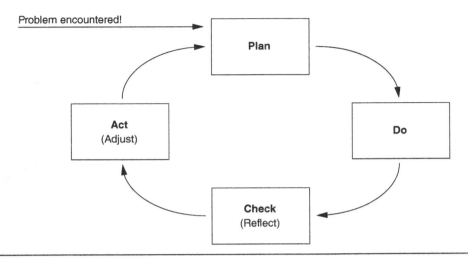

Figure 3.1.1.3-1   Deming PDCA wheel.

that, you begin again with analysis and a plan, and so on around the wheel until you get the outcome, the improvement you predicted. Once the actual outcome matches the expected outcome, you've closed the loop on a process improvement. And you've learned more about a particular part of your process.

At least it works that way in theory.

Closing the Loop in the Real World

In practice, where people work in the process, *no* improvement is safe from being cut short, diluted, modified, or, in general, messed with. Think of this as the downside of human creativity, if you like. The implication is this: For consistent execution, and to keep the improvement loop closed, any process that involves people needs to be monitored. That's true for newly installed processes as well as changes made in response to problems. Please note that monitoring is not solely for compliance with a design or standard; it should also include observing and talking with those doing the work to find opportunities for improvement.

Keeping in mind that people are a potentially endless source of process variation, the elements of closed-loop lean thinking in the real world might look more like the following example.

First, define standardized work for the elements in the process. In repetitive processes, this is straightforward. Where tasks can vary from cycle to cycle, as in many office or administrative processes, standardized work could be defined procedures for handling the variety of tasks likely to be encountered in the department. For example, a customer service operation could have standard procedures for handling complaints about products or services, issuing return authorizations, applying discounts, modifying schedules, changing orders in process, and so on. With standards in place, you can readily see variation from standards when monitoring the process.

Second, when variations occur, capture information about them right then and there. In manufacturing, variations might manifest as stoppages, defective parts or units, or shortages. Variations of this sort often are symptoms of vulnerabilities or weaknesses in processes and, as such, are among the best next areas for focusing improvement activity. In customer service or help desk operations, complaints are a valuable source of data on failure to meet expectations. With customer complaints, closed-loop thinking calls for recording and providing complaint or failure data to the appropriate group. Various forms of production tracking charts are particularly useful for capturing information. Where feasible, visual methods for tracking production or logging problems are best for immediately raising accountability and stimulating corrective action.

The next steps are problem solving, root cause analysis, and PDCA: Plan the improvement, do the plan, check actual outcomes with what you expected, and act accordingly. If the outcome was unexpected, repeat the steps. If actual and expected outcomes align, revise the standardized work and communicate the change.

Does this identify a solution to a problem? Yes. Does it close the loop? No!

Leader Standard Work Closes the Loop

Leader standard work provides a structure and routine that help leaders shift from a sole focus on results to a dual focus on process plus results (Mann 2010). In a lean implementation that includes a lean management system, you'll find standardized work for leaders. The primary intent of leader standard work is to guarantee the integrity of the standardized lean production process. That's true for an initial lean process design as well as for backstopping process changes, improvement by improvement. With solid accountability for integrity of a new or systematically modified process design, the PDCA loop stays closed. See Figure 3.1.1.3-2.

Leader standard work, to be effective, includes standardized tasks up through the chain of command for monitoring standardized work or procedures. Closer to the value-adding task level, more of a leader's time will be accounted for by his or her standardized work, with more frequent monitoring of adherence to standardized work for production and support tasks. Going up the chain of command, process monitoring shifts to spot checks of task-level standardized work processes, as well as subordinate leaders' adherence to their standardized work.

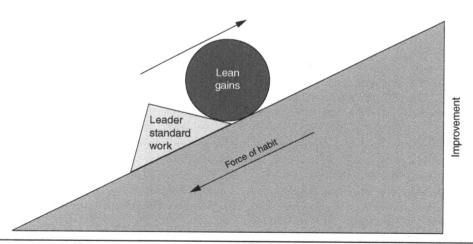

Figure 3.1.1.3-2   Leader standard work keeps the improvement loop closed.

Incorporating PDCA-derived process changes in task- and leader-level standardized work is a critical step in sustaining the change. It is the first step in communicating the change, by putting it in forms and formats familiar and readily communicated to others elsewhere in the organization who are involved with or affected by it.

Remember, no loop remains closed without a defined, structured process to keep it that way. One of the paradoxes in lean is that ultimately the loop-closing or backstopping process depends on disciplined adherence to the process, reinforced by the individual at the top of the organization. When the person in that position maintains the discipline of following his or her standardized work and holds others accountable for theirs, he or she maintains closed-loop thinking and practices, along with the organization's opportunity to learn from its own experience.

3.1.2. CONSTANCY OF PURPOSE

The *Cambridge Advanced Learner's Dictionary* (2010) defines an *organization* as "a group of people who work together in a structured way for a shared purpose." Following this definition, without a shared purpose, there is no organization. There is only a group of people who come to work and most likely head in different directions as they focus on what they each believe is important.

The first of W. Edwards Deming's (1986) 14 Points for Management, constancy of purpose, refers to the need for leaders to clearly define the organization's fundamental purpose in terms of continually improving the value provided to customers. The purpose guides the strategy and objectives and must never change.

Although a fairly simple concept on the surface, constancy of purpose has many dimensions that are critical to the success of an organization. The *value* is why the organization exists, and its products and services are *how* it provides value. Focusing on product and service offerings as the purpose can cause a company to become too narrowly focused and reject new and better ways to provide value to its customers.

Where would manufacturers of typewriters or slide rules be today had they defined their purpose in terms of the value rather than the product they offered? A typewriter manufacturer that defined its purpose as continually finding easier ways for people to create and edit documents would have been more likely to explore the possibility of offering word processing software or keyboards as personal computers began to make their way onto the scene.

Another important aspect of the focus on value to customers is that it does not focus on financial gain for the organization. According to Peter Drucker (1993, 59), "Profit is not the explanation, cause or rationale of business behavior and business decisions, but the test of their validity."

In addition to being clear and unchanging, an organization's purpose must, in some way, be inspiring. People need to feel that they are contributing to something important with the significant amount of time they spend at work. Table 3.1.2-1 presents some examples of purpose statements that are clear and focus on value rather than products or financial returns.

An obvious but extremely challenging aspect of constancy of purpose is that the organization's leaders maintain a never-ending commitment to the purpose. This means that the level of commitment does not waiver during the inevitable

3.1.2

Table 3.1.2-1 Purpose statement examples.

- To be the earth's most customer-centric company; to build a place where people can come to find and discover anything that they might want to buy on-line. (Amazon)

- To be the world's best quick service restaurant experience. Being the best means providing outstanding quality, service, cleanliness, and value, so that we make every customer in every restaurant smile. (McDonald's)

- To organize the world's information and make it universally accessible and useful. (Google)

- To so develop airplane design and construction that today's spectacular feat of bravery will become tomorrow's accepted mode of speedy transportation—inexpensive, dependable, safe! (Boeing—written in 1927)

- Nucor Corporation is made up of more than 21,000 team members whose goal is to take care of customers. We are accomplishing this by being the safest, highest quality, lowest cost, most productive, and most affordable steel and steel products company in the world. We are committed to doing this while being cultural and environmental stewards in our communities where we live and work. We are succeeding by working together. (Nucor Steel)

distractions that companies face on a regular basis, like recession, acquisitions, rapidly rising material costs, or a host of other issues.

A midsized manufacturer of oil and gas exploration and production equipment had defined its purpose in terms of serving the needs of the oil and gas industry. During a downturn in business, the company had an opportunity to bid on a fairly large contract to provide equipment to a beverage producer. The technology needed was similar, and the company could perceivably provide the equipment with slight modifications to its designs. The CEO vehemently rejected the idea because beverage manufacturing was outside the company's focus and expertise (i.e., its purpose). He feared that learning a new industry and serving a new type of customer would be a distraction to the company's constancy of purpose. It should be noted that it was strongly believed that, unlike the typewriter example earlier, the downturn in the oil and gas industry was a normal downturn and not the result of a dying technology. Instead of pursuing the new business, the company focused its efforts on developing new technology for oil and gas production to be ready when the market recovered. When it did, the company's new products were successful and the company's market share increased dramatically.

An organization that remains committed to its customers by definition remains committed to improvement. A lean process is a natural progression of a commitment to constancy of purpose and, as such, is not dependent on economic conditions or whatever else is going on at any given time. Improvement must occur at all times and become ingrained into the culture and systems of the organization.

3.1.2.1. Focus on Results

When an organization clearly understands its purpose, it understands its stakeholders and measures success in terms of meeting their needs. This implies gaining a clear understanding of the needs of the stakeholders and identifying measures to determine how well the company is creating value.

Care must be taken to ensure that the results are closely tied to the company's purpose. Too often, financial results get the most focus, and then actions become very short term in nature. If the purpose is defined in terms of providing—and continually improving—value to customers, then results must be defined in terms of how well this is being done. Although profits can be a measure of how well the company is meeting customer needs, the relationship is long term. Companies can improve profits in the short term through actions that have nothing at all to do with meeting customer needs.

An excellent example is Nucor Corporation, whose purpose statement was listed in Table 3.1.2-1. Nucor clearly defines results as customer satisfaction, safety, quality, cost, productivity, and environmental protection.

In another example, in addition to a clearly focused mission statement, a small global manufacturing organization defined its vision as "Clearly the Best!" It further defined "the best" as being the following:

- 95%+ on-time delivery to the customer's requested date

- 8+ inventory turns/year

- 90% of customers rate the company as "best" when compared with competitors

- 20% of company time is spent on improvement (personal skills or company processes)

- Customer returns < 0.01%

By clarifying the vision, the company's leaders have determined which results are critical to the company's success. The measures given here made up the company's dashboard, and the senior leadership team reviewed progress quarterly. As the company improved and its environment changed, its definition of "Clearly the Best!" was modified to keep pace.

In a lean environment, the Plan-Do-Check-Act (PDCA) cycle naturally focuses attention on results. Whether used for process improvement or business planning, the cycle begins with quantifying the target, carrying out plans or tests, and regularly comparing the results of the tests with those of the target. Determining which results are important is done at the outset of the process, and the cycle ensures that plans are aligned with desired results.

A significant benefit of using the PDCA approach to business planning (often referred to as hoshin kanri or policy deployment; see Section 3.2.2) is that the results measure the success of the company's planning process. If the "Check" step shows that the company is successful in implementing its plans but the results are not showing improvement or meeting targets, then the planning process needs to be evaluated to determine the reason for the disconnect.

3.1.2.2. Focus on Waste Elimination

In the simplest terms, *waste* is anything an organization does for which its customers do not pay. When a company is focused on its purpose of providing value to customers, it must constantly work to identify and eliminate waste within its operation and improve its offering.

A simple concept on the surface, focusing on waste reduction often requires a different level of thinking and a cultural shift within the organization. The traditional approach focuses on cost-cutting to improve performance, while lean thinking companies follow a waste elimination approach to improvement. Although both methods lead to reduced costs, the lean approach considers reduced costs to be the *effect* of eliminating waste, while cost-cutting focuses solely on costs rather than considering a cause-and-effect relationship.

In order to drive a consistent lean culture, a focus on waste elimination requires people to become intimate with what the customers value in the company's products and services so they can better determine what constitutes waste and work to reduce it. As waste is eliminated, costs are reduced, leading to other benefits such as improved quality, reduced lead time, and improved safety.

Alternatively, a focus on cost-cutting does not truly consider the impact on the customer. Costs are reduced based on directive rather than as a result of improvement. Whereas cost reductions that are the result of improvement activities tend to be sustained into the future, the benefits from cost-cutting actions are often short term. Since many cost-cutting initiatives reduce expenses that do not appear to add immediate value (e.g., training, maintenance activities, and exempt/nondirect employees), the impact of the reductions is eventually offset by increases in quality problems, lack of resources, and equipment problems.

The cultural change involved in a shift to a focus on waste elimination requires a variety of actions by company leaders, such as having clear and consistent expectations as well as aligning rewards and measures with the new direction. As mentioned earlier, there must be constancy of purpose toward waste reduction, meaning that the commitment and focus must be constant, not start-and-stop based on current conditions.

3.1.2.3. Focus on Value to Customer

Organizations focused on their purpose operate with their customers' best interests in mind. They never stop working to understand what customers value, and they use the information gained to continually improve the products and services they provide.

Focusing on value provided to the customer requires an approach different from traditional thinking. It is important to think beyond the products and services the company offers and focus on the *value* that the products and services provide. When value is viewed in this manner, dialogue with customers can bring about positive changes and innovations.

As an example, a manufacturer of calibration instrumentation had always maintained a focus on its products rather than the value its products provided. As a result, the company continued to develop products with higher levels of accuracy at higher prices. Although surveys showed that customers were willing to pay more for products with higher accuracy, revenues rarely changed when new products were introduced. After the company organized into product teams, its dialogue with customers began to change. Instead of market surveys, a cross-functional team began making regular visits to facilities of the company's largest customers and witnessed the products in use. They quickly learned that speed (including setup, calibration, and disconnect) was much more important than higher accuracy. This information, which was never considered in market surveys, completely changed the company's approach to product development and resulted in more successful product launches.

In addition to improving product development, the knowledge gained from focusing on customer value can help people better understand what adds value and what does not. Analyzing the value stream for waste becomes much easier when those involved understand the customer's point of view.

The first step in mapping a value stream is to identify the customer and define the value that the stream defines. Without a focus on customer value, mapping will become an internally focused exercise. Further, if the team is not focused on customer value, any waste identified will be nothing more than a guess. A focus on customer value is a fundamental element that must exist before attempting lean. Pursuing lean without it will, at best, result in an unsustainable effort.

Lean-thinking organizations realize that *it's all about the customer*. The Voice of the Customer (VOC) is in the forefront when making major decisions, as well as when pursuing improvement activities. The focus on customer value is evident throughout the company, not just with those who directly interact with customers.

3.1.3. SOCIAL RESPONSIBILITY

A focus on waste elimination is very well aligned with social responsibility. In addition to lowering costs for the company, reductions in materials and energy used by the company benefit the environment. Generally, eliminating waste lowers a company's impact on the environment. As the cost of raw materials rises, along with the logistical costs associated with transporting them, the fewer materials a company uses, the more competitive it will be. By reducing waste, an organization can reduce its usage of materials and gain a distinct advantage over its competitors.

Also, as environmental protection becomes a bigger social and political issue, the costs of regulation, including permits, fines, and public relations, make it more important for businesses to focus on social responsibility. As with reducing costs, the chance of success in reducing environmental impact greatly increases when it is the result of a holistic approach to improvement rather than an isolated initiative.

When an organization focuses on all of its stakeholders, it understands that the environment and the community are critical to its success. The environment ensures a future for the company by providing its supply of raw materials; the community in which the company operates provides employees for the company, a place for those employees to live, and an infrastructure in which to operate.

REFERENCES

Cambridge Advanced Learner's Dictionary. 2010. Cambridge, UK: Cambridge University Press.

Deming, W. Edwards. 1986. *Out of the Crisis*. Cambridge, MA: MIT Press.

Dennis, Pascal. 2007. *Lean Production Simplified: A Plain Language Guide to the World's Most Powerful Production System*. New York: Productivity Press.

Drucker, Peter. 1993. *Management: Tasks, Responsibilities and Practices*. New York: HarperBusiness.

Mann, David. 2010. *Creating a Lean Culture: Tools to Sustain Lean Conversions*. 2nd ed. New York: Productivity Press/Taylor and Francis Group.

3.2

Processes for Developing Consistent Lean Enterprise Culture

Section 3.1 looked at the principles of creating a consistent lean culture. This section explores the processes or systems needed in order to achieve and maintain a lean culture. To begin, an organization needs to integrate its information and reporting systems, including how it creates flow, how it creates a business improvement system, and how it shares information. The second portion of this section explores how management aligns the organization through a shared process known as policy deployment to implement breakthrough initiatives and drive results.

3.2.1. ENTERPRISE THINKING

We have all seen this situation before: Decide among what's best for you, your boss, your department, or someone else competing for the same scarce resources. This situation starts with a lack of enterprise thinking.

To more deeply understand what is meant by the term "enterprise thinking," we need to first explore the life cycle of an organization. Most companies start up with a great deal of enthusiasm, innovation, and spirit. This entrepreneurial spirit is contagious and attracts us to want to get in on the ground floor. People are pumped up, but at the same time they have no idea of the structure needed to support this spirit.

Over time structure creeps in, and at first it is supportive of the organization's spirit. At some point, though, structure begins to create increased bureaucracy, and this starts to create a new set of problems. Once the structure is unwieldy enough, it begins to constrain the spirit of creativity and can even reward some unproductive behaviors. A great start-up with an intense customer focus can eventually turn into an institution that no longer considers the customer as its main reason for existence (see Figure 3.2.1-1).

At the heart of high performance is a supportive, nurturing environment that rewards collaboration, innovation, and a healthy dissatisfaction with the status quo.

Organizations that have lost track of their entrepreneurial spirit may actually reward people for dysfunctional behaviors. For example, when budget season springs upon us, some department managers work hard to get a piece of the pie for their own benefit but are unwilling to sacrifice for the greater good.

One such company (a tier-one automotive supplier) was choosing between investing in equipment that would make its product better and investing in making the repair operation faster. As the budget season commenced, a pivotal moment

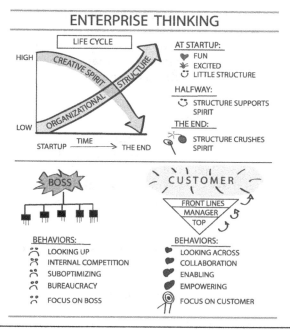

Figure 3.2.1-1   Enterprise thinking—organizational structure, spirit, and focus diagram.

occurred when someone decided to invest in repairing product faster instead of getting it right the first time (eliminating the need for repair). In three short years this company was on the ropes and over 1500 people lost their jobs. While one poor decision was likely not the reason for closing this plant, a lack of enterprise thinking opened a space for frequent silo behaviors.

Enterprise thinking might have had us ask these questions instead:

- What's best for the customer?

- What's best for the overall organization?

- What's best for people?

- What's best for product?

- What's best for our environment?

- And, how to balance all of these?

By working with the minimum structure possible, people are given leeway to choose the best course of action. Focusing on customer needs ensures internal collaboration since it takes everyone working together to succeed in a competitive marketplace.

When a company starts any cost-reduction initiative, it is usually reactive in nature and can result in a focus that ensures customer dissatisfaction—just when customers are of most importance. Consider the boss announcing to the team, "We saved $3 million last year—someone uncork the champagne!" and then someone else chimes in, "Wait a minute, our on-time delivery has dropped to an all-time low and we just lost half of our customer base."

3.2.1

Realignment toward a customer focus through collaborative internal working relationships must be considered a pivotal moment in any organization's life cycle. The key is to enable the people working in an organization to focus on and serve the customer. By removing barriers that prevent organizational excellence, we can create some of the conditions conducive to enterprise thinking.

3.2.1.1. Organize around Flow

Linear thinking often results in the misguided conclusion that the sum of the parts of an organization equals performance of the system. Traditional organizations typically have multiple layers of management that were thought to be needed for better control. It makes sense in traditional thinking to monitor and optimize individual parts of the organization. The thinking is that by accruing each department's results and holding functional department managers responsible for individual performance, the overall objectives will somehow be met. This adds to the perception of "what gets measured gets improved."

Unfortunately for the linear thinkers, focusing on performance at the functional level leads to an endless focus on blame for lack of performance. "Who is responsible?" is their mantra, instead of, "What causes our problems and how can we fix them together?"

The higher up you go in a traditional organization chain of command, the less likely that person is to know and understand what it is like to be on the front lines. This disconnection with the current reality makes it easier to say no when someone asks for funding for making improvements.

In a lean organization, frontline workers typically report to an area leader who in turn reports to the plant manager or value stream manager, which eliminates the need for the traditional department manager. By removing layers of control, the plant manager can focus on the system of work as a whole—an interconnected web of internal customer and supplier relationships. In this environment, information flows freely since there are fewer filtering mechanisms, and, most importantly, people are held accountable for organizational performance as a whole, not individual performance.

When you think about a production system, at its most fundamental and basic level it is converting raw materials to finished product that a customer would like to purchase. Removing many sources of non-value-added work is an important focus for lean organizations. For example, when employees are working to "the cadence" (aka takt time) in a lean organization, there is not much "extra" time for hunting around for parts.

Organizing around flow may introduce a position—the water spider. You may have heard the mantra "Treat frontline workers like surgeons." The water spider is the person who ensures that value-added frontline workers spend most of their time creating customer value and not hunting around for parts or dealing with a tangled mess from suppliers. Water spiders replenish raw materials as needed following standard work loops throughout the facility.

The water spider position is a great learning opportunity for high-potential employees since it exposes the person to the entire production system. Many consider it a stepping stone to the area leader position. When you think about it, water spiders are suppliers to the frontline workers because they deliver parts just in time and move racks around to make it easier to produce product. Water spiders typically get involved in real-time decision making and problem solving, and find themselves in the unique position of being a conduit for information flow.

Organizing around flow is all about eliminating traditional boundaries between internal customers and suppliers. For example, a food manufacturer that introduced office cells in accounts payable found that there were two basic types of invoices entering the value stream: (1) high volume–low complexity and (2) low volume–high complexity. The people in the accounts payable department moved from functional experts, who were responsible for individual vendors, to generalists, who could handle any task within the two cells. Job rotation ensured that people were cross trained and learned to appreciate the needs of customers, since one day they would be a supplier and the next day they would be the customer.

Before the introduction of office cells in the department, a clerical error by a team member often snowballed, as an invoice gets processed later. By instituting "fitness for use" checks, the quality of work improved since output was checked by both the person doing the work and the next person in line before using it (input). This single-piece flow ensured that problems were highlighted and corrected immediately. This resulted in fewer calls from suppliers asking for an update since the lead time was reduced from two weeks to about two days, and late invoices were virtually eliminated.

The concept of lean in the office is depicted in Figure 3.2.1.1-1.

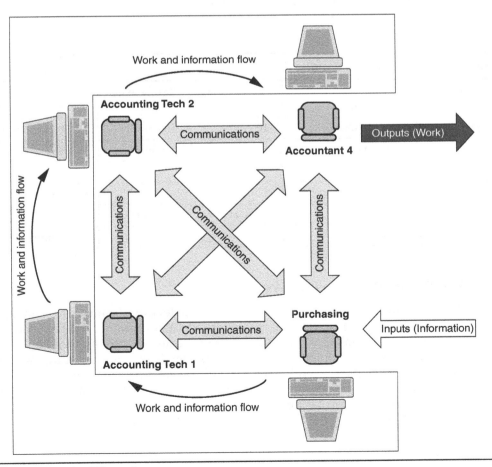

Figure 3.2.1.1-1 Office cells.

3.2.1.2. Integrated Business System and Improvement System

Finance function involvement is a key to starting and sustaining lean. The standard costing model has remained relatively unchanged since it was introduced, when mass production was the norm. The problem with standard costing is that it muddies the waters by allocating costs to overhead costs that are absorbed into the cost of the product (typically by standard direct labor hours). At the end of the month, actual costs are compared with standard costs, and these differences are allocated into different categories of variances (material, usage, labor, overhead absorption). Standard costing models drive behaviors since people respond to what questions they are asked and what they believe leadership desires. Imagine trying to get to the root cause of a variance to budget if you are a frontline leader. This is why it is important to integrate business systems with improvement systems.

Box scores are one way to help make better decisions regarding quotes, profitability, make/buy, and product rationalization that many companies face to stay in business. A typical box score has three major sections: operational, capacity, and financial. Box scores are used in many applications, including weekly value stream performance reporting toward achieving the goals, sourcing decisions for a potential new sales order under different scenarios, or purchasing additional machines (see Table 3.2.1.2-1).

Table 3.2.1.2-1   Box score example.

Box score section	Element	Current state (before lean)	Future state (lean)	Estimated benefit
Operational	Process time	106 minutes	100 minutes	6% reduction
	Lead time	646 minutes	240 minutes	63% reduction
	First-yield pass	57%	93%	61% improvement
Capacity	Value-added time	16%	42%	163% improvement
Financial	Revenue	$500,000	$500,000	—
	Profit	$50,000	$60,000	20% improvement

3.2.1.3. Reconcile Reporting Systems

When starting any lean journey, it takes time to develop the measures and reporting systems needed to quantify improvements. For example, a major food manufacturer was wholeheartedly implementing lean in 2008, and its teams were deeply involved in implementing and sustaining lean. An interesting thing happened when people started looking carefully at the financial numbers. The plant controller was very focused on accumulating the savings from the company's lean journey. At the same time, the manufacturing manager was also interested in quantifying the improvements being made. Even some staffers were asked to provide a summary of the impact from this effort. And the senior vice president in charge of manufacturing was interested in this as well.

So there we had it: People from one end of the business to the other were interested in the same thing. So what difference did lean make for the manufacturer?

What was found was that if you combined everyone's quantifiable savings, all together they saved well over $1 million. Since it was their first year, everyone knew that it wasn't really possible, so they were all wondering what the total impact of the lean effort truly was.

The answer came during one of the touch points with the senior leadership. Maintenance had just reported on how it put in vending machines for perishable parts and how those machines were monitored by the suppliers in real time. This eliminated the need to put in orders for expensive tooling, while keeping a usage record. Suppliers had a vested interest in keeping the vending machines full of tooling, and this led to less out-of-stock situations. Only authorized personnel could use the vending machines, which kept control of expenses. Also, since the tool room personnel were freed up to focus on serving maintenance personnel, tool room service levels increased and the maintenance team reported a healthy savings.

A material usage team reported next, and it had discovered a way to save on materials using a visual technique for monitoring weights. Overages were reduced while meeting the requirements of the United States Department of Agriculture (USDA), schools, and the Food and Drug Administration (FDA). This resulted in a rather large savings.

The lean teams reported next, and they were working on reducing waste. Team members had been weighing scrap containers and had reported a drastic reduction in the amount of product thrown out. This added up to a considerable sum as well. In addition, many new ideas came from gemba walks; team members had a steady stream of opportunities to improve.

The director of manufacturing (who was very enlightened) stood up and said, "Folks, we need to put everything that we're doing under one umbrella, and let's call that lean." It was the beginning of the total reconciliation of the reporting systems. No longer were people all going out independently trying to quantify the efforts lean was having on the overall organization. Instead, they were all focused on the same thing: sustaining lean. True to its nature, the lean transformation took them to a place they didn't anticipate. The number-one rule, *We are all in this together*, had been realized.

Are costs the only thing a lean effort will impact on an organization's metrics? Of course, senior leadership is held accountable for costs, and it only makes sense to work on what the boss wants. But are there other things that are just as important as financial measures? One could say that the financial impact of lean is only a trailing indicator of the efforts by those making daily improvements happen. Everyone needs to recognize that results emanate from the efforts and creativity of the frontline workers. Therefore, measures such as employee engagement, team spirit, turnover, absenteeism, and new ideas submitted are important as well.

Ultimately we are seeking direct costs that describe how well the value stream is functioning for the customer. By creating timely reports that are easy to understand, frontline workers can make better real-time decisions. For example, at what time will this run be completed? Or, what is the number-one quality defect happening today? Only by reconciling the reporting system and making it resonate with the front lines will this be possible.

Measures and reports must be relevant to the work being performed so that the people doing the work can better grasp the situation. Reporting systems must be integrated and roll up to enterprise metrics that make sense for the overall organization, and they also must make it easy for people working in the value streams to focus on improving the daily work.

3.2.1.4. Information Management

A value stream map shows a high-level process flow that includes everything needed to create value for a customer. Most standard accounting processes do not identify product categories that customers buy. They simply categorize costs by department, instead of categorizing product costs on a value stream or product line basis. Table 3.2.1.4-1 helps clarify the differences in approaches.

Lean accounting (see Section 4.2.1.5, "Lean Accounting") categorizes costs by value stream at the product line level. Costs in a value stream include expenses

Table 3.2.1.4-1 Costing.

Principle	Traditional cost accounting	Lean accounting
Performance measurements	• Measure outcomes, not processes • Drive non-lean behaviors • Are too late and too complicated	• Motivate action • Drive continuous improvement • Are visual, simple, actionable
Value stream accounting	• Many people do not understand the reports • Data gathering and transactions are complex and wasteful	• Timely-weekly • Easy-to-understand reports • Less work
Decisions and budgets	• Product and service costs are misleading and inaccurate • Focus on quoting, make/buy, financial impact of lean profitability	• Real numbers • Better decisions • Fully understood • Up-to-date • Box score
Transactions	• Involve thousands of transactions • Are complex and wasteful • Impede improvement	• Understand the "why" behind decisions • Eliminate problems • Eliminate transactions
Target costing	• Price = Cost + Margin • No understanding of customer value • Unfocused cost cutting	• Profit = Price – Cost • Deep understanding of value • Focus lean improvements to achieve targets • Integrated with strategy

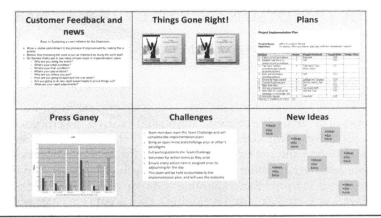

Figure 3.2.1.4-1   Example of center for excellence.

to produce and ship a product as well as costs related to servicing and collecting payments from customers. Therefore, corporate overhead costs are hidden from internal value stream reports. The reason is that those costs are not controllable costs for employees working within the value stream.

Visual information boards go a long way in creating a common understanding of what is important to the frontline worker and how he or she fits into the whole. For example, consider a "center of excellence" for information management purposes (see Figure 3.2.1.4-1).

Team meetings are held directly in front of center of excellence boards, using the board itself as an agenda. Other things to note:

- Progress, problems, and plans are discussed while standing in front of the board.

- An early goal should be to transfer ownership of improvement plans to the team and to celebrate early signs of engagement, best performance, and helpful behaviors.

- Another goal should be to increase the frequency of team meetings while reducing the time spent in meetings. This is accomplished by holding "standing" meetings at the team board. People will get down to business and focus on the problems if they are not seated and facing one another.

- The board will soon become a central point of communication for the team and will be used to generate new ideas as well.

- Leaders are responsible for giving the team feedback as to what constitutes a priority and the rationale for not approving some ideas. Also, leaders should consider prioritizing the next wave of efforts for the team.

- Rewarding individuals reinforces competitive behaviors, whereas rewarding the team reinforces team behaviors. So, choose consequences carefully.

3.2.1.4

3.2.2. POLICY DEPLOYMENT/STRATEGY DEPLOYMENT

*Leaders establish the vision for the future and set the
strategy for getting there.*

—John P. Kotter

Policy deployment or *strategy deployment* (aka hoshin kanri) is the process of driving the organization's vision down to the tactics that align actions for achievement of results. It is the formation of the policies and strategies, the alignment of these within the organization, and the consistent pursuit of improvement that set lean organizations that use hoshin apart from others. Genuine and correct application of policy deployment will provide the linkage for developing a consistent lean enterprise culture.

Since hoshin kanri first appeared in the late 1960s, it has been a system of management in which the annual policy set by a company is passed down through the organization and implemented across all departments and functions in this system (Kondo 1998).

Organizations use many different methods to create their strategic direction, ranging from no planning at all to full policy deployment. Table 3.2.2-1 gives a brief review of some of these methods.

Table 3.2.2-1 Methods to create a strategic direction.

Method	Advantages	Disadvantages
No planning method	• Saves time • Failure comes as a complete surprise	• Probably won't stay in business • The company has no clear direction
"Hope" as a strategy	• It may make you feel good	• Hoping does not create results
Whatever the boss says	• Pleases the boss • Can't get in trouble if you do what the boss wants	• Unless the boss is omniscient, how would he or she have all the answers? • Little or no buy-in • Can change direction at any time
Operation plan, budgeting, marketing plan	• At least there is some type of planning	• How do you know that you are spending your resources on the most important initiatives? • Is this real planning or an educated guess? • Typically these plans are separate and not connected
Management by objective (MBO)	• When the numbers are achieved, management gets their bonuses • The boss is happy	• Things can be made worse by the methods used to reach the numbers • Can be short-term thinking • May pit one department against another • "Win at all cost" mentality

How do any of these styles develop a consistent, good culture? Typically, they don't. Policy deployment drives correct behaviors and engagement to bring about real change that will lift an organization above its competitors.

3.2.2.1. Scientific Thinking as a Strategy Process

> *It is useful to remind everyone that you are experimenting in order to see obstacles and to learn from them what you need to work on in order to achieve the target condition.*
>
> —Mike Rother, *Toyota Kata: Managing People for Improvement, Adaptiveness, and Superior Results*

Policy deployment is based on the scientific method of Plan-Do-Check-Act (PDCA). The planning process is not a once-a-year technique. By following PDCA the organization has the opportunity to improve, enhance, or even change when appropriate and necessary. The scientific method means that a company is willing to experiment or test a hypothesis in order to achieve superior results. By using a rigorous approach to experiments, the company can learn and grow in a low-risk environment.

Plan

Of course, policy deployment is about creating the strategic plan (including driving the changes to get the results). The planning portion of hoshin has many elements, including reviewing the previous year's plan and performing hansei (self-reflection). Many organizations review their vision, mission, and values to ensure that they are still aligned with their "True North." Another step may include performing an environment scan of items that may affect the organization, covering economic, social-demographic, technological, legal/political, and competitive subjects and more. This is all to prepare the top management team to create the top longer-term (three to five years) breakthrough strategies that will vault the company ahead of the competition. From here the executives pass this information to the appropriate department, person, or team for further development (see Section 3.2.2.3, "Dynamic Give and Take").

Do

The "Do" phase is where the actual execution of the plan occurs. It is important during this phase to closely monitor actions that lead to the "Check" phase. Many times during the planning process impediments are discovered. These hurdles need to be overcome during this phase.

Check

During the "Check" phase of PDCA it may come to light that the hypothesis did not pan out. This is a learning moment. If during this phase the results are exactly what was expected, then no new learning was achieved.

Act

If the results expected did not materialize, then the action would be to discover lessons learned, find a root cause, and apply scientific thinking to create a new hypothesis and return to the "Plan" phase. If the results expected were verified during the "Check" phase, then standardization must occur to sustain the gains (or at least prevent them from slipping back).

In order for an organization to grow or try innovative approaches, the scientific method must become an essential part of policy deployment.

3.2.2.2. Series of Nested Experiments

To create innovative or groundbreaking achievements—the ones that set you above your competition—a consistent, planned scientific approach of nested experiments is required. By using a series of experiments, keeping all variables constant but one, the organization can truly begin to understand the cause and effects of its actions. This method is simple to teach and understand. A more complex method like design of experiments (DOE) may be used, but there is a larger risk to an organization while performing the test.

When creating the strategy plan, not all variables are known; in other words, how or what to implement is not always clear-cut. Let's say that the top management of an organization decides that they want to enter a completely new market. Not all the variables are known about how to execute this strategy, so a set of experiments will need to be created to find the best path for implementation. Marketing may have information related to this new market, but a low-risk approach may be to try a pilot program in a region or customer segmentation. A hypothesis like, "We can sell 3000 units in this new territory in the next three months" is proposed. A marketing plan is created and then carried out. For instance, it is proposed that the initial advertisement for the product will be carried out by a localized pay-per-click program on the internet. By monitoring the sales in relation to the number of clicks (click-through rate), the company gains valuable feedback regarding the program's effectiveness. Let's say that the company sold 50 units over two weeks using this method. It doesn't have to abandon this method, but it may consider performing another nested experiment. This time the company decides to perform A-B split testing of the ads that appear. They run both ads over two weeks and find that ad "A" produced sales of 40 units and ad "B" produced sales of 10 units. Realizing that ad "A" produced better results, the company runs a new A-B split test by revamping ad "B" as "B_{new}." This time ad "A" produces sales of 40 units and ad "B_{new}" produces sales of 100 units. The company can continue this method until it finds the most effective ad to help reach its goal.

3.2.2.3. Dynamic Give and Take

To help deploy the policies or strategies created by upper management, they need to be moved down to the next level. The departments or groups work on them and then send them back up to make sure they are in alignment with management. This is known as *catchball*: the strategy is thrown to the group below, they create their plan, and then they throw it back up for feedback (see Section 3.3.2 for more details). This continues at all levels of an organization until the implementation plans are driven all the way down to gemba and the value-adders.

As part of this dynamic give and take, each group must always consider:

- What is value for the customer (internal and external)?

- What is best for the value stream (not just one person, area, division, or department)?

- How do we properly allocate resources to achieve the desired results?

This give and take allows the organization to set the direction and then let the people closest to implementation determine the plan of action. This monitoring ensures alignment throughout the organization, and everyone knows his or her role in achieving his or her goals.

3.2.2.4. Forming Consensus

To fully engage and implement your strategic plan, it is important to build consensus from top to bottom and within teams. *Consensus*, as used here, is an outcome that all team members can support or live with and that no one opposes. Everybody might not be totally satisfied with the decision, but it is still supported by all concerned. It is not a unanimous vote or a majority vote. If you had to wait for a unanimous vote, you may never get everyone on board; and a "majority wins" vote could lead to team members not fully supporting the idea or plan.

To build consensus, consider the following:

- No silent disagreements or passive-resistant behavior

- Sufficient time

- Active participation of all team members

- Skills in listening

- Seeing others' point of view

- Creative thinking

- Open-mindedness

- Sharing all available information

- Process oriented (not people)

By coming to consensus about the plan, the teams can move forward with implementation. This is especially important during plan development and the catchball phase.

3.2.2.5. Align Strategies and Execution

A key advantage of using policy deployment is discovering the strength of the alignment among the long-term strategies, the short-term projects, the measures and metrics, and the teams deploying the action plans. One of the main tools to visually show these relationships is the X-matrix. Dr. Ryuji Fukuda created the X-matrix as a way to help organizations align the entire company with the strategies

(Hamilton and Wardwell 2010, 79). There are many adaptations of the X-matrix, but a typical high-level X-matrix has six main sections (see Figure 3.2.2.5-1):

1. Long-term (three to five years) goals or strategies

2. Near-term (one to two years) goals or strategies

3. Current projects

4. Measures or metrics

5. Department or team members involved

6. Correlation areas or "correlation corners"

The key to showing alignment occurs in the "corners." The management team comes to consensus on the level of correlation of the different sections (very strong, important, weak, or none); this shows and emphasizes the alignment throughout the entire plan. Simple symbols are used to show the intensity of correlation (see Table 3.2.2.5-1).

By being able to see the correlations, the entire organization can trace and prioritize the most important initiatives. If a particular strategy, project, or measure does not correlate well with others, it might not be a good fit for the organization—especially if it cannot be traced back to long-term initiatives.

Another method of gaining alignment is to use a tree diagram (see Figure 3.2.2.5-2), where the high-level strategies are the trunk, and the near-term strategies down to the tactics are the roots. By connecting the high-level strategies all the way down to the tactical level, everyone in the organization can see his or her role in achieving the organization's breakthrough goals. An additional benefit of using a tree diagram is that it shows the "how" and the "why." Reading from the top down shows how we are going to get things done, and reading from the bottom up shows why we are doing these actions.

3.2.2.6. Standard Work for Strategy Communication—How We Think and Talk

After the plan is created and alignment is validated, effective communication is crucial for keeping everything on track. How we act and talk is noticed every day. Going to gemba and talking with the value-adders to see if they understand the goals and objectives, coaching or mentoring supervisors and managers, and practicing what we preach are all part of leader standard work.

Two additional elements are critical during this phase: (1) consistent reviews and (2) a communication plan. Planned reviews are essential for the organization to apply PDCA and the scientific method. Team leaders may need to perform reviews and updates on a weekly to monthly time frame. Managers should review plans at least on a monthly basis. Formal executive management reviews may occur quarterly. The closer to the action, the more frequent the reviews will occur. Creating leader standard work for these reviews is important, including the schedule and how reviews are performed.

Creating a communication plan regarding policy deployment is another application of standard work. A communication plan can be a one-page document that shows the contact person, the key message, the target audience, methods of communication, resources, desired results, status, and effectiveness (see Table 3.2.2.6-1).

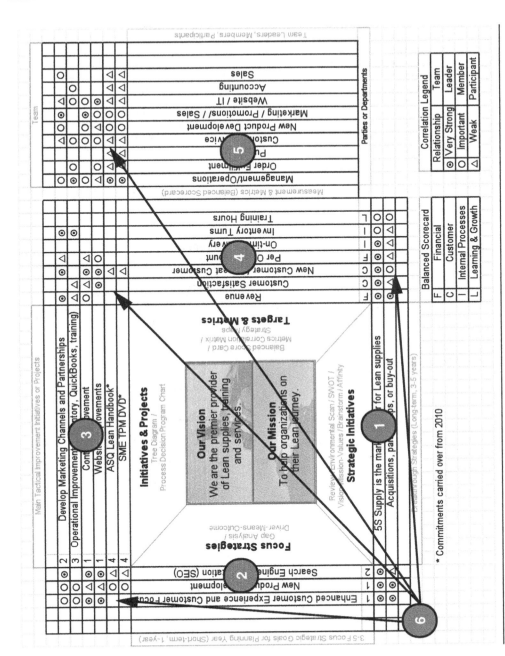

Figure 3.2.2.5-1 X-matrix example.

Table 3.2.2.5-1 Correlation symbols.

Relationship (Sections 1–4)		Team (Section 5)
⊙	Very strong	Leader
○	Important	Member
△	Weak	Participant

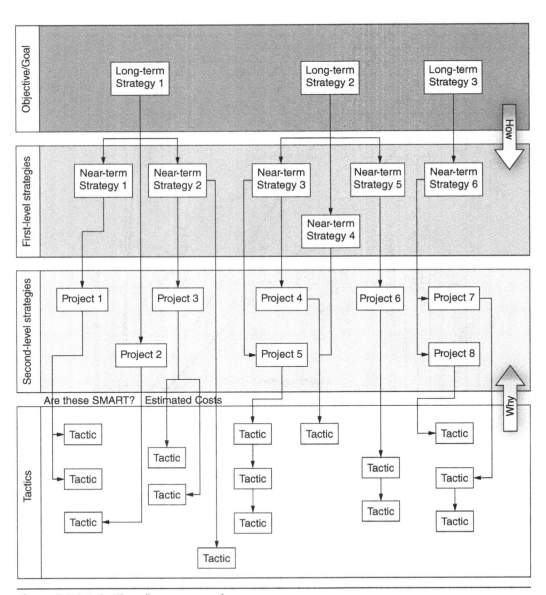

Figure 3.2.2.5-2 Tree diagram example.

Table 3.2.6-1 Communication plan example.

					Date reviewed	XX/XX/XX	Reviewed by		Justin Tyme	
Hoshin Communication Plan										
ID	Leader	Date	Key message	Target audience	Method(s) of communication	Resources required (time, people, budgets)	Desired results	Percent complete	Effectiveness rating
1	George A.	XX/XX/XX	What is policy deployment?	Managers, supervisors, and hourly employees	Town hall meetings, department meetings, newsletter, one-on-one	15-minute sessions each week for 4 weeks	Everyone has a basic understanding of policy deployment and its purpose	50	"B"
2	Jenifer	XX/XX/XX	Progress reviews	Supervisors and value-adders	Small team meetings	Half-hour meeting each week	To make sure teams are on track	0	
3	Jean	XX/XX/XX	Planning forms for implementation	Managers and supervisors	Demonstration	Standard work training kit, training room	Dedicated execution of the plan	0	
4	Joanne	XX/XX/XX	Role of innovation	Supervisors	Brainstorming session, role-playing	2-hour meeting	New way of thinking	100	Very good
5	George P.	XX/XX/XX	How *you* affect the strategy	Value-adders	Small group meetings	20 minutes each session	Employees understand their role in achieving our goals	75	Needs improvement
6	Tony	XX/XX/XX	Quarterly reviews	Executive management	Quarterly status meeting	15 minutes	Understand the importance of removing roadblocks	50	On track

3.2.2.6

3.2.2.7. Resource Deployment and Allocation

All organizations have the same issues when it comes to limited resources such as time, people, and budgets. There are several ways to help ensure that resources are allocated for the benefit of the customer and the value streams. The first one is to utilize the X-matrix (see Section 3.2.2.5, "Align Strategies and Execution"). By finding the correlations among strategies, tactics, and team members, better decisions can be made regarding resource allocation and deployment. Although robust methods that calculate return on investment, net present value, and internal rate of return and other methods may show the best allocation of resources for the monetary return, this type of analysis may inadvertently skip over other, longer-lasting benefits like teamwork and creating a lean culture. A simple tool to use is the effort and impact matrix. Using a scale like low-medium-high, the team can come to consensus on the effort it would take to complete a project and the overall impact it would have. Even though this method is subjective, it can still help an organization determine low-effort, high-impact projects. Other tools that can be used include A3 reports and Gantt charts. Remember, one of the best ways to get results fast is to perform kaizen events to implement projects.

REFERENCES

Hamilton, Bruce, and Pat Wardwell. 2010. *E2 Continuous Improvement System*. Boston: GBMP.

Kondo, Yoshio. 1998. "Hoshin Kanri—a Participative Way of Quality Management in Japan." *The TQM Magazine* 10 (6): 425–31.

3.3

Consistent Enterprise Culture Techniques & Practices

In Section 3.2, the processes of communication and policy deployment were emphasized. This section focuses on the how-to tools to make this happen, including A3 storytelling and catchball (throwing the plan back and forth to get input and build buy-in), and looks at how to move resources around when needed.

3.3.1. A3

A3, or "A san" in Japanese, literally means a paper size defined by ISO 216 as 11 × 17 inches (297 × 420 mm). A3 in lean terminology means learning, sharing, or knowledge-capturing documentation using an A3 format. Traditionally, an A3 was drawn by hand on A3 paper, but with the pervasiveness and ease of computing, more and more A3s are documented on programs such as Microsoft Excel, Microsoft Word, Visio, or similar. The purpose of the A3 is not so much in formatting or how it looks, but in the knowledge captured, the process problem analyzed/ solved, or the mentoring/learning that occurs in the A3 documentation process.

The true origin of A3 is not fully known, but it is believed to have originated with Toyota in application of the Plan-Do-Check-Act (PDCA) cycle of experimentation in continuous improvement. During the A3 process, the mentor or coach asks the mentee or learner to define the background and current state or situation. This information is usually placed in the upper left of the A3 page. Below that is the desired state or goals to be achieved. In the lower left is the analysis of the current situation or problem (Figure 3.3.1-1).

The upper right of the A3 page contains the countermeasures or actions proposed or implemented to move the process or situation to the next level of improvement. Below that are any specific future actions, and in the lower right are the control steps to preserve the new current state. This is necessary to ensure that standard work is in place and that no deterioration or backsliding occurs between now and when the next PDCA experiment is undertaken to improve the process in the future.

The exact format of an A3 is not important. The journey of discovery, knowledge, and learning is the true value of the A3 thinking process. The documentation of the A3 by the learner and coaching by the mentor create an invaluable process of capacity development (Figure 3.3.1-2). Two key references that can help those new to A3 thinking are *Managing to Learn* (2008), by John Shook, and *Understanding A3 Thinking* (2008), by Durward Sobek.

Define—background/current state	Plan—propose countermeasures
Describe what is happening and why it is important	Develop actions to move toward target condition

Plan—set future-state goals or target	Do—complete actions
Determine the target condition or future state to be achieved	Execute countermeasures to determine impact

Plan—analyze	Act—standardize
Analyze the current processes to fully understand root cause of challenge	Create standard work, set up monitoring or controls to maintain new current state/standard work

Figure 3.3.1-1   Sample A3 format.

Issue: 4 pts of leverage theory

Background/Buisness Case: Fundamental technology used on Donjoy knee braces.

Key Words: 4 pts, four, points, leverage, anterior drawer

Author/Date: Rich Gildersleeve/ August 20, 2007

Current Condition/Reason for Technology

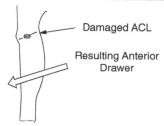

Damaged ACL

Resulting Anterior Drawer

Problem Analysis: When ACL is compromised, tibia can slide forward (anterior drawer) and cause knee instability, compromising activities of daily living and sporting participation. Also increased potential for additional damage to knee soft tissues.

References:
Donjoy ACL bracing literature and promotional materials.

Target Condition/Trade-Off Curves

Femoral Rotation

Tibial Rotation

F Ray   Ray

$\ell \quad \ell \quad \ell \quad \ell$

Ray F

$\Sigma\, Fy = Ray - F = 0$
$\Sigma\, Ma = \ell - Ray = 0$
$Ray = 1/2\, F$
$Ray = 1/2\, F$

4 Points of Leverage

$E/2$
$-F/2$
$FR/2$
$-FR/2$

V Shear Diagram

M Moment Diagram

Counter Measures/Actions/Features
Four points of leverage shown allow dynamic support of damaged ACL with posteriorly directed moment and shear of tibia and anteriorly directed moment and shear of femur.

Implementation Plan
What   Who   When   Outcome

All Donjoy ACL braces over last 20 years have successfully employed this concept.

Cost: n/a

Benefit: n/a

Figure 3.3.1-2   Sample A3 for knowledge capture.

Source: Adapted from original courtesy of Richard Gildersleeve, DJO Global, 2007.

3.3.1

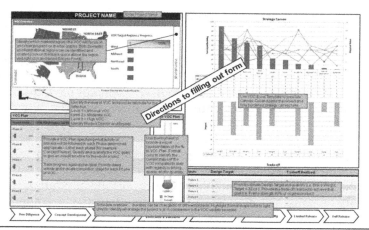

Figure 3.3.1-3 Sample A3 for VOC with Instructions to complete.
Source: Courtesy of DJO Global, 2011.

The key purpose of the A3 process is to engender (1) a style of thinking that is rigorous and thorough, (2) communication that focuses on hard data and vital information, and (3) problem solving that is collaborative and objective. Lean companies are also using A3 thinking to do much more within their organization (Figure 3.3.1-3). Some other examples of A3 thinking are the following:

- Capturing Voice of the Customer (VOC)

- Project management

- Vendor capabilities

- New product or process concepts

- Technology mapping

3.3.2. CATCHBALL

A common way to set goals in a lean-minded organization is through strategic policy deployment, or hoshin kanri. Policy deployment (also known as hoshin planning) is an approach to cascading goals and objectives from the board or company leadership throughout the organization in a specific method. The method is typically very well organized throughout the levels of the company to ensure tight alignment of all affected personnel to effectively complete the objectives in a specified cadence.

One of the key techniques used in policy deployment is the collaborative practice of catchball. The term "catchball" comes from the concept that a strategy or objective may be outlined by the company leadership but then rather than implementing it as dictated, the objective is "thrown" to the lower levels of the organization to review, discuss, and adjust it. After the objective is refined by the team, it is "thrown" back to the company leader(s) to review and discuss again. This can go back and forth several times as the objective or strategy is further refined. The tossing of the idea back and forth is compared to that of a team playing catch with a ball.

The advantage to catchball is that it seeks to create a better solution through team development and eventual team ownership, rather than an objective that has been "decreed" by management regardless of unknown potential impacts to the entire organization. Companies that have used catchball have found that strategies are better understood by the entire organization, have the potential problems already identified, and, in many cases, provide a quicker implementation than the traditional, strict, top-down approach of management by objectives (MBO).

Proponents of catchball find that it creates organizational alignment and informed completion of company initiatives. Another advantage is that it tends to eliminate the NETMA syndrome (No one ever tells me anything), which plagues too many organizations even today. Catchball participants feel more engaged and that they are part of the solution to the company's challenges; this process helps build more ownership throughout the organization as well.

The frequency with which catchball is performed within an organization can be daily on a more localized basis, for example, within a site or department/functional area. In terms of broader strategy setting, it is often performed annually, and even semiannually or quarterly in fast-moving organizations. Regardless of the cadence, the power of catchball is evident in its growing popularity within lean organizations around the world.

3.3.3. REDEPLOYMENT OF RESOURCES

Any continuous improvement program is doomed to fail if employees who are no longer needed in the now-improved process are let go. A common edict within lean-minded companies is that *no one will lose his or her job as a result of our continuous improvement program*. Without this understanding, it is extremely difficult to build participation and buy-in from employees on kaizen blitzes, Lean-Sigma projects, and the like.

That being said, what do you do with the "extra" people you now have available after improving the process? The most common scenarios follow, and usually, but not always, in this order:

1. Reduce temporary workers (if applicable)

2. Reduce overtime (if employees are easily retrained or already capable of being redeployed within the work area)

3. Retrain and redeploy to where demand is required

4. Absorb redeployed employees through reduced replacement from normal attrition

5. Provide for growth without hiring additional labor (assumes growth)

Scenarios 1 through 3 are the most common. Scenario 4 is preferred over the first three scenarios, as the impact is minimal to payroll and full-time employees, excluding some level of retraining for different work. Scenario 5 is the most preferred, with growth provided on a consistent labor cost basis. This means actual profitability growth if this is sustained. The ideal scenario for a company is continued revenue growth with either consistent or reduced expenses.

Lean is often credited with being the vehicle by which an organization can build capacity for growth at little to no expense. To make this work, processes and work cells or functions that now require fewer people than before provide the "new" employees to handle the additional volume driven by the sales increase. The requirement for the organization is to understand that redeployment will be required (in the absence of rapid growth).

Since training will be required in any scenario, requiring flexibility in the workforce, lean organizations find great benefits in having a detailed cross-training program in each functional area, department, or site. Through cross training, the ability to redeploy resources is accomplished with relative ease, assuming the existing workers already possess the required skill sets. Figure 3.3.3-1 shows a sample cross-training matrix for an operations team.

Quick reviews of cross-training matrices can provide instant insight into where training is sufficient or required. A good cross-training matrix can greatly assist with redeployment of resources when required.

Another means to provide flexibility is job rotation. As the saying goes, walk a mile in someone's shoes and you'll better understand their experiences. This applies to daily work and interactions as well. Companies that have had supervisors, leads, or technicians rotate to different teams, functions, shifts, or departments have found great benefit in better teamwork, enhanced process knowledge, and a more complete value stream understanding.

Flexibility does not stop with people. Machines in a lean organization also need to be flexible. Setups should be accomplished in less than 10 minutes preferably and cannot run just for the sake of utilization or efficiency. Many lean organizations have found that smaller, more flexible machines provide the needed output without the large capital cost. However, what if you already own the machine and it works perfectly, even though it is not right-sized? Unless space is dictating reinvestment in a smaller machine, it's OK to leave the machines as they are and create flow up to them and from them, retaining them as a monument operation. Replacement can be had when it is financially prudent to do so.

Most companies find sufficient success in redeploying machines previously dedicated to a specific department to their new cell team locations. Frequently, organizations find themselves split into functionally common departments such as cutting, machining, welding, and so on. These departments do not always fit the lean, one-piece flow concept and have to be redeployed, much as the people who run them do. Retraining may or may not be needed as machines are further deployed to their new homes.

Finally, capital in the form of company cash may need to be redeployed in a lean transformation. The most common form of capital redeployment is that of inventory to cash. While the balance sheet for accounting purposes counts both inventory and cash as an asset, all agree that cash is more flexible. The challenge is to make sure that the cash made available through increased inventory turns/lower inventory is reinvested in the business to support further lean improvements.

3.3.3

3.3.3

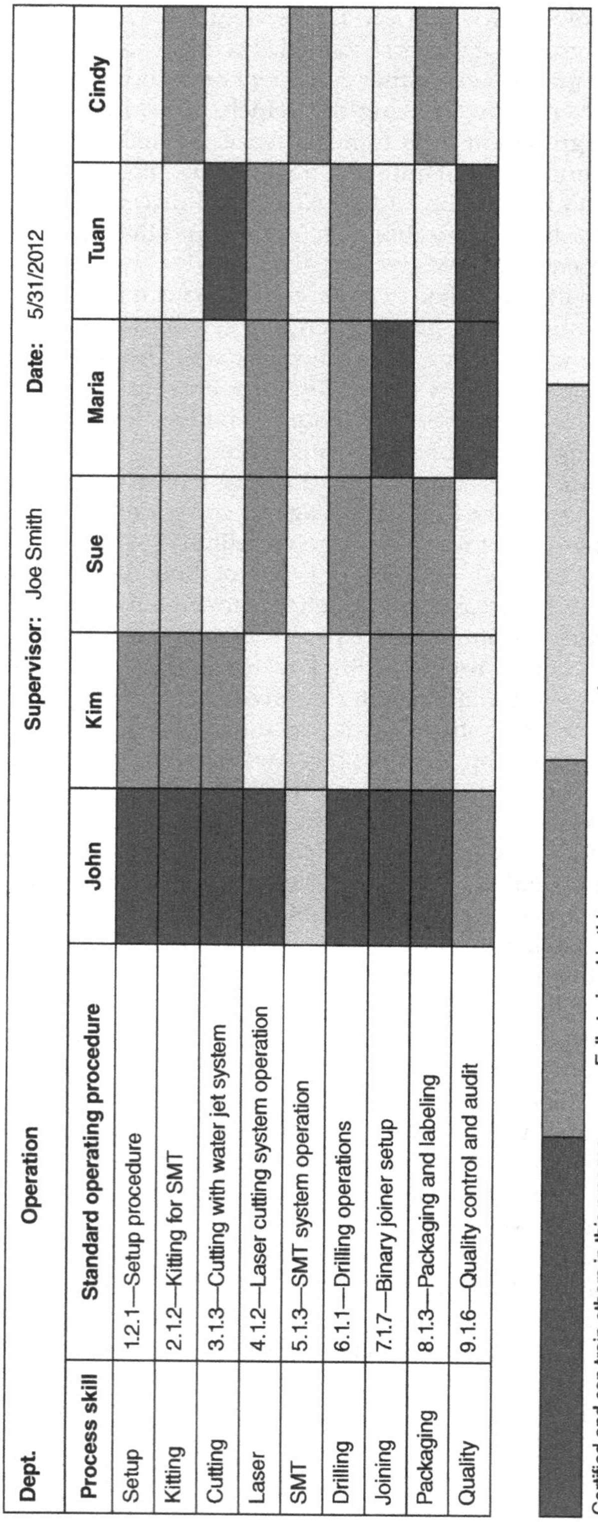

Dept.	Operation					Supervisor: Joe Smith	Date: 5/31/2012
Process skill	Standard operating procedure	John	Kim	Sue	Maria	Tuan	Cindy
Setup	1.2.1—Setup procedure						
Kitting	2.1.2—Kitting for SMT						
Cutting	3.1.3—Cutting with water jet system						
Laser	4.1.2—Laser cutting system operation						
SMT	5.1.3—SMT system operation						
Drilling	6.1.1—Drilling operations						
Joining	7.1.7—Binary joiner setup						
Packaging	8.1.3—Packaging and labeling						
Quality	9.1.6—Quality control and audit						

Certified and can train others in this process   Fully trained in this process   In progress on this process   Not trained on this process

Figure 3.3.3-1 Cross-training matrix.

Module 4
Business Results

4.1. Principles of Business Results
4.2. Measurement Systems
4.3. Key Lean Related Measures

However beautiful the strategy, you should
occasionally look at the results.

—Winston Churchill

As a lean student, one should realize that doing lean for lean's sake is not the appropriate reason for implementing these principles, processes, or systems. There must be results. Results give us evidence or proof that what we are doing is correct. This is a fundamental part of scientific thinking and the Plan-Do-Check-Act methodology. This section covers the measures that matter to the customer and therefore matter to your organization and looks at how to set up these systems and measures that are distinctive to lean.

4.1

Principles of Business Results

Measures have one primary purpose: to help you continually improve business results. Measures help you evaluate whether your operation is performing well and generating value-producing outcomes with minimal costs and waste. Additionally, measures indicate whether your employees are productive, satisfied, and planning to stick around. Measures give you feedback on whether customers are willing to repeat business with you. Properly designed, your measures tell you whether you are generating sufficient revenues, profits, and financial returns. With just a few carefully selected indicators, your measures will tell you, at a glance, whether you are winning or losing. You can make rapid, timely decisions on where to invest your time and resources to achieve needed gains.

With good measures directed toward business results, you can more easily:

- Identify and eliminate waste and inefficiency

- Find and eliminate bottlenecks in your work flows

- Understand what customers really want and ensure that you are meeting their needs and building loyalty and repeat business

- Help employees see how they contribute to work flows, and use feedback to continually improve processes

- Promote accountability and action with your team

- Relate and connect the elements in the value chain, leading to greater gains with less effort

With good measures, you set targets that make sense to your customers, employees, and stakeholders. You help everyone understand how efforts align toward results. Most importantly, you gain back some of your most valuable resources: your time, energy, and attention. As a result, you will have better visibility on progress toward your goals, less anxiety from wondering if you're doing the right things, and better tools for communicating progress to your stakeholders and employees.

4.1.1. CREATE VALUE FIRST TO DRIVE PERFORMANCE

Begin with the end in mind.

—Stephen Covey, *The 8th Habit:*
From Effectiveness to Greatness

Customers are the recipients of the value, services, and products that you produce. You must satisfy customers to reach your targets for sales and profits. More importantly, you must keep customers coming back in order to achieve targets for growth. Naturally, you want to measure results associated with your customers. However, most people fall into the trap of measuring only customer satisfaction.

All of us have been swamped in the past few years with surveys and phone calls asking for satisfaction ratings. Your car dealer, credit card company, and dentist want you to fill out a comment card. This frenzy for measuring customer satisfaction has led to a growth of firms that track customer satisfaction. You often see these results touted in ads: "Ranked #1 in customer satisfaction for six straight years." Tracking all that data and giving out customer satisfaction awards is big business. People in the customer satisfaction business fail to let you in on a little secret: Customer satisfaction measures rarely tell anyone anything specifically meaningful. In fact, customer satisfaction data are often misleading or dangerous, as they lead a management team to erroneously believe it is doing a good job.

I recall a presentation at a measurement conference a few years ago when a senior vice president of a major airline outlined the process for gathering customer satisfaction data. It was an exhaustive process, with comment cards, phone surveys, and ratings gathered by gate attendants. The vice president proudly reported that customer satisfaction showed steady gains for the past few quarters. The next week, I chuckled when I read in the business news that the airline had lost several hundred millions of dollars in the previous quarter and was preparing for major layoffs due to record annual losses. So much for satisfied customers.

There's the issue: Customer satisfaction has little direct relation to sales and revenues. Satisfied customers may like what you offer and may even like your company. However, their feedback says nearly nothing about whether they will do business with you again. Even more, it doesn't tell you whether customers will tell other potential customers to do business with you.

Instead of customer satisfaction, two alternative indicators may be more beneficial:

- Customer loyalty
- Aspects of customer value

Customer loyalty is the indicator that customers will return to do business with you, even when competitors pursue them for business. Customer loyalty comes when you pay attention to the aspects that customers value—and when customers perceive high value from your products and services.

4.1.1

For example, Lexus concentrates on customer loyalty and consistently enjoys high customer loyalty ratings. People who buy Lexus automobiles have a very strong tendency to buy Lexus cars again. The customers are satisfied, but it goes beyond that; given the competition for luxury automobile buyers, Lexus buyers tell Lexus that they are very likely to buy again. Actual repurchase behavior supports their intent.

In just 20 years, Lexus has established a solid reputation and created an upscale image; it repeatedly tops industry surveys related to quality, service, and value. Lexus knows that its customers value three aspects of its automobiles:

1. Quality, as perceived as an automobile with few defects

2. Dependability and reliability

3. Service

Quality is emphasized, with each vehicle designed to approximately 500 specific product standards, known as "Lexus Musts," on criteria such as leather seat stitching. Lexus consistently leads in statistics compiled on reliability. At dealerships, service employees are instructed to follow the "Lexus Covenant," which states that "Lexus will treat each customer as we would a guest in our home" (Carroll 2011, 106).

4.1.1.1. Measure What Matters to the Customer

If you measure what matters to your customers, you will find opportunities to align, streamline, and simplify work processes.

For example, a team that delivers training products and services for an electronics manufacturer measured three dimensions of service that it attributed to customer value:

- Timeliness of delivery

- Technical accuracy of the information provided

- Percentage of orders fulfilled on request

From feedback on these three measures, the team felt that it was doing a great job. Requests were filled quickly, and customers rarely noted technical errors. However, during a forum with the team's top 20 customers, customers complained about poor service.

Digging into customers' complaints, the team discovered three aspects of value not previously tracked:

1. Specialist availability

2. Specialist courtesy

3. Specialist accuracy

The team realized that its measures focused on the technical aspects of services but overlooked the human elements. The team worked with customers to define the right measures and to establish targets for availability (responses within four hours), courtesy (9.5 on a 10-point scale), and accuracy of information (100% accurate). The team changed its customer measures and began realizing big improvements in customer relations, referrals, and sales.

Customers really want solid relationships with their suppliers. It is best to continually interact with your customers to gauge and monitor what they truly value.

4.1.1.2. Measure Normal versus Abnormal Conditions—(Triggers Response)

Sometimes a shift in measurement is needed to more appropriately define when actions need to occur. For example, a firearms manufacturer and recipient of the 2009 Malcolm Baldrige National Quality Award for Excellence monitored shipping accuracy for several years, defined as the percentage of shipments properly filled and sent to customers on schedule. The company was satisfied with shipping accuracy rates approaching 99% for years, but realized that any shipment incorrectly filled was costly and affected customer loyalty. The company added a measure to monitor cost per return, working to eliminate any defects from the order fulfillment and shipping process. Better visibility on defective shipments created focus on abnormal conditions and supported analyses on why shipments were incomplete or late (Carroll 2011).

4.1.1.3. Guidelines for Measurement Categories

Many managers and work teams suffer from data floods and information droughts. The constant barrage of reports, e-mails, phone calls, and meetings usually fails to provide the meaningful feedback busy people need to make rapid and appropriate decisions.

A lean enterprise uses a set of measures to achieve better results through improved alignment, visibility, and feedback. It is worth taking time to define the right indicators to track, a concise set that can be checked at a glance for how things are going and where to take action.

While your indicators will vary according to your processes, outputs, industry, and so on, there are generally five categories to consider when developing, tracking, and using key indicators to monitor business results:

1. Competitive impact

2. Quality

3. Cycle time

4. Cost and productivity

5. People development

Competitive Impact

Your indicators should provide feedback on whether you are meeting customers' expectations in the aspects of value. Customers' expectations and perception of value are defined by *needs* and *wants*.

To attract customers, you must first satisfy the *need*. If you are delivering accounting services, your customers *need* your services to be compliant with the standards of accounting, mathematically accurate, timely, and legible. You won't be in business long if you're not satisfying needs.

But just satisfying customers' *needs* won't distinguish your organization. You must satisfy *wants* to keep customers coming back. For accounting services,

4.1.1.3

customers want you to be pleasant, prompt, and attentive to their individual requests. However, customers' wants vary. You must ensure that you know what they are and that you measure your ability to deliver.

The easiest way to determine whether you are satisfying customers' wants is to ask. This can be done through several methods:

- Face-to-face interviews

- Phone interviews

- Feedback cards

- Customer complaints

- Service contracts

- Negotiations

- Custom-designed questionnaires

- Careful listening during any customer interaction

- Voice of the Customer (VOC) (see Section 4.2.1.6, "Voice of the Customer")

Listen carefully every time you have contact with your customers. What are they really seeking that would excite them and create loyalty:

- Ease of use?

- The best price?

- Superior service and attentiveness?

- Something unique?

The point is to consider operations measures (Voice of the Process) that truly provide insight into what customers value. Ask yourself the following:

- Do you truly know your customers' expectations?

- Do your measures provide feedback on the important aspects of your products and services?

- Does your work team receive the feedback and know what levels it needs to achieve to satisfy customers, fulfill value expectations, and build loyalty?

Similarly, your indicators should provide feedback on whether customers are acting on their perceived loyalty and value perceptions. Are customers renewing contracts, purchasing from you repeatedly, and even referring other customers to you?

Additionally, you want some type of external validation of comparisons of your customers' perceptions and rankings. Consider the example of MEDRAD, a company that specializes in developing and servicing medical devices. MEDRAD developed and refined a lean set of customer indicators to match its lean enterprise, focusing on three aspects of customer value:

1. Finished product quality, as measured by on-time shipments and defects when delivered

2. Fast resolution of customer complaints

3. Accessibility, as measured by prompt answers to calls and questions

MEDRAD (2010) benchmarks results against other leaders in its industry and consistently outperforms industry standards. MEDRAD also maintains industry-leading levels of customer engagement and customer referrals.

Quality

You can keep customers coming back by delivering quality. It is surprising how many firms fail to define and track the quality of their products and services. Often, executives struggle with declines in customers and profits, yet they never look at their work processes to examine problems within their own company.

Whether providing medical supplies, legal services, or new homes, your organization must be able to answer five important questions about its operations:

1. How many goods or services do we produce?

2. What does it cost us to produce the goods or services (per unit)?

3. How many defects or rejections are we producing?

4. How long does it take us to produce our goods or services?

5. How well do we satisfy customers' requirements or expectations?

A large toy manufacturing firm that was suffering with declining sales decided to pull the product development, engineering, production, marketing, and sales teams together to find the problem. They created flow throughout the entire process and defined indicators for each area. Each team gathered data, developed graphs, and shared results. Looking at the feedback, they immediately had their answer: Product development had not produced a single output—a new product concept—in more than 12 months. The entire process had a bottleneck at the start, and no one knew it until the chart went on the wall. Production, marketing, and sales knew they were working with products that were stale and tired by consumer standards, but they did not realize the root cause of their problem until that moment. To start, they tracked the volume of outcomes produced by the operation. Then, they considered how they measure defects. Defects can be, simply, anything that does not meet customers' requirements or expectations. For example, a defect for a florist would be a delivery that is late, spoiled, or rejected by a customer. A defect for a retail manager would be an angry customer leaving the store, a returned item, or a damaged item. A defect measure for a car dealership would be the number of cars not ready on a promised date, the number or percentage of service complaints, or the number of cars damaged during transport.

As another example, when a large pizza chain promises "delivery within 30 minutes or the pizza is on us," a late delivery is a defect and it costs the company money. The team needs to know how many late deliveries occur.

Defects cost your organization money—probably more than you realize. Many studies point out that firms that don't measure their defects have costs that are 40%–60% higher than firms that track defects (Archambeau 2004). This is a direct hit to your bottom line.

Honeywell Federal Manufacturing & Technologies (FM&T), which provides management, infrastructure, and services to the US Department of Energy, recognizes that any defects within its entire value chain affect performance and costs. In an attempt to remove costly defects from its work processes, FM&T closely monitors the on-time deliveries and quality performance of its suppliers, product and

4.1.1.3

service delivery performance, job orders completed trouble-free, and customer complaint corrective actions.

Cycle Time

The measure for "how long it takes" is known as *cycle time*. Start with the fundamentals of what you produce. How long (hours, days, weeks, or months) does it take to produce the good or service? This may not be a meaningful measure for businesses in which customers are more concerned with quality over speed (e.g., architectural firms) or businesses in which time is built in to the service (e.g., massage therapists; 30-minute massages can't be streamlined and delivered in 20 minutes with the same level of customer expectation). However, if you produce goods and services repetitively and can benefit from shortening the time to produce your outcomes, you need a measure of cycle time. For example, Nucor Steel monitors time from customer order to order fulfillment. Boeing knows how long—both in days and in labor-hours—it takes to manufacture an airplane.

There are several ways to measure cycle time, and each operation needs to define the measures appropriate to its product or service. For example, McDonald's restaurants cannot speed up the time it takes to cook a hamburger, but it can (and does) measure how many meals are served per hour. Similarly, a marketing research firm may not be able to easily track how long it takes to conduct each study, but it should know how many studies are produced—and sold—each quarter annually.

Cost and Productivity

Productivity can be defined as cost per units produced. Manufacturing businesses usually have no problem defining productivity, as the production counts are easily tallied and expenses can be determined. The ratio of goods produced to costs expended usually gives this indicator.

However, some organizations struggle with a productivity measure because units produced may be difficult to define, particularly with service businesses or healthcare. For example, in a legal firm, what is the real service unit—a client? a case? a verdict? For medical care, is a service unit a patient, an office visit, or a billable transaction? Similarly, costs may not be easily attributed to each unit.

Additionally, it's hard to break out the costs for each service unit, as some accounting systems are not set up to provide the information you need.

For example, a team of managers responsible for installing large business phone systems was faced with competitors that were handily garnering business from this firm. To turn this problem around, the managers defined several indicators to understand current operations. (It turned out that the managers had hundreds of indicators and dozens of monthly reports, but no one knew what all the indicators meant. Data flood, information drought!) When they dug out the cost per installed phone system, the managers realized they were losing money on every installation. Plus, their costs were 20% higher than the competitors'. No one knew this until they compiled and analyzed the measures. It took a few weeks, but the managers were able to bring costs into line and compete in their industry and region, thereby bringing customers back into the fold.

People Development

You need to measure employee indicators, but satisfaction indicators don't give the entire picture. Employees may be satisfied, but are they productive? Are they producing goods and services that customers value? Are they developing value-added skills? Are they getting what they need to be productive? Are they helping one another? Do they understand how to contribute to business results?

Research conducted by the Gallup Organization with more than 200,000 managers identified six questions that you should ask employees regularly. Employees' responses on these six questions have a direct correlation with sales, profits, and productivity:

1. Do I know what is expected of me at work?

2. Do I have the materials and equipment I need to do my work properly?

3. At work do I have the opportunity to do what I do best every day?

4. In the last seven days have I received recognition or praise for good work?

5. Does my supervisor or someone at work seem to care about me as a person?

6. Is there someone at work who encourages my development?

Consider using these six questions as a basis for people development indicators. Measuring employees' ability and behaviors in sustaining a positive, productive working environment is a key element. Review your employee goals and define indicators in the employee category that will help create a positive, productive environment.

You want feedback in three areas of people development:

1. The employee's impact on customers, especially in relation to the loyalty and referral indicators described in the competitive impact category

2. The employee's impact on the business, such as number of units produced or number of defects eliminated

3. The employee's impact on other employees, especially the ability to help others be more productive and profitable

Most managers understand the importance of all three areas but too often still measure the wrong employee indicators. Too many measures crop up on things like "employee's willingness to change" or "employee's attitude," attributes that are difficult to measure and even harder to improve. Employees come with unique capabilities and strengths. You really want to see if employees will use their strengths, ingenuity, and resources to accomplish goals.

The first step is to figure out the measure of the employee's desired results in relation to customers' needs and wants. Don't think about what is included in employees' job descriptions and duties, but what they produce that customers value—what do employees get paid to do? For example, specialists in customer call centers are traditionally measured on number of calls per day or average length of call. Instead of traditional measures, consider what customer service representatives are paid to do, such as:

- Prevent customers from defecting to competitors
- Sell additional products and services
- Prevent customers' problems from escalating
- Resolve complaints in a friendly, competent way

4.1.1.3

Relate employees' actions and outcomes to the three things that are important for you to know about your customers:

1. How likely are customers to purchase our products and services in the future?

2. How likely are customers to recommend our company to a friend or colleague?

3. How strongly do customers agree that our company deserves their loyalty?

Focus on perceptions of a productive environment and employees' readiness and willingness to do good work.

Lean Measures

As you develop and improve measures to support your lean enterprise and continuous improvement, ask yourself these questions to maintain your focus on useful measures and results:

- Is this a measure that I can count, quantify, and graph?
- Will this measure give me useful, actionable feedback?
- Is this a measure I can influence or affect?
- Will my customers and work team customers care about the outcome of the measure?

As your measures and feedback improve, you will notice many opportunities for improvement. Here are five actions for you to take your team's performance and results to the next level:

1. Take complete and personal responsibility for your measures and results

2. Review your measures and results regularly

3. Continually verify customers' expectations

4. Experiment and innovate

5. Take action on priorities

You will see the intangibles—morale, trust, loyalty, and commitment—improve as well. You will see your team's energy and drive increase. Accept these as intangibles, but keep the focus on the tangibles: measurable business results.

REFERENCES

Archambeau, Shellye. 2004. "What Is Your Company's Cost of Poor Quality?" *Quality Digest*. August. http://www.qualitydigest.com.

Carroll, Becky. 2011. *The Hidden Power of Your Customers: Four Keys to Growing Your Business through Existing Customers*. Hoboken, NJ: John Wiley & Sons.

Honeywell Federal Manufacturing & Technologies. Application for the 2009 Malcolm Baldrige National Quality Award. US Department of Commerce.

MEDRAD. 2010. *Malcolm Baldrige National Quality Award Application*. US Department of Commerce.

4.2

Measurement Systems

How you go about measuring your lean system is just as important as what you measure. It is critical to align your measurements with your customer needs, understand how to create goals and objectives, analyze the results for improvement, and report these back to your organization.

4.2.1. MEASUREMENT

Measurement is defined as "a method of determining quantity, capacity, or dimension" (*American Heritage Science Dictionary* 2011). While the concept seems simple, collecting accurate measures of a quantity, capacity, or dimension requires an accurate definition of the measure, discipline, and consistency. Many practitioners learn very quickly that accurate and consistent measurements relative to a definition are easier said than done.

Measurement systems need to be precise and accurate. The *precision* of the measurement system is the degree to which the measure is consistant relative to the other measurements that have been made, and the *accuracy* of the measurement is the degree to which the measure of the exactness of the measurement is relative to a known standard. The measure of precision is called the reliability of the measure, and the measure of accuracy is referred to as the repeatability of the measure.

Lean practitioners want to monitor a process using visual indicators. Therefore, the people closest to the process are the best informed about the state of the process, and they are the best qualified to manage the process. For these reasons we often see higher levels of management present at the locations where the work is performed (gemba). In this paradigm it is critically important that process discipline be meticulously enforced and corrective actions implemented immediately.

In this section we will overview the role of measurement systems as a means of monitoring a process and assessing the effectiveness of corrective action plans. We will also look at the linkages between measurements taken at the process level and the quality or value that is perceived by the customer.

4.2.1.1. Understand Interdependencies between Measures and Measurement Categories

Measurement categories diverge between discrete measures, referred to as attribute measures, and continuous measures, referred to as variables data. Generally speaking, *attribute measures* involve counts of individual items, or categories for classification, for example, the number of students in a classroom. The set of natural numbers is frequently used to quantify the number of objects.

In contrast, *variables data* are used to quantify a measure where the quantity, capacity, or dimension is not a countable number. The set of real numbers is often used to quantify a measure using variables data. For example, the cycle time to complete a task or build a product is a measure captured with a real number. A practitioner refers to the collection of these measures as variables data.

Lean processes are results oriented. An effective lean process is designed to enable participants and stakeholders to visually monitor the success of the process. Sometimes the process can be monitored visually without data, and other times data are used to quantify the state of the process. We refer to the key performance indicators (KPIs) of a process as the measures, and the measurements of other process attributes as metrics.

When data are used to examine the success of the process, the nature of the observation links the measurement system to the measurement categories. For example, a production process may track the number of nonconformities. The number of nonconformities is attribute data, and the measurement system might employ a statistical process control chart called an *np* chart to ensure that the rate of nonconformities is limited to random cause variation. In the event that the level of nonconformities is attributed to special cause variation, then the out-of-control corrective action plan must be executed immediately to ensure that the process continues to flow without interruption. This is a very important point since a lean process, by definition, does not have a significant amount of slack in its design. The result is that process participants must watch the processes with their trained eyes to ensure that the product produced in each production cycle is within acceptable specifications.

In contrast, if the process is controlled by regulating variables that influence the rate of successful production, then the measurement system may be based on continuous measurements. One example is in the production of semiconductor devices, where the process is managed through the regulation of gas pressure and gas temperature to estimate the rate of mass flow. The gas pressure and gas temperature measurements are each a continuous variable. In this case the measurement system might assess special and random cause variation using a multivariate statistical process control (SPC) chart so that the process operators can simultaneously assess the variations in both temperature and pressure to determine whether the rate of mass deposition is within acceptable levels.

Another way to look at measurement systems and categories is to look at whether the metrics are leading, real time, or lagging.

In the case of the manufacture of the semiconductor devices, the metrics that measure the temperature and the pressure are a *leading* or forward-looking indicator of the amount of mass deposited on a surface; they are also a leading indicator of product quality since the proportion of conforming product is determined by the thickness of the material deposited. Once again, those closest to the process are the most informed about the state of the process and the most able to quickly implement corrective actions as needed. Another example of a leading indicator is the percentage of budget used for a project. This will give you a heads-up whether you are above or below the projected amount.

Real-time measures are best for value-adders. The ability to know whether the process, product, or service is correct right away is always best. An operator shouldn't have to wait until the monthly report on scrap comes out before he or she hears for the first time that something he or she did was wrong. Another example of a real-time measure is takt time (see Section 2.3.1.4). The operator knows right away if he or she is ahead or behind.

Lagging measures seem to be the most common. These are the score after the fact. Typically, with lagging measures things can't be changed to correct the outcome. Many managers' reports (i.e., monthly reports) are lagging. Lagging measures may be good for looking at trends.

A quick baseball analogy may help show the difference among leading, real-time, and lagging measures:

> Leading—the pitch count. Managers may use the pitch count (the number of pitches thrown) to gauge how many more good throws the pitcher has left. Let's say that a particular pitcher has 60 throws in him for the game. When the pitch count nears 60, the manager may have the bullpen start to warm up a reliever.

> Real-time—the speed of the pitch. Managers will watch the speed of the pitcher's fastball to see how well the pitcher is throwing. If the pitcher's fastball is usually around 99 mph and it drops to 90 mph, something may be wrong with the pitcher's arm.

> Lagging—the final score of the game. Win or lose, there is not much a manager can do for that particular game.

Now, in this same analogy you can see that the frame of reference from which one is looking is very important. A lagging indicator of win/lose may not help the manager much for that specific game, but string these together over time and the general manager may look at it from the standpoint of trading players or changing coaches.

4.2.1.2. Align Internal Measures with What Matters to Customers

There are many ways to link process measures with customer expectations. The simplest is to ask the customer what he or she wants, when he or she wants it, and the relative importance of each item provided as in critical to quality (CTQ) or Voice of the Customer (VOC). Using a lean thought process, a practitioner can work backward from the customer to the measures that quantify the quantity, capacity, or dimension of the product. Since products are outcomes of a process, the process measures that represent the key performance indicators (KPIs) of the process can be associated with the measures on the product and, consequently, the expectations of the customer.

When the customer expectations are prioritized, the relative importance of each product measure can be associated with a corresponding prioritized product measure. Therefore, a production process can be aligned with customer expectations by setting the KPIs in-line with the expectations of the customer.

Consider the production of gasoline. Most customers take for granted that the quality of their gasoline is very high. They have come to expect that there will be relatively low water content in the gasoline. How does the quality of the gasoline have low water content? The answer rests with the regulation of the temperature and pressure levels when the gasoline is produced. This simple example demonstrates the linkage between the process metrics and the pressure and temperature of the fluid in the process, with the resulting water content of the gasoline. The water content is part of the measure of product quality, and product quality drives customer satisfaction. This is a simple example where customer satisfaction can be linked directly to the management of the production process and visualized using metrics and KPIs.

4.2.1.3. Measure the Results from the "Whole" System

A lean practitioner is concerned with the maximization of value and the minimization or complete elimination of waste. When internal measures are aligned with customer needs, any activities of the process that do not contribute to an increase in customer value are a candidate for elimination or automation. The lean community measures the results from the whole system using a number of metrics, like the percentage of value-added cycle time. The same principle is extended from the process throughout the value chain, with the goal of delivering exactly what the customer wants, when the customer wants it.

There was a time when organizations were inwardly focused. A product or service was developed, the cost to produce it was determined, a percentage of profit was added, a price was set, and everyone watched to see what would happen. Lean thinking completely changed this paradigm. Current world-class companies recognize that there is a market price for a product or service, and there is a responsibility on the part of the company to develop it in a way that maximizes the value to the customer for the price that the customer is willing to pay.

The production of Japanese automobiles is an excellent example. Toyota recognized that the cost of a vehicle could be reduced by using crumple zones designed to absorb energy in the event of a vehicle impact. This approach was radically different from the approach employed by American and European manufacturers, which followed a design that incorporated significantly greater amounts of steel in the vehicle body. The result is that Toyota was able to produce a car that met customer needs and expectations at a lower cost while still enabling Toyota to make a profit. This same type of approach has been used many times since this example to continually examine the value chain and the value stream to determine which vehicle services and components actually add customer value.

Another illustration of lean principles is in the educational system. Consider the development of an engineer. The progression of a student from the time that individual begins his or her education as a young child to his or her graduation from college is a combination of value chains and value streams. Many people don't realize that the continuous review of academic programs for the integration and removal of course content is actually an exercise in value chain and value stream management. In order to ensure the quality of the engineer that is produced, the educational managers evaluate the value added at each step in the educational process. The quality is examined in terms of the relevance of the material and the relevant contribution of the material along with the cost of education. This is another simple illustration of measuring the results from the whole system.

4.2.1.4. Measure Flow and Waste

Efficient production techniques employ the concept of single-piece flow. A product can be thought of as being enhanced with value-added activities as it seamlessly flows through a production process. At each step of the process the practitioners should try to identify and eliminate the seven sources of waste that Taiichi Ohno identified (see Section 2.1.2.2).

A true lean deployment does not depend on a measurement of the waste that was eliminated; instead, a true lean deployment postulates that these seven forms of waste exist in all organizations and then seeks to extinguish them wherever they occur. However, in practice, most lean deployments are a blend of lean principles with measurement systems that are aligned with organizational results. An example of the linkage between process metrics and the warranty cost is the result of production and distribution of defective product.

Since the warranty cost is an item listed on a firm's balance sheet, the cost of defective product can be measured directly. The cost of warranty returns is a direct cost to the manufacturer, and this cost comes at the sacrifice of profits. Warranty costs can be traced to specific product failures. Specific product failures are traceable to manufacturing defects, poor material quality, or bad product design. Many times, bad product design originates from poorly captured and documented product requirements. No matter where the missed opportunity originated, the waste is measurable and traceable to the flow of the product from the start of the design process, through production, and into the hands of the customer.

Another example is the direct cost of scrap in a production process. This cost is a measurable loss to the firm that results from poor quality of the materials, or the design and management of the production process, or both. One key performance indicator that captures the level of scrap is first pass yield. A clever practitioner can associate first pass yield with departmental budgets and with the balance sheet of the firm. Consequently, the reduction in scrap or warranty costs can have a traceable and measurable impact on an increase in the profitability of a firm.

These two simple examples illustrate the relationship between the measurement of flow and the level of waste. This is a very important relationship to understand since many process and product improvement efforts require management support. Without a strong statement that makes the business case for launching an improvement initiative, any corrective actions are likely to fail.

4.2.1.5. Lean Accounting

The purpose of lean accounting is to support the lean enterprise as a business strategy. It seeks to move from traditional accounting methods to a system that measures and motivates excellent business practices in the lean enterprise. Good lean enterprises use lean accounting as part of their measurement system.

Introduction

There are two main thrusts for lean accounting. The first is the application of lean methods to the company's accounting, control, and measurement processes. This is no different from applying lean methods to any other processes. The objective is to eliminate waste, free up capacity, speed up the process, eliminate errors and defects, and make the process clear and understandable.

The second (and more important) thrust of lean accounting is to change the accounting, control, and measurement processes so that they motivate lean change and improvement, provide information that is suitable for control and decision making, provide an understanding of customer value, correctly assess the financial impact of lean improvement, and are themselves simple, visual, and low-waste.

Lean accounting does not require traditional management accounting methods like standard costing, activity-based costing, variance reporting, cost-plus pricing, complex transactional control systems, and untimely and confusing financial reports. These are replaced by the following:

- Lean-focused performance measurements

- Simple summary direct costing of the value streams

- Decision making and reporting using a box score

- Financial reports that are timely and presented in plain language that everyone can understand

- Radical simplification and elimination of transactional control systems by eliminating the need for them

- Driving lean changes from a deep understanding of the value created for the customers

- Eliminating traditional budgeting through monthly sales, operations, and financial planning processes

- Value-based pricing

- Correct understanding of the financial impact of lean change

As an organization becomes more mature with lean thinking and methods, it recognizes that the combined methods of lean accounting create a lean management system designed to provide the planning, the operational and financial reporting, and the motivation for change required to prosper the company's ongoing lean transformation.

The vision for lean accounting includes the following:

- Provide accurate, timely, and understandable information to motivate the lean transformation throughout the organization, and for decision-making leading to increased customer value, growth, profitability, and cash flow

- Use lean tools to eliminate waste from the accounting processes while maintaining thorough financial control

- Fully comply with generally accepted accounting principles (GAAP), external reporting regulations, and internal reporting requirements

- Support the lean culture by motivating investment in people, providing information that is relevant and actionable, and empowering continuous improvement at every level of the organization (Maskell and Baggaley 2006, L2)

Why Lean Accounting Is Needed

Lean accounting provides accurate, timely, and understandable information that can be used by managers, salespeople, operations leaders, accountants, lean improvement teams, and others. The information gives clear insight into the company's performance, both operational and financial. The lean accounting reporting motivates people in the organization to move lean improvement forward. It is often stated that what you measure is what will be improved. Lean accounting measures the right things for a company that wants to drive forward with lean transformation.

Lean accounting is itself lean. The information, reports, and measurements can be provided quickly and easily. It does not require the complex systems and wasteful transactions usually used by companies. The simplicity of lean accounting frees up the financial people and the operational people so that they can become more actively involved in moving the company toward its strategic goals. The role of the financial professional moves from the traditional bookkeeper and reporter to more of a strategic partner with the company leaders.

At a deeper level, lean accounting matches the cultural goals of a lean organization. The simple and timely information empowers people at all levels of the organization. The financial and performance measurement information is organized around value streams and thereby honors the lean principle of value stream management. The emphasis on customer value is also derived from the principles of lean thinking. The way a company accounts and measures its business is deeply rooted in the culture of the organization. Lean accounting plays an important role in developing a lean culture within an organization.

Traditional Accounting vs. Lean Accounting

Everybody working seriously on the lean transformation of their company eventually bumps up against the company's accounting systems. Traditional accounting systems (particularly those using standard costing, activity-based costing, or other full absorption methods) are designed to support traditional management methods. As a company moves to lean thinking, many of the fundamentals of its management system change, and traditional accounting, control, and measurement methods become unsuitable. Some examples of this are the following:

- Traditional accounting systems are large, complex processes requiring a great deal of non-value work. Lean companies are eager to eliminate this kind of non-value work. Traditional accounting systems provide measurements and reports like labor efficiency and overhead absorption that motivate large batch production and high inventory levels. These measurements are suitable for mass production–style organizations but actively harmful to companies with lean aspirations.

- Traditional accounting systems have no good way to identify the financial impact of the lean improvements taking place throughout the company. On the contrary, the financial reports will often show that bad things are happening when a very good lean change is being made. One example of this is that traditional reporting shows a reduction in profitability when inventory is reduced. Lean companies always make significant inventory reductions and the accounting reports show negative results.

- Traditional accounting reports use technical words and methods like "overhead absorption" and "gross margin." These reports are not widely understood within most organizations. This may be acceptable when the financial reports are restricted to senior managers, but a lean company seeks to empower the entire workforce. Clear and understandable reporting is required so that people can readily use the reports for improvement and decision making.

- Traditional companies use standard product or service costs that can be misleading when making decisions related to quoting, profitability, make/buy, sourcing, product rationalization, and so forth. Lean companies seek to have a clearer understanding of the true costs associated with their processes and value streams.

There are, of course, traditional methods for overcoming some of these issues and problems. Indeed, few of the methods of lean accounting are new ideas. They are mostly adaptations of methods that have been used for many years and have been codified into a lean management system designed to support the needs of lean-thinking organizations.

Where to Apply Lean Accounting

Like most lean methods, lean accounting was developed to support manufacturing companies, and thus most of the implementation of lean accounting has been within manufacturing organizations. Lean accounting has moved beyond manufacturing and is now applied in other industries, such as financial services, healthcare, government, and education.

The Tools of Lean Accounting

Lean Performance Measurements

Much of the control of production (and other) processes is achieved by visual performance measurements at the shop-floor and value stream levels. These measurements eliminate the need for the shop-floor tracking and variance reporting favored by traditional cost accounting systems. There are at least three levels of operational performance measurements linking the executive strategies to the detailed work in production and support processes (see Table 4.2.1.5-1).

Table 4.2.1.5-1 Operational performance measure linkages.

Measurements	Purpose	Plan-Do-Check-Act improvement	Typical frequency
Company or plant	Enable the senior managers of the company to monitor achievement of the company's strategy	Strategy deployment	Monthly
Value stream	Track the performance of the value stream and provide information to drive continuous improvement	Continuous improvement	Weekly
Cell and process	Enable the cell team to monitor and control its own activities	Identify and eliminate defects	Hourly or by shift

Financial Reports for Lean Operations

Value Stream Costing

Cost and profitability reporting is achieved using *value stream costing*, a simple summary direct costing of the value streams. The value stream costs are typically collected weekly, and there is little or no allocation of "overheads." This provides financial information that can be clearly understood by everybody in the value stream, which in turn leads to good decisions, motivation for lean improvement across the entire value stream, and clear accountability for cost and profitability. Weekly reporting also provides excellent control and management of costs because they can be reviewed by the value stream manager while the information is still current.

Plain Language Financial Statements

Lean accounting provides financial reports that are readily understandable by anyone in the company. The income statements are in *plain language*, and the information is presented in a way that is no more complicated than a household budget. Plain language income statements are easy to use because they do not include misleading and confusing data relating to standard costs and hosts of incomprehensible variance figures. When used in meetings, plain language financial statements change the question from "What does this mean?" to "What should we do?"

Box Score Reporting

Box scores are used widely within lean accounting. The standard format of the box score shows a three-dimensional view of value stream performance, operational performance measurements, financial performance, and how the value stream capacity is being used (see Figure 4.2.1.5-1). The capacity information shows how much of the capacity within the value stream is used productively, how much is used for nonproductive activities, and how much is available for use. The box score shows the value stream performance on a single sheet of paper, using a simple and accessible format.

Making Decisions without the Use of Product or Process Costs

Most companies using lean accounting do not need to calculate a product cost. The reasons for needing a standard product or service cost are eliminated by using the information from value stream accounting and the box scores.

Making Decisions Using Box Scores and Value Stream Cost Information

Routine decision making—including quotes, profitability, make/buy, sourcing, and product rationalization—is achieved using simple yet powerful information readily available from the box score. There is no need to use a standard cost again for these important decisions. The box score in Figure 4.2.1.5-1 shows an example of this method for decision making related to sourcing of a new product.

Value stream box score for weekly performance reporting—Caspian Company PA Motors Current

		5-Feb	12-Feb	19-Feb	26-Feb	5-Mar	12-Mar	19-Mar	26-Mar	GOAL 31-Mar
Operational	Units per person	27.26	23.91	24.66	24.21	27.24				35.2
	On-time shipment	96.2%	98.2%	98.5%	97.6%	97.2%				98.0%
	First time thru	42%	44%	43%	47%	54%				62%
	Dock-to-dock days	12.50	11.9	10.94	9.33	8.90				8.0
	Average cost	$115.78	$115.78	$114.62	$112.66	$111.74				$86.47
	AP days – AR days	8.0	8.0	8.0	8.0	8.0				8.0
Capacity	Productive	32%	32%	32%	31%	31%				22%
	Nonproductive	62%	62%	62%	56%	56%				37%
	Available capacity	6%	6%	6%	13%	13%				41%
Financial	Revenue	$366,487	$321,499	$331,546	$325,481	$366,240				$325,000
	Material costs	$112,196	$97,818	$100,875	$99,030	$111,431				$98,883
	Conversion costs	$115,564	$100,743	$99,833	$99,463	$112,198				$86,825
	Inventory	$310,622	$295,712	$271,857	$231,848	$221,163				$198,798
	Value stream profit	$138,727	$122,938	$130,838	$126,988	$142,611				$139,291
	Value stream ROS	37.85%	38.24%	39.46%	39.02%	38.94%				42.86%
	Hurdle Rate	−8.15%	−7.76%	−6.54%	−6.98%	−7.06%				

46.00%

Figure 4.2.1.5-1 Box score example.

4.2.1.5

The box score method is flexible to meet the needs of different kinds of decisions, but uses the same underlying approach that we do not try to calculate a fully absorbed product cost. Instead, the impact of these decisions on the value stream as a whole is used to assess the suitability of each of our choices. When used with standard decision-making processes, this leads to better understanding and better decisions.

Product or Service Costing

Under most circumstances it is not necessary to calculate product or service costs. Companies employing lean accounting methods recognize that standard costs and other methods for fully absorbed product or service costing lead to poor decisions and motivate anti-lean behavior. These companies also find that there is no need to calculate a product cost, because all the uses of product costs within traditional companies can be addressed in lean accounting using simpler and better methods. If a product cost is required, there are simple methods within lean accounting that can be used.

External Reporting

Lean accounting fulfills the needs of cost and management accounting, and also financial accounting. Lean accounting completely replaces traditional accounting for both internal reporting and external reporting.

Closing the Books

The primary collection of revenue and costs is done using value stream costing, and (typically) weekly value stream income statements are used by the value stream managers to control costs and to work to reduce costs. External reporting is achieved by taking the monthly value stream income statements and the financial statement for the support people and adding them together to get the consolidated financial report for the company or division as a whole. This month-end close provides financial reports for the company that can be used for all external reporting. There is usually a requirement for some "below the line" adjustments to bring the income state in line with GAAP. The "bottom line" of the adjusted statement will be the same as the traditional statements.

Inventory Valuation

Lean accounting contains a number of methods for valuing inventory that are simple, accurate, and often visual. Several of these methods do not require any computer-based inventory tracking.

Compliance with Regulatory Requirements

Lean accounting fully complies with all statutory and GAAP in the United States and Europe. Lean accounting also complies with the increasingly popular International Accounting Standards (IAS), which is seeking to create a single worldwide approach. When moving from traditional accounting methods to lean accounting, there is no "change of accounting," because the external reporting outcome of lean accounting uses the same accrual-based actual costing required by GAAP and statutory regulations.

Further Simplifying the Accounting Processes

Transaction Elimination

Traditional companies use complex, transaction-based information systems like MRPII or Enterprise Systems (enterprise resource planning) to maintain financial and operational control of their processes. Lean organizations bring their processes under good control using lean methods, visual control, low inventories, and short lead times; most importantly, lean organizations identify and resolve the root causes of the problems that create the lack of control. Once these root causes have been addressed and the process has been brought under control, it is no longer necessary to use these complex and wasteful transactional systems and they can be gradually eliminated. Other kinds of service companies, like banks, healthcare, and insurance, have similarly transaction-heavy processes that can be radically simplified through the use of lean methods of control.

Accounting Controls

Lean accounting provides a full measure of accounting controls, and, even though the processes are very much simplified, its methods fully comply with all accounting regulations, including Sarbanes-Oxley.

Focusing on Customer Value

Target Costing

Target costing is the tool for understanding how the company creates value for the customer and what must be done to create more value. Target costing is used when new products are being designed and/or when the value stream team needs to understand the changes required to increase the value for the customers. The outcome is a series of initiatives to create more value for the customer and to bring the product costs in line with the company's needs. These improvement initiatives encompass sales and marketing, product design, operations, logistics, and administrative processes within the company.

Value-Based Pricing

The first of the five principles of lean thinking is value to the customer (Womack and Jones 2003). The prices of products and services are set according to the value created for the customer. Lean accounting includes methods for calculating the amount of value created by a company's products and services, and this knowledge is used to establish prices. The price of a product is unrelated to the cost of manufacturing and supplying that product. The price of a product or service is entirely determined by the amount of value created by the product in the eyes of the customer. Lean accounting methods enable value-based pricing.

4.2.1.5

4.2.1.6. Voice of the Customer

Voice of the Customer (VOC) is the ongoing, regular measurement of the needs and expectations of those who purchase or use your products or services. It differs from the in-process measurements found in lean such as cycle time, first pass yield, and overall equipment effectiveness, which are sometimes called Voice of the Process (VOP) (see Figure 4.2.1.6-1).

In the figure, the inputs (people, material, equipment, methods, and environment) are transformed during the process into outputs that go to the customers. In principle, two feedback loops are at work: VOP and VOC. VOP measurements are used to control the process and ensure that the output satisfies the requirements of the customer. VOC identifies and measures those customer requirements. Both measurement systems should be ongoing with a regular frequency. However, VOC cannot effectively be used for control for several reasons:

- It is too slow

- It takes too long to collect

- It typically is expensive

- VOC measurements are typically hard to interpret for those working in the process because they are stated in customer terms and not in the terms of the producers

The VOC is translated into key process indicators (KPIs), which are then used as part of the VOP. These KPIs are used to control the process by determining whether the products, as they are produced, meet customer requirements in terms of quality (first pass yield), delivery (cycle times or lead times), and value (cost measures such as full-time-equivalent).

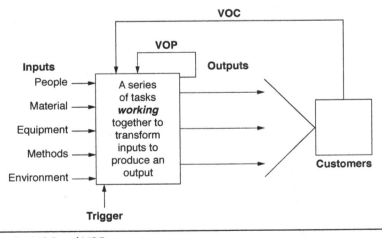

Figure 4.2.1.6-1   VOC and VOP.

The Importance of the VOC in Lean

Lean is about getting rid of waste. Waste is anything that does not add value—particularly anything for which the customer is unwilling to pay. Therefore, the customer defines value in our lean value stream, and the VOC is the means by which we collect the data. These data tell us what is and what is not of value to customers. In this sense, then, the VOC is foundational to all lean improvement efforts.

Measuring the VOC

Just as with all lean improvement efforts, we need to go to gemba. In this case, the source is not where the work is being done within the process or value stream but where the customer is using our products or services. Too many times the only source of VOC information is the order that the customer places and any complaints or warranty costs when the customer is not satisfied with the products or services received. In both cases, this feedback is too late. Although order databases and complaint and warranty systems are a necessary part of the VOC, they do little to help drive prevention and, in particular, define what is and what is not value.

The first step is to understand who your customers are. This is typically done by performing a Pareto analysis (aka 80/20 analysis) that shows the products and services you provide, and who is purchasing and using them. Typically 80% of your products and services are purchased and used by 20% of your customers. Not all of your customers have the exact same needs and expectations. Customer segmentation classifies customers into groupings based on similar requirements. This is done together with the Pareto analysis and the selection of the key value streams. Data are then collected on the needs and expectations of each customer segment (see Table 4.2.1.6-1).

Once the segmentation is completed, it is refined using the Plan-Do-Study-Act (PDSA) cycle, as shown in Figure 4.2.1.6-2.

Once the customers of a given value stream have been identified, a combination of the following methods is used to understand the "why" of the customer:

- Observing customers as they are using your products or services

- Open discussions with customers as to what their needs and expectations are

- Why customers have those needs

- What customers' objectives or goals are with respect to using your products or services

It is critical that we understand "why" because as producers we have the technology, means, and knowledge to satisfy those goals or objectives in many different ways—ways customers would probably not be aware of. This sets the stage for innovative new products or services, particularly for needs that remain unspoken but are articulated through customer behaviors. A classic example is the Canon personal copier, which was developed after employees were observed staying after work to use the company copier to make their own copies.

4.2.1.6

Table 4.2.1.6-1 Examples of VOC in lean applications.

Sector	Value stream area	Customer	Customer segments	VOC measurment	Method	Frequency
Manufacturing	Car assembly	Car owner	Region, Income, Gender, Age, Fleet	Interior noise	Drive clinics	Quarterly
Healthcare	Clinical services	Patient	Location, Income, Gender, Age, Type of Insurance	Satisfaction	Interview	Weekly
Service	Restaurants	Paying guest	Location, Income, Gender, Age, Avocations	Facial expressions, body language	Observations by host	Daily
Government	Airport transportation security	Traveler	Gender, Age, Impairments, Class of Travel	Personal security and comfort	Interview	Weekly
Education	Elementary schooling	Parents or guardians	Income, Age, Marriage Status, Education Level, Country of Origin	Satisfaction and involvement	Individual conferences with teacher	Quarterly

4.2.1.6

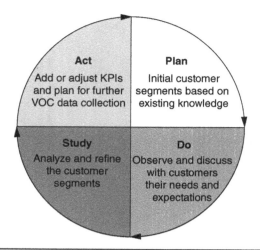

Figure 4.2.1.6–2   PDSA for VOC.

4.2.2. GOAL AND OBJECTIVE SETTING

> *Objectives are not fate; they are direction. They are not commands; they are commitments. They do not determine the future; they are means to mobilize the resources and energies of the business for the making of the future.*
>
> —Peter Drucker, *Management Tasks, Responsibilities, and Practices*

One of the most critical and most misunderstood aspects of a lean implementation is the process for setting goals and objectives. Goals and objectives are very important for communicating expectations to team members and driving improvement, but extreme care must be taken to ensure that everyone's efforts are focused in a consistent direction. When the process is not carefully thought out to ensure alignment, the organization can end up fragmented and suboptimized.

By definition, goals are broad and general, whereas objectives (or subgoals) are more specific, actionable, and intended to contribute to the achievement of a goal. Basically, goals are tied to the vision, and objectives are means to achieve a goal.

As an example, suppose an organization defined as its vision, "To provide the highest-quality, lowest-cost products in the automotive industry—respected by our customers for reliability and recognized by our team members as a great place to work."

It may set a goal to become recognized as the safest company in the industry. The goal is directly tied to the vision through the desire to become recognized "as a great place to work," since a safe work environment contributes to being a great place to work.

The goal is clear, but it's too large to be directly actionable. To become a reality, it must be broken down into actionable and measurable objectives (as shown

Table 4.2.2-1   Example of goal with associated objectives.

Vision	Goal	Objectives
To provide the highest-quality, lowest-cost products in the automotive industry—respected by our customers for reliability and recognized by our team members as a great place to work	Become recognized as the safest company in the industry	• Implement a safety audit process by Q2 • Institute preventive safety training workshop for managers and engineers by Q2 • Modify management bonus system to include safety component • Institute gemba walk process for managers by Q1 • Begin 5S process in factories by Q3 • Implement safety improvement suggestion program by Q3

in the right side of Table 4.2.2-1). The objectives can now be assigned to teams to begin working on improving safety through specific actions.

Goals, Objectives, and PDCA

Like many activities typically associated with a lean implementation, the Plan-Do-Check-Act (PDCA) cycle, when done correctly, greatly improves the goal-setting process. At the outset of the process, the desired goal is determined, as well as the organization's current performance in relation to the goal. The goal needs to be defined clearly enough for the team to understand the intent and develop a plan to move the process, system, or organization from the current situation to the desired goal. As the plan is implemented, results are checked against the goal to determine whether the changes are actually resulting in improvement. If results are not as expected or desired, the plan is changed in order to continue moving toward the target.

Figure 4.2.2-1 presents an overview of PDCA applied to goal setting using the safety goal example. After the leadership team begins highlighting the importance of reducing TRIR and assigns objectives, it can meet regularly to review (or *check*) results against the goal of becoming the safest company in the industry. The process can be adjusted depending on whether the results show improvement toward the goal.

PDCA can also be applied to each of the objectives. Those involved in the objectives begin the process by establishing metrics to measure progress against their efforts. For example, the team working on creating and delivering the preventive safety training workshop can measure progress against the target date, attendance, and implemented changes resulting from the workshop. As progress is measured, changes to the workshop material or class size, for example, can be made if the desired results are not being met.

As the organization begins thinking in terms of the PDCA process, understanding goals and objectives and how to measure progress toward their achievement

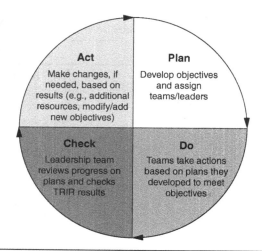

Figure 4.2.2-1 PDCA and goals.

becomes much more natural. Rather than general discussions and generalizations, conversations about improvement opportunities often begin with agreement on what success will look like for the organization.

It should be noted that not everything critical to organizational improvement can be accurately measured. Attempting to measure the costs associated with fear in the workplace or a poor planning process can result in frustration, increased stress, and a lack of success. Aligning a desired improvement (or goal) with the vision and following the process for setting objectives, however, can greatly improve the ability to succeed.

4.2.2.1. SMART (Specific, Measurable, Achievable, Realistic, Timely)

One method to help an organization improve is to apply the SMART process for setting objectives. SMART objectives include the following characteristics:

- Specific: The target is clearly specified, including the desired result and the reasons for pursuing the objective (i.e., aligning the objective with the goal and the organization's vision).

- Measurable: One or more measures are identified to enable the team to track progress throughout the effort and to know when the objective is achieved.

- Achievable: The individuals assigned the objective have the ability to influence or change the process(es) involved.

- Realistic: The capability of the process is considered to ensure that the objective is taken seriously and that it is achievable within the given time frame. Stretch objectives can benefit the organization and motivate action, but only if they are deemed realistic and meaningful.

- Timely: A realistic date or time period is defined within which the objective to be accomplished is acceptable to the person(s) responsible.

In Table 4.2.2-1, the leadership team identified that it was important for the organization to be respected as a great place to work. With this in mind, the team developed the goal of becoming recognized as the safest company in the industry. Several objectives were assigned to move the company from its existing level of safety performance to the point where it would become recognized as the safest company in the industry.

One of the objectives was to implement a gemba walk process for managers by the end of the first quarter. Making this a SMART objective, and thereby increasing the chances for success, would include the following:

- Being very clear in identifying that the objective includes getting managers to spend more active time on the factory floor with a focus on safety. Also, clarifying the link between the goal of becoming recognized as the safest company in the industry and being respected as a great place to work provides alignment with the organization's high-level direction. (*Specific*)

- Instituting a requirement that each manager receive coaching in the gemba walk process in the first quarter and begin conducting two gemba walks per month beginning in the second quarter provides a measure to know that the objective has been achieved. (*Measurable*)

- Assigning the objective to a cross-functional team of lean professionals, safety personnel, human resources representatives, and production team members ensures that the appropriate people are involved to make the objective successful. Also, instituting the requirement that all managers must conduct at least two gemba walks per month, and including it within their bonus plans, further increases the probability of success. (*Achievable*)

- Communicating the connection among gemba walks, safety, improvement, and the company's vision helps clarify the reasons behind developing the objective. Also, increased visits by the leadership team to the shop floor and continual emphasis on the importance and benefits of gemba walks will help. Finally, making sure that participating in gemba walks is not optional—that is, that there are no valid reasons for not achieving at least two walks per month—shows the seriousness of the objective. (*Realistic*)

- Providing enough time to develop an effective process and provide coaching to managers given the company's other priorities while communicating the time frame within which the objective must be completed increases the chances that people will be able to meet the desired objective. (*Timely*)

4.2.2.2. Tied to the Customer

It is important that goals and associated objectives be set in a way that achievement will benefit internal and external customers. Ensuring that people focus their efforts on satisfying the needs of those they serve can benefit teamwork and result in improvements in quality, costs, and delivery of products or services to external customers.

In Table 4.2.2-1, making the organization's factories the safest in the industry will lead to making the company a great place to work, and being a great place to work is directly tied to being respected by customers and providing the highest-quality and lowest-cost products in the industry.

To achieve any sustainable level of success with a lean effort requires an obsession with satisfying customers. In addition to emphasizing a customer focus and coaching people on how to do it, goals, measures, and objectives must absolutely be tied to continually improving customer satisfaction to show the seriousness of the effort.

When goals are developed and objectives are assigned, it is critical that they in some way be aligned with meeting internal or external customer needs. In Table 4.2.2-1, the leadership team developed an objective to institute a preventive safety workshop. The initial step for the team assigned this objective is to identify the customers of the training, which in this case could include the managers, shop-floor workers, and possibly human resources team members. Developing the plan to implement the workshops must include discussions with the customers to ensure that the final product meets their needs.

Focusing on customers when setting goals and objectives helps provide a framework with which to ensure alignment between the efforts of teams and people. When the process is not tied to customers and not aligned with meeting their needs, the organization becomes fragmented and objectives tend to conflict with one another. The result is a breakdown in teamwork and suboptimization of the company's results.

With lean, it is all about the customer. Tying goals and objectives to customers ensures that the effort does not become too inwardly focused and does not spend valuable resources on efforts that, in the long run, do not matter.

4.2.3. ANALYSIS—UNDERSTAND WHAT MOVES THE DIAL ON MEASURES

There is a phrase that says, "From the trivial many come the vital few." Simply put, there are many possible factors that can influence a process, but there are a relatively smaller number of factors that have a significant influence on a process. Therefore, a lean practitioner will identify those factors that significantly influence the outcome of a process and then learn how to control those factors in order to control the process.

There are a number of ways that a lean practitioner can determine which factors are the most influential. A powerful approach is to tap the knowledge of subject matter experts or line workers. Some of the techniques employed include failure mode and effects analysis (FMEA) or failure mode, effects, and criticality analysis (FMECA), or data collected from the facilitated group discussion using nominal group technique. A more formal technique for identifying the most influential factors involves the application of statistical methods—for example, a screening experiment, an assessment of the statistical significance of the coefficients associated with the factors in an analysis of variance (ANOVA), or the variable of a regression model. The practitioner needs to ensure that the factors are causal factors and not simply association; however, an understanding of the relationship between these factors and their influence on the process is an important step in learning how to manage the process.

Regardless of the approach, after the practitioner has identified the most influential factors, the process can be managed by controlling those factors—and these factors "move the dials on measures."

4.2.4. REPORTING

One major theme in the practice of lean is the idea of transparency—specifically, learning to see where problems are taking place or where the process is deviating from standards. Reporting communicates the process effectiveness by informing process stakeholders about the velocity of product flow, backlogs, excess production, quality problems, and so on. The reporting can take place using simple charts that are either manually or electronically produced, or the reporting may come from more elaborate systems.

4.2.4.1. Visible Feedback Real-Time

Real-time data may be visualized in a variety of ways in a lean environment. Some methods involve the use of andon signal devices, display boards, or red-yellow-green indicators. An example of a simple visual process monitor feedback is a gauge marked with green for normal operation and red for abnormal operation. Anyone who walks by the gauge can tell at a glance whether the process is operating correctly. Another example includes the use of a solution that enables communication of key performance indicators (KPIs) across the process, throughout the enterprise, or across the value stream.

The key point is that there isn't one correct technique or approach—it is about understanding that questions need to be answered. This information can be used to answer those questions and then develop a means to communicate the information to the people who need to know, when they need to know it, and to a location where it will be most useful.

For example, mobile devices have now been integrated into solutions so that process stakeholders and frontline personnel have immediate access to real-time data describing the state of the process. If there are quality or performance issues, the process can react faster.

REFERENCES

American Heritage Science Dictionary, s.v. "measurement." http://ahdictionary.com/word/search.html?q=measurement&submit.x=60&submit.y=18. Accessed January 7, 2011.

Maskell, Brian, and Bruce Baggaley. 2006. "What's Lean Accounting All About?" *Target Magazine* 22(1).

Womack, James P., and Daniel T. Jones. 2003. *Lean Thinking: Banish Waste and Create Wealth in Your Corporation*. 2nd ed. New York: Free Press.

4.3

Key Lean Related Measures

Having the right measures, or metrics, is critical to the success of implementing and sustaining a lean enterprise. Measures promote knowledge transfer within an organization by providing the right information, in the right form, to the right people, when they need it. This allows for the promotion of fact-based decision making at all levels of the organization to drive the continuous improvement behavior that is crucial in building a lean culture.

As characterized in the book *Learning to See*, "measures should provide meaningful information for managing a lean operation, and must not be counterproductive to lean goals" (Rother and Shook 2009, 89). During the lean journey, we find that our traditional measures of organizational management often do not provide us with the information necessary to effectively manage value streams. Therefore, a new set of measures is necessary to continue the pursuit of perfection.

Rother and Shook (2009, 89) identify three principles as guidelines to which lean measures for performance should adhere:

- Principle 1: Measures should encourage desired behavior by the front lines.

- Principle 2: Measures should provide information for senior managers to make decisions.

- Principle 3: Principle 1 takes precedence over Principle 2.

The fundamental idea is that measures within a lean organization must be for everyone and not just top management. An organization should understand the purpose of a given measurement. What behavior is the organization attempting to drive? The purpose of the measurement is to define the performance criteria that align with organizational strategy. This unites everyone, at different levels and within different functions, toward the same goals. The main goal is to eliminate waste throughout the organization through continuous improvement. As the saying goes, you cannot improve what you do not measure.

Lean measures can be broken down into the following five categories:

1. Quality

2. Delivery

3. Cost

4. Financial impact

5. Competitive impact

From a measurement perspective, the lean organization is pursuing perfection by providing a product and/or service that a customer wants (quality), when he or she wants/needs it (delivery), at a price he or she is willing to pay for it (cost). This is value in the eyes of the customer.

$$\text{Total customer value} = \text{Quality} + \text{Delivery} + \text{Cost}$$

However, to be successful, the organization must accomplish this without harming its long-term stability (financial impact), and it must do it better than its competition (competitive impact).

4.3.1. QUALITY

As previously discussed, the quality of products and services is directly correlated to value in the eyes of the customer. Any product or service that does not meet the requirements of the customer will be perceived as non-value-added, or defective. Therefore, poor quality of products and services must be measured and eliminated.

However, the traditional measures of poor quality (e.g., percent defective, units scrapped, or errors) focus on the product/service only at a given point in the process and do not take into account the flow of the product/service from beginning to end. The principle behind lean measures is to incorporate not only quality waste but also the disruption of flow of quality to the product/service throughout the organization's processes to provide total customer value (quality + delivery + cost). While defective product and services are considered waste, the lean organization focuses on the total elimination of waste by viewing the total impact of poor quality on the processes. Rather than tracking simplistic measures, such as defects and scrap, lean measures track the impact of poor quality on cost and delivery as well. Two lean quality measures are rework and first pass yield.

4.3.1.1. Rework

Womack and Jones (2003, 51) identify *rework* as a measure of what resources it takes to correct work that was done that was either incorrect from a technical standpoint or failed to meet the needs and expectations of the customer. Rework is a result of the muda (waste) created due to rejects that must be repaired. Rejects and errors interrupt the flow of products and services. In large batch-and-queue operations, rejects can require expensive rework. By tracking how much rework an organization performs, lean leaders can monitor the waste created by defective products and services.

Rework can be measured a number of ways depending on the type of organization (e.g., units reinspected, units repaired, raw material quantities reprocessed, documentation errors corrected, orders modified, number of design changes, and hours of rework). In most lean organizations, rework is the monetary amount or cost associated with resources used to correct defective product or services. If a batch of product is found to contain a defect during quality management inspections, the cost associated with employees performing a 100% inspection on that batch would be considered part of the rework measure. Monitoring costs associated with rework normalize the measure to take into account varying degrees of batch size, inspection complexity, and the number of inspectors performing the work. Rework cost also takes into account additional parts or raw materials that must be used to repair defective product.

The same can be stated about administrative and service processes in which errors create rework. Rework may consist of the generation of additional paperwork, time to correct documentation, and the number of persons whose time was involved in the correction of paperwork. Any organizational function that deals with administrative tasks, such as accounting, scheduling, purchasing, and engineering, can have rework generated due to documentation errors. In a clinical setting, an error can create unnecessary tests, doctor visits, and retesting. It can also increase the risk of harm to the patient.

The idea is for an organization to continually improve in order to eliminate rework, or the waste associated with rejects/repairs. For a lean enterprise, the reduction of rework indicates the following is being accomplished:

- Batch sizes are reduced, thereby reducing the number of units requiring inspection when a defect is found. This is indicative of an organization that is improving processes to incorporate the one-piece flow technique. Reducing batch sizes inherently reduces the costs associated with reworking a batch.

- Continuous improvement efforts to incorporate lean practices and principles, such as poka-yoke, jidoka, and root cause elimination, are successful in reducing defects or the impact of defects. Reducing defects and errors reduces the costs associated with reworking/repairing defective products or services.

Rework causes the organization to incur additional costs that it would not have taken on if the original product or service had met customer requirements. This adds to the cost of the product or service, or in most cases reduces its profitability. This is how rework takes into account the impact to the cost value in the eyes of the customer. The resources used to perform rework are resources; they are not performing value-added tasks. Therefore, resources for value-added tasks to produce a product or service when the customer demands it become more constrained. This is how rework takes into account the impact to the delivery value in the eyes of the customer.

4.3.1.2 First Pass Yield

Another quality measure of process performance, *first pass yield* (FPY) is a measure of the organization's ability to "do things right the first time." To understand FPY, one must understand the concept of Little's law.

As defined by Dennis (2007), Little's law states:

$$\text{Cycle time} = \text{Work-in-process} \div \text{Throughput}$$

or

$$\text{Throughput} = \text{Work-in-process} \div \text{Cycle time}$$

where

Throughput = The average output of a process per unit time.

Cycle time = The average time for one part or service to be completed, from the beginning of a process to the end of a process (additional information provided in the cycle time measure).

Work-in-process (WIP) = The inventory accumulated between the start and end points of a process. This can also be considered "things in process."

WIP consists of inventory (e.g., parts, assemblies, raw material, documentation, and patients in clinical settings), both "good" and "bad," and defects.

$$\text{Throughput} = \text{WIP} \div \text{Cycle time}$$

Good product/Service outcomes   Defects/Rework

As previously discussed, defects create rework. The rework measure already monitors the waste created by defective product. Rework is a measure of poor quality. However, we are now interested in good quality and the flow of good quality product and services throughout our processes. This can be accomplished with the FPY measure by determining how much of the total process throughput consists of product or services "done right the first time" over a specific period of time; in other words, the percentage of the throughput of a process that consists of "good" product or service outcomes, excluding those that are defects or reworked.

$$FPY = \frac{\text{Total units processed} - \text{Rejects or reworks}}{\text{Total units processed}}$$

For a service organization, FPY may look something like this:

$$FPY = \frac{\text{Total persons served} - \text{Errors or reorders}}{\text{Total persons served}}$$

For example, XYZ Manufacturing produces a welded assembly of two components, Part A and Part B. On a single day, Shift 1 has a total throughput of 1347 welded units, with 57 designated as requiring rework or defective. Shift 2 has a total throughput of 1567 welded units, with 21 designated as requiring rework or defective. Shift 3 has a total throughput of 1245 welded units, with 82 designated as requiring rework or defective. For each shift, the FPY is:

$$FPY \text{ (Shift 1)} = 1290 \div 1347 = 0.958 \text{ or } 95.8\%$$

$$FPY \text{ (Shift 2)} = 1546 \div 1567 = 0.987 \text{ or } 98.7\%$$

$$FPY \text{ (Shift 3)} = 1163 \div 1245 = 0.934 \text{ or } 93.4\%$$

To calculate the FPY of the process for the entire day, add the total number of "good" welded components and divide by the total throughput across all shifts, or:

$$\frac{1290 + 1546 + 1163}{1347 + 1567 + 1245} = 0.962 \text{ or } 96.2\%$$

4.3.1.2

However, FPY across an entire value stream is calculated differently. FPY considers only what goes into each process step and what comes out. Therefore, FPY for an entire value stream is the product of all FPYs of each process step in a value stream. Take the following value stream process steps and their respective FPY for each step:

Value stream FPY is:

Injection Molding FPY × Welding FPY × Assembly FPY × Finishing FPY

or

$$FPY_{value\ stream} = 99.8\% \times 75.2\% \times 86.3\% \times 95.3\% = 61.7\%$$

4.3.2. DELIVERY

Delivery in lean starts with the Voice of the Customer (VOC) and, more specifically, what value is to the customer. Of the three basic measures of value—good (quality), fast (time), and cheap (cost)—a customer is first willing to pay the agreed price. The customer also expects the quality agreed to and delivery on time. The product or service provider works to minimize its cost in ensuring the agreed-upon quality and on-time delivery. The discussion then becomes favored toward a push batch system or one of single-piece continuous flow. While having lots of work-in-process (WIP) may make one feel comfortable, excess WIP causes tampering, defects, rework, excess inventory costs, and delay in delivery. By focusing first on lean flow methods that are fairly easy to apply, such as takt time and managing lead time, the product or service provider can more effectively and efficiently provide the product or service at a lower overall cost while meeting the delivery expectations of the customer. This can bring "quick win" improvements.

Terms for the methods of lean flow include customer demand, cycle time or process cycle time, actual work time or available operating time, takt time, lead time, average completion rate or average exit rate, and WIP. Applying the methods of lean flow also includes consideration of the elimination of waste (muda); reduction of fluctuation (mura), which is best managed with variability reduction, just-in-time, and leveling (heijunka); and minimization of overburden (muri), which is best managed through work flow, work standardization, and the application of takt time. By applying the different cures for muda, mura, and muri, with a focus on producing to customer demand with a managed takt time, the product or service provider can meet the customer's delivery requirements.

$$\text{Takt time} = \frac{\text{Actual work time (AWT) or time available per shift}}{\text{Customer demand}}$$

Let's walk through in more detail how to calculate takt time, starting with customer demand.

Since lean starts with understanding customer value, we will focus on lean flow on delivery or customer demand. *Customer demand* is, as expected, the number of units demanded over a period of time, often expressed in units required per day. For example, over five days, customers order 144, 216, 156, 196, and 162 Toe-Flexors from the Lean Mean Exercise Machine Company.

The average customer demand is (144 + 216 + 156 + 196 + 162 = 874) Toe-Flexors/5 days, which equals an average customer demand or average daily order of 175 Toe-Flexors (rounded to whole units). (Please note that, statistically, a larger sample such as 25–30 orders is needed; however, 5 orders is used here to simplify the explanation.)

$$\text{Average customer daily demand} = \frac{144 + 216 + 156 + 196 + 162}{5}$$

$$\text{Average customer daily demand} = 175$$

Next, the Lean Mean Exercise Machine Company needs to plan for variability in customer demand. There are several ways to do this, and a few are presented here for reference only (see Appendix B, "Lean Knowledge Certificate & Lean Bronze Certification Recommended Reading," for more information). One of the easiest ways to manage variability is to consider the variability effects of customer demand based on the maximum and average daily orders:

$$\text{Customer demand variability percent} = (\text{Maximum daily order} - \text{Average daily order} / \text{Maximum daily order}) \times 100$$

$$\text{Customer demand variability percent} = (216 - 175/216) \times 100$$

$$\text{Customer demand variability percent} = 41/216 \times 100$$

$$\text{Customer demand variability percent} = 19\%$$

$$\text{Customer demand variability percent} = 20\% \text{ (with adjustment factor)}$$

The two main points, regardless of the method of planning for variability in customer demand, are (1) that any of these methods utilize samples, and samples are short term, and (2) that customer demand changes as it wishes to, not as we plan. Therefore, set the adjusted customer demand based on variability as a pilot and then monitor and adjust for dramatic shifts. Additional considerations for changes in customer demand are seasonality and other cyclic conditions that do not produce a demand in the stable state but instead fluctuate to different levels over time. For example, the demand for lawn mowers is higher in the spring than in the winter. Also note that different components may have different customer demand and that processes operate at different rates, so consider these areas of variation as well.

Actual work time (AWT) or available operating time (AOT) is the operating hours available based on working regular time, excluding overtime, meals, and breaks. For AWT we normally do not deduct maintenance time, preventive maintenance time, scheduled meetings, cleanup time, setup time, or any planned or unplanned downtime. The Lean Mean Exercise Machine Company has allocated AWT, excluding nonworking time such as meals and breaks, as a daily shift of 8 hours (7 actual work hours, 30 minutes for lunch, and two 15-minute breaks). The most common unit for expressing takt time is minutes, so we often need to convert the time metric to minutes.

$$AWT = 8 \text{ hour shift (or 480 minutes)}$$

$$\text{lunch} = 30 \text{ minutes}$$

$$\text{breaks} = 2 \times 15 \text{ minutes}$$

$$AWT = 7 \text{ hours (or 420 minutes per shift)}$$

$$AWT = \frac{7 + 7 + 7 + 7 + 7}{5}$$

$$AWT = 7 \text{ hours (or 420 minutes per shift)}$$

Consider that some theories state that the AWT based on working regular time—excluding overtime, meals, and breaks and not including maintenance time, preventive maintenance time, scheduled meetings, cleanup time, setup time, or any planned or unplanned downtime—would be considered the basis and input for calculating a theoretical takt time. If you consider, in particular, planned preventive maintenance, scheduled meetings, or other monument events as an automatic reduction of the available time, then you could consider these as a reduction of available time. This would produce an actual takt time based on more realistic parameters that in turn calculate the real time available and therefore require a faster takt rate to meet demand. Whichever parameters you decide to exclude from available time (meals, breaks, preventive maintenance, etc.), you should be consistent across your operations and facilities so that you can compare the metrics of similar operations. Note, though, that if you are comparing against benchmarks, the benchmark has most likely excluded meals and breaks. It may be best, then, to plan with monuments (meals, breaks, and planned and conducted regular preventive maintenance) when calculating available time so that your true run rate to meet customer demand is understood.

4.3.2.1. Takt Time

Takt time is the amount of time required to produce a part or service based on customer demand. *Takt* is the German word for the rhythm or beat that an orchestra conductor moves his or her baton to regulate the speed, beat, or timing at which musicians play. So, in kind, it is the rhythm with which a product or service provider should pace the work to meet customer demand. Important takt time rules include the following:

- Takt time is the time required between the completion of successive units at the end of the process providing the product or service

- Takt time is calculated for each process step or position and is used to pace the work

- Takt time in an environment of unstable demand is extremely difficult

- Takt time must be updated with demand changes

Takt time (expressed in minutes per unit) =

AWT per time period/Customer demand for Toe-Flexors per time period

Takt time = (420 minutes/day)/(210 Toe-Flexors/day) = 2 minutes per Toe-Flexor

$$\text{Takt time} = \frac{420 \text{ minutes}}{210}$$

Takt time = 2 minutes per piece (or 120 seconds)

Some companies express takt time in seconds per piece (versus minutes). This may become important during takt awareness.

So, in this example, the flow rate through each process step must be less than or equal to two minutes per Toe-Flexor, or a backlog will be developed with respect to meeting customer demand.

Takt Awareness

Another key lean measurement used by operators and team leaders is *takt awareness*. It's a way for the people closest to the process to determine whether the process is on time, late, or ahead. Takt awareness allows the operators to adjust their speed to meet the takt time. If an operator notices that the cycle time (see Section 4.3.2.2) is longer than the takt time, the pieces will be late. For example, the operator on process step 3 notices that it took 122 seconds to complete the task that normally takes 114 seconds. In this situation, the operator has standardized options based on the situation and organization. It may be as simple as working a little faster on the next piece, asking for help from the team lead (pulling the andon cord), working a little into the break time, or following whichever standards the company creates. This is a very powerful, visual tool to maintain even flow, pace, or rhythm. This reduces the unevenness of mura.

4.3.2.2. Cycle Time

Cycle time or *process cycle time* is the amount of time to complete one unit (standard work sequence), or simply the amount of time for a task to be completed. Cycle time is calculated for each process step. For machine cycle time, both machine run

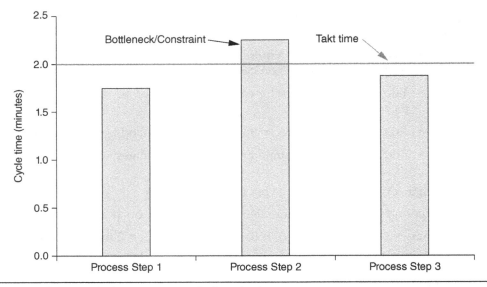

Figure 4.3.2.2-1 Takt time–process cycle time chart.

time and setup time internal to the machine are included. Cycle time is calculated using the actual hours expended by the number of people working on the activity. For the Lean Mean Exercise Machine Company, the process cycle time for the three process steps is 1.8 minutes, 2.3 minutes, and 1.9 minutes per Toe-Flexor. Takt time is 2 minutes per Toe-Flexor, which appears as the line at 2 minutes in Figure 4.3.2.2-1. Any process step taking longer than the takt time is a constraint or bottleneck in the process and prevents the overall process from meeting customer demand.

The goal is to ensure that process cycle time is less than takt time. When takt time is greater than process cycle time for a process step, capacity is wasted, and idle time or waiting (a form of waste [muda]) is present. When takt time is less than cycle time for a process step, one or more bottlenecks are present and therefore additional capacity or resources are needed. When takt time is equal to process cycle time for a process step, the work is balanced. If the process has a constraint, then a quick improvement may be leveling work across the process steps.

Takt time begins the movement in lean flow toward single-piece continuous flow. A pitfall of the push batch system is the false comfort of allowing for or planning WIP in the process. A way to both understand the effect of WIP in the process and manage WIP is with lead time or process lead time (PLT). PLT is also known as Little's law, where PLT = WIP / AWT.

$$\text{Little's law or process lead time (PLT)} = \frac{\text{WIP}}{\text{AWT}}$$

For the Lean Mean Exercise Machine Company, the current bottleneck of process step 2 takes 2.3 minutes per operation (Table 4.3.2.2-1). AWT is 420 minutes per day; therefore, the average completion rate (ACR) (unit complete per time

Table 4.3.2.2-1 Overproduction or bottleneck.

Process	PCT	Number of units per shift	Issue
Process 1	1.8 min.	233	Overproduction
Process 2	2.3 min.	183	Bottleneck
Process 3	1.9 min.	221	Overproduction

unit) or exit rate is 183 Toe-Flexors per day. Process step 3 takes 1.9 minutes per operation, and the ACR is 221 Toe-Flexors per day. At the end of the day, the Lean Mean Exercise Machine Company will have a buildup of 39 Toe-Flexors in WIP in front of process step 2.

4.3.2.3. Lead Time

By definition, the *process lead time* (PLT) is the average time it takes the next unit to enter and then exit the overall process. For the three processes of the Toe-Flexor operation, we might expect to see a Toe-Flexor every six minutes by adding up each of the times for the three process steps, but it really doesn't happen that way:

PLT = WIP / ACR for Toe-Flexors

PLT = 39 Toe-Flexors / (1 Toe-Flexor / 2.3 minutes)

PLT = 39 × 2.3 minutes = 89.7 minutes

When the next Toe-Flexor enters process step 2, it will be 89.7 minutes before it exits, assuming first-in, first-out (FIFO). This, of course, gets worse as WIP builds up in front of process step 2. By visual assessment as well as the time values provided, we can see that the total time for the three steps is 6 minutes per Toe-Flexor. If we balanced or leveled the line, then, on average, we would be operating each process step at 2 minutes per Toe-Flexor. Customer demand requires a takt time of 2 minute per Toe-Flexor, so if we leveled resources, our operation would be in harmony and no WIP would be present.

PLT does not have to be used in considering flow through the production processes as shown in the example of the Toe-Flexors, but for the most part it is. A broader consideration should be the concept of total lead time. *Total lead time* includes placement of an order and receipt of just-in-time supplies, production time, shipping time, and receipt time. Essentially, how long does it take to meet the customer's needs? We usually exclude transit time; for example, 2 minute shipping of a Toe-Flexor may not be practical; however, colocation of facilities is sometimes a solution. We want to include order processing. For example, if the order processing time on average for each Toe-Flexor was 10 minutes, we would not meet the customer demand of 2 minutes per Toe-Flexor. The point being that you may need to consider more than the production processes when considering process time to meet customer demand.

4.3.3. COST

Many lean practitioners are cautious when discussing cost metrics. It is often said that the goal of lean is the complete elimination of waste and should not be an initiative to reduce costs. However, this is not entirely true. While the fundamental principle of lean is the complete elimination of waste in all forms, part of being a sustainable business is being able to make a profit. The traditional business equation:

$$\text{Profit}_{\text{fixed}} = \text{Selling price} - \text{Actual cost}$$

no longer applies in today's competitive environment. This is where companies fixed the profit and adjusted the selling price based on actual costs. In today's environment, customers are more knowledgeable about products and services, and they have more choices. Customers now have more buying power, whereas before companies had the selling power of raising the prices of goods and services to increase profit. The traditional business equation has changed to:

$$\text{Selling price}_{\text{fixed}} = \text{Profit} + \text{Actual cost}$$

where the selling price is fixed by the customer. Today, companies must now either reduce profit or reduce actual costs of making the product or providing the service. To remain sustainable, the organization cannot reduce profits, at least not over the long term. Therefore, the only long-term choice is to reduce the actual costs. As one can see, cost reduction becomes the driving force behind an organization's decision to begin the lean journey. Organizations choose lean since focusing on the complete elimination of waste results in a reduction of costs. This is typically why cost reduction is given as the foremost reason for organizations to adopt lean initiatives. Cost reduction as a driving force in the decision to "go lean" should not be confused with the main principle of lean, which is the complete elimination of waste.

4.3.3.1. Inventory Turns

Taiichi Ohno viewed the muda (waste) of overproduction as the root cause of many of manufacturing's problems with cost reduction. While economies of scale was the driving force for mass production (produce as much as possible in a short period of time to reduce overall costs of a product or service), this created the waste of overproduction. Overproduction results in inventory, and inventory is products or services that are not sold. This means organizations are holding this inventory somewhere, and there are costs associated with having inventory on hand. These may consist of, but are certainly not limited to, warehouse costs, additional workers and machines to move the inventory, hidden product and service problems, cost of cycle counting, and the time value of money—a dollar today is not worth the same as a dollar in the future.

According to Womack and Jones (2003), in *Lean Thinking*, the measure of inventory is not only the best lean measure but also the simplest. Inventory should be at a level that supports a given demand to customers. It is impossible to operate as a lean business or as a lean enterprise consisting of extended value streams without increasing the flow of value from raw materials to customers and reducing inventories. Notice that there is no mention of "zero" inventory or the complete elimination of inventory. This is because inventory comes in a number of forms. Some inventory is necessary, like raw materials, work in process (WIP), and finished goods. Some inventory is necessary only in given circumstances, like buffer stock, safety stock, and shipping stock. The concern with inventory is not having an inventory, but having an *excess* of inventory (or the contrary—not having enough inventory). So, how can we measure inventory in such a way that it incorporates the flow of product and services to the customer?

The idea of inventory in a lean organization is the ability to turn inventory around to sell to the customer. The measure of that ability is called inventory turns. *Inventory turns* are the amount of goods "sold" during a specific period of time divided by the average amount of inventory during that same period.

$$\text{Inventory turns} = \frac{\text{Cost of goods "sold" during a period of time}}{\text{Average cost of inventory during the same time period}}$$

Using the cost of goods sold, prior to adding any overhead/administrative costs, removes variations associated with profits and focuses on the cost of inventory used to meet customer demand. But why is average cost of inventory important? As an example, say that a company's process requires a total cost of raw material inventory of $300,000 to produce to demand for a 30-day period (month). The cost of goods sold is $300,000 per month. The company has two choices:

Scenario A: The company receives $300,000 of raw material inventory once per month and stores it in a warehouse until use. The reorder schedule is once per month.

Scenario B: The company receives $100,000 of raw material inventory three times per month (every 10 days) and stores it in a smaller warehouse until use. The reorder schedule is three times per month.

In both scenarios, the company utilizes a one-day spot check of inventory turns during the month—what it considers its monthly inventory turns measure.

In Scenario A, the company had a cost of goods sold of $300,000 for the month of April. The company performs its spot check of inventory turns on April 30, when it has just received its monthly shipment of $300,000 of raw materials. This results in an inventory turn of 1 for the month of April.

$$\text{Inventory turns} = \$300,000 \div \$300,000 = 1$$

This is not very good. So manufacturing and purchasing get together and decide to change the date the raw materials shipment is received to the first of the month, after the inventory spot check. This allows the company to have $10,000 (given the demand is $10,000 per day) in inventory on hand when the spot check is performed, resulting in an inventory turns measure of 30.

$$\text{Inventory turns} = \$300,000 \div \$10,000 = 30$$

This gives better results, but was waste really eliminated? Let us now look at Scenario B. Given the same spot check being performed on April 30, the inventory on hand would be $100,000 if the shipment of raw materials came in that day. This would result in:

$$\text{Inventory turns} = \$300,000 \div \$100,000 = 3$$

And if the receipt of raw material was changed to the day after the spot check, it would result in:

$$\text{Inventory turns} = \$300,000 \div \$10,000 = 30$$

These examples show how the traditional system of spot checking inventory and measuring total inventory levels do not provide an adequate picture. This spot-check inventory can be manipulated too easily without any waste reduction being accomplished. Now let us look at the inventory turns based on the average cost of inventory over that period of time:

$$\text{Average cost of inventory}_{\text{Scenario A}} = \frac{\$300,000 \text{ (cost of monthly inventory)}}{30 \text{ days}} = \$10,000$$

$$\text{Average cost of inventory}_{\text{Scenario B}} = \frac{\$300,000 \text{ (cost of monthly inventory)}}{30 \text{ days}} = \$10,000$$

Therefore, the inventory turns for both scenarios now become:

$$\text{Inventory turns} = \frac{\text{Cost of goods ``sold'' (30 days)}}{\text{Average cost of inventory (30 days)}} = \frac{\$300,000}{\$10,000} = 30$$

By using the average cost of inventory, the data are normalized and cannot be easily manipulated by changing receipt dates or dates that inventories are performed. However, we know that additional costs are associated with inventory. The cost of a warehouse for $300,000 worth of raw material carries greater overhead costs than that of a right-sized warehouse for $100,000 of the same raw material. Because inventory turns do not take into account overhead costs associated with the cost of goods sold, other lean measures are used to identify other wastes associated with inventory, such as waiting.

4.3.3.2. Queue Time

Womack and Jones (2003) define *queue time* as the time a product spends in a line awaiting the next design, order-processing, or fabrication step. The product can be a finished good, subassembly (work-in-process), or a person in a service line. Queue time can also be a measure of the duration a customer is on hold on the telephone.

$$\text{Queue time} = \text{Duration of product/person remains in queue}$$

Queue time can be calculated a number of ways depending on the process:

- Technical support hotline: the duration of time from when the automated telephone system answers the call to the point when the next available service representative takes the customer off hold

- Manufacturing: the duration of time from when a part is placed into inventory to the point it is used at the next process step

- Manufacturing: the duration of time from when a finished good is placed in inventory to the point it is shipped to the customer

- Retail: the duration of time from when a product is placed on the shelf to the point it is purchased by a customer

- Hospital or doctor's office: the duration of time from when a patient checks in at the admissions desk to the point the patient is seen by the triage nurse/doctor (time spent in the waiting room)

- Restaurant: the duration of time from when a customer orders a meal to the point the meal is prepared

Often, the average queue time can be calculated by dividing the total number in the queue by the demand of the downstream process step. Consider the technical support hotline example. Let's say that 10 technical support representatives are available at any given time. The average time it takes to help a customer is five minutes. Therefore, the downstream "demand" is two per minute. Given that the number of calls into a call center fluctuates, the queue time fluctuates. If the call center has 20 customers on hold, the queue time becomes

$$\text{Queue time} = 20 \text{ callers} \div 2 \text{ callers/minute} = 10 \text{ minutes}$$

If the call center has 10 customers on hold, the queue time becomes

$$\text{Queue time} = 10 \text{ callers} \div 2 \text{ callers/minute} = 5 \text{ minutes}$$

Automated call systems can track these measures instantaneously. This is why you often hear how long you will be on hold until the next representative is available when you are on an automated system.

Queue time works much the same way in a manufacturing environment. For instance, an inventory amount of 1000 units is located between process step A and process step B. If process step B is the downstream process and the demand/pull is 1 per second, the average queue time is 1000 seconds at that inventory point.

Queue time can also be used in administrative functions, such as engineering. Queue time can be calculated based on the duration from when an engineering change request, or design change, document is submitted to the engineering department to the point it is assigned or pulled by an engineer to begin work on it. In office environments, the paper trail often has queues in the form of inboxes (physical and e-mail).

Using our example for inventory turns, we can see how to utilize this measure to identify when we have excessive levels of inventory. Average daily demand for raw material is $10,000 ($300,000 of raw material needed per 30-day period). Therefore, the scenarios now look like this:

Scenario A

$$\text{Queue time} = \frac{\text{Maximum inventory in queue}}{\text{Demand}} = \frac{\$300,000}{\$10,000 \text{ per day}} = 30 \text{ days}$$

Scenario B

$$\text{Queue time} = \frac{\text{Maximum inventory in queue}}{\text{Demand}} = \frac{\$100,000}{\$10,000 \text{ per day}} = 10 \text{ days}$$

We can now see that the flow of product through the process in Scenario A is much slower than the product flow in Scenario B. Queue time can bring to the forefront those areas within a value stream that may have overproduction waste in downstream processes, unleveled production, or too high of inventory levels. As queue time decreases, the flow of the product/service through a value stream improves closer to one-piece flow.

4.3.3.3. Wait Time (Delays)

While queue time is related to inventory/overproduction muda (waste), wait time is related to waiting muda (waste). According to Liker (2004, 28), waiting, or time on hand, is:

> Workers merely serving as watch persons for an automated machine, or having to stand around waiting for the next processing step, tool, supply, part, etc., or just plain having no work because of no stock, lot processing, delays, equipment downtime, and capacity bottlenecks.

Therefore, *wait time* is simply the measure of the duration of time a person or process is waiting due to unplanned delays (e.g., equipment downtime, no parts, and automated machine operating). Wait time can also be measured in service organizations or functions when automated systems like computers are processing information and the service representative is waiting for the next process step.

In a value stream, if the process steps are not leveled, there is wait time associated when the downstream process is much faster than the upstream process. For instance, take a look at the following process with the cycle time for each step identified:

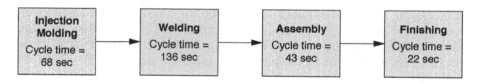

In this process, if each step is performed by a single machine and operator in a one-piece flow, the wait time for the operator at the assembly process step is:

$$\text{Wait time} = \text{Cycle time}_{\text{welding}} - \text{Cycle time}_{\text{assembly}} = 136 - 43 = 93 \text{ seconds per part}$$

This is an example of wait time due to a capacity constraint (bottleneck) within the process.

Another example of wait time is if, during the previous process, the injection molding process step runs out of plastic pellets. Now, the wait time is from the last part produced until the next part is produced after the plastic pellets are supplied, dried (or prepared for molding), and the barrel is purged. This wait time can be added together with the wait times of all the downstream processes that are waiting due to parts from injection molding not being supplied. This sort of wait time is widely associated with equipment availability and equipment downtime.

4.3.3.4. Overall Equipment Effectiveness (OEE)

Measurement of equipment efficiency has been a long-standing traditional measure of productivity in manufacturing. Reliability measures have included failure rate, mean time to repair (MTTR), mean time between failures (MTBF), and availability. However, over time these measures have become numbers that are reported without understanding what was included or missed in the measurement. As manufacturers progressed with their lean journeys, it was realized that these traditional measures of efficiency were covering up many of the root causes of lost efficiency because they were not getting all the information about the process or equipment. Manufacturers need a measure that includes all the information of downtime, lost production, and quality associated with processes and equipment.

Overall equipment effectiveness (OEE) has become known as the leading measure of equipment, process, labor, and plant efficiency. OEE takes into account all the significant losses of productivity and incorporates them into a metric that shows the complete picture of efficiency. OEE also places these productivity losses into groups to aid in root cause analysis and focus improvement efforts. This is why OEE has become a key measure for total productive maintenance (TPM) activities.

OEE has three main factors: availability, performance, and quality. These measures are utilized to track the efficiency and effectiveness of processes and equipment. The idea of OEE is to consider the amount of time the equipment is making good product and comparing that with the total time possible the equipment could theoretically make good product.

OEE calculation begins with determining the amount of time the facility is open for operation—the potential available time. *Potential available time* is the theoretical total time possible that the equipment, process, labor, and plant could make good product, or hours (time) of potential operation. For a facility that operates 24 hours a day 7 days a week, the potential available time for one week is:

$$\text{Potential available time} = 24 \text{ hours} \times 7 \text{ days} = 168 \text{ hours}$$

4.3.3.4

For a facility that operates 24 hours a day 5 days a week, the potential available time for one week is:

Potential available time = 24 hours × 5 days = 120 hours

Potential available time can be based on a single day, week, month, quarter, year (annually), or any time frame the organization wants to calculate OEE on a given frequency.

Once potential available time is calculated, planned downtime should be determined. *Planned downtime* includes all times that should be removed from the OEE calculation because they are times when the equipment is not planned to run production (e.g., the facility is closed, scheduled downtime due to maintenance activities, lunch breaks, or customer demand is met and the equipment is shut down as to not create overproduction muda). Assume the equipment is shut down during lunch breaks for one hour each shift, there are three shifts per day, the equipment operates only during the week (no weekend operation), and all scheduled maintenance activities occur on the weekend. The planned downtime is:

$$
\begin{aligned}
\text{Planned downtime} \; &= \; \underset{\text{Lunch breaks}}{(1 \text{ hr} \times 3 \text{ shifts})} \; + \; \underset{\text{Weekend}}{(24 \text{ hr} \times 2 \text{ days})} \\
&= 3 \text{ hours} \qquad\qquad + \; 48 \text{ hours} \\
&= 51 \text{ hours}
\end{aligned}
$$

Planned available time—the time that a process, equipment, labor, assembly line, plant, and so on, is planned to be in production making good product—can now be calculated.

Planned available time = Potential available time − Planned downtime

While potential available time is the potential usage of equipment (potential capacity), planned available time is the actual time that the equipment is expected, or planned, to be making good product (planned capacity). Planned available time is where the OEE measure begins to take shape. The next step is to analyze the inefficiencies and productivity losses that occur during planned available time. Inefficiencies and productivity losses are broken down into three groups:

1. Unplanned downtime loss

2. Performance loss

3. Quality loss

Unplanned downtime loss is the sum of the losses of equipment availability due to unplanned stoppage of production over a period of time. The period of time should be the same as that used in the calculation of potential available time and planned available time. Examples may include running out of material/parts, changeovers, and equipment failures. Usually, events included in unplanned downtime are those that have significant recovery time and are usually long enough to be documented for tracking. Events that last longer than a significant number of cycles and/or takts (several minutes) may be included in this loss group. With

4.3.3.4

unplanned downtime loss calculated, equipment actual operating time can be determined.

$$\text{Actual operating time} = \text{Planned available time} - \text{Sum of all unplanned downtime losses}$$

Availability, the first factor of OEE, is the percentage of time that equipment, the process, labor, or the production line is operating compared with the planned time of operation, or:

$$\text{Availability} = \frac{\text{Planned available time} - \text{Sum of all unplanned downtime losses}}{\text{Planned available time}}$$

or

$$\text{Availability} = \frac{\text{Actual operating time}}{\text{Planned available time}}$$

Performance loss, the second group of productivity losses, is the sum of losses during equipment operation due to factors that cause the equipment to operate at less than the maximum designed efficiency over a period of time. Examples may include wear, operator inefficiency, material variations, part jams, and so on. Dirty equipment or residue buildup can also have an impact on optimized equipment operation. This is also true for office equipment, computer systems/servers, and measurement equipment. Some automated equipment is capable of tracking the number of machine faults and the recovery time for each fault. In these cases, performance loss can be easily calculated electronically. With performance loss captured, equipment actual performance time can be determined.

$$\text{Actual performance time} = \text{Actual operating time} - \text{Sum of all performance time losses}$$

While actual operating time is the planned performance of equipment as designed (designed performance), actual performance time is the efficiency level at which the equipment actually performs during operation (actual performance).

Performance, the second factor of OEE, is the percentage of time of actual performance (net operating time) that equipment, the process, labor, or the production line runs during operation compared with the designed performance of operation (actual operating time), or:

$$\text{Performance} = \frac{\text{Actual operating time} - \text{Sum of all performance losses}}{\text{Actual operating time}}$$

or

$$\text{Performance} = \frac{\text{Actual performance time}}{\text{Actual operating time}}$$

Performance can also be calculated based on equipment/process cycle times:

$$\text{Performance} = \frac{\text{Designed cycle time}}{(\text{Actual operating time} \div \text{Total units production})}$$

where designed cycle time is the minimum cycle time that the equipment/process was designed for operation under optimal, or ideal, circumstances. Performance can also be calculated based on the traditional measure of production efficiency:

$$\text{Performance} = \frac{(\text{Total units production} \div \text{Actual operating time})}{\text{Designed production efficiency}}$$

where designed production efficiency is the set standard run rate (typically for traditional financial calculations) of a machine or process. However, this measure is sometimes greater than 100%. Therefore, to limit the impact to the OEE calculation, this measure of performance is topped at 100%.

Quality loss, the third group of productivity losses, is the sum of quality losses during equipment operation due to defects and rework. This is simply the percentage of good production, or first pass yield. With quality loss captured, equipment first pass yield, or first pass yield, can be determined.

$$\text{Quality} = \text{FPY} = \frac{\text{Total units processed} - \text{Rejects or reworks}}{\text{Total units processed}}$$

Quality, the third and final factor of OEE, is first pass yield. In simplest terms, OEE is a ratio of first pass yield to planned available time. However, OEE is calculated by multiplying the three factors:

$$\text{OEE} = \text{Availability} \times \text{Performance} \times \text{Quality}$$

Figure 4.3.3.4-1 is a visual representation of OEE.

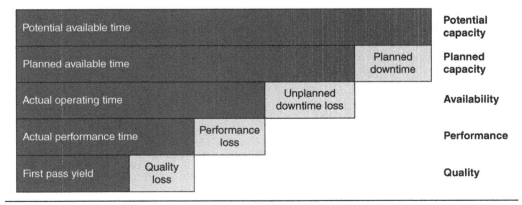

Figure 4.3.3.4-1 A visual representation of OEE.

Consider the following example for a single shift in a manufacturing facility:

Factor	Data
Shift length	12 hours = 720 min.
Breaks	2 at 15 min. = 30 min.
Lunch break	1 at 30 min. = 30 min.
Total downtime losses	68 min.
Designed cycle time	0.55 sec per unit
Total units production	41,056 pieces
Rejected units	312 pieces
Reworked units	1848

$$
\begin{aligned}
\text{Planned downtime} &= \text{Breaks} \quad + \quad \text{Lunch break} \\
&= 30 \text{ min.} \quad + \quad 30 \text{ min.}
\end{aligned}
$$

$$
\begin{aligned}
\text{Planned available time} &= \text{Potential available time} \quad - \text{Planned downtime} \\
&= 720 \text{ min.} \qquad\qquad\quad - \; 60 \text{ min.} \\
&= 660 \text{ min.}
\end{aligned}
$$

$$
\begin{aligned}
\text{Actual operating time} &= \text{Planned available time} \quad - \text{Sum of all unplanned} \\
&\qquad\qquad\qquad\qquad\qquad\qquad\quad \text{downtime losses} \\
&= 660 \text{ min.} \qquad\qquad\qquad\; - \; 68 \text{ min.} \\
&= 592 \text{ min.}
\end{aligned}
$$

$$
\begin{aligned}
\text{Availability} &= \frac{\text{Actual operating time}}{\text{Planned available time}} = \frac{592 \text{ min.}}{660 \text{ min.}} \\
&= 0.897
\end{aligned}
$$

$$
\begin{aligned}
\text{Performance} &= \frac{\text{Designed cycle time}}{(\text{Actual operating time} \div \text{Total units production})} \\
&= \frac{0.55 \text{ sec per unit}}{(592 \text{ min.} \div 41{,}056 \text{ units})} = \frac{0.55 \text{ sec per unit}}{0.87 \text{ sec per unit}} \\
&= 0.632
\end{aligned}
$$

$$
\begin{aligned}
\text{Quality} = \text{First pass yield} &= \frac{\text{Total units production} - \text{Rejects or reworks}}{\text{Total units processed}} \\
&= \frac{41{,}056 - 312 - 1848}{41{,}056} = 0.947
\end{aligned}
$$

$$
\begin{aligned}
\text{OEE} &= \text{Availability} \times \text{Performance} \times \text{Quality} \\
&= 0.897 \qquad\quad \times \; 0.632 \qquad\quad \times \; 0.947 \\
&= 0.537 \\
\textbf{OEE} &= \textbf{53.7\%}
\end{aligned}
$$

4.3.3.4

The following table is the general industry accepted world-class goals for OEE and its different factors:

OEE factor	World-class goal
Availability	90.0%
Performance	95.0%
Quality	99.9%
Overall OEE	**85.0%**

OEE can also be used to compare the three factors across various shifts. Simply comparing the previous shift example with a second shift, TPM teams can internally benchmark across shifts to identify specific areas for improvement.

Table 4.3.3.4-1 allows for identification of potential areas of improvement. For example, shift 2 may experience additional unplanned work stoppages, such as running out of parts, or may have difficulty performing changeovers from one product to another. The TPM team could investigate and determine that creating standard work for changeovers based on shift 1 may bring shift 2 availability up near shift 1 and world-class levels. Both shifts show difficulty meeting world-class performance, so the TPM team may focus on bringing the equipment back up to the original design state through 5S activities and maintaining it with revised preventive/predictive maintenance.

OEE can also be used as a measure at the value stream and plant levels. Two methods are commonly used for these calculations: average and weighted average. The average method is simpler to calculate, but one should be cautious that the processes and value streams have similar planned available times. Otherwise, the measure may be skewed by one process/value stream scheduled to operate at a significantly less amount of time than others in the calculation. Observe the comparison in Table 4.3.3.4-2.

However, when considering the planned available times for each process/value stream, we get a different OEE result using the weighted average method. See Table 4.3.3.4-3.

Planned available time (Process A) = 720

Planned available time (Process B) = 360

Table 4.3.3.4-1 OEE by shift comparison.

OEE factor	Shift 1 example	Shift 2 example	World-class goal
Availability	89.7%	70.1%	90.0%
Performance	63.2%	75.6%	95.0%
Quality	94.7%	90.3%	99.9%
Overall OEE	**53.7%**	**47.9%**	**85.0%**

Table 4.3.3.4-2 Average method of calculating value stream OEE.

OEE factor	Process A or Value Stream A	Process B or Value Stream B	Average method
Availability	75%	90%	(75% + 90%) ÷ 2 = 82.5%
Performance	85%	90%	(85% + 90%) ÷ 2 = 87.5%
Quality	95%	90%	(95% + 90%) ÷ 2 = 92.5%
Overall OEE	**60.6%**	**72.9%**	82.5% × 87.5% × 92.5% = **66.8%**

Note: Overall OEE is calculated by multiplying the averages of the factors and not by averaging the OEEs of the processes/value streams.

Table 4.3.3.4-3 Weighted average method of calculating value stream OEE.

OEE factor	Process A	Process B	Average method
Availability	75%	90%	[(75% × 720) + (90% × 360)] ÷ (720 + 360) = 80.0%
Performance	85%	90%	[(85% × 720) + (90% × 360)] ÷ (720 + 360) = 86.7%
Quality	95%	90%	[(95% × 720) + (90% × 360)] ÷ (720 + 360) = 93.3%
Overall OEE	**60.6%**	**72.9%**	80.0% × 86.7% × 93.3% = **64.7%**

The primary goal of OEE is to have a measure to identify areas of focus to reduce/eliminate the six most common causes of inefficiency in manufacturing, also known as the Six Big Losses. Table 4.3.3.4-4 summarizes these losses and how they relate to the OEE measure.

While OEE originated for use with manufacturing operations to monitor equipment, machines, and automated production, it can also be utilized to monitor labor-intensive operations (e.g., manual assembly, administrative duties, and service functions). By modifying the definitions of each factor (availability, performance, and quality) for labor-intensive processes, OEE can be utilized as an effective measure for service and administrative functions. This can be called *overall labor effectiveness* (OLE). See Table 4.3.3.4-5 for examples within labor-intensive functions.

Consider the example shown in Table 4.3.3.4-6. Notice that all individual calculations previously identified were not utilized. Automated and equipment-heavy processes have standard metrics and methods of calculating availability (uptime), performance (cycle time), and quality (first pass yield) due to the similarity of automated and equipment-related processes. Because manual labor-intensive processes vary in many ways (e.g., by industry, function, and requirements), more flexibility is needed in calculating availability, performance, and quality. For instance, absenteeism may not be a significant factor for availability in an accounting office process, but it would be considered in a restaurant kitchen or emergency room.

4.3.3.4

Table 4.3.3.4-4 The Six Big Losses.

Six Big Losses category	OEE loss category	Examples
Equipment breakdowns	Unplanned downtime loss	• Tooling failures • Unplanned maintenance • General breakdowns • Equipment failure • Preventive maintenance that occurs during planned available time
Setup and adjustment delays	Unplanned downtime loss	• Changeovers • Setup • Material/parts shortages • Operator absenteeism • Significant alignments and adjustments • Start-up time • Meetings/training • Facility/utility problems • Experimentation
Idling and minor stoppages	Performance loss	• Product flow obstructed • Overload of components/parts • Part or component jams • Machine faults • Misfeeds • Sensor misaligned or blocked • Equipment cleaning
Reduced speed	Performance loss	• Slower than design speed • Wear • Operator inefficiency • Dirt or residue
Process defects	Quality loss	• Defects scrapped • Defects reworked/repaired • Product damaged (scrapped) • Product expired (scrapped)
Reduced yield	Quality loss	• Defects resulting from start-up • Rework/repairs from start-up • Product damage (scrapped) from start-up

4.3.3.4

Table 4.3.3.4–5 Overall labor efficiency definitions.

OEE factor	Individual calculations	Individual calculation example
Availability	Utilization	Traditional labor utilization metrics such as time when personnel is out for training, meetings, and other organization-sponsored activities. Expressed as a percentage of actual personnel time versus planned, or standard, personnel time.
	Absenteeism	Shortage of personnel due to absences, illness, medical leave, etc. Expressed as a percentage of actual personnel time versus planned, or standard, personnel time. Can also be the percentage calculated from actual number of persons by the planned number of persons.
	Scheduling and downtime	Downtime due to material stoppage, idle time, shift changeovers, equipment failures (personnel cannot perform task due to computer crash). Calculated the same as OEE availability = Uptime ÷ Planned available time.
Performance	Tool availability	Minor stoppages or delays caused by misplaced tools and job aids, tool wear and damage, missing or misplaced work instructions, and any other instance of slowed performance as a result of missing information and tools required to perform a task. This emphasizes the importance of 5S. This can be the ratio of time to perform a task with all the right tools and instructions at the point of use versus the time of performing the task where the tools and instructions are not at the point of use. Actual cycle time compared with ideal cycle time.
	Training and skills	Inefficiency as a result of personnel not knowing how to do the tasks they are assigned. This takes into account employee skills and task experience/knowledge. This can be calculated by comparing actual cycle times with ideal cycle times.
	Support	This is the measure of support staff required versus actual support staff used. For instance, the amount of time, supervision, technical staff, and quality staff required to perform a task under optimal personnel conditions compared with less than optimal conditions. This can be the result of training a new hire, equipment failure, equipment setup, changeovers, etc.
Quality	Knowledge	This is first pass yield considering defects and rework as a result of personnel failing to understand that their task(s) impact quality of the product or service. This can also be the result of personnel not stopping a process when a defect is identified.

4.3.3.4

Table 4.3.3.4-5 Overall labor efficiency definitions. *(continued)*

OEE factor	Individual calculations	Individual calculation example
Quality	Correct work	This can be a measure of the percentage of personnel utilizing the correct tools and instructions to complete a task. This can be calculated by performing an assessment of an employee during a task or process. This is a measure of the percentage of time or tasks that were performed per work instructions correctly. This can also be the first pass yield considering defects and rework as a result of personnel failing to perform tasks correctly.
	Fatigue	Typically as production rates are increased by supervision (goals or behind schedule), quality of the product or service decreases due to personnel fatigue. This can be an *estimated* calculation based on cycle times for tasks that are faster than takt time where exceeding customer demand (overproduction) decreases the quality percentage. For example, for every cycle time 5% faster than takt time, quality decreases by 5%, or to 95% first pass yield.

Table 4.3.3.4-6 OLE example.

OEE factor	Examples of individual calculations used	Individual calculation example	OEE factor calculation
Availability	Utilization: 4 persons per 8-hour shift (7 hours with lunch and breaks), with each person having 30 minutes of training	$[1680 - (4 \times 30)] \div 1680$ $= 0.929$	92.9% × 100% × 97.4% = 90.5%
	Absenteeism: 4 persons required for process, no one was absent	$4 \div 4$ = 1.00 or 100%	
	Scheduling: Equipment was down for 10 minutes of total possible time of 390 minutes (420 − 30)	$380 \div 390$ $= 0.974$	
Performance	Tool availability: Ideal time for service is 20 minutes; service average actual time is 29 minutes due to searching for supplies	$20 \div 29$ $= 0.689$	68.9%
Quality	Knowledge: A total of 14 services performed; 1 task required rework due to documentation correction	$13 \div 14$ $= 0.929$	92.9% × 78.6% = 73.0%
	Correct work: A total of 70 tasks performed (5 tasks per service), 28 tasks observed, 6 tasks not performed per standard work	$(28 - 6) \div 28$ $= 0.786$	

For the previous example, calculating OEE remains the same once availability, performance, and quality are defined:

$$OEE = \text{Availability} \times \text{Performance} \times \text{Quality}$$
$$= 90.5\% \quad \times 68.9\% \quad \times 73.0\%$$
$$= 45.5\%$$

4.3.3.5. Changeover Time

Since it is a form of downtime, changeover time is included in the OEE analysis as part of the availability factor. In most cases, changeover time is the major contributor of unplanned downtime loss, and thus it is also considered a key lean measure. As defined by Marchwinski and Shook (2006, 8),

> Changeover is the process of switching from the production of one product or part number to another in a machine (e.g. a stamping press or molding machine) or a series of linked machines (e.g. an assembly line or cell) by changing parts, dies, molds, fixtures, etc. (Also called setup.) Changeover time is measured as the time elapsed between the last piece in the run just completed and the first good piece from the process after the changeover.

Simply put, *changeover time* is the amount of time needed to stop producing one product or service and start producing a different product or service. Traditionally, changeover time is the contributing factor that determines batch size due to the economical impact changeover downtime has on a process. This means that in traditional mass production, the longer the changeover time, the larger the batch size. Therefore, most lean companies strive to make changeover times as short as possible in order to be able to make more frequent changeovers and reduce batch sizes as they pursue one-piece flow.

Since changeovers are waste, the idea is to eliminate the time the machine, process, or system is down while a changeover is being performed. While it is not always possible to eliminate changeover time, in a majority of the instances it can be reduced. This is the premise behind Shigeo Shingo's single minute exchange of dies (SMED). In the 1950s and 1960s, Shingo developed the method of setup reduction, where internal setup operations were separated from external setup operations (see Section 2.3.7.2, "Quick Changeover/Setup Reduction (SMED)").

Changeover time can be measured in a number of ways. It can be measured using a percentage like that determined during the OEE calculation. It can be measured based on the actual time to perform the changeover. It can also be calculated in costs associated with a changeover (e.g., personnel usage, scrap created during start-up). No matter the unit of the changeover measure, changeover time begins when the last good part or service is completed and ends when the first good part or service is started at normal cycle time and efficiency.

Consider the following example from an assembly process. The customer demand of the assembly process for a single week is identified in Table 4.3.3.5-1, where the current schedule has the process making batch quantities the size of the stated product's weekly demand.

There is a total of 1260 minutes per day of operation. The current changeover time between products is 120 minutes. Assuming no other downtime loss, actual

4.3.3.5

Table 4.3.3.5-1 Example: customer demand of the assembly process for a single week.

Product	Monday	Tuesday	Wednesday	Thursday	Friday
A	1000				
B		5000			
C			2000		
D				1500	
E					500

Table 4.3.3.5-2 Example: total daily changeover time per day after standard scheduling.

Changeover	Time (minutes)
A to C	40
C to D	40
D to B	120
B to E	60
E to A	120
Total	380

Table 4.3.3.5-3 Example: changeover times.

Changeover	Time (minutes)
A to C	10
C to D	10
D to B	25
B to E	15
E to A	25
Total	75

operating time is 1140 minutes per day. With a current changeover time of 120 minutes between products, it would not be possible to level the schedule in order to produce all five products each day (120 minutes $\times$ 5 products = 600 minutes). Let's consider that Products A, C, and D are like products, and Products B and E are like products. This allows changeovers between A, C, and D to be shortened to 40 minutes, and the changeover between B and E to be shortened to 60 minutes through a change in scheduling. This is still 380 minutes (see Table 4.3.3.5-2) of changeover time per day, which is not reduced enough for a daily level scheduling.

Table 4.3.3.5-4 Example: level schedule.

Product	Monday	Tuesday	Wednesday	Thursday	Friday
A	200	200	200	200	200
C	1000	1000	1000	1000	1000
D	400	400	400	400	400
B	300	300	300	300	300
E	100	100	100	100	100

Now imagine a kaizen event is conducted to optimize changeover time. After the event, the changeover times look like Table 4.3.3.5-3, and a level schedule could be achieved per Table 4.3.3.5-4.

There are some factors that should be considered from this example. Total changeover time was reduced from 120 minutes each day to 75 minutes each day. This allows for additional actual operating time, which creates added capacity. Another factor to consider is the changeover costs. Say the original changeover costs were $10,000 per changeover, for a total of $50,000 in changeover costs per week. However, if the new schedule was created without reducing the changeover costs, the new weekly changeover costs would be $250,000, which is most likely not economically feasible. This is why both time and monetary units should be considered when evaluating this measure.

4.3.4. FINANCIAL IMPACT

It is known that lean typically results in significant improvements in operations. Organizations may observe, however, that financial benefits are not as immediately recognizable or are recognized to the same degree as operational measures. This causes some executives to question the benefit behind a lean initiative. It comes down to different perspectives between people who work in finance and those who work in operations. A language barrier between these two groups needs to be broken down for lean to be successful in the long term. The easiest way to break down that barrier is to begin with something both groups should be able to relate to, *flow*. By now, operations people should understand the principle behind product flow. Product flow is similar to cash flow. Operations must look at cash as finance's product, and finance must see raw materials, work-in-process (WIP), and finished product as cash.

4.3.4.1. Cash Flow

The idea of flow is centered on the conversion of raw material to product or the speed in which a service can be completed—in other words, reducing the time from purchasing resources to selling product, or speeding up *cash flow*. Cash flow is a combination of both operational measures and financial-based measures, as shown in Table 4.3.4.1-1.

4.3.4.1

Table 4.3.4.1-1 Lean measures associated with cash flow.

Measure	Type	Description
Dock-to-dock days	Operational	This is the amount of time from the receipt of material, or a service is requested, to the shipment of the finished product, or the completion of a service, to the customer. It is calculated by dividing the numbers of parts in a facility (raw material, WIP, and finished products) by the average rate the end productions are produced in a given value stream. Usually expressed in the number of finished products per day.
First pass yield	Operational	This is the percentage of total finished product that passes through the value stream without being repaired, reworked, or scrapped.
On-time shipment	Operational	This is the measure of the percentage of the correct finished product being shipped on the correct shipment date and in the correct order. Simply the ratio of total shipments that are made on time that meet order requirements to the total number of shipments from a value stream.
Floor space	Operational	Defined as the square footage of space that a given value stream takes up. This includes not only value added production areas, but also areas for inventory (raw material, WIP, and finished product).
Sales per person	Operational	A measure of the productivity and value created by a given value stream. This measure is calculated by dividing revenue generated (shipped and invoiced) from a value stream during a period of time by the average number of full-time employees. Full-time employees is an equivalency metric based on resource hours including management.
Average cost per unit	Operational	A measure of the total costs of a value stream for a given period divided by the total number of finished product shipped during that same period. The costs include labor, support, materials, and all other costs incurred by the value stream.
Inventory value	Financial	This is the value of inventory (raw material, WIP, and finished product) of the value stream at the end of a given period. This is no different than what is normally recorded by accounting on company books.
Revenue	Financial	A measure of the invoiced amounts for finished product shipped from a value stream during a given period. This is no different than what is normally recorded by accounting on company books.
Material cost	Financial	This is the cost of materials consumed for production during a given period. This is no different than what is normally recorded by accounting on company books.
Conversion costs	Financial	A measure of the costs incurred in a value stream during a period of time that it takes to operate the value stream and convert raw materials to finished product.
Profits	Financial	This is the revenue subtracted by the cost of sales (material costs plus conversion costs). This is essentially cash flow.

4.3.4.1

Essentially, profits based on the value stream differ from profits as defined by traditional accounting. Traditional accounting matches the expenses for product sold with the revenue earned during a period of time to calculate gross profits. However, the traditional accounting cash flow calculation does not take into account the flow of product in and out of inventory. This means that some periods will experience high revenues from the sale of product out of inventory while manufacturing expenses may be low due to slowed production as a result of increased inventory level. This results in a scenario of high revenues and low costs, and thus higher gross profit, giving a false sense of increased cash flow. The opposite is also misleading. The next period, production will increase to raise the inventory levels while sales may be steady or slowed. In this case, revenue will be low while costs are high, resulting in a low gross profit or even a loss for that period, giving a false sense of decreased cash flow. The latter is what typically happens when a lean improvement is made in an organization. This may cause a chief financial officer to panic and question the decision to implement lean. However, the reduction of inventory is a one-time expense that will eventually be eliminated as production steadily matches demand, or sales, and in the long term will result in an improved financial bottom line. Within lean accounting, the cash flow is stabilized when inventory levels are reduced and production matches demand.

Traditional cash flow can get even more complicated when standard costs for different types of products are introduced into the equation. When costs are standardized based on product type and not value stream, the fluctuations in cash flow can be even greater. Lean accounting standardizes the costs of product based on where they are produced. Therefore, as additional products are introduced into a lean cell for production, the cost of manufacturing the different products is the same within that cell. Within lean accounting, as product costs are standardized within a production cell, the cash flow becomes more stabilized. This is why increased cash flow is an important financial benefit of lean. Expensing costs of a value stream as materials are consumed and resources are used is equivalent to traditional cash flow calculations but more accurate of the actual flow of the conversion of purchased materials to product sales within the value stream.

4.3.5. COMPETITIVE IMPACT

> *Competition is the keen cutting edge of business,*
> *always shaving away at costs.*
>
> —Henry Ford

The world has obviously changed since the days of Henry Ford's concerns about competition to his Model T. Thomas Friedman (2005), in his book *The World Is Flat*, provides a thought-provoking account of how, in the modern world, the internet has blurred local, national, and even international boundaries. As technology changes manifest at the speed of light, competition is now a global phenomenon impacting every business of every size within every industry. Thus, addressing the competitive impact on our businesses is no longer a choice; it is a clear and present danger that needs immediate attention if the business is to exist.

In this era of global competition resulting from a "flat world," lean is a time-tested tool that can help corporations realize a definite competitive edge in their respective markets. Correctly applying lean thinking makes the following possible in order to stay competitive:

- Loyalty from customers

- Appreciation of true assets of the organization

- Business profitability

Loyalty from Customers

> *The single most important thing to remember about any enterprise is that there are no results inside its walls. The result of a business is a satisfied customer.*
>
> —Peter Drucker

Lean technology, at its core, is the wise use of software and other systems to eliminate waste at every point in a manufacturing or business process, that is, the value stream.

The sole focus of lean is to create value for the customer by providing excellent quality products or service, at minimal costs and at optimal speed.

Excellent Quality Product or Service

A lean organization ensures customer satisfaction of both its internal and external customers by optimizing the following:

- *Internal quality* by reducing scrap and rework, and by increasing the first pass yield

- *External quality* by ensuring that only error-free products, services, and information are provided to customers

Minimal Costs

A lean organization ensures customer satisfaction by reducing the following:

- *Internal costs* by reducing inventory, increasing overall equipment effectiveness (OEE), reducing change over time, significantly increasing "value added activities" that change the form, fit, or function of a product or service throughout the supply chain, and eliminating all non-value added activities and wastes (Krueger 2004)

- *Customer costs* by passing on some of the savings to the customers by controlling and reducing internal costs

Optimal Speed

A lean organization ensures customer satisfaction by optimizing the following:

- *Internal lead times* by building strong supply chain relationships, eliminating queue times and wait times (delays), and optimizing the individual process cycle times

- *Customer delivery times* by reducing the internal lead times and optimizing shipping and distribution channels

Appreciation of True Assets of the Organization

> *Lean is about people, not techniques.*
>
> —Adil Dalal, "Keep It Simple"

Developing the assets for competitive impact requires both employee involvement and employee empowerment.

Employee involvement is achieved by getting individuals engaged in activities like kaizen, 5S, and brainstorming. The goal of involvement is to improve productivity, quality, cost, delivery time, safety, the environment, and morale (PQCDSM) (Dennis 2007, 110).

People are the prime appreciating asset in any organization (Dalal 2011). Some companies use this notion as a slogan, but only a few lean organizations truly believe it. Employee empowerment is achieved by getting individuals engaged in decision making. To help employees become capable of making good business decisions, it is critical to invest in training and development, creating a fear-free and stress-free environment. When we invest in employees—that is, provide the right environment for growth, free of stress and external pressures—they are able to provide results far better than we could ever imagine. People who are highly motivated tap into the core of their creativity and achieve results beyond their wildest dreams (Dalal 2011).

Toyota is one of the leading lean organizations that not only believe this to be true but also act on their beliefs. Teruyuki Minoura, managing director of global purchasing at Toyota, emphasizes that "developing people is the starting point for monozukuri at Toyota. There can be no successful monozukuri (making things) without hitozukuri (making people)" (Toyota, n.d.).

Business Profitability

> *Profit in business comes from repeat customers,*
> *customers that boast about your project or service,*
> *and that bring friends with them.*
>
> —W. Edwards Deming

Since customer loyalty and repeat orders are directly proportional to business profits, another significant benefit of lean is the positive cash flow generated due to the financial impact of lean initiatives undertaken by the corporation.

4.3.5

A core element of lean is a just-in-time (JIT) system, which ensures flexible responsiveness. The production strategy of JIT strives to improve a business's return on investment by reducing in-process inventory and associated carrying costs. A JIT system operates according to a pull system, takt time, and one-piece flow, which allows for a defect-free, timely response to customer demand.

Increasing market share can be one of the most important objectives of a business. The main advantage of using market share as a measure of business performance is that it allows a better understanding of competitive advantage irrespective of variables such as the state of the economy or changes in tax policy. Lean companies stand a better chance of getting a bigger market share, which is defined as the total available market or market segment serviced by a company.

In *Lean Thinking*, James Womack and Daniel Jones (2003, 144) provide some great case studies of corporations like Wiremold and Lantech that demonstrate the impact of lean technology on business profits.

How can corporations gauge their competitiveness?

One of the tools lean corporations use to improve their products and services is benchmarking. Benchmarking helps a company measure the impact of competition. Internal and strategic benchmarking, as well as generic cross-industry studies, enable lean companies to gauge the competition. Benchmarking gives companies more opportunities to provide value to their customers. The reason for this is that lean focuses on value from a customer's point of view.

Thus, lean provides a significant competitive advantage to the operations, has a direct impact on competitiveness in this increasingly global market and on customer satisfaction, and provides opportunities for organizations to create "customers for life" (Womack and Jones 2003, 235).

4.3.5.1. Customer Satisfaction

If you work just for money, you'll never make it, but if you love what you're doing and you always put the customer first, success will be yours.

—Ray Kroc, *McDonald's*

Customer satisfaction as a key lean-related measure helps us circle back to the original premise of delivering value from the customer's point of view. There are several measures and methods of determining customer satisfaction (or dissatisfaction) beyond those already discussed in Section 4.3 (quality, lead time, delivery, etc.):

- Voice of the Customer (VOC)—listening to your customers to help improve your processes, creating new or innovative products or services based on their input, and focusing on what is important to them is a key element of customer satisfaction.

- Benchmarking—finding world-class organizations in areas where your organization would benefit and then learning from those companies to improve your systems. "Benchmarking is a waste of time for managers that understand lean thinking. Lean benchmarkers who discover their performance is superior to their competitors' have a natural tendency to relax" (Womack and Jones 2003, 48).

- Surveys—creating, sending, and analyzing periodic customer satisfaction surveys is a common way to receive feedback. However, the response rate is low, and the delay in sending and receiving the surveys may render some of the information useless.

  - After-use surveys—send surveys after the use of the product or service to obtain specific feedback. This is now common on websites, and customers can give a rating and write a review.

- Repeat orders—receiving a repeat order from a customer is a sign that you have probably met their most basic needs. If they become an advocate for your product or service, you should find out what it is that you are doing well and parlay that to other customers.

- Recommendations, endorsements, awards or kudos—tracking positive press about your organization may give an indication of customer satisfaction.

- Complaints—this can include the number, size or impact, dollar value, and so on. Complaints are obviously after-the-fact, but it is the successful resolution that can make all the difference to your customer.

Not Understanding the Customer's Point of View

There are times organizations do what they want without regard to the impact on the customer. Consider a company whose automated menu takes several minutes to navigate and doesn't even have the choice that the customer wants. Having this automated service may simplify things for the company, but it can frustrate or even lose a customer. Another example is the company that tries to direct the customer to its website to complete the transaction instead of tying up a customer service representative. This may work fine, but if the company's website is unclear or difficult to navigate, then once again it's lost a customer.

Caveat of Measures

Using these key measures for *improvement* is what this is about, not the measures themselves. For example, in the course of getting your car repaired, the dealer mentions that you will receive a survey in a few days and asks you to put down all "10s." Of course, the dealer wants the highest score possible, but by finagling the system it is not receiving correct feedback. "It's a lot easier to fix the score, than fix the store" (Womack 2011, 118).

I once saw floor personnel at a hospital wearing pins that said "Ask me about a 10." So I had to ask what that meant. It was explained to me that the patient survey scores had been low lately, and the personnel wanted the patients to give them better scores. I asked if this was used to improve either their process or the patient's satisfaction. The answer I received was, "Neither, but it will help the executives get their bonuses if the scores increase."

New Frontiers—Social Media

Social media is a great way to find, solicit, and gain feedback about your product or service. This is a newcomer to the game compared to other traditional methods like surveys. Monitoring Facebook, Twitter, or blog comments can give the company valuable feedback on its products or services. In fact, this can be much closer to real-time feedback than traditional surveys. As people become savvier with social media outlets like Twitter, they can instantly report a great experience to their potentially thousands of followers.

REFERENCES

Dalal, Adil. 2011. *The 12 Pillars of Project Excellence: A Lean Approach to Improving Project Results.* Boca Raton, FL: CRC Press.

Dennis, Pascal. 2007. *Lean Production Simplified: A Plain-Language Guide to the World's Most Powerful Production System.* 2nd ed. New York: Productivity Press.

Friedman, Thomas. 2005. *The World Is Flat: A Brief History of the Twenty-First Century.* New York: Farrar, Straus and Giroux.

Krueger, Kaye. 2004. "Value-Added vs. Non-Value-Added Activities." http://www.wisc-online.com/Objects/ViewObject.aspx?ID=eng11104.

Liker, Jeffery. 2004. *The Toyota Way: 14 Management Principles from the World's Greatest Manufacturer.* New York: McGraw-Hill.

Marchwinski, Chet, and John Shook. 2006. *Lean Lexicon.* 3rd ed. Version 3.0. Cambridge, MA: Lean Enterprise Institute.

Rother, Mike, and John Shook. 2009. *Learning to See.* Version 1.4. Cambridge, MA: Lean Enterprise Institute.

Toyota. n.d. "The Toyota Production System." http://www.toyotageorgetown.com/tps.asp.

Womack, James P. 2011. *Gemba Walks.* Cambridge, MA: Lean Enterprise Institute.

Womack, James P., and Daniel T. Jones. 2003. *Lean Thinking: Banish Waste and Create Wealth in Your Corporation.* 2nd ed. New York: Free Press.

Appendix A
Lean Certification Body of Knowledge

Appendix A

LEAN CERTIFICATION
BODY OF KNOWLEDGE RUBRIC VERSION 3.0

	WEIGHTINGS PER EXAM		
	Lean Bronze (tactical)	Lean Silver (integrative)	Lean Gold (strategic)
MODULE 1			
1. Cultural Enablers	15%	20%	25%
1.1. Principles of Cultural Enablers	3%	4%	5%
1.1.1. Respect for the individual			
1.1.2. Humility			
1.2. Processes for Cultural Enablers	4%	8%	12%
1.2.1. Planning & Deployment			
1.2.2. Create a sense of urgency			
1.2.3. Modeling the lean principles, values, philosophies			
1.2.4. Message Deployment — Establishing vision and direction			
1.2.5. Integrating Learning and Coaching			
1.2.6. People development — Education, training & coaching			
1.2.7. Motivation, Empowerment & Involvement			
1.2.8. Environmental Systems			
1.2.9. Safety Systems			
1.3. Cultural Enabler Techniques and Practices	8%	8%	8%
1.3.1. Cross Training			
1.3.2. Skills Assessment			
1.3.3. Instructional Goals			
1.3.4. On-the-Job Training			
1.3.5. Coaching & Mentoring			
1.3.6. Leadership Development			
1.3.7. Teamwork			
1.3.8. Information Sharing (Yokoten)			
1.3.9. Suggestion Systems			
MODULE 2			
2. Continuous Process Improvement	60%	30%	15%
2.1. Principles of Continuous Process Improvement	15%	10%	6%
2.1.1. Process Focus			
2.1.2. Identification & Elimination of Barriers to flow			
2.1.2.1. Flow & the Economies of Flow			
2.1.2.2. 7 Wastes (Muda), Fluctuation (Mura), and Overburden (Muri)			
2.1.2.3. Connect & Align Value added work fragments			
2.1.2.4. Organize around flow			
2.1.2.5. Make end-to-end flow visible			
2.1.2.6. Manage the flow visually			
2.1.3. Match rate of production to level of customer demand — Just-in-Time			
2.1.4. Scientific thinking			
2.1.4.1. Stability			
2.1.4.2. Standardization			
2.1.4.3. Recognize Abnormality			
2.1.4.4. Go and See			
2.1.5. Jidoka			
2.1.5.1. Quality at the source			
2.1.5.2. No defects passed forward			

	WEIGHTINGS PER EXAM		
	Lean Bronze (tactical)	Lean Silver (integrative)	Lean Gold (strategic)
2.1.5.3. Separate man from machine			
2.1.5.4. Multi-process handling			
2.1.5.5. Self detection of errors to prevent defects			
2.1.5.6. Stop and Fix			
2.1.6. Integrate Improvement with Work			
2.1.7. Seek Perfection			
2.1.7.1. Incremental continuous improvement (Kaizen)			
2.1.7.2. Breakthrough continuous improvement (Kaikaku)			
2.2. Continuous Process Improvement Systems	**20%**	**10%**	**7%**
2.2.1. Visual Workplace			
2.2.1.1. 5S standards and discipline			
2.2.2. Lot size reduction			
2.2.3. Load leveling			
2.2.4. 3P Production Process Preparation			
2.2.5. Total Productive Maintenance (including predictive)			
2.2.6. Standard Work			
2.2.7. Built-in feedback			
2.2.8. Strategic Business Assessment			
2.2.9. Continuous Improvement Process Methodology			
2.2.9.1. PDCA			
2.2.9.2. DMAIC			
2.2.9.3 Problem Solving Storyboards			
2.2.10 Quality Systems			
2.2.10.1 ISO and Other standards			
2.2.11 Corrective Action System			
2.2.11.1. Root Cause analysis			
2.2.12. Project Management			
2.2.13 Process design			
2.2.14 Pull System			
2.2.15 Knowledge Transfer			
2.3. Continuous Process Improvement Techniques & Practices	**25%**	**10%**	**2%**
2.3.1. Work Flow Analysis			
2.3.1.1. Flowcharting			
2.3.1.2. Flow Analysis Charts			
2.3.1.3. Value Stream Mapping			
2.3.1.4. Takt Time Analysis			
2.3.2. Data Collection and Presentation			
2.3.2.1. Histograms			
2.3.2.2. Pareto Charts			
2.3.2.3. Check Sheets			
2.3.3. Identify Root Cause			
2.3.3.1. Cause & Effect diagrams (Fishbone)			
2.3.3.2. 5-Whys			
2.3.3.3. Failure Mode and Effects Analysis			
2.3.4. Presenting Variation Data			
2.3.4.1. Statistical Process Control Charts			
2.3.4.2. Scatter and Concentration Diagrams			
2.3.5. Product and Service Design			
2.3.5.1. Concurrent Engineering			

	WEIGHTINGS PER EXAM		
	Lean Bronze (tactical)	Lean Silver (integrative)	Lean Gold (strategic)
2.3.5.2. Quality Function Deployment			
2.3.5.3. Product or Process Benchmarking			
2.3.5.4. Design for Product Life Cycle (DFx) — cradle to cradle			
2.3.5.5. Variety Reduction — product and component			
2.3.5.6. Design for Manufacturability			
2.3.6. Organizing for Improvement			
2.3.6.1. Kaizen Blitz Events			
2.3.7. Countermeasure Activities			
2.3.7.1. Mistake and Error Proofing (Poka Yoke)			
2.3.7.2. Quick Changeover/Setup Reduction (SMED)			
2.3.7.3. One Piece Flow			
2.3.7.4. Right sized equipment			
2.3.7.5. Cellular Flow			
2.3.7.6. Sensible Automation			
2.3.7.7. Material Signals (Kanban)			
2.3.7.8. Source Inspection			
2.3.8. Supply Processes External			
2.3.8.1. Supplier managed inventory			
2.3.8.2. Cross-docking			
2.3.8.3. Supplier Assessment and Feedback			
2.3.8.4. Supplier Development			
2.3.8.5. Supplier Benchmarking			
2.3.8.6. Logistics			
2.3.9. Supply Processes Internal			
2.3.9.1. Material Handling			
2.3.9.2. Warehousing			
2.3.9.3. Planning and Scheduling			
MODULE 3			
3. Consistent Lean Enterprise Culture	10%	20%	30%
3.1. Principles of Consistent Lean Enterprise Culture	5%	7%	11%
3.1.1. Systemic Thinking			
3.1.1.1. Part-whole relationships are clear and explicit through holistic thinking			
3.1.1.2. The organization evolves as necessary to accommodate future conditions through dynamic thinking			
3.1.1.3. Closed-loop thinking to assure effective feedback of organizational learning			
3.1.2. Constancy of Purpose			
3.1.2.1. Focus on Results			
3.1.2.2. Focus on Waste Elimination			
3.1.2.3 Focus on Value to customer			
3.1.3. Social Responsibility			
3.2. Processes for Developing Consistent Lean Enterprise Culture	3%	6%	11%
3.2.1. Enterprise Thinking			
3.2.1.1. Organize around flow			
3.2.1.2. Integrated business system and improvement system			
3.2.1.3. Reconcile reporting systems			
3.2.1.4. Information management			
3.2.2. Policy Deployment/Strategy Deployment			

	WEIGHTINGS PER EXAM		
	Lean Bronze (tactical)	Lean Silver (integrative)	Lean Gold (strategic)
3.2.2.1. Scientific thinking as a strategy process			
3.2.2.2. Series of nested experiments			
3.2.2.3. Dynamic give and take			
3.2.2.4. Forming consensus			
3.2.2.5. Align strategies and execution			
3.2.2.6. Standard work for strategy communication — how we think and talk			
3.2.2.7. Resource deployment and allocation			
3.3. Consistent Enterprise Culture Techniques & Practices	**2%**	**7%**	**8%**
3.3.1. A3			
3.3.2. Catchball			
3.3.3. Redeployment of Resources			
MODULE 4			
4. Business Results	**15%**	**30%**	**30%**
4.1. Principles of Business Results	**4%**	**10%**	**12%**
4.1.1. Create Value first to drive performance			
4.1.1.1. Measure what matters to the customer			
4.1.1.2. Measure normal versus abnormal conditions — (triggers response)			
4.1.1.3. Guidelines for Measurement Categories			
* Customer demand and characteristics			
* Customer retention			
* Waste			
* People Development Measures			
* Quality			
* Cost and Productivity			
* Competitive Impact			
4.2. Measurement Systems	**3%**	**10%**	**12%**
4.2.1. Measurement			
4.2.1.1 Understand interdependencies between measures and measurement categories			
4.2.1.2 Align internal measures with what matters to customers			
4.2.1.3 Measure the results from the 'whole' system			
4.2.1.4 Measure flow and waste			
4.2.1.5 Lean Accounting			
4.2.1.6. Voice of the Customer			
4.2.2. Goal and Objective Setting			
4.2.2.1. SMART (Specific, Measurable, Achievable, Realistic, Timely)			
4.2.2.2. Tied to the customer			
4.2.3. Analysis — Understand what moves the dial on measures			
4.2.4. Reporting			
4.2.4.1. Visible feedback real-time			
4.3. Key Lean Related Measures	**8%**	**10%**	**6%**
4.3.1. Quality			
4.3.1.1. Rework			
4.3.1.2. First Pass Yield			
4.3.2. Delivery			
4.3.2.1 Takt Time			
4.3.2.2 Cycle Time			

	WEIGHTINGS PER EXAM		
	Lean Bronze (tactical)	Lean Silver (integrative)	Lean Gold (strategic)
4.3.2.3 Lead Time			
4.3.3 Cost			
4.3.3.1 Inventory turns			
4.3.3.2 Queue time			
4.3.3.3 Wait time (delays)			
4.3.3.4 Overall Equipment Effectiveness (OEE)			
4.3.3.5 Changeover Time			
4.3.4 Financial Impact			
4.3.4.1. Cash Flow			
4.3.5 Competitive Impact			
4.3.5.1. Customer Satisfaction			

Appendix B

Recommended Reading for Lean Certification Exam Preparation

These are the core reference materials upon which the exams for Lean Certification are based. The exam is an open-book format. You may bring the exam reading books with you when you take your test.

LEAN KNOWLEDGE CERTIFICATE & LEAN BRONZE CERTIFICATION RECOMMENDED READING

Dennis, Pascal. 2007. *Lean Production Simplified: A Plain-Language Guide to the World's Most Powerful Production System.* 2nd ed. New York: Productivity Press, ISBN: 9781563273568 (The first edition of *Lean Production Simplified*, ISBN: 1563272628 is also acceptable).

Graban, Mark. 2009. *Lean Hospitals: Improving Quality, Patient Safety, and Employee Satisfaction.* Boca Raton, FL: CRC Press, ISBN: 9781420083804.

Imai, Masaaki. 1997. *Gemba Kaizen: A Commonsense, Low-Cost Approach to Management.* New York: McGraw-Hill, ISBN: 0070314462.

Rother, Mike, and John Shook. 2003. *Learning to See: Value Stream Mapping to Create Value and Eliminate Muda.* Cambridge, MA: Lean Enterprise Institute, ISBN: 0966784308.

Womack, James P., and Daniel T. Jones. 2003. *Lean Thinking: Banish Waste and Create Wealth in Your Corporation.* 2nd ed. New York: Free Press, ISBN: 0743249275.

LEAN SILVER CERTIFICATION RECOMMENDED READING

Fiume, Orest J., and Jean E. Cunningham. 2003. *Real Numbers: Management Accounting in a Lean Organization.* Durham, NC: Managing Times Press, ISBN: 0972809902.

Lareau, William. 2002. *Office Kaizen: Transforming Office Operations into a Strategic Competitive Advantage.* Milwaukee, WI: ASQ Quality Press, ISBN: 0873895568.

Liker, Jeffrey. 2003. *The Toyota Way: 14 Management Principles from the World's Greatest Manufacturer.* New York: McGraw-Hill, ISBN: 0071392319.

Mascitelli, Ronald. 2004. *The Lean Design Guidebook: Everything Your Product Development Team Needs to Slash Manufacturing Costs.* Northridge, CA: Technology Perspectives, ISBN: 0966269721.

Version 4.0, May 2011.

Maskell, Brian H., and Bruce Baggaley. 2003. *Practical Lean Accounting: A Proven System for Measuring and Managing the Lean Enterprise* [Book and CD ROM]. New York: Productivity Press, ISBN: 1563272431.

Ohno, Taiichi. 1988. *Toyota Production System: Beyond Large-Scale Production*. Cambridge, MA: Productivity Press, ISBN: 0915299143.

LEAN GOLD CERTIFICATION RECOMMENDED READING

Ford, Henry. 1988. *Today & Tomorrow*. Cambridge, MA: Productivity Press, Reprinted June 1988, ISBN: 0915299364.

Hawken, Paul, Amory Lovins, and L. Hunter Lovins. 2000. *Natural Capitalism: Creating the Next Industrial Revolution*. Back Bay Books, ISBN: 0316353000.

Henderson, Bruce A., and Jorge L. Larco. 1999. *Lean Transformation: How to Change Your Business into a Lean Enterprise*. Richmond, VA: Oaklea Publishing, ISBN: 0964660121.

Mann, David. 2005. *Creating a Lean Culture: Tools to Sustain Lean Conversions*. New York: Productivity Press, ISBN: 563273225.

Womack, James P., and Daniel T. Jones. 2005. *Lean Solutions: How Companies and Customers Can Create Value and Wealth Together*. New York: Free Press, ISBN: 0743277783.

Appendix C

Lean Glossary of Terms

Lean is the foundation of a high-performance enterprise. In the simplest of terms, lean is the elimination of waste, and it is one of the biggest opportunities for improvement. The following glossary of terms will assist the reader in understanding lean concepts.

5S—Five Japanese words that begin with the letter "S" and translate to English as *Seiri* = Sort, *Seiton* = Set in order, *Seiso* = Shine, *Seiketsu* = Standardize, *Shitsuke* = Sustain. Collectively, they mean maintaining an orderly, well-inspected, clean, and efficient working environment.

5-Whys—A simple principle of determining the root cause of a problem by asking "why" after each scenario to drive deeper and into more detail to get to the root cause of an issue.

7 Wastes—Taiichi Ohno's original enumeration of the seven wastes:

1. Overproduction
2. Time on hand (waiting)
3. Transportation
4. Processing itself (overprocessing)
5. Stock on hand (inventory)
6. Movement
7. Making defective product

An eighth waste often added is waste of human potential or underutilized people.

andon—A Japanese word meaning "light" or "lantern." An andon is a light triggered by an abnormal condition or machine breakdown. It is a form of communication indicating that human intervention is required. It often resembles a stoplight (red = stop, yellow = caution, green = go). Another type is the andon cord, where an operator pulls a cord to notify management of an abnormal situation.

andon board—A visual control device in a production area, typically a lighted overhead display, indicating the current status of the production system and alerting team members to emerging problems, for example, "takt" awareness displays.

A3—International sized paper (11 × 17 inches) that has a visual, concise description, or a report for use with problem solving, status updates, and proposals. It is read from top to bottom, left to right, and tells a story. The author takes ownership of the issue and uses this format to gather current information, analyze it, create a target condition, plan, and follow up with metrics to create a solid solution to a problem that builds buy-in from the stakeholders. A3 follows the Plan-Do-Check-Act methodology.

autonomation (jidoka)—Combining human intelligence with automation so that equipment is able to detect defects, alert personnel of the abnormality, and immediately stop production.

balanced line—See **line balancing**.

batch-and-queue—Producing more than one piece and then moving the pieces to the next operation before they are needed—the opposite of single-piece or one-piece flow.

bottleneck—Any resource whose capacity is less than the demand placed on it.

cell—The layout of machines of different types for performing different operations in a tight sequence, typically in a U-shaped pattern. Cellular production permits single-piece flow, line balancing, and flexible deployment of human effort by means of linked multi-machines working efficiently based on takt time. Cell operators (who are cross trained) may handle multiple processes, and the number of operators changes when the customer demand rate changes.

change agent—The catalytic champion who moves firms and value streams from batch-and-queue manufacturing to flow manufacturing.

changeover—Assigning a production device to perform a different operation or setting up a machine to make a different part number than the previous part. Examples include installation of a new type of tool in a metal working machine, a different paint in a painting system, a new plastic resin and a new mold in an injection molding machine, new software in a computer, and so on. In service, it applies to converting from performing one service to performing a different service.

changeover time—The time required to modify a system or workstation, usually includes both teardown time for the existing condition and setup time for the new condition. Also, the time from the last good piece of the current run to the first good piece of the next run.

constraint—Anything that limits a system from achieving higher performance, or throughput. Alternate definition: the bottleneck that most severely limits the organization's ability to achieve higher performance relative to its purpose/goal.

continuous flow—A production system in which products flow continuously rather than being separated into lots or batches. No work-in-process is built up. In the purest form, each step completes its task just as the following process step needs the item and the lot size is one. Also known as "one-piece flow," "make one, move one," and "one by one flow."

continuous improvement—A philosophy of making frequent and small changes to processes, the cumulative results of which lead to high levels of quality, cost, and efficiency and include ongoing actions to find ways to improve processes, decrease variation, decrease cycle time, and improve effectiveness of the organization.

countermeasure—Corrective action taken to address abnormalities or problems that cannot be eliminated immediately. Countermeasures are put in place to protect the process from the problem. They are considered temporary fixes until solutions to completely eliminate the problem are implemented. They are sometimes referred to as a "target condition" or "future state."

cycle—(1) A sequence of operations repeated regularly. (2) The time necessary for one sequence of operations to occur.

cycle time—(1) The time required to complete one cycle of an operation. If cycle time for every operation in a complete process can be reduced to equal takt time, products can be made in single-piece flow. (2) The time elapsing between a particular point in one cycle and the same point in the next cycle.

equipment availability—The percentage of time a process (or equipment) is available to run. This is sometimes called "uptime."

error detection—A hybrid form of error-proofing. It means that a bad part can be made, but it will be caught immediately and corrective action will be taken to avoid another bad part from being produced. A device is put in place that detects when a bad part is made and then stops the process. This is used when error-proofing is too expensive or not easily implemented.

error-proofing—See **poka-yoke**.

external setup—Procedures that can be performed while a machine is running.

FIFO—"First-in, first-out," meaning that material produced by one process is consumed in the same order by the next process. A FIFO queue is filled by the supplying process and emptied by the customer process; when a FIFO lane fills up, production is stopped until the next (internal) customer uses up some of that inventory.

First pass yield (FPY)—Also referred to as "quality rate." The percentage of units that complete a process and meet quality guidelines without being scrapped, rerun, retested, reworked, returned, or diverted into an off-line repair area. FPY is calculated by subtracting the defective units from the units entering the process and dividing by the total number of units entering the process.

flow—The accomplishment of steps within a value stream so that a product or service proceeds from the beginning of the value stream to the customer without waste. Also known as "flow production."

gemba—A Japanese term that translates to "real place," as in where the action is; in lean it is where value-adding occurs. It has been adapted to mean the workplace, or the shop floor in manufacturing. Often used as a phrase—"go to the gemba," meaning when an abnormality occurs, management should go to the place where the abnormality occurred and gather information for corrective action.

gemba walk—A learning and coaching moment between a lean sensei and a student to look for abnormal conditions, waste, or opportunities for improvement.

hansei—A Japanese term that means one's honest reflection, as in reviewing an event to capture lessons learned and see how to improve.

heijunka—A method of leveling production for mix and volume.

hoshin kanri—A strategic decision-making tool for the selection of initiatives, projects, and tasks to achieve breakthrough goals. This method aligns and designates people and resources for completion, and establishes metrics to track progress and verify sustainment. Also called "policy deployment."

information flow—The task of disseminating information for taking a specific product from order entry through scheduling to delivery. See also **value stream**.

inspection—Comparing product or component against specifications to determine whether the product or component meets requirements.

internal setup—Procedures that must be performed while the machine is stopped.

inventory—The money the firm has invested in purchasing things it intends to sell (raw materials, buffer stock, work-in-process, safety stock, and finished goods).

jidoka—A device that stops production and/or equipment when an abnormal or defective condition arises. Any necessary improvements can be made by directing attention to the stopped equipment and the worker who stopped the operation. The jidoka system has faith in the worker as a thinker and gives all workers the right to stop the line on which they are working. Also called "autonomation."

just-in-time (JIT)—A philosophy that has the elimination of waste as its ultimate objective. To achieve this goal, each operation must be synchronized with subsequent operations. The concept refers to the manufacturing and conveyance of only what is needed, when it is needed, and in the amount needed. Originally developed by the Toyota Motor Company as a production system, it is also known as the "Toyota Production System," "lean manufacturing," and "lean production system."

kaikaku—Typically translated as "innovation," is also described as "radical improvement," "major process redesign," and "reformation." Kaikaku changes may include major redesigns of product, part manufacture, or facility layout or business processes. Due to their inherent magnitude of change, kaikaku innovations require radical thinking, more time to implement, extensive planning and coordination, time commitment of people supporting, and (often) significant financial investment. Kaikaku is often associated with revolutionary change, as opposed to kaizen, which is associated with evolutionary change.

kaizen—A Japanese word or term meaning "change for the better" or "continuous improvement." Continuous, incremental improvement of an activity to create more value with less waste. Many Japanese facilities view kaizen as the process of continually making incremental changes and not as a single, separate event. Kaizen also strives to ensure quality and safety. A true kaizen environment promotes continuous improvement by everyone, every day. Kaizen is often associated with evolutionary change, as opposed to kaikaku, which is associated with revolutionary change.

kaizen event—A short, focused team-based improvement project that achieves breakthrough results. Also called "kaizen blitz," "rapid kaizen," "quick kaizen," and "kaikaku."

kanban—Meaning "sign board." A communication tool (e.g., open space, two-bin, and kanban cards) that ensures that every operation produces only the amount that will be used in the next step of the process. Kanban serves as instruction for both production and replenishment.

leader standard work—Work that provides a structure and routine for process management, specifically for core tasks and routines of leaders and management.

lead time—(1) The time required for one piece to move all the way through a system of processes, from start to finish. (2) The time from when the order is taken until the item is shipped.

lean—A systematic approach to identifying and eliminating waste (non-value-added activities) through continuous improvement by flowing the product at the pull of the customer in pursuit of perfection.

Lean Champion—Subject matter expert in the tools of lean typically chosen to lead lean training, lean projects, and the lean transformation.

lean enterprise—Any organization that continually strives to eliminate waste, reduce costs, and improve quality, on-time delivery, and service levels.

lean production—The opposite of mass production.

line balancing—A process in which work elements are evenly distributed and staffing is balanced to meet takt time.

load leveling—A technique for balancing product mix and volume to capacity available.

manufacturing resource planning (MRP II)—Uses the elements of material requirements planning (MRP) plus capacity planning and a finance interface to translate operations planning into financial terms; also a simulation tool to assess alternate production plans.

mass production—Large-scale manufacturing with high-volume production and output; implies traditional methods (even pre-computer-era methods), with departmentalized operation and reliance on "economies of scale" to achieve low per-unit costs.

material requirements planning (MRP)—A computerized system typically used to determine the quantity and timing requirements for production and delivery of items (for both customers and suppliers). Using MRP to schedule production at various processes will result in "push" production, since any predetermined schedule is only an estimate of what the next process will actually need.

milk run—The routing of supply and/or delivery vehicles to make multiple pickups and/or deliveries at multiple locations to reduce transportation waste.

mistake-proofing—See **poka-yoke**.

muda—A Japanese term translated as "waste." Elements that do not add value to the product or service.

mura—A Japanese term meaning "irregularity" or "variability," "unevenness."

muri—A Japanese term meaning "strain," either physical or mental, or "overburden."

non-value-added—Activities or actions taken that add no real value to the product or service, making such activities or actions a form of waste. See also **value-added**.

one-piece flow—One work piece flows from process to process in order to minimize muda in a just-in-time production system.

overall equipment effectiveness (OEE)—The product of a machine's operational availability, performance efficiency, and first pass yield. See also **total productive maintenance**.

point-of-use storage (POUS)—Storing information, items, materials, parts, and tools near where they are used.

poka-yoke—Also known as "mistake-proofing." In Japanese, *poka* means "inadvertent error," and *yoke* means "prevention." The implementation of simple, low-cost devices or innovations that can either detect abnormal situations before they occur in a process or, if they do occur, stop the operation or equipment and prevent the production of defective units.

product family—A group of related products or services that can be produced or performed using like and/or similar processes interchangeably.

production (analysis) board—A board located at the job site on which hourly production targets are recorded along with the actual production achieved. A production board is a good example of visual management. Also known as "60-minute board."

production leveling—See **load leveling**.

production smoothing—See **load leveling**.

productivity—A measurement of output for a given amount of input(s). Increases in productivity are considered critical to raising living standards.

pull—A system of cascading production and delivery instructions from downstream to upstream activities in which the upstream supplier does not produce until the downstream customer signals a need. The opposite of push. Also known as "pull production."

push—A system of production in which the upstream supplier produces as much as it can without regard to the actual demand of the downstream processes and sends it to the downstream processes whether they need it or not. The opposite of pull. Also known as "push production."

queue time—The amount of time a product or customer (in service) spends in line awaiting the next process step.

quick changeover—The ability to change dies, tooling, and fixtures rapidly (usually in minutes) so that smaller batch sizes can be produced effectively.

right-size—Matching tooling, manpower, and equipment to the job and space requirements of lean production; it is different from "down-size."

runner—A person on the production floor who paces the entire value stream from the pickup and delivery of materials to kanban utilization. Also known as a "material handler" or a "water spider."

shadow board—A board painted to indicate which tool belongs where and which tools are missing. A visual management tool.

single minute exchange of dies (SMED)—A series of techniques pioneered by Shigeo Shingo for changeovers of production machinery in less than 10 minutes. The long-term objective is always zero setup, in which changeovers are instantaneous and do not interfere in any way with continuous flow. (SMED = Changing dies in a single digit, meaning nine minutes or less, rather than a single minute).

single-piece flow—Products proceed, one complete unit at a time, through various operations in design, order-taking, and production, without interruptions, backflows, or scrap. In lean manufacturing, this is the antithesis of batch-and-queue production.

spaghetti diagram—A drawing that shows the layout and flow of materials, information, and people in a work area and is commonly used to uncover motion and transportation wastes.

standardization—A system of using policies and common procedures to manage processes.

standard work—A precise description of each work activity specifying cycle time, takt time, the work sequence of specific tasks, and the minimum inventory of parts on hand needed to conduct the activity. All jobs are organized around human motion to create an efficient sequence without waste.

supermarket—The storage locations of the parts before they go on to the next operation. They are managed by predetermined maximum and minimum (or order point and order quantity) inventory levels.

takt time—The available production time divided by the rate of customer demand. The heartbeat of any lean system, takt time sets the pace of production to match the rate of customer demand.

theory of constraints—A management philosophy that stresses removal of constraints to increase throughput while decreasing inventory and operating expenses.

throughput—The rate the system generates money through sales (or the conversion rate of inventory into shipped product).

total productive maintenance (TPM)—A system to ensure that every machine in a production process is able to perform its required tasks so that production is never interrupted. Uptime is maximized, along with machine performance and first pass yield. See also **overall equipment effectiveness**.

value—A capability provided to a customer at the right time at an appropriate price, as defined in each case by the customer.

value-added—Activities or actions taken that add real value to the product or service. See also **non-value-added**.

value stream—The set of actions required to take a specific product from raw material to finished good per customer demand, concentrating on information management and physical transformation tasks.

value stream mapping—The process of creating a drawing of the value stream using icons that show the information flow and material flow of a process family (similar processing steps) in an organization.

visual management—The placement in plain view of all tools, parts, production activities, and indicators of production system performance so that everyone involved can understand the status of the system at a glance. This is a concept whereby managers can tell immediately whether production activities are proceeding normally. Lines, signs and labels, andons, kanbans, production boards, painted floor, and shadow boards are typical visual control tools.

waste—Any activity that consumes resources but creates no value. Any activity that uses equipment, materials, parts, space, employee time, or other corporate resources beyond the minimum amount required for value-added operations and for which the customer is unwilling to pay. See **muda**.

work-in-process (WIP)—Incomplete products or services that are awaiting further processing prior to being forwarded to the customer as finished product or completed services.

Index

Page numbers followed by *f* or *t* refer to figures or tables, respectively.

Q

Belong to the Quality Community!

Established in 1946, ASQ is a global community of quality experts in all fields and industries. ASQ is dedicated to the promotion and advancement of quality tools, principles, and practices in the workplace and in the community.

The Society also serves as an advocate for quality. Its members have informed and advised the U.S. Congress, government agencies, state legislatures, and other groups and individuals worldwide on quality-related topics.

Vision

By making quality a global priority, an organizational imperative, and a personal ethic, ASQ becomes the community of choice for everyone who seeks quality technology, concepts, or tools to improve themselves and their world.

ASQ is...

- More than 90,000 individuals and 700 companies in more than 100 countries

- The world's largest organization dedicated to promoting quality

- A community of professionals striving to bring quality to their work and their lives

- The administrator of the Malcolm Baldrige National Quality Award

- A supporter of quality in all sectors including manufacturing, service, healthcare, government, and education

- YOU

Visit www.asq.org for more information.

ASQ Membership

Research shows that people who join associations experience increased job satisfaction, earn more, and are generally happier*. ASQ membership can help you achieve this while providing the tools you need to be successful in your industry and to distinguish yourself from your competition. So why wouldn't you want to be a part of ASQ?

Networking

Have the opportunity to meet, communicate, and collaborate with your peers within the quality community through conferences and local ASQ section meetings, ASQ forums or divisions, ASQ Communities of Quality discussion boards, and more.

Professional Development

Access a wide variety of professional development tools such as books, training, and certifications at a discounted price. Also, ASQ certifications and the ASQ Career Center help enhance your quality knowledge and take your career to the next level.

Solutions

Find answers to all your quality problems, big and small, with ASQ's Knowledge Center, mentoring program, various e-newsletters, *Quality Progress* magazine, and industry-specific products.

Access to Information

Learn classic and current quality principles and theories in ASQ's Quality Information Center (QIC), *ASQ Weekly* e-newsletter, and product offerings.

Advocacy Programs

ASQ helps create a better community, government, and world through initiatives that include social responsibility, Washington advocacy, and Community Good Works.

Visit www.asq.org/membership for more information on ASQ membership.

*2008, The William E. Smith Institute for Association Research

ASQ Certification

ASQ certification is formal recognition by ASQ that an individual has demonstrated a proficiency within, and comprehension of, a specified body of knowledge at a point in time. Nearly 150,000 certifications have been issued. ASQ has members in more than 100 countries, in all industries, and in all cultures. ASQ certification is internationally accepted and recognized.

Benefits to the Individual

- New skills gained and proficiency upgraded
- Investment in your career
- Mark of technical excellence
- Assurance that you are current with emerging technologies
- Discriminator in the marketplace
- Certified professionals earn more than their uncertified counterparts
- Certification is endorsed by more than 125 companies

Benefits to the Organization

- Investment in the company's future
- Certified individuals can perfect and share new techniques in the workplace
- Certified staff are knowledgeable and able to assure product and service quality

Quality is a global concept. It spans borders, cultures, and languages. No matter what country your customers live in or what language they speak, they demand quality products and services. You and your organization also benefit from quality tools and practices. Acquire the knowledge to position yourself and your organization ahead of your competition.

Certifications Include

- Biomedical Auditor – CBA
- Calibration Technician – CCT
- HACCP Auditor – CHA
- Pharmaceutical GMP Professional – CPGP
- Quality Inspector – CQI
- Quality Auditor – CQA
- Quality Engineer – CQE
- Quality Improvement Associate – CQIA
- Quality Technician – CQT
- Quality Process Analyst – CQPA
- Reliability Engineer – CRE
- Six Sigma Black Belt – CSSBB
- Six Sigma Green Belt – CSSGB
- Software Quality Engineer – CSQE
- Manager of Quality/Organizational Excellence – CMQ/OE

Visit www.asq.org/certification to apply today!

ASQ Training

Classroom-based Training

ASQ offers training in a traditional classroom setting on a variety of topics. Our instructors are quality experts and lead courses that range from one day to four weeks, in several different cities. Classroom-based training is designed to improve quality and your organization's bottom line. Benefit from quality experts; from comprehensive, cutting-edge information; and from peers eager to share their experiences.

Web-based Training

Virtual Courses

ASQ's virtual courses provide the same expert instructors, course materials, interaction with other students, and ability to earn CEUs and RUs as our classroom-based training, without the hassle and expenses of travel. Learn in the comfort of your own home or workplace. All you need is a computer with Internet access and a telephone.

Self-paced Online Programs

These online programs allow you to work at your own pace while obtaining the quality knowledge you need. Access them whenever it is convenient for you, accommodating your schedule.

Some Training Topics Include

- Auditing
- Basic Quality
- Engineering
- Education
- Healthcare
- Government
- Food Safety
- ISO
- Leadership
- Lean
- Quality Management
- Reliability
- Six Sigma
- Social Responsibility

Visit www.asq.org/training for more information.